Great value accommodation – all at £12 … t

BED & … AST

CONTENTS

Designed and published by the Wales Tourist Board, Brunel House, Cardiff CF2 1UY, Wales.

Written by Roger Thomas Freelance Services.

Printed in Britain. Distributed overseas by the British Tourist Authority.

 ISBN 1 85013 024 8.

NORTH WALES

Within a mere half-hour of leaving the coast, those driving through this dramatically varied part of Wales can be high in the mountains. North Wales was made for touring holidays. Gentle, green borderlands serve as a counterpoint to Snowdonia's rocky peaks. On the coast you'll come across a string of lively seaside resorts and – in complete contrast – the peaceful bays and beaches of the Isle of Anglesey and Llŷn Peninsula. There are so many places to visit, too – everything from mighty medieval castles to vast slate caverns.

The North Wales coast resorts have a well-deserved reputation for their good-value family holidays. And as well as providing all the expected seaside entertainments, they also double up as handy touring centres.

Llandudno, a stylish resort of rare charm and character, has the largest number of hotels and guest houses in Wales and a brand-new attraction in the form of Ski Llandudno, a dry ski slope and exciting toboggan run. Neighbouring Colwyn Bay, with its fine sands and wealth of attractions – including a Mountain Zoo – is a super family resort. And there's more great entertainment at colourful Rhyl (the weather's always fine here thanks to its marvellous Sun Centre complex) and sandy Prestatyn, with its new multi-leisure Nova Centre.

Perhaps you'd prefer to head for North Wales's two coastal 'Areas of Outstanding Natural Beauty', the Isle of Anglesey and Llŷn Peninsula. Anglesey is an island fringed by low cliffs, rocky foreshores and sweeping, dune-backed beaches. Stay at one of the many pretty little resorts – such as Benllech or Moelfre – which dot the coast. Visit famous Llanfair P. G. with its new craft centre.

Llŷn has a personality all of its own. Explore its remote coves and untamed headlands from one of its seaside villages or water-sports centres. Porthmadog, at the gateway to Llŷn, is a good touring centre. Places to stay on the peninsula itself include castle-crowned Criccieth, Pwllheli, Abersoch and Nefyn.

Mount Snowdon gives its name to the Snowdonia National Park. Within the 845-square-mile park there are country towns and stone-built villages dwarfed by surrounding summits, boulder-strewn mountain passes and sheltered vales, cascading rivers, forests and moorlands. Good touring centres include Betws-y-Coed, Llanwrst, Llanberis and pretty Beddgelert.

Snowdonia's mountains decline into green hills and fertile valleys further eastwards. Historic Denbigh, Ruthin and Llangollen, home of the International Musical Eisteddfod, stand amongst lovely, hilly landscapes, within a stone's throw of the Hiraethog moors and the breezy borderland Clwydian Hills, another 'Area of Outstanding Natural Beauty'.

PLEASE SKI
IN CONTROL
AT ALL TIMES

MID WALES

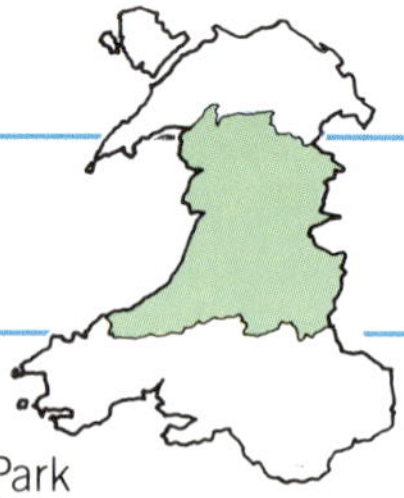

You'll be following in the footsteps of some seasoned travellers when you explore this unchanging, unhurried region. The Mid Wales drovers of the last century journeyed over remote hills and mountains on their way to market in England. Some of their old routes can today be followed by car – the Abergwesyn Pass, which winds its way over the wildly beautiful 'roof of Wales', is a classic example.

Exhilarating Abergwesyn is one of the many memorable motoring routes in green, peaceful Mid Wales. And since this is Wales's quietest holiday region, you'll be free from all hustle and bustle.

The busiest scene you're likely to come across is on market day, when the country comes to town. Along the great curve of Cardigan Bay, the atmosphere's the same. Mid Wales's small, friendly seaside resorts fit in perfectly. Stay at Aberystwyth, a place full of period charm. Or make for happy-go-lucky Barmouth and Tywyn. Further south, it's still quite easy to imagine the days of the sailing ketch and windjammer from the picturesque quaysides at New Quay and Aberaeron.

Although the Snowdonia National Park takes its name from the North Wales summit, the lion's share of the park – 500 of its 845 square miles – lies within Mid Wales. Mighty Cader Idris stands at the park's southern gateway, with handsome Dolgellau and the cool, green glades of the Coed-y-Brenin Forest in its shadow.

All in all, Mid Wales offers no less than 3,000 square miles of hills, forests, lakelands and mountains. In contrast to the Snowdonia Park's highlands, the undulating border country in the east is a patchwork of green enlivened by a scattering of striking black-and-white farmsteads.

Dolgellau, Machynlleth, Bala and Tregaron are ideal centres from which to venture into the lofty Cambrian Mountains. Welshpool and Newtown are pleasant border towns. Whilst Llandrindod Wells, a perfectly preserved Victorian Spa resort, is on the doorstep of the moody, spectacular Mid Wales lakelands.

Go red kite spotting or deep sea fishing. Climb to the top of Harlech Castle for the view to end all views. Explore vast tracts of untrodden countryside on foot or horseback – or even by narrow-gauge railway.

There are woollen mills hidden deep in the country where traditional Welsh tapestries are still woven. And during your travels, be sure to call in at two villages with a difference – bizarre, beautiful Portmeirion (there's nowhere else quite like it) and the futuristic National Centre of Alternative Technology.

KARINDA

SOUTH WALES

This is a holiday region with something for everyone – and not a few surprises. Some come to South Wales for its marvellous bays, headlands and beaches. Others are attracted to the great outdoors of the Brecon Beacons National Park, or the cosmopolitan appeal of Wales's capital city.

But that's not all. South Wales is also peppered with powerful castles such as giant Caerphilly and Pembroke. There are resorts large and small, cheerful and quiet, and attractions of all kinds including showcaves and wildlife parks. There's even a fascinating glimpse into our industrial beginnings in the friendly 'Valleys', an area of dramatic – and unexpected – beauty.

The Pembrokeshire Coast National Park is acknowledged as one of Europe's finest stretches of coastal natural beauty. It winds its way for over 180 miles across clifftops teeming with seabirds and along untouched sandy beaches washed by clear seas. Stay at picturesque Tenby, the sailing centre of Saundersfoot, or peaceful places such as tiny St. David's or Newport.

The wide, open spaces of the Brecon Beacons National Park attract country lovers. This park is an area of big skies, ice formed summits, wooded gorges, waterfalls and lakes, with a huge choice of outdoor activities. Explore the park from medieval Brecon, Llandovery or Crickhowell, where the stagecoaches used to stop.

There's more magnificent countryside to the east along the history-laden border. Monmouth, birthplace of Henry V, stands at the gateway to the loveliest part of the Wye Valley, a thickly wooded stretch of 'Outstanding Natural Beauty'. Further west, there are more magical vales around Carmarthen and Newcastle Emlyn, where you'll stumble across ruined castles and traditional woollen mills, and maybe see Wales's coracle fishermen in action . . . or, in complete contrast, enjoy an action-packed visit to the new Oakwood Leisure Park, near Narberth, with its imaginative rides and attractions.

The balmy, breezy Gower Peninsula was the first area in Britain to enjoy 'Outstanding Natural Beauty' status. And don't miss nearby Swansea, with its traditional fresh-foods market – the finest in Wales – and smart new marina and Maritime Quarter on the redeveloped waterfront.

Glamorgan's cliff-backed Heritage Coast and the traditional family resorts of Porthcawl and Barry separate Swansea from Cardiff, Wales's capital city. Cosmopolitan Cardiff really makes an impression. It's full of splendid sights, including an ornate city-centre castle, truly outstanding Civic Centre, St. David's Concert Hall, theatres and magnificent museums such as the open-air Welsh Folk Museum, St. Fagans.

EASY GOING

Take a look at the map – it really brings home the fact that Wales is so easy and quick to get to. Wales's ease of access is a real plus-point. Journey times are usually not more than a handful of hours – so travelling time, and costs, are kept to an absolute minimum.

BY CAR

North Wales has benefited tremendously from the up-graded A55 Expressway, parts of which are to motorway standard, which connects with the M53, M56 and M6. This Expressway gives access to the major coastal resort area and has also reduced travelling times to Anglesey and the Llŷn Peninsula.

Mid Wales is easily accessible from the M5 and M6 via the M54 and a number of other very convenient routes. South Wales enjoys excellent motorway links. The M4 now runs continuously from London right into South-West Wales. From the Midlands and North, use the M5/M50.

BY COACH

Fast and comfortable express coach services link almost all major towns and cities in England and Scotland to Wales – and they're competitively priced, too. For full details, contact your local National Express office, travel agent or bus station.

BY TRAIN

Journey times by rail can be spectacularly low – well under two hours, door-to-door, from London (Paddington) to Cardiff by Inter-City 125, for example. Speedy 125 trains also link Birmingham, Sheffield, York and Newcastle with Cardiff, and regular express services from the Midlands and West Country connect with the main South Wales line to Swansea, Carmarthen and beyond.

There's a fast, regular service from London (Euston) to Holyhead, calling in at the North Wales resorts. This coast is also served by direct services from Manchester, Liverpool and Hull.

Mid Wales's coast and country are accessible by two scenic rail routes. There's the Cambrian Coast line, running along Cardigan Bay from Aberystwyth to Pwllheli, which connects with mainline stations at Shrewsbury. The Heart of Wales line also runs from Shrewsbury through tranquil countryside to Llanelli and Swansea.

Check with British Rail for details – and ask about the holiday saver and discount fares that may be available. Travelling to Mid Wales? Then ask about the 'Explorer' ticket which gets you there and also allows unlimited 'Pass Cambria' travel (see 'Out and About' section for further information). Details from BR Travel Centres in London, Birmingham and Manchester or Chiltern Trains,
P.O. Box 10, Chinnor, Oxon, OX9 4UJ.
(Tel: 0844 – 52198).

BY SEA

Direct car ferry services operate between the Irish Republic and Wales on the following routes: Dublin to Holyhead (B&I), Dun Laoghaire to Holyhead (British Ferries-Sealink), Rosslare to Fishguard (British Ferries-Sealink combined) Rosslare to Pembroke Dock (B&I) and Cork to Swansea (Swansea/Cork Ferries).

OUT AND ABOUT IN WALES

Travelling around Wales is a real pleasure. Motorists can make the most of a network of attractive routes which are blissfully traffic-free. Wales's narrow-gauge 'Great Little Trains' and British Rail's scenic coast and country lines offer something special in the way of rail travel (details of the narrow-gauge unlimited travel 'Wanderer' ticket from 'Great Little Trains', c/o Talyllyn Railway, Wharf Station, Tywyn, Gwynedd. Tel: 0654 – 710472).

Local coach companies run many day and half-day excursions from venues throughout Wales. Just keep an eye out locally. And if you want to travel the length of the country, ask about the north-south Traws Cambria service.

The 'Pass Cambria' ticket, mentioned earlier, allows unlimited travel on all forms of public transport in Mid Wales. Details from Welsh Country Holidays,
Ladywell House, Newtown, Powys.
(Tel: 0686 – 626965) or Tourist Information Centres locally.

HOW TO BOOK

GENERAL GUIDELINES

When making an enquiry or booking, you should always state:

1. The dates you wish to stay, together with any alternatives.
2. The number of people in your party.
3. Any special requirements that you may need (such as terms for children, special diets, facilities for pets etc.).

If the establishment can provide you with the accommodation required, you should always confirm your booking in writing as soon as possible, enclosing any deposit that may be necessary.

HOLIDAY HOTLINE

Take advantage of our Holiday Hotline. Many of the establishments in this guide can be booked through our central Hotline service. It's free and easy-to-use. Just telephone one of the three numbers shown here, stating your requirements.

BOOKING DIRECT

You can 'phone or write, using the booking and enquiry form at the back of this guide. If you 'phone, follow it up with a letter of confirmation enclosing the agreed deposit.

PRICES

Minimum and maximum prices quoted throughout this publication cover the complete range of holiday seasons, from low to peak period. All prices are inclusive of VAT at the current rate. Please remember that the prices and other specific information quoted in this guide were supplied to the Wales Tourist Board by the establishments and operators listed during April-June 1987 for subsequent publication. So do check all prices and facilities before confirming your booking.

DEPOSITS

Please note that some establishments may request payments in advance from clients. This may occur at hotels or motels, particularly when there is no written or confirmed reservation or in cases where guests arrive with little or no luggage. Most establishments will ask for deposits when a written reservation is being made.

LATE ARRIVALS

Guests who have made prior bookings and who intend arriving late can help by 'phoning the establishment well in advance with details of the intended time of arrival.

CANCELLATIONS

When you confirm a booking and accept the conditions of that booking, bear in mind that you are entering into a legally binding contract with the proprietor of the establishment. This entitles the proprietor to compensation if you fail to take up the accommodation. Accordingly, if you have to change your travel plans and cancel a booking, remember that it is in your interest to advise the proprietor, manager or owner immediately.

TOURIST INFORMATION CENTRES

When you're out and about in Wales, make use of the Wales Tourist Board's network of Tourist Information Centres. They all offer a bed-booking reservation service, whilst major centres also provide a book-a-bed-ahead scheme which enables you to travel to your destination with all accommodation arrangements made in advance. A list of Tourist Information Centres appears at the back of this guide.

GREAT VALUE ACCOMMODATION

Looking for somewhere small and friendly in which you're really made to feel at home? Then look no further. Wales's small hotels and guest houses have a long tradition of offering honest-to-goodness budget accommodation – and you'll be pleasantly surprised by the improved facilities and standards of comfort which many of these modestly-priced places now provide, all for up to only £12 a night.

Traditionally speaking, nothing can beat Wales's farmhouse accommodation. Farmhouse holidays have become really popular in Wales. By staying down on the farm you'll sample, first-hand, a flavour of the rural way of life – quite literally, for wholesome, home-cooked food is usually the order of the day.

LOOK OUT FOR THE AWARD WINNERS

AWARD

Guest houses and farmhouses are both eligible for the Wales Tourist Board's Farm and Rural Guest House Award. This coveted Award recognises and rewards superior standards of accommodation.

Long gone are the days when a guest house or farmhouse simply hung a 'bed and breakfast' sign on the gate and hoped for the best. The personal service is still there, of course, but today it's allied to real flair, expertise and comfort.

Many of the places listed in this guide now offer that important something extra in the way of standards and facilities. Look out for the distinctive Award symbol in the accommodation listings. It's your sign that the guest house or farmhouse has features such as washbasins in all bedrooms and full central heating (or an alternative fixed source of heating). It also means that the establishment is in the capable hands of people who have successfully completed a guest house or farmhouse tourism training course.

ALL CHECKED OUT

All holiday accommodation in this guide – every hotel, guest house and farmhouse – has been checked out by the Wales Tourist Board. Each establishment has been personally visited by a Board representative to confirm and verify its facilities and services. In essence, we make sure that the features which the establishment lays claim to are, in fact, all present and correct. This means that you can book safe in the knowledge that the accommodation has been thoroughly checked out – so that you can check in with confidence when you arrive.

CROWNS TO HELP YOU CHOOSE

Not only do we personally check everything out. We also classify the accommodation by using the 'Crown' system. A nationwide scheme adopted by the Wales, English and Scottish Tourist Boards Crown classifications reflect the levels of facilities, equipment and services provided at each individual hotel, guest house and farmhouse.

CROWN CATEGORIES EXPLAINED

It's so straightforward. The higher the Crown rating, the greater the range of facilities, equipment and services on offer. Please note that a high classification does not necessarily imply that the quality on offer is superior to that available at an establishment with less Crowns.

L LISTED

Relatively simple accommodation satisfying the Wales Tourist Board's minimum standards, with a limited range of facilities and services. Specifically:

1. Bedrooms are of reasonable size and meet basic (minimum) Wales Tourist Board standards for furnishings and equipment. Beds are made daily and basic toiletries provided.
2. Breakfast is provided either in bedrooms or more usually in a dining room.
3. Public areas are cleaned daily and there is adequate heating according to season.
4. At least one fully equipped bathroom available for every 15 guests (other than guests having rooms with private bathrooms or wash handbasins).

Better equipped accommodation with a wider range of facilities, especially in bathrooms. Specifically, all 'Listed' requirements plus:

1. Higher standard of bedroom furnishings and equipment including washbasins or private bathrooms with hot and cold running water.
2. At least one bathroom for every 10 guests (other than those with private bathrooms).
3. Lounge area with adequate chairs; access to telephone.
4. Reception area or bell to call for attention.
5. Tourist information available.

Accommodation offering a more extensive range of equipment, facilities and services (the latter in particular). Specifically, all 'One Crown' requirements plus:

1. Dining/breakfast room usually separate from lounge.
2. Early morning tea/coffee served in bedrooms on request (unless beverage making facilities in bedroom).
3. Early morning call (or alarm clock) on request.
4. Colour TV in lounge – if no TV in bedrooms.
5. Hot drinks available on request in evening (unless beverage making facilities in bedroom or nearby).

Well-appointed accommodation with a higher proportion of en-suite facilities. Specifically, all 'Two Crown' requirements plus:

1. At least one-third of bedrooms with private bath or shower and WC en-suite.
2. Bedrooms have fixed heating with automatic and individual controls.
3. Lounge area separate from bar or TV lounge.
4. Hair drier, iron and shoe cleaning facilities available.
5. Pay telephone.

Particularly well-appointed accommodation with a wide range of facilities and services, most bedrooms with en-suite facilities etc. Specifically, all 'three crown' requirements plus:

1. At least three-quarters of bedrooms with private bath or shower and WC en-suite.
2. Colour TV and radio in bedrooms.
3. Lounge service until midnight.
4. 24-hour access to hotel.
5. Room telephone capable of external calls.

Exceptionally well-appointed accommodation with an extensive range of facilities and services. Specifically, all 'four crown' requirements plus:

1. All bedrooms with private bath with fixed shower attachment and WC en-suite.
2. Direct-dial telephone in bedrooms.
3. Room service available.
4. All night lounge service and night porter.
5. 24-hour return service for laundry (except at weekends).

ALL ABOUT THIS GUIDE

This introductory page marks the start of the guide's accommodation listings. The places to stay are grouped within three main regional sections – North, Mid and South Wales. Each regional section is subsequently divided into smaller areas. North Wales, for example, is split into five parts – Anglesey, Coast Resorts, Llŷn, Snowdonia and Clwyd. It's all explained, with the help of a map, on the next page.

These smaller areas are broken down into alphabetical listings of resorts, towns, etc. The accommodation appears under each relevant destination, listed under 'Hotels', 'Guest Houses' or 'Farmhouses'.

Each destination includes a map reference which enables you to pinpoint its location on the gridded maps of Wales.

Key to Symbols

P	Car Parking off-street or Garage available.
(dog)	Dogs accepted by arrangement.
(knife and fork)	Evening Meal available by prior arrangement.
(bed)	The number of bedrooms available.
1-12	The period the establishment is open during the year is denoted by numbers, e.g. 1-12 means open all year, January to December inclusive. 4-10 means open April to October inclusive.
AWARD	Wales Tourist Board Award recipient.

CHOOSING YOUR HOLIDAY AREA

The accommodation entries begin on page 18. We've divided them up first by region – North, Mid and South Wales – and then by area. It's all explained here. Take a look at the map, and also the information on the previous page. Everything is presented in a way which enables you to turn straight to the part of Wales that interests you.

NORTH WALES

1. Isle of Anglesey.
2. North Wales Coast Resorts.
3. Llŷn – Snowdon's Peninsula.
4. Snowdonia Mountains & Coastline.
5. Clwyd Countryside & Heritage.

MID WALES

6. Meirionnydd.
7. Ceredigion.
8. Montgomeryshire.
9. Heart of Wales.

SOUTH WALES

10. Pembrokeshire.
11. The Vales of Dyfed.
12. Brecon & the Beacons.
13. Swansea, Mumbles & Gower.
14. Cardiff & the South Wales Coast.
15. Vale of Usk & Wye Valley.
16. South Wales Valleys.

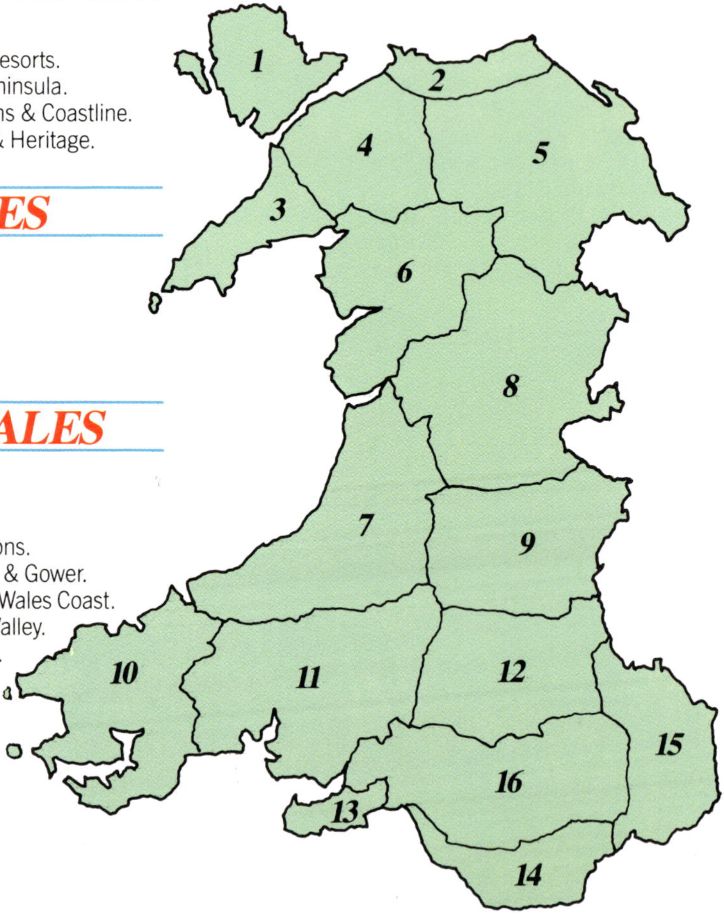

NORTH WALES

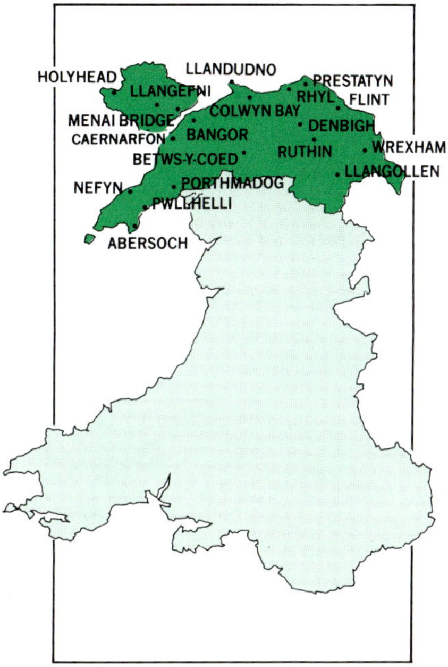

There's more than enough here to guarantee memorable holidays for everyone. North Wales' assets and attractions are as long as Llandudno pier. There's the magnificent Snowdonia National Park, with the highest mountains in England and Wales. Nearby, there are colourful, popular resorts which spell out fun for all the family – though there's no hint of hustle or bustle along the peaceful Isle of Anglesey or the Llŷn Peninsula. North Wales's attractions and activities are legion – and legendary. There's everything here from medieval castles to cable cars, slate caverns to butterfly farms.

The resorts extend a big welcome. In stylish Llandudno's case, it includes the biggest selection of hotels in Wales. Cheerful Colwyn Bay (the children will love its Mountain Zoo), Rhyl and Prestatyn are super family resorts. Rhyl's weather, by the way, is always fine thanks to its imaginative Sun Centre complex.

Bring your bucket and spade – and also your map of the mountains. Snowdonia's rugged peaks, rushing rivers and lakes are only a stone's throw away from the sea. Further east, explore heather-covered moorlands and the rolling, rounded Clwydian Hills, an official 'Area of Outstanding Natural Beauty'. Soak up the sights at Llangollen and Betws-y-Coed. Or go back in time at historic Denbigh and Ruthin.

Visit some of Europe's greatest castles – mighty Caernarfon, moody Conwy and Beaumaris, to name but three. Ride narrow-gauge railways, call in at craft shops, go walking, sailing, swimming or climbing. Or simply get away from it all by escaping to two more 'Areas of Outstanding Natural Beauty' – the uncrowded sands and small resorts around the Isle of Anglesey or the lovely, lonely bays and dramatic cliff scenery along the Llŷn Peninsula.

ISLE OF ANGLESEY

There's an unmistakable island atmosphere here. Although connected to mainland Wales by road and rail bridges, Anglesey is at least one step removed from the outside world's hustle and bustle. Its resorts are small, quaint and quiet. And you'll have a 125 mile coastline almost all to yourself.

Anglesey's coastal fringes – sometimes sandy, other times rocky, always lovely – are one of Wales's officially designated 'Areas of Outstanding Natural Beauty'. Delightful resorts such as Rhosneigr, Trearddur Bay, Amlwch, Moelfre and Red Wharf Bay complement their surroundings perfectly. Beaumaris is a handsome little sailing centre with a most impressive castle – Wales's finest according to some.

There's more finery at the opulent stately home of Plas Newydd, and a wealth of prehistory at mysterious stone tombs scattered all over the island. And don't miss the world's longest place-name, conveniently shortened to Llanfair P. G. by the canny locals – nor the village's brand-new crafts complex.

Beaumaris
Map Ref Ae3

Coastal resort on the Isle of Anglesey. Magnificent 13th-century castle, 15th-century Tudor House, Victorian Gaol and enchanting Museum of Childhood. Yachting centre. Golf course, excellent fishing. Ideal touring centre for Snowdonia. Sixth-century Penmon Priory nearby. Superb views over the Menai Strait towards the mountains horizon on the mainland.

Guest Houses

2 Greenbank
Llandegfan, Anglesey, Gwynedd,
LL59 5YD.
Tel: (0248) 713108.

Superbly situated overlooking Menai Strait with views of Snowdonia. Close to historic town of Beaumaris. Two twins and one double room. Washbasins and tea making facilities. Residents' lounge with colour T.V. Evening meal optional. Ideally located for touring Anglesey and the North Wales coast.

	Single Room per one person B&B		Double Room for two persons B&B		3
	MIN £ 7.95	MAX £	MIN £ 15.80	MAX £	OPEN 3-10

Farmhouses

Dinmor
Penmon, Beaumaris, Anglesey,
Gwynedd, LL58 8SN.
Tel: (0248) 78395.

Dinmor is a smallholding with panoramic views over Snowdonia, 3½ miles from Beaumaris in Area of Outstanding Natural Beauty. Three family rooms with hot and cold water. Open fire in sitting room. Vegetarians catered for. Home baked bread, free range eggs. Warm friendly atmosphere. Charted walks, riding, fishing, bird watching. Victorian house off the beaten track.

	Single Room per one person B&B		Double Room for two persons B&B		3
	MIN £ 9.50	MAX £ 10.00	MIN £ 17.00	MAX £ 19.00	OPEN 1-12

Plas Cichle
Beaumaris, Anglesey, Gwynedd,
LL58 8PS.
Tel: (0248) 810488.

A working farm where animals graze in beautiful parkland, close to historic town of Beaumaris and the Menai Strait. Period farmhouse accommodation in double and family rooms. Tea making facilities. Large lounge. Colour T.V. Log fire. Separate dining room. Emphasis on wholesome food. Local activities, water sport, golf, riding.

	Single Room per one person B&B		Double Room for two persons B&B		3
	MIN £ 8.00	MAX £ 9.00	MIN £ 20.00	MAX £ 22.00	OPEN 4-10

Benllech
Map Ref Ad2

Popular holiday village standing above a sweeping bay on Anglesey's east coast. Four miles of good sands, safe bathing, sailing, bowling, walking, etc. Cliffs nearby rich in fossils.

Hotels

Hafod Wyn Hotel and Restaurant
Benllech Bay, Anglesey, Gwynedd,
LL74 8SD.
Tel: (0248) 852357.

Hafod Wyn is a family-run hotel offering accommodation of a good standard. Our rooms are en-suite, have beverage facilities and colour T.V.'s. We have a restaurant, comfortable bar lounge with pool table and residents' lounge. We are ideally situated for beaches, boating, golfing, fishing, horse riding, walking and touring Snowdonia. Fire certificate. Parking.

	Single Room per one person B&B		Double Room for two persons B&B		6
	MIN £ 12.00	MAX £ 12.00	MIN £ 24.00	MAX £ 24.00	OPEN 1-12

Brynsiencyn
Map Ref Ad4

A waterside hamlet on the Isle of Anglesey looking across the Menai Strait. Bodowyr Burial Chamber, Plas Newydd stately home and Sea Zoo nearby.

Farmhouses

Cefn Arthen Farm
Brynsiencyn, Llanfairpwll, Anglesey,
Gwynedd, LL61 6SZ.
Tel: (024873) 223.

Cefn Arthen is a modern working farm and a good centre for touring North Wales. Good home cooking using home grown vegetables. Warm Welsh welcome with views of Snowdonia. Evening meal by arrangement. Situated near beach, sea. Zoo 15 miles. Ferry at Holyhead for Ireland and railway station with the longest name in Wales.

	Single Room per one person B&B		Double Room for two persons B&B		2
	MIN £ 7.50	MAX £ 7.50	MIN £ 15.00	MAX £ 15.00	OPEN 3-10

Plas Trefarthen
Brynsiencyn, Anglesey, Gwynedd,
LL61 6SZ.
Tel: (024 873) 379.

Plas Trefarthen is a large Georgian country house standing in an Area of Outstanding Natural Beauty on the shores of the Menai Strait and overlooking Snowdonia. Close to Plas Newydd. All bedrooms with bathrooms en-suite. Most food served is produced on the farm. There is a full size snooker table plus fishing. Real Welsh welcome guaranteed. Self catering available.

	Single Room per one person B&B		Double Room for two persons B&B		5
	MIN £ 11.00	MAX £ 12.00	MIN £ 22.00	MAX £ 24.00	OPEN 1-11

Tyddyn Goblet
Brynsiencyn, Anglesey, Gwynedd,
LL61 6TZ.
Tel: (024 873) 296.

Character farmhouse set back 200 yds from A4080 road. Private ground floor family suite, double and twin bedroom with own shower room and toilet. First floor bedroom and bathroom. Evening dinner optional. All dishes home cooked to a high standard. Ideal base for touring the North Wales coast, Snowdonia and Anglesey. Brochure: Mrs Williams.

	Single Room per one person B&B		Double Room for two persons B&B		3
	MIN £ 7.50	MAX £ 8.50	MIN £ 15.00	MAX £ 17.00	OPEN 1-11

Cemaes Bay

Map Ref Ac1

Quaint and uncommercialised village on the Isle of Anglesey. Boating, swimming and fishing.

Guest Houses

Treddolphin Guest House

Beach Road, Penrhyn, Cemaes Bay,
Gwynedd, LL67 0ET.
Tel: (0407) 710388. C/Res: (0492) 534626

Commanding a panoramic coastal view. All bedrooms have hot & cold, and shower. Four family rooms, two twin, two double. Visitors' lounge. Colour T.V. Centrally heated. Fire certificate. Ample parking. Beach only yards away. Children welcome, half price when sharing parents' room. Free baby sitting. Free evening tea and biscuits. For a welcoming service ring Roberta and Harold Williams.

P	Single Room per one person B&B		Double Room for two persons B&B		8
	MIN £ 9.00	MAX £ 9.00	MIN £ 16.00	MAX £ 16.00	OPEN 1-12

Farmhouses

Tyddyn Llwyd

Llanfwrog, Holyhead, Anglesey,
Gwynedd, LL65 4YN.
Tel: (0407) 730639.

Get away from it all in the peace and quiet of a secluded farmhouse in unspoilt North West Anglesey, near beautiful sandy beaches. Spacious family accommodation comprising one double bedded and one bunk bedded room with own shower and toilet facilities. Colour T.V. Good home cooking. Only ten miles from ferry port of Holyhead.

P	Single Room per one person B&B		Double Room for two persons B&B		2
	MIN £ 6.50	MAX £ 9.00	MIN £ 13.00	MAX £ 18.00	OPEN 5-10

Holyhead

Map Ref Aa2

On Holy Island, this is a port for Irish ferries. Sailing centre and sailing school. Sea angling, cliff and hill walking in the surrounding area. Sea-birds and coastal flora to be enjoyed on a walk down the 350 steps to the South Stack lighthouse nearby.

Hotels

Crown Hotel

Bodedern, Anglesey, Gwynedd,
LL65 3TU.
Tel: (0407) 740734.

An ideal holiday bed and breakfast base, just off the A5, 6 miles east of Holyhead. Beautiful traditional family pub with well appointed bedrooms. All have T.V., washbasins and full central heating throughout. Traditional beers. Ample parking. Bar meals. Facilities for children. Parties/coaches by prior arrangement.

P	Single Room per one person B&B		Double Room for two persons B&B		6
	MIN £ 11.50	MAX £	MIN £ 23.00	MAX £	OPEN 1-12

Guest Houses

Bryn Awel

Edmund Street, Holyhead, Anglesey,
Gwynedd, LL65 1SA.
Tel: (0407) 2948. [L]

Centrally situated, five minutes walk from car ferry, five minutes shops. Double, family and single rooms, special rates children. T.V. lounge, video. Dining room with separate tables. Central heating. Sandy beaches nearby. Ideal for touring North Wales, Snowdonia and North Wales coast. Well situated for day trips to Ireland.

P	Single Room per one person B&B		Double Room for two persons B&B		4
	MIN £ 8.50	MAX £ 9.00	MIN £ 17.00	MAX £ 18.00	OPEN 1-12

Yr Hendre

Porth-y-Felin Road, Holyhead,
Anglesey, Gwynedd, LL65 1AH.
Tel: (0407) 2929.

Situated opposite park. Within few minutes drive of car ferry and station, Holyhead promenade at bottom of road. 5 minutes walk into town centre. Large bedrooms with hot and cold, shaver points, tea/coffee facilities, full central heating. Dining room and lounge with colour T.V. Private parking. Full English breakfast however early. Brochure available.

P	Single Room per one person B&B		Double Room for two persons B&B		3
	MIN £ 9.00	MAX £ 9.00	MIN £ 18.00	MAX £ 18.00	OPEN 1-12

Oakleigh

4 Walthew Avenue, Holyhead,
Gwynedd, LL65 1AF.
Tel: (0407) 2941. [L]

Very convenient for ferry, railway and bus station. Situated on the seafront, we offer double, twin and single bedrooms, television lounge complimented by full English breakfast under the personal supervision of Barbara Simms. Handy for town and park, also country walks and fishing.

P	Single Room per one person B&B		Double Room for two persons B&B		3
	MIN £ 9.00	MAX £ 10.00	MIN £ 18.00	MAX £ 20.00	OPEN 1-12

Tan-y-Cytiau Country Guest House

South Stack Road, Holyhead,
Anglesey, Gwynedd, LL65 1YH.
Tel: (0407) 2763.

The house offers a friendly and comfortable atmosphere set in lovely gardens. Spacious rooms with panoramic views, situated on slopes of Holyhead mountain. R.S.P.B. Reserve ideal for birdwatching and walking. Convenient for ferry terminal for Ireland. Excellent golf course nearby and good sailing area. Home cooking using fresh produce.

P	Single Room per one person B&B		Double Room for two persons B&B		7
	MIN £ 11.00	MAX £ 12.00	MIN £ 22.00	MAX £ 24.00	OPEN 1-10

Witchingham Guest House

20 Walthew Avenue, Holyhead,
Anglesey, Gwynedd, LL65 1AF.
Tel: (0407) 2426.

Warm and friendly welcome in family-run guest house, close to sea, five minutes from car ferries. Also five minutes town centre. Hot and cold in all rooms. Full central heating. Double, single or family rooms available. One family room en-suite. Guests' T.V. lounge. Evening meal available if ordered before 3.00 p.m. Full Fire Certificate.

P	Single Room per one person B&B		Double Room for two persons B&B		4
	MIN £ 9.00	MAX £ 9.00	MIN £ 17.00	MAX £ 17.00	OPEN 1-12

Farmhouses

Tŷ Mawr Farmhouse

Valley, Anglesey, Gwynedd,
LL65 3HH.
Tel: (0407) 740235. [L]

Welsh granite farmhouse, ideally situated off main A5 road, 5 miles Holyhead/Dublin ferry. On 250 acre dairy farm. Splendid views across Anglesey towards Snowdonia. 1 mile from sea, shops, ideal for all water sports and fishing. Good base for touring North Wales. Colour T.V. room, table tennis, garden. Always a warm welcome. Children catered for.

P	Single Room per one person B&B		Double Room for two persons B&B		4
	MIN £ 10.00	MAX £	MIN £ 20.00	MAX £	OPEN 4-9

Llanerchymedd
Map Ref Ac2

A central Anglesey village with access to beaches of all kinds along the island's coast. Din Lligwy, the remains of an ancient fortified village, are nearby.

Farmhouses

Drws-y-Coed
Llanerchymedd, Anglesey, Gwynedd, LL71 8AD.
Tel: (0248) 470473.

Modern farmhouse peacefully situated in beautiful wooded countryside with panoramic views of Snowdonia. Centrally situated for beaches, golf, fishing and leisure centres. Bedrooms with tea making facilities, radios. Two bedrooms with bathroom en-suite. Central heating, log fire. Children welcome. Games room. Free pony rides. Rough shooting available on 250 acre farm. Good food. Fire certificate.

P ✕	Single Room per one person B&B		Double Room for two persons B&B		3
	MIN £ 10.00	MAX £ 12.00	MIN £ 20.00	MAX £ 24.00	OPEN 1-12

Llwydiarth Fawr
Llanerchymedd, Isle of Anglesey, Gwynedd, LL71 8DF.
Tel: (0248) 470321.

AWARD

Georgian mansion, secluded, woodlands, luxurious. Set in 750 acres farmland, centrally situated. Ideal for touring the island, walks and private fishing. Four beautifully appointed bedrooms, all with H/C, shaver points, tea/coffee making facilities, en-suite available. Full central heating. Two sitting rooms with log fires. Spacious dining room with separate tables. Emphasis on farmhouse fare. Personal attention and a warm Welsh welcome. Brochure available.

P ✕	Single Room per one person B&B		Double Room for two persons B&B		4
	MIN £ 10.00	MAX £ 10.00	MIN £ 20.00	MAX £ 20.00	OPEN 1-12

Llanfair P.G.
Map Ref Ad3

Its full name is Llanfairpwllgwyngyllgoger-ychwyrndrobwlltlantysiliogogogoch or "St. Mary's Church by the white aspen near the violent whirlpool and St. Tysilo's Church by the red cave." Excellent craft centre. Plas Newydd stately home nearby.

Guest Houses

Sarn Faban Guest House
Penmynydd Road, Llanfair Pwll, Anglesey, Gwynedd, LL61 5AZ.
Tel: (0248) 712410. L

Situated one mile off Menai Bridge and Strait. Easy access to Expressway en route for Ireland. Five bedrooms centrally heated, including family room. Television lounge. Warm Welsh welcome with good home cooking. Children welcome.

P 🐕 ✕	Single Room per one person B&B		Double Room for two persons B&B		5
	MIN £ 8.50	MAX £ 8.50	MIN £ 17.00	MAX £ 17.00	OPEN 1-12

Llangefni
Map Ref Ad3

Administrative capital of Anglesey, a market town and shopping centre. Excellent touring base, as all the island's coastline is within a radius of 15–20 miles. Many prehistoric monuments nearby. Theatre and sports centre. Trout fishing on the Cefni reservoir nearby.

Guest Houses

Argraig
Llangristiolus, Bodorgan, Isle of Anglesey, Gwynedd, LL62 5PW.
Tel: (0248) 724390.

Situated in a rural setting with panoramic views of Anglesey and Snowdonia. Half mile (0.8 km) west of A5 trunk road on B4422. Ideal for ferry traffic or touring. Family room, double room, both with hot and cold, central heating, tea/coffee facilities. Dining room. Lounge, T.V. Children welcome, reductions for under twelves. A warm welcome awaits you.

P	Single Room per one person B&B		Double Room for two persons B&B		2
	MIN £ 8.00	MAX £ 9.00	MIN £ 16.00	MAX £ 18.00	OPEN 1-12

Farmhouses

Bryn Hyfryd
Bethel, Bodorgan, Anglesey, Gwynedd, LL62 5AB.
Tel: (0407) 840496. L

Perfect location for birdwatching, sea or freshwater fishing, windsurfing, walking. Ideal for quiet holiday, but within easy reach of shops and many beautiful beaches. Centrally heated modernised farmhouse, two twin rooms, one double room. Good home cooking using our own organically grown produce as available. Open all year. Reduced rates for pensioners and children.

P ✕	Single Room per one person B&B		Double Room for two persons B&B		3
	MIN £ 9.00	MAX £ 9.50	MIN £ 18.00	MAX £ 19.00	OPEN 1-12

Trer'ddôl Farm
Trevor, Llanerchymedd, Anglesey, Gwynedd, LL71 7AR.
Tel: (0248) 470278.

AWARD

A true Welsh welcome assured at this former historic 17th century manor house, centrally situated – 200 acres of freedom. Free riding and participation in farm activities, preparing cattle for "showing", etc. Spacious bedrooms, H & C, tea making facilities. Cosy lounge, log fires. Separate tables in dining room. Homely atmosphere with emphasis on traditional farmhouse fare and cleanliness. Brochure available.

P 🐕 ✕	Single Room per one person B&B		Double Room for two persons B&B		4
	MIN £ 10.00	MAX £ 12.00	MIN £ 18.00	MAX £ 20.00	OPEN 1-11

Menai Bridge
Map Ref Ad3

The first town encountered upon crossing the Menai Strait to Anglesey over Telford's magnificent Suspension Bridge, looks out over the mountains of Snowdonia on the mainland. Tegfryn Gallery provides examples of work by contemporary Welsh Artists. Pili Palas butterfly farm nearby.

Guest Houses

Glan-y-Don
St. George's Road, Menai Bridge,
Isle of Anglesey, Gwynedd.
LL59 5EP.
Tel: (0248) 713087.

Pamper yourself at Pam's waterside guest house with its homely atmosphere backed by first class service, comfort, central heating. Full access to bedroom/T V lounge throughout day. Fire certificate. Try scrambled eggs with chives on wholemeal toast, fish dish or "full fried" with fresh coffee. Excellent centre for touring beautiful Anglesey and Snowdonia, affording golf, fishing, beaches.

P	Single Room per one person B&B		Double Room for two persons B&B		5
	MIN £	MAX £	MIN £ 17.00	MAX £ 18.00	OPEN 1-12

Rhoscolyn
Map Ref Ab3

Picturesque sandy bay near this small village not far from Holyhead. Excellent sailing facilities on nearby Trearddur Bay, and safe swimming.

Guest Houses

The Old School
Rhoscolyn, Holyhead, Gwynedd.
LL65 2RQ.
Tel: (0407) 741593.

Minutes away from Rhoscolyn and Trearddur Bay beaches, golf, fishing and nature walks. The rooms have colour T.V., radio/alarm clocks, hot and cold, tea/coffee making facilities and central heating. Small guest house with beautiful country views and high standard of accommodation. English or continental breakfast.

P	Single Room per one person B&B		Double Room for two persons B&B		3
	MIN £ 9.00	MAX £	MIN £ 18.00	MAX £	OPEN 4-10

Rhosneigr
Map Ref Ab3

Anglesey seaside village. Swimming, golf, horse riding. Barclodiad y Gawres burial chamber.

Guest Houses

Engedi House
Bryngwran, Rhosneigr, Gwynedd.
LL65 3RR.
Tel: (0407) 720498. L

A warm welcome awaits you at this guest house on the A4080 to Rhosneigr. Double, twin and single bedrooms available. Situated close to beautiful bays. An ideal base for touring the magnificent Isle of Anglesey coastline, North Wales coast and Snowdonia. Bird watching, surfing and golf locally.

P	Single Room per one person B&B		Double Room for two persons B&B		3
	MIN £ 7.50	MAX £ 8.00	MIN £ 15.00	MAX £ 16.00	OPEN 1-12

Garreg Lwyd
Pencarnisiog, Rhosneigr, Gwynedd,
LL63 5SD.
Tel: (0407) 810365. L

Country house with relaxed atmosphere. Views over Snowdonia and Llŷn Peninsula. Ideally situated for touring. Nearby sandy beaches. Good home cooking. All rooms have tea and coffee making facilities. The house is fully centrally heated. Table licence held. Children welcome. Pets by arrangement only. Optional evening meal. Log fire in the lounge.

P	Single Room per one person B&B		Double Room for two persons B&B		4
	MIN £ 9.00	MAX £ 9.00	MIN £ 18.00	MAX £ 18.00	OPEN 1-11

Farmhouses

Cae'r Brenin
Bodedern, Anglesey, Gwynedd,
LL65 3PE.
Tel: (0407) 741147.

A warm Welsh welcome awaits you at Cae'r Brenin. Our guests are offered tasteful and comfortable accommodation with hospitality to match. Sample a taste of Wales with our home cooked meals. Spacious lounge with log fire, exposed beamed ceiling. Cae'r Brenin is ideal for family holidays or short weekend breaks. Two crown.

P	Single Room per one person B&B		Double Room for two persons B&B		3
	MIN £ 9.00	MAX £ 9.00	MIN £ 18.00	MAX £ 18.00	OPEN 1-12

Trearddur Bay
Map Ref Aa2

Holiday area on Holy Island, near Holyhead. Activities available – golf, sailing, fishing, swimming.

Hotels

Highground Hotel
off Ravenspoint Road, Trearddur Bay,
Isle of Anglesey, Gwynedd,
LL65 2YY.
Tel: (0407) 860078.

Magnificent panoramic coastal views are a feature of Highground, the ideal venue for family holidays, sporting activities, or relaxing breaks. A family run, licensed hotel, Highground offers a warm and friendly atmosphere. All bedrooms have colour T.V. and coffee/tea facilities, with central heating throughout. Access/Visa welcomed. For brochure contact the resident proprietors.

P	Single Room per one person B&B		Double Room for two persons B&B		7
	MIN £ 12.00	MAX £ 12.00	MIN £ 24.00	MAX £ 24.00	OPEN 1-12

Guest Houses

Moranedd Guest House
Trearddur Road, Trearddur Bay,
Anglesey, Gwynedd, LL65 2UE.
Tel: (0407) 860324.

Moranedd is a lovely house with a sun patio overlooking three quarters of an acre of garden. Only five minutes stroll to the beach, shop, sailing and golf clubs. The bedrooms are large and centrally heated and all have washbasins and tea making facilities. AA and RAC listed.

P	Single Room per one person B&B		Double Room for two persons B&B		6
	MIN £ 10.00	MAX £ 10.00	MIN £ 20.00	MAX £ 20.00	OPEN 1-12

NORTH WALES COAST RESORTS

This coastline shows off its popular personality everywhere. For a start there's elegant Llandudno, perfectly framed between two headlands. This is a resort of rare style which has moved with the times – recent additions include a dry ski slope – without sacrificing its Victorian and Edwardian elegance. Its seafront promenade is particularly splendid, the finishing touch provided by a decorative pier.

The beaches all along this coast are superb. Make the most of the sands at Colwyn Bay, a friendly family resort with a whole range of attractions including a famous Mountain Zoo. There's more great value enjoyment at Rhyl. This colourful resort has even managed to improve on its enviable sunshine record by guaranteeing the weather in its Sun Centre, a marvellous leisure complex which has a swimming pool with real waves and a tropical beach area. And nearby Prestatyn, with its miles of safe, flat sands and brand-new Nova multi-leisure centre, is also perfect for family holidays.

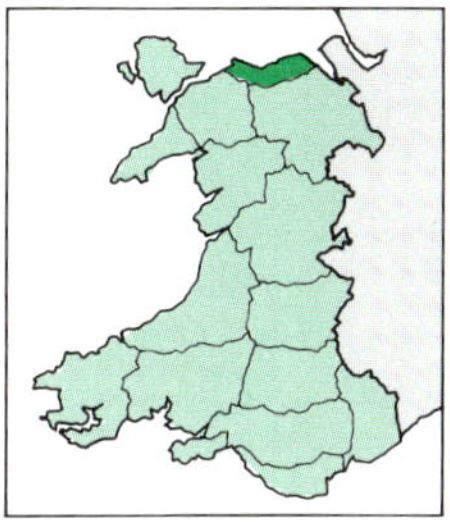

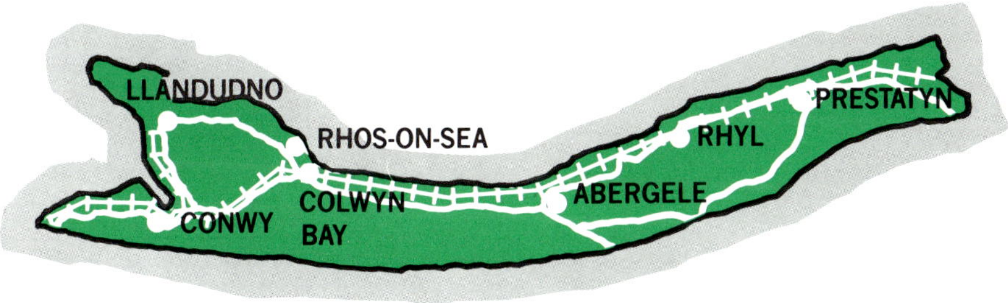

Abergele
Map Ref Bd4

Convenient centre for exploring the North Wales coastal resorts. Wooded walks nearby. 18-hole golf course, livestock market. Miles of sands at nearby Pensarn.

Guest Houses

The Haven Guest House
Towyn Road, Belgrano, Abergele,
Clwyd, LL22 9AB.
Tel: (0745) 823534.

The Haven is a friendly guest house with single, double and family rooms all with central heating, hot and cold water, shaver points and tea making facilities. Lounge with colour T.V. Dining room has separate tables. Access to rooms and lounge at all times. Cliff and Barbara Pilley give you a very warm welcome.

Single Room per one person B&B		Double Room for two persons B&B		4
MIN £	MAX £	MIN £	MAX £	OPEN
7.50	7.50	15.00	15.00	1-12

Colwyn Bay
Map Ref Bb4

Attractive bustling seaside resort. Pier, promenade, amusements. Convenient touring centre for Snowdonia and Anglesey. Leisure centre, mountain zoo. Golf, riding and sports well catered for. Wide range of hotels and guest houses.

Hotels

Haven Villa Private Hotel
Hillside Road, Colwyn Bay, Clwyd,
LL29 7EL.
Tel: (0492) 531931.

Friendly, small, family hotel. Certificate of merit for food/hygiene. RAC listed. Hot and cold all rooms. English and continental breakfast. Fourteen choice menu. Bar in restaurant. Licence. Evening meal optional. A change of scene is a tonic and North Wales is beautiful – so come on, treat yourselves and have a break. You will feel better for it!

Single Room per one person B&B		Double Room for two persons B&B		5
MIN £	MAX £	MIN £	MAX £	OPEN
7.00	8.00	14.00	16.00	1-12

Holcombe Hotel
9 Grosvenor Road, Colwyn Bay,
Clwyd, LL29 7YF.
Tel: (0492) 530423.

Croeso Cymreig – Welsh welcome at our eight bedroom detached, licensed hotel situated in one of the most desirable residential parts of town, yet close to all amenities. Bedrooms with colour T.V.'s, tea/coffee facilities. Heating in all bedrooms, some en-suite, two on ground floor. Ideal for touring North Wales.

Single Room per one person B&B		Double Room for two persons B&B		8
MIN £	MAX £	MIN £	MAX £	OPEN
8.00	11.00	16.00	22.00	1-12

Penrhyn Hotel
2 Mostyn Road, Colwyn Bay, Clwyd,
LL29 8PB.
Tel: (0492) 532227.

A friendly Welsh welcome awaits you. Central for touring North Wales, within walking distance of railway and bus stations, beach, shops and Eirias park. Licensed bar. Food highly recommended. Lounge with colour T.V. All bedrooms have H & C, shaver points, radios and baby listening. Car parking. Fire certificate. Les Routiers approved. Write/telephone for colour brochure.

Single Room per one person B&B		Double Room for two persons B&B		6
MIN £	MAX £	MIN £	MAX £	OPEN
10.00	12.00	20.00	24.00	1-12

Stanton House
33 Whitehall Road, Rhos-on-Sea,
Colwyn Bay, Clwyd, LL28 4ET.
Tel: (0492) 44363.

Family, licensed hotel open all year. Central heating. Bedrooms en-suite available. Tea making facilities, T.V. and reading lounge. Beach 100 yards. Ideal base for Snowdonia, Conwy, Bodnant Gardens. Early and late season breaks. Excellent cuisine. B & B and half board terms. Special terms for children sharing room with parents. AA*. Send for brochure.

Single Room per one person B&B		Double Room for two persons B&B		11
MIN £	MAX £	MIN £	MAX £	OPEN
10.00	11.50	20.00	23.00	1-12

Westwood
51 Princes Drive, Colwyn Bay,
Clwyd, LL29 8PL.
Tel: (0492) 532078.

Handy for beach, bus/railway stations, shops, theatre, Eirias park, Welsh Mountain Zoo. Excellent base for touring North Wales. All bedrooms have hot/cold, shaver points, central heating, colour T.V., tea/coffee making facilities. Licensed. Home cooking, including chef's special. Refreshments all day. Special rates children/senior citizens. Parking. Fire certificate. Open all year.

Single Room per one person B&B		Double Room for two persons B&B		9
MIN £	MAX £	MIN £	MAX £	OPEN
9.00	11.00	18.00	22.00	1-12

Guest Houses

Crossroads Guest House
Coed Pella Road, Colwyn Bay,
Clwyd, LL29 7AT.
Tel: (0492) 530736.

Family-run, well established Victorian guest house with considerable charm and relaxing atmosphere. Although in the town centre there are scenic views of the mountains and woods. All bedrooms have hot drinks and colour T.V. facilities, heating, H & C. The only guest house approved for accommodation in the borough by Les Routiers Good Value Guide.

Single Room per one person B&B		Double Room for two persons B&B		4
MIN £	MAX £	MIN £	MAX £	OPEN
8.00	8.50	16.00	17.00	1-12

Pinehurst
42 Greenfield Road, Colwyn Bay,
Clwyd, LL29 8EW.
Tel: (0492) 533873.

Licensed, family-run guest house. Open all year. Bed and breakfast with evening meal optional. Good home cooking. T.V. lounge. Centrally heated throughout. Close to beach and town centre. Ideal base for touring North Wales. Families welcome. Children half price. Free babysitting service.

Single Room per one person B&B		Double Room for two persons B&B		4
MIN £	MAX £	MIN £	MAX £	OPEN
7.00	8.00	14.00	16.00	1-12

Conwy
Map Ref Bb4

Strong medieval atmosphere here – mighty castle and complete town walls on the riverbank and many interesting historic buildings. Popular fish quay. Three bridges spanning the river, many waymarked footpaths. Gateway to Snowdonia. Good range of accommodation.

Hotels

Cyfnant Private Hotel
Henryd Road, Conwy, Gwynedd,
LL32 8HW.
Tel: (0492) 592442.

A warm friendly welcome awaits you at Cyfnant. Small licensed hotel, about 10 minutes walk from Conwy castle and harbour. Ideally situated for golf, sailing, fishing, riding. 5 bedrooms all with hot and cold, shaver points, T.V. 4 with private shower. Lounge with colour T.V. AA and RAC listed. Fire certificate held. Private parking.

Single Room per one person B&B		Double Room for two persons B&B		5
MIN £	MAX £	MIN £	MAX £	OPEN
9.50	10.50	20.00	22.00	3-10

Glyn Isa Hotel

Ro-wen, Nr. Conwy, Gwynedd,
LL32 8TB.
Tel: (0492) 650242.

Sixteen acres and trout lake. Georgian country house. Three rooms, luxury bath, shower en-suite. Beautifully furnished and decorated house. Close to the picturesque castled town of Conwy and Betws-y-Coed which is a walker's delight, with waterfalls, craft shop, golf course and restaurants.

P	Single Room per one person B&B		Double Room for two persons B&B		5
	MIN £ 10.00	MAX £ 12.00	MIN £ 20.00	MAX £ 24.00	OPEN 1-11

Llys Llewelyn

Mount Pleasant, Conwy, Gwynedd,
LL32 8NY.
Tel: (0492) 593257.

Detached Victorian house in a large private garden. We offer good value, good food and service with a smile. We aim to provide a comfortable room with colour T.V., tea/coffee maker, private shower, and front rooms have excellent views of Conwy castle. Lounge, dining room with licensed bar. Ideal base for touring.

P	Single Room per one person B&B		Double Room for two persons B&B		9
	MIN £ 10.75	MAX £ 12.00	MIN £ 21.50	MAX £ 24.00	OPEN 1-12

Myrtlewood Hotel

Penmaenmawr Road, Llanfairfechan,
Gwynedd, LL30 0PN.
Tel: (0248) 680735.

Myrtlewood is situated in 1 acre of grounds, overlooking Aberconwy Bay and Puffin Island. Fifteen miles radius of the hotel are the ancient towns of Caernarfon, Conwy and Beaumaris, with their famous castles. Pony trekking, golf, fishing and sailing are all available locally.

P	Single Room per one person B&B		Double Room for two persons B&B		10
	MIN £ 8.00	MAX £ 9.00	MIN £ 16.00	MAX £ 18.00	OPEN 1-12

Guest Houses

Angorfa Guest House

25 Cadnant Park, Conwy, Gwynedd,
LL32 8PR.
Tel: (049 263) 593280.

Quiet area close to town. Double, twin, family rooms. Ample toilet facilities. T.V. lounge. Bedtime drinks if required. Separate tables in dining room. Fire certificate. Central heating. Golf, riding close by. Access to rooms during day. Ideal touring centre. Parking on premises. Reduced rates for children sharing parents' room. S.a.e. please, Mrs. E. V. Williams.

P	Single Room per one person B&B		Double Room for two persons B&B		5
	MIN £	MAX £	MIN £ 17.00	MAX £ 17.00	OPEN 1-11

Cefn

Tyn-y-groes, Nr Conwy, Gwynedd,
LL32 8TA.
Tel: (0492) 650233.

Lovely 17th century country house set in 4 acres of grounds. Quiet and secluded in a rural and picturesque setting. Magnificent views of the Conwy Valley and Snowdonia. Three lovely bedrooms, all with en-suite facilities. Comfortable lounge with beams and inglenook fireplace. Ideal touring centre. Scenic drives, walks, castle, river, short drive to coast.

P	Single Room per one person B&B		Double Room for two persons B&B		3
	MIN £ 9.00	MAX £ 10.50	MIN £ 18.00	MAX £ 21.00	OPEN 1-12

Llys Gwilym Guest House

3 Mountain Road, Cadnant Park,
Conwy, Gwynedd, LL32 8PU.
Tel: (0492 59) 2351.

Friendly guest house makes ideal base for Snowdonia and coastal day visits. Short walk to Conwy and castle. Single, double and family rooms with hot and cold, shaver points. Colour T.V. lounge. Separate dining room. Licensed bar. AA and RAC listed. Fire certificate held. Evening meals by arrangement. Central heating. Resident proprietors Mr and Mrs Field.

P	Single Room per one person B&B		Double Room for two persons B&B		6
	MIN £ 9.50	MAX £ 10.50	MIN £ 18.00	MAX £ 20.00	OPEN 1-12

The Old Ship (16th Century Licensed) Guest House

28 High Street, Lancaster Square,
Conwy, Gwynedd, LL32 8DE.
Tel: (0492) 596445.

Relaxation and comfort assured in delightful 16th century surroundings. Situated within Conwy's historic town walls close to all amenities. All bedrooms have central heating, colour television, hand basins, tea and coffee facilities. Some rooms have private shower and toilet. We pride ourselves on the quality of our substantial home cooked breakfasts. Warm welcome guaranteed.

P	Single Room per one person B&B		Double Room for two persons B&B		6
	MIN £ 10.50	MAX £	MIN £ 21.00	MAX £	OPEN 1-12

Sunnybanks Guest House

Woodlands, Llanrwst Road, Conwy,
Gwynedd, LL32 8LT.
Tel: (0492) 593845.

Set in beautiful gardens with its own car park, our friendly guest house is situated high off main road, four minutes walk from Conwy Castle. Hot and cold in bedrooms. Good home cooking. T.V. lounge. Licensed restaurant. Off season rates. Ideal base for walking, riding, golf, fishing, sailing.

P	Single Room per one person B&B		Double Room for two persons B&B		7
	MIN £ 8.50	MAX £ 10.50	MIN £ 17.00	MAX £ 19.00	OPEN 1-12

Farmhouses

Garth Fawr Farm

Llangystennin, Llandudno Junction,
Gwynedd, LL31 9JF.
Tel: (0492) 44646.

A peaceful farmhouse offering 3 comfortable rooms. Hot and cold, shaver points and central heating in all rooms. Guests have private T.V. lounge and bathroom. Full breakfast and evening refreshments. Children under 11 at reduced rates. Situated midway between Conwy and Colwyn Bay at gateway to Snowdonia. For further details contact Mrs Margaret Williams.

P	Single Room per one person B&B		Double Room for two persons B&B		3
	MIN £ 8.50	MAX £ 10.00	MIN £ 17.00	MAX £ 20.00	OPEN 4-9

Glyn Uchaf

Conwy Old Road, Dwygyfylchi, Nr.
Penmaenmawr, Gwynedd, LL34 6YS.
Tel: (0492) 623737.

Situated on hillside in 10 acres of National Park land at the bottom of Sychnant Pass. Dining room, T.V. lounge, two bedrooms. Good home cooking. Home grown produce. Dogs welcome and horses stabled. Central for most activities. Reductions for children. An idyllic holiday setting.

P	Single Room per one person B&B		Double Room for two persons B&B		2
	MIN £ 10.50	MAX £ 12.00	MIN £ 17.00	MAX £ 21.00	OPEN 1-12

Henllys Farm

Llechwedd, Conwy, Gwynedd,
LL32 8DJ.
Tel: (0492) 593269 L

Ideally placed for touring Snowdonia and the North Wales coast, 1½ miles from Conwy. Colour T.V. lounge. Bathroom with bath and shower. One double, one family room with hot and cold, shaver point, tea and coffee making facilities. Evening meal. Good home cooking. Magnificent views of the countryside. 200 acre mixed working farm. AA listed. Send s.a.e. to Mrs. C. Roberts.

P	Single Room per one person B&B		Double Room for two persons B&B		2
	MIN £ 9.50	MAX £ 10.50	MIN £ 19.00	MAX £ 21.00	OPEN 4-10

Llandudno
Map Ref Bb3

The premier coastal resort of North Wales. Two beaches, good shops, a wide selection of hotels and guest houses. All the facilities a holiday maker needs for sports and entertainment. There are donkey rides, Punch and Judy, ski slope plus a pier and promenade. Visit the Great Orme and ride the Cabin lift and Tramway.

Hotels

Ashby Hotel
31 Church Walks, Llandudno,
Gwynedd, LL30 2HL.
Tel: (0492) 75608.

Two Crowns. Convenient both shores. Open all year. Separate tables. En-suites available. Licensed bar. T.V. lounge. Fire certificate held. Tea making, radio alarms, shaver points, H and C all rooms. Childrens' reductions.

Single Room per one person B&B		Double Room for two persons B&B		8
MIN £ 8.50	MAX £ 9.50	MIN £ 17.00	MAX £ 19.00	OPEN 1-12

Ashfields Hotel
32 Deganwy Avenue, Llandudno,
Gwynedd, LL30 2YB.
Tel: (0492) 79220.

Friendly family-run hotel, high standard food, comfort and service. On level, close to shops, beach, entertainment, skiing. Colour T.V. lounge, attractive dining room, licensed. Car park. Central heating. Modern bedrooms with colour T.V. and teasmades. Open all year. Evening meal on request. Discount for children, mid-week bookings. Send s.a.e. to Colin and Gwen Hicklin.

Single Room per one person B&B		Double Room for two persons B&B		10
MIN £ 8.00	MAX £ 9.00	MIN £ 16.00	MAX £ 18.00	OPEN 1-12

Banham House Hotel
2 St. David's Road, Llandudno,
Gwynedd, LL30 2UL.
Tel: (0492) 75680.

Select, fully central heated licensed hotel. Delightful T.V. lounge and a dining room with cocktail bar and excellent à la carte and table d'hôte menus. All bedrooms are tastefully decorated, have colour T.V., tea making facilities. En-suite rooms available. Open all year. You are assured of a warm welcome from the proprietors Tony and Tricia Sharpe.

Single Room per one person B&B		Double Room for two persons B&B		8
MIN £ 10.00	MAX £	MIN £ 20.00	MAX £	OPEN 1-12

The Bay Court Hotel
North Promenade, Llandudno,
Gwynedd, LL30 2LP.
Tel: (0492) 77356.

Situated on the seafront opposite pier entrance. The hotel offers magnificent panorama of Llandudno Bay. An ideal setting for visitors to Llandudno. Close to shops, entertainment, Happy Valley. Completely on the level. En-suite rooms, family rooms available. Generous children's reductions. Licensed bar. Excellent food. T.V. in rooms. Full central heating.

Single Room per one person B&B		Double Room for two persons B&B		11
MIN £ 8.50	MAX £ 10.50	MIN £ 17.00	MAX £ 19.00	OPEN 3-10

Brannock Hotel
36 St. David's Road, Llandudno,
Gwynedd, LL30 2UH.
Tel: (0492) 77483.

Situated between both shores, close to shops, railway station, etc. Car parking. Central heating. Separate tables. Open all year (except Christmas). Colour T.V. and tea/coffee making facilities in all rooms. Some rooms en-suite. Varied home cooking with choice of menu. Access to rooms at all times. Senior citizens discount. AA and RAC listed.

Single Room per one person B&B		Double Room for two persons B&B		7
MIN £ 9.00	MAX £ 11.00	MIN £ 18.00	MAX £ 22.00	OPEN 1-12

Brigstock Hotel
1 St. David's Place, Llandudno,
Gwynedd, LL30 2UG.
Tel: (0492) 76416.

Situated in the garden area of town, on the level, close to all amenities and entertainment. Choice of menu at all meals. Licensed bar. Separate T.V. lounge. Private bathrooms available. Colour T.V. and tea/coffee making in all bedrooms. Full central heating. Car park. AA/RAC listed. Any day to any day, your choice.

Single Room per one person B&B		Double Room for two persons B&B		10
MIN £ 9.50	MAX £ 10.50	MIN £ 19.00	MAX £ 21.00	OPEN 3-11

Bron Orme Private Hotel
54 Church Walks, Llandudno,
Gwynedd, LL30 2HL.
Tel: (0492) 76735.

Privately owned hotel AA* RAC*. Licensed. Only few minutes from promenade and town centre. Comfortable residents' lounge with panoramic views over town and bay. Colour television. Centrally heated bedrooms with hot and cold, shaver points and comfortable furnishing. Large south facing patio overlooking lawns and gardens. Short or long stay, any day booking welcomed.

Single Room per one person B&B		Double Room for two persons B&B		9
MIN £ 9.00	MAX £ 10.00	MIN £ 17.00	MAX £ 19.00	OPEN 1-12

Bryn Rosa
16 Abbey Road, Llandudno,
Gwynedd, LL30 2EA.
Tel: (0492) 78215.

"Bryn Rosa" is a small and friendly family-run hotel, conveniently situated for all amenities. Colour T.V. and tea making facilities in all bedrooms, some en-suite. Good home cooking with choice of menu. We serve a full English breakfast and five course dinner. Central heating. Free car park. AA listed. Credit cards accepted.

Single Room per one person B&B		Double Room for two persons B&B		7
MIN £ 8.00	MAX £ 9.50	MIN £ 16.00	MAX £ 19.00	OPEN 3-11

Carmel Private Hotel
17 Craig-y-Don Parade, Promenade,
Llandudno, Gwynedd, LL30 1BG.
Tel: (0492) 77643.

3 crowns. Highly recommended small private hotel ideally situated on seafront between the two Ormes. All pleasant airy bedrooms (some en-suite) with tea/coffee making facilities, have sea or mountain views, fitted carpets, bedhead lights and shaving points. Full central heating and fire precautions installed. Evening meal optional. Free car park on the premises.

Single Room per one person B&B		Double Room for two persons B&B		10
MIN £ 9.00	MAX £ 11.00	MIN £ 18.00	MAX £ 24.00	OPEN 4-10

Cleave Court Private Hotel
1 St. Seiriol's Road, Llandudno,
Gwynedd, LL30 2YY.
Tel: (0492) 77849.

Small family-run private hotel, situated in most quiet and pleasant garden area of the town with flat and easy access to shores, shops and all amenities. Colour T.V. lounge. Separate tables in dining room. Home cooking. All rooms hot and cold, shaver points. RAC listed. Fire certificate.

Single Room per one person B&B		Double Room for two persons B&B		5
MIN £ 10.00	MAX £ 11.00	MIN £ 20.00	MAX £ 22.00	OPEN 1-12

The Crickleigh Hotel
37/39 Lloyd Street, Llandudno,
Gwynedd, LL30 2YG.
Tel: (0492) 75926. L

Crickleigh is a detached, licensed hotel, situated in the most residential area of Llandudno. We are fortunate in being between the two shores on the level with no hills to climb. We do our best to welcome guests and ensure that you will have a very pleasant, enjoyable stay, with good wholesome food.

Single Room per one person B&B		Double Room for two persons B&B		15
MIN £ 11.50	MAX £ 12.00	MIN £ 23.00	MAX £ 24.00	OPEN 1-12

Epperstone Hotel

15 Abbey Road, Llandudno,
Gwynedd, LL30 2EE.
Tel: (0492) 78746.

A beautifully appointed centrally heated detached hotel in its own grounds with car park, situated between the two shores with Orme views. Open all year. Licensed. Eight well appointed bedrooms within a spacious elegant Edwardian house which has a majestic mahogany staircase, intimate dining room and a relaxing lounge. Excellent cuisine. 24 hour service.

Single Room per one person B&B		Double Room for two persons B&B		8
MIN £ 8.50	MAX £ 9.50	MIN £ 17.00	MAX £ 19.00	OPEN 1-12

Hatfield Hotel

12 St. David's Road, Llandudno,
Gwynedd, LL30 2UL.
Tel: (0492) 76518.

The Hatfield is a small, friendly family-run early 20th century hotel, situated in the rural part of Llandudno but close to all amenities. Offering good home cooked food. Centrally heated throughout, and cleanliness is a top priority. Personal service by the resident proprietors to make sure all our guests are happy and comfortable.

Single Room per one person B&B		Double Room for two persons B&B		10
MIN £ 8.50	MAX £ 9.50	MIN £ 17.00	MAX £ 19.00	OPEN 4-10

Heath House Hotel

Central Promenade, Llandudno,
Gwynedd, LL30 1AT.
Tel: (0492) 76538.

Les Routiers recommended family-run seafront hotel, open all year. All bedrooms have central heating, radio, telephone, room call and baby listening. Ground floor bedrooms. Delightful air conditioned Tudor style "No Smoking" dining room, choice menus. Colour television lounge, attractive bar with dance floor and cabaret entertainment in season. Eight rooms available at rate quoted.

Single Room per one person B&B		Double Room for two persons B&B		22
MIN £	MAX £	MIN £ 24.00	MAX £	OPEN 1-12

Hotel Messina

Hill Terrace, Llandudno, Gwynedd,
LL30 2LS.
Tel: (0492) 75260.

Fantastic situation close all amenities. Single, double and family rooms. Reductions for children. Rooms hot and cold, tea making facilities, T.V.'s, en-suite. Ideal centre for touring, fishing, golfing. Visit new dry ski slope, toboggan run. Special rates. Licensed bar. Home cooking. Midweek, weekend breaks. Open Xmas, New Year. Ring or write for brochure.

Single Room per one person B&B		Double Room for two persons B&B		12
MIN £ 10.00	MAX £ 12.00	MIN £ 20.00	MAX £ 24.00	OPEN 1-12

Karden House Hotel

16 Charlton Street, Llandudno,
Gwynedd, LL30 2AN.
Tel: (0492) 79347.

Family-run licensed hotel. Centrally situated close to sea, shops, bus and railway stations. We offer friendly service and excellent food. Spacious heated bedrooms, some on ground floor. Tea/coffee making facilities. No supplement for single rooms. Special rates for children sharing parents room. Free baby laundry service. Comfortable T.V. lounge and separate bar.

Single Room per one person B&B		Double Room for two persons B&B		12
MIN £ 7.50	MAX £ 10.00	MIN £ 15.00	MAX £ 20.00	OPEN 1-12

Kenmore Private Hotel

28 Trinity Avenue, Llandudno,
Gwynedd, LL30 2SJ.
Tel: (0492) 77774.

An attractive corner property, situated in a pleasant residential area with gardens to front and side. Spacious comfortably furnished rooms with tea makers, etc. Level walking to both shores and all amenities. Ideally situated whether touring North Wales or simply having a few relaxing days in Llandudno. Personal and friendly service from the proprietors Miriam and Dennis Butters.

Single Room per one person B&B		Double Room for two persons B&B		10
MIN £ 8.50	MAX £ 9.50	MIN £ 17.00	MAX £ 19.00	OPEN 2-11

The Linden Private Hotel

10 Church Walks, Llandudno,
Gwynedd. LL30 2HG.
Tel: (0492) 77684. L

The Lindens is a family-run hotel with a homely atmosphere and is highly recommended. It is situated in a supreme position at the foot of the Great Orme, close to pier, prom, gardens and all amenities. Shops 2 mins away. Hot/cold water and shaver points in all rooms. Colour T.V. Lounge. Residential Licence.

Single Room per one person B&B		Double Room for two persons B&B		18
MIN £ 8.50	MAX £ 9.50	MIN £ 17.00	MAX £ 19.00	OPEN 1-12

Mariners Lee

9 Clarence Road, Craig-y-Don,
Llandudno, Gwynedd, LL30 1TA.
Tel: (0492) 77513. L

Small family-run licensed hotel. Full central heating. 8 bedrooms each equipped with colour T.V., free tea and coffee making facilities, shaver points, washbasins with hot and cold water. T.V. lounge. Separate tables in dining room. Access to rooms all day. Close to beach and all amenities. Reductions for senior citizens and children.

Single Room per one person B&B		Double Room for two persons B&B		8
MIN £ 6.50	MAX £ 7.50	MIN £ 13.00	MAX £ 15.00	OPEN 1-11

Nant-y-Glyn Hotel

59 Church Walks, Llandudno,
Gwynedd, LL30 2HL.
Tel: (0492) 75915.

Nant-y-Glyn is a comfortable 10 bedroomed hotel located in quiet yet convenient position. Good food and a warm welcome assured. Full central heating. Just 300 yards from pier, close to shops, entertainment, ski slopes. Our secluded sun terrace has lovely views over Snowdonia. Excellent base for touring, walking, fishing, with four good golf courses close by.

Single Room per one person B&B		Double Room for two persons B&B		10
MIN £ 8.00	MAX £ 9.00	MIN £ 16.00	MAX £ 18.00	OPEN 1-12

Northgate Hotel

Central Promenade, Llandudno,
Gwynedd, LL30 1BB.
Tel: (0492) 77701.

Situated on central promenade close to town centre, theatres, swimming pool, pier, children's amusements, fishing, golf. Parties catered for. Open all year. Dining room and lounge overlook the bay. Bar with residential licence. Family rooms with reductions for children. Intercom, radio and baby listening all rooms. Tea making facilities. Colour T.V. Full central heating.

Single Room per one person B&B		Double Room for two persons B&B		12
MIN £ 9.90	MAX £	MIN £ 19.00	MAX £ 24.00	OPEN 1-12

Norwich House Hotel

122 Mostyn Street, Llandudno,
Gwynedd, LL30 2SW.
Tel: (0492) 77972. L

A family-run hotel. Situated one minute from promenade, pier and shopping centre. Offering licensed bar, bar snacks, optional evening meal, all home cooking. Colour televisions, tea and coffee facilities in all bedrooms. Television lounge. Family rooms, child minding service. Reduced rates for children. Full fire certificate. Props: Carol and Tony Griffiths.

Single Room per one person B&B		Double Room for two persons B&B		10
MIN £ 9.50	MAX £ 9.50	MIN £ 19.00	MAX £ 19.00	OPEN 1-12

Nuneham House Hotel

12 South Parade, Llandudno,
Gwynedd, LL30 2LN.
Tel: (0492) 77369.

Family-run hotel adjacent pier and beach. Residential and restaurant licence. All rooms have tea making facilities. T.V.'s on request. Large proportion of rooms en-suite. Choice of menu, snacks served until 23.00. Sauna/sunbed. From £12.00 per day D.B.B.

Single Room per one person B&B		Double Room for two persons B&B		14
MIN £ 10.00	MAX £ 12.00	MIN £ 20.00	MAX £ 24.00	OPEN 2-11

Oak-Alyn Hotel

Deganwy Avenue, Llandudno,
Gwynedd, LL30 2YB.
Tel: (0492) 76497.

Family-run. RAC*/AA*. Situated town centre. Ample parking own car park. Real home cooking, varied menu. Comfortable rooms with colour T.V., drink making facilities. Well stocked bar. All rooms have own toilet, bath/shower. Midweek or weekend bookings taken. Book now for great value for money. Ring (0492) 76497 for brochure.

Single Room per one person B&B		Double Room for two persons B&B		14
MIN £	MAX £	MIN £	MAX £	OPEN
11.50		23.00		3-12

St. Katherine's

Church Walks, Llandudno, Gwynedd,
LL30 2HL.
Tel: (0492) 70329.

Situated in a quiet position yet only a few minutes from both beaches and shops.
St. Katherine's is a family-run hotel with an impeccable reputation. We can also offer climbing, walking and dry ski slope. Weeks or weekends.

Single Room per one person B&B		Double Room for two persons B&B		8
MIN £	MAX £	MIN £	MAX £	OPEN
10.00	12.00	18.00	24.00	4-11

Sunnycroft Private Hotel

4 Claremont Road, Llandudno,
Gwynedd, LL30 2UF.
Tel: (0492) 76882.

Situated 5 minutes from both shores. Family-run licensed hotel under new management. Full central heating, dining room, television lounge, bar. Evening meal optional. Twelve bedrooms, all with tea making facilities. Ground floor bedroom for elderly/disabled. Noted for our high standards of cleanliness and cuisine. Open all year. Fire certificate. Children 2-12 half price.

Single Room per one person B&B		Double Room for two persons B&B		12
MIN £	MAX £	MIN £	MAX £	OPEN
8.50	8.50	17.00	17.00	1-12

Tan y Marian Private Hotel

87 Abbey Road, West Shore,
Llandudno, Gwynedd, LL30 2AS.
Tel: (0492) 77727.

Charming small hotel. Perfect situation at foot of the Great Orme. Only yards from Llandudno's beautiful West Shore. Lovely scenery, sandy beaches, two golf courses nearby. Something for everyone. Pleasant well furnished bedrooms, C.H., tea making facilities, some en-suite rooms. Licensed. Parking. Excellent meals. Reduced rates for children. Dogs by arrangement.

Single Room per one person B&B		Double Room for two persons B&B		8
MIN £	MAX £	MIN £	MAX £	OPEN
9.00	11.00	17.00	20.00	3-10

Thorpe House Hotel

3 St. David's Road, Llandudno,
Gwynedd, LL30 2UL.
Tel: (0492) 77089.

Friendly, family-run small hotel with special rates for small parties. Full central heating. Residential licence. Family rooms with children 50% discount. All bedrooms with handbasins, some en-suite. Central for shops, beaches, entertainment. Good home cooking. Free transport from station or coach. Three fine golf courses in area, theatre, bowling greens. Ideal touring.

Single Room per one person B&B		Double Room for two persons B&B		10
MIN £	MAX £	MIN £	MAX £	OPEN
9.50	10.50	19.00	21.00	1-11

Warwick Hotel

56 Church Walks, Llandudno,
Gwynedd, LL30 2HL.
Tel: (0492) 76823.

The Warwick has a tradition of a friendly, welcoming service and guests are sure of comfortable and relaxed surroundings to enable them to take full advantage of Llandudno's invigorating climate. Only a few minutes walk to beach, pier and shopping centre. Some en-suite rooms with T.V. available. Lounge bar. Central heating. Tea/coffee facilities. Brochure available.

Single Room per one person B&B		Double Room for two persons B&B		17
MIN £	MAX £	MIN £	MAX £	OPEN
11.00	12.00	22.00	24.00	4-10

Westbourne Hotel

8 Arvon Avenue, Llandudno,
Gwynedd, LL30 2DY.
Tel: (0492) 77450.

Double fronted private hotel, very central on flat ground. Colour T.V. in bedrooms. Central heating and tea making facilities. Licensed bar. Chef proprietor. Some bedrooms with private facilities, including ground floor. Near to all amenities. Children and pensioner reduced rate. Open Christmas. 4 day Christmas special. Send s.a.e. to Mrs Jones for brochure.

Single Room per one person B&B		Double Room for two persons B&B		13
MIN £	MAX £	MIN £	MAX £	OPEN
10.50	11.50	21.00	23.00	3-12

Whitefriars Hotel

10 Abbey Road, Llandudno,
Gwynedd, LL30 2EA.
Tel: (0492) 76287.

Situated within minutes from shopping centre, pier, Haulfre gardens, Happy Valley and West Shore. Lovely, spacious old house. Two floors only. Licensed bar with small dance floor. Television lounge. Separate tables in dining room. Free tea/coffee making facilities and colour television in all bedrooms. 8 rooms en-suite. All home cooking, food plentiful.

Single Room per one person B&B		Double Room for two persons B&B		13
MIN £	MAX £	MIN £	MAX £	OPEN
10.00	11.00	20.00	22.00	3-10

White Heather Hotel

St. George's Place, Llandudno,
Gwynedd, LL30 2NR.
Tel: (0492) 76421.

White Heather has been owned and managed by the family for 40yrs, thus assuring all guests a friendly, personal service. Heating to all bedrooms. Full fire certificate. Own keys. Passengers lift. T.V. lounge. Reading lounge. Ballroom. Bar. Sun verandah. Some rooms en-suite. Tea/coffee facilities all rooms. Some rooms colour T.V. Brochure on request.

Single Room per one person B&B		Double Room for two persons B&B		39
MIN £	MAX £	MIN £	MAX £	OPEN
10.00	12.00	20.00	24.00	4-10

Willowmere Private Hotel

4 – 6 Maelgwyn Road, Llandudno,
Gwynedd, LL30 2YN.
Tel: (0492) 76888.

An attractive family-run hotel with parking on the premises. Central heating throughout. Excellent cuisine in a spacious dining room and comfortable T.V. lounge and lounge bar with warm atmosphere. Situated between both shores and close to the shops. Well centred for activities concerning all ages. Half price for children sharing with adults.

Single Room per one person B&B		Double Room for two persons B&B		17
MIN £	MAX £	MIN £	MAX £	OPEN
8.00	9.00	16.00	18.00	1-12

Guest Houses

Alvastrada

24 Caroline Road, Llandudno,
Gwynedd, LL30 2JY.
Tel: (0492) 78229. L

Close to railway/coach stations, promenade, shopping centre, entertainments, sports facilities. Family, double, single rooms. Access all day. Large lounge, colour T.V. Bathroom with shower and W.C. Separate W.C. Central heating. Fire certificate. Parking space. Payphone. Available on request: evening refreshments, packed lunches, early morning tea, tea/coffee facilities. Evening meals.

Single Room per one person B&B		Double Room for two persons B&B		7
MIN £	MAX £	MIN £	MAX £	OPEN
7.00	8.00	13.50	15.50	1-12

Ashbourne Guest House
6 Rosebery Avenue, Craig-y-Don,
Llandudno, Gwynedd, LL30 1TF.
Tel: (0492) 77610.

A small established guest house ideally situated in Craig-y-Don. All four tastefully furnished bedrooms, one with en-suite, are on the first floor. An inviting dining room with separate tables where excellent home cooking is served. For relaxing, a luxuriously furnished lounge with colour T.V. Ashbourne is a must for flower lovers.

Single Room per one person B&B		Double Room for two persons B&B		4
MIN £	MAX £	MIN £ 17.00	MAX £ 21.00	OPEN 4-10

Belmont Guest House
18 Clifton Road, Llandudno,
Gwynedd, LL30 2YH.
Tel: (0492) 77179. L

Family-run business, situated 5 minutes walk beaches/town centre. Hot & cold, shaver points all rooms. Guests lounge with colour T.V., video. Good home cooking with daily choice of menus for dinner. Separate tables. Family rooms available. Reductions for children. Sorry no pets. Fire certificate.

Single Room per one person B&B		Double Room for two persons B&B		5
MIN £ 7.00	MAX £ 7.50	MIN £ 14.00	MAX £ 15.00	OPEN 1-9

Branstone
14 Llewelyn Avenue, Llandudno,
Gwynedd, LL30 2ER.
Tel: (0492) 76448.

Situated 200 yards from beach, our family managed hotel is licensed and has a reputation for good food, personally prepared by the proprietor. Hearty breakfasts to choose from, 5 course dinner with choice. Colour T.V. lounge. Hot and cold, shaver points, bedside lights all rooms. Own keys. Access all times. Midday, evening snacks. Your comfort our priority.

Single Room per one person B&B		Double Room for two persons B&B		10
MIN £ 8.50	MAX £ 9.50	MIN £ 17.00	MAX £ 19.00	OPEN 1-12

Bryn Hazel Guest House
10 Harcourt Road, Craig-y-Don,
Llandudno, Gwynedd, LL30 1TU.
Tel: (0492) 75098. L

Friendly guest house on level ground in quiet road, close to bowling green, park, tennis courts. Short distance to beach, shops and entertainments. Comfortable colour television lounge. Single, double and family rooms available. Reductions for children. Access to rooms at all times. Fire certificate granted. Full central heating. Open all year. Sorry no pets.

Single Room per one person B&B		Double Room for two persons B&B		7
MIN £ 6.50	MAX £ 7.00	MIN £ 13.00	MAX £ 14.00	OPEN 1-12

Bryn Tawel
19 St. David's Road, Llandudno,
Gwynedd, LL30 2UL.
Tel: (0492) 77979. L

Friendly guest house situated on the level within walking distance of both shores. Highest standard of cuisine. Separate tables in dining room. Comfortable lounge. Colour T.V. Personal attention at all times. Diets catered for. Midweek bookings. Central heating. Tea making facilities. Access to rooms at all times.

Single Room per one person B&B		Double Room for two persons B&B		8
MIN £ 8.00	MAX £ 8.50	MIN £ 16.00	MAX £ 17.00	OPEN 1-12

Cunliffe
Gogarth Road, West Shore,
Llandudno, Gwynedd, LL30 2AP.
Tel. (0492) 70257. L

Situated in a quiet cul-de-sac of Great Orme's Road. Within walking distance of the main entertainment and shopping centre. One minute from the beach. Two golf courses within a mile. Bedrooms centrally heated, hot and cold, razor points, tea making facilities. Good home cooking. Separate tables. Television lounge.

Single Room per one person B&B		Double Room for two persons B&B		4
MIN £ 7.50	MAX £	MIN £ 15.00	MAX £	OPEN 4-11

Dolwen Guest House
7 St. Mary's Road, Llandudno,
Gwynedd, LL30 2UB.
Tel: (0492) 77757.

Situated on the level near town centre. Beautifully appointed house. Bedrooms with hot and cold, razor points. Lounge with colour T.V. Separate dining room. Central heating. Good home cooking, evening meals optional. Children welcomed.

Single Room per one person B&B		Double Room for two persons B&B		3
MIN £ 7.00	MAX £ 8.00	MIN £ 7.00	MAX £ 14.00	OPEN 4-10

Elgin Lodge
14 Abbey Road, Llandudno,
Gwynedd, LL30 2EA.
Tel: (0492) 78486.

Ideally situated within close reach of shopping centre and beach in quiet pleasant area. Small private car park. All rooms with shaver point and hot and cold. Central heating. T.V. lounge. Pleasant dining room with good home cooking and personal service of the proprietors.

Single Room per one person B&B		Double Room for two persons B&B		8
MIN £ 8.00	MAX £ 9.00	MIN £ 16.00	MAX £ 18.00	OPEN 1-12

Glenvine Guest House
45 Church Walks, Llandudno,
Gwynedd, LL30 2HL.
Tel: (0492) 75850.

A small homely guest house, situated at foot of Great Orme. Highly recommended, plentiful food and warm friendly atmosphere. Families welcome, reduced rates. Large garden, swings, slide and climbing frame. Panoramic views. Full central heating. Shower or en-suite some bedrooms. Tea and coffee facilities, colour T.V.'s all bedrooms. T.V. lounge. Games room.

Single Room per one person B&B		Double Room for two persons B&B		6
MIN £ 8.75	MAX £ 9.00	MIN £ 17.00	MAX £ 18.00	OPEN 1-10

Granby Guest House
Deganwy Avenue, Llandudno,
Gwynedd, LL30 2DD.
Tel: (0492) 76095.

Centrally situated near town centre and beaches. Family-run guest house offering family, double and twin rooms, some with private facilities, colour T.V., tea makers. We offer a varied choice of menu, special diets catered for. Parking space. Cosy bar. Mid-week booking, also mini breaks available. AA listed. British Relais Routier recommended.

Single Room per one person B&B		Double Room for two persons B&B		8
MIN £ 10.50	MAX £ 11.00	MIN £ 19.00	MAX £ 20.00	OPEN 4-10

Hampton House
1 Claremont Road, Llandudno,
Gwynedd, LL30 2UF.
Tel: (0492) 860588. L

Situated five minutes from town centre in quiet, residential area. Bedrooms with hot/cold, razor points, colour T.V., central heating. T.V. lounge. Residential licence. Good home cooking. Reduced rates for children. Car parking space. All bedrooms have tea making facilities. Warm and friendly atmosphere. Family-run business.

Single Room per one person B&B		Double Room for two persons B&B		7
MIN £ 8.00	MAX £ 8.00	MIN £ 15.00	MAX £ 15.00	OPEN 3-12

Hayley House
22 Church Walks, Llandudno,
Gwynedd, LL30 2HG.
Tel: (0492) 79249.

Small guest house with full central heating, situated close to pier, beach, town, ski slope and Great Orme tram. All bedrooms have vanity units, shaver points, tea making facilities. Good home cooking, separate tables, television lounge, shower facilities. Reduced rates for children under 14 sharing parents room. Fire certificate held. Our best attention assured.

Single Room per one person B&B		Double Room for two persons B&B		6
MIN £ 7.50	MAX £ 8.50	MIN £ 15.00	MAX £ 17.00	OPEN 1-12

Heatherdale

30 St. David's Road, Llandudno,
Gwynedd, LL30 2UL.
Tel: (0492) 77362. L

A homely family-run guest house with a friendly atmosphere. Situated in one of Llandudno's loveliest areas between shores and convenient to all amenities. All bedrooms with colour televisions, tea/coffee facilities, storage heaters. Qualified chef proprietor provides excellent food. Personal attention is assured.

Single Room per one person B&B		Double Room for two persons B&B		8
MIN £ 10.00	MAX £ 10.00	MIN £ 18.00	MAX £ 18.00	OPEN 1-12

Hollybank

9 St. David's Place, Llandudno,
Gwynedd, LL30 2UG.
Tel: (0492) 78521.

Central and close to all amenities. Free lock-up car parking. Central heating. Spacious single, double and family bedrooms, all with hot and cold, shaver points. Warm welcome with highly recommended home cooking. Separate tables. Colour T.V. Fire certificate. Children welcome, ½ price if sharing with parents. Babysitting. Birdwatching and local tours organised.

Single Room per one person B&B		Double Room for two persons B&B		6
MIN £ 7.50	MAX £ 8.50	MIN £ 15.00	MAX £ 17.00	OPEN 4-10

Imbros Guest House

37 Bryniau Road, Llandudno,
Gwynedd, LL30 2EZ.
Tel: (0492) 77922. L

Situated on West Shore, walking distance from town centre. Single, double, family rooms available. Special rates for children. Colour T.V. lounge. Central heating. Full fire certificate. H & C, tea making facilities.

Single Room per one person B&B		Double Room for two persons B&B		3
MIN £ 7.00	MAX £ 7.00	MIN £ 14.00	MAX £ 14.00	OPEN 3-10

The Kestrel

25 Deganwy Avenue, Llandudno,
Gwynedd, LL30 2YB.
Tel: (0492) 75108.

Located in the heart of Llandudno, level and convenient for all amenities, main shopping centre, conference and entertainment centres. Close to two golf courses, both seashores, dry ski slope and bus and rail terminals. All bedrooms en-suite with colour television, teamaker, clock radio. Central heating throughout. Full English breakfast. Four course candlelit dinners. Limited car parking.

Single Room per one person B&B		Double Room for two persons B&B		10
MIN £ 11.00	MAX £ 12.00	MIN £ 22.00	MAX £ 24.00	OPEN 3-10

Lincoln Villa

23 Trinity Avenue, LLandudno,
Gwynedd, LL30 2SJ.
Tel: (0492) 79686. L

Lincoln Villa is ideally situated on the level between both shores and minutes from town centre, beaches and entertainments. All bedrooms have hot and cold water, razor sockets, central heating and tea makers. Comfortable lounge with colour television. Good home cooking with full English/Welsh breakfast. Evening meal by arrangement. Fire certificate has been granted.

Single Room per one person B&B		Double Room for two persons B&B		5
MIN £ 8.00	MAX £ 9.00	MIN £ 16.00	MAX £ 18.00	OPEN 4-10

Maldon Guest House

12 Clifton Road, Llandudno,
Gwynedd, LL30 2YH.
Tel: (0492) 79503. L

Centrally situated on the level. Five minutes sea and shops. Central heating, hot and cold, shaver points all bedrooms. Tea makers. Children welcome. Home cooking with choice of menu, separate tables. Licensed bar. Television lounge. Full fire certificate.

Single Room per one person B&B		Double Room for two persons B&B		5
MIN £ 9.50	MAX £ 9.50	MIN £ 19.00	MAX £ 19.00	OPEN 3-11

Plas Brith

38 Church Walks, Llandudno,
Gwynedd, LL30 2HN.
Tel: (0492) 79991. L

Detached house of character within minutes walk of two shores and town centre. Situated at foot of the Great Orme. Bedrooms with hot and cold, razor points, some with private shower. Colour T.V., central heating. Good home cooking and homely atmosphere. Separate tables in spacious dining room. Cocktail bar. Midweek bookings.

Single Room per one person B&B		Double Room for two persons B&B		7
MIN £ 7.50	MAX £ 9.00	MIN £ 15.00	MAX £ 18.00	OPEN 3-11

Rose-Tor Licensed Guest House

124 Mostyn Street, Llandudno,
Gwynedd, LL30 2SW.
Tel: (0492) 70433.

Rose-Tor is decorated throughout with great flair and creates a calm, relaxing atmosphere. All bedrooms are en-suite with central heating, colour T.V., telephone, clock/radio, tea/coffee units, also hairdryers. Our restaurant offers a table d'hôte menu, also bar meals served all day until 12 p.m. in our cosy licensed bar.

Single Room per one person B&B		Double Room for two persons B&B		9
MIN £ 12.00	MAX £	MIN £ 23.00	MAX £	OPEN 1-12

St. David's Guest House

32 Clifton Road, Llandudno,
Gwynedd, LL30 2YH.
Tel: (0492) 79216. L

Situated between the two shores of Llandudno close to all amenities. The St. David's offers hot and cold in all bedrooms. Colour T.V. lounge, homely atmosphere, excellent food service. Access at all times. Open all year and Christmas. We assure you that we do our best to ensure the comfort of all our guest. Brochure from Mrs. Jill Martin.

Single Room per one person B&B		Double Room for two persons B&B		7
MIN £ 9.00	MAX £ 9.50	MIN £ 18.00	MAX £ 19.00	OPEN 1-12

Prestatyn

Map Ref Be3

North-east Wales family seaside resort, with good selection of holiday centres. All kinds of entertainment at the superb Nova Centre and Royal Lido. Heated outdoor pool, sailing, swimming on the long, sandy coastline.

Guest Houses

Hawarden House

13-15 Victoria Road, Prestatyn,
Clwyd, LL19 7SW.
Tel: (074 56) 4226. L

Situated on main North Wales coast, five minutes from beach. Home from home service and cooking. Prestatyn town 2 minutes walk, Nova Swimming Pool and bars 5 minutes away. T.V. and central heating in all rooms. Children and dogs welcome. T.V. lounge. Own keys, can come and go at your leisure. Fire certificate held.

Single Room per one person B&B		Double Room for two persons B&B		6
MIN £ 7.50	MAX £ 7.50	MIN £ 15.00	MAX £ 15.00	OPEN 1-12

Marine Court

4-6 Marine Road, Prestatyn, Clwyd,
LL19 7HD.
Tel: (074 56) 6825.

A spacious house personally run in a friendly family atmosphere. We guarantee cleanliness and good home cooked food, as well as complying fully with the two crown requirements. Central for town centre (bus, railway station), hillside walks (Offa's Dyke), beach with new Nova indoor fun pool, cabaret complex. Illustrated brochure.

Single Room per one person B&B		Double Room for two persons B&B		10
MIN £ 7.50	MAX £ 9.00	MIN £ 15.00	MAX £ 18.00	OPEN 1-12

Roughsedge House

28 Marine Road, Prestatyn, Clwyd,
LL19 7HD.
Tel: (07456) 87359.

Situated close to main railway, Offa's Dyke footpath, Pontins and Presthaven Sands holiday camps. Offering friendly service and home cooked foods, special diets are welcomed. All rooms contain washbasins, tea and coffee making facilities and are furnished to a high standard. Centrally heated with open lounge fire in winter. Children welcome.

Single Room per one person B&B		Double Room for two persons B&B		6
MIN £ 8.00	MAX £ 8.50	MIN £ 15.00	MAX £ 16.00	OPEN 1-12

Rhos-on-Sea

Map Ref Bc4

Village linking Llandudno and Colwyn Bay with promenade, beach and golf.

Hotels

Whitehall Hotel

Cayley Promenade, Rhos-on-Sea,
Colwyn Bay, Clwyd, LL28 4EP.
Tel: (0492) 47296.

Friendly family-run licensed hotel on the beautiful Cayley promenade at Rhos-on-Sea. Lovely bay views. Close to all local amenities. Ideal touring area. 14 bedrooms with heating, tea trays, H & C, shaver points. (6 with shower, W/C and colour T.V.). Cosy bar. Separate T.V. lounge. High standard of catering. Choice of menu. AA/RAC*.

Single Room per one person B&B		Double Room for two persons B&B		14
MIN £ 11.50	MAX £	MIN £ 23.00	MAX £	OPEN 4-10

Guest Houses

The Cedar Tree

27 Whitehall Road, Rhos-on-Sea,
Colwyn Bay, Clwyd, LL28 4HW.
Tel: (0492) 45867.

Comfortable, friendly guest house, 300 yards promenade, convenient Snowdonia National Park, Bodnant, Conwy. Colwyn Bay railway/coach stations within one mile. Private parking. En-suite facilities all bedrooms. Central heating. Tea making facilities. Family rooms available. Special rates for children sharing parents room. Excellent cuisine, separate tables. Attractive lounge with colour television. Fire certificate to latest standards.

Single Room per one person B&B		Double Room for two persons B&B		7
MIN £ 10.00	MAX £ 11.50	MIN £ 20.00	MAX £ 23.00	OPEN 1-11

Gwylfa

79 Everard Road, Rhos-on-Sea,
Colwyn Bay, Clwyd, LL28 4HA.
Tel: (0492) 44760.

Pleasantly situated in the village of Rhos-on-Sea, only 300 yards from promenade. Licensed guest house with comfortable T.V. lounge, attractive dining room with separate tables. All bedrooms on first floor with tea making facilities. Excellent food. Children welcome, 16 and under half price. Write or phone Barbara or Paul Lyon for brochure.

Single Room per one person B&B		Double Room for two persons B&B		6
MIN £ 8.50	MAX £ 9.50	MIN £ 17.00	MAX £ 19.00	OPEN 1-12

Sunnyside

146 Dinerth Road, Rhos-on-Sea,
Colwyn Bay, Clwyd, LL28 4YT.
Tel: (0492) 44048. L

A warm welcome awaits you at our comfortable guest house situated in the town of Rhos-on-Sea, adjacent to Colwyn Bay and Llandudno, offering ample shopping facilities, miles of excellent coastline and close to the mountains of Snowdonia. Lovely country views from our establishment, with good home cooked breakfasts and excellent value accommodation.

Single Room per one person B&B		Double Room for two persons B&B		2
MIN £ 8.00	MAX £ 12.00	MIN £ 16.00	MAX £ 24.00	OPEN 6-9

Rhyl

Map Ref Bd4

Major North Wales coast resort. Extensive holiday caravan parks offering all round entertainment. The Sun Centre is a major attraction, also funfair and Marine Lake park. Safe swimming, sailing. An ideal seaside holiday resort for the whole family.

Hotels

Plastirion Private Hotel

45-48 East Parade, Rhyl, Clwyd,
LL18 3AW.
Tel: (0745) 53170.

Situated adjacent to Rhyl's Suncentre and opposite the rock gardens and beach. Shaver points, tea making facilities in all rooms. Party bookings a speciality at party terms. T.V. lounge, games room, bar. Parking for twelve cars.

Single Room per one person B&B		Double Room for two persons B&B		49
MIN £ 9.30	MAX £ 10.50	MIN £ 18.60	MAX £ 21.00	OPEN 4-10

West Cliffe Hotel

88 West Parade, Rhyl, Clwyd,
LL18 1HW.
Tel: (0745) 53705. L

Pleasant family-run seafront hotel. Licensed bar. Passenger lift. En-suite rooms available. Children welcome and catered for. Excellent food, home cooking.

Single Room per one person B&B		Double Room for two persons B&B		18
MIN £ 9.00	MAX £ 11.00	MIN £ 18.00	MAX £ 24.00	OPEN 3-11

West Shore Hotel

74 West Parade, Rhyl, Clwyd,
LL18 1HN.
Tel: (0745) 51499. L

Situated on the seafront in Rhyl. Nice large bedrooms, all with handbasins with H & C water. Hotel has a licensed bar. Open all the year round. Small parties catered for. Reduced rates for children. Fire certificate held. Send for a brochure from the above address.

Single Room per one person B&B		Double Room for two persons B&B		17
MIN £ 8.00	MAX £ 10.00	MIN £ 15.00	MAX £ 21.00	OPEN 1-12

Guest Houses

Arncliffe

100 Crescent Road, Rhyl, Clwyd,
LL18 1LY.
Tel: (0745) 53634. L

Centrally situated five minutes to sea front, pleasure beach and all amenities. All rooms have hot and cold water, shaver point. Tastefully decorated throughout. T.V. room. Separate dining room. Free baby listening service. Families welcome. Good home cooking. Reduced rates early and late season. Reduced rates for children. Parking nearby. RAC listed.

Single Room per one person B&B		Double Room for two persons B&B		6
MIN £ 7.50	MAX £ 8.50	MIN £ 15.00	MAX £ 17.00	OPEN 1-11

Beechroyde Guest House

27 Palace Avenue, Rhyl, Clwyd,
LL18 1HS.
Tel: (0745) 50159.

Situated only 7 doors from promenade. Close to all amenities. Popular west end. Good home cooking. Separate tables. Evening drinks and snacks available. Shaver points, hot and cold all rooms. Own door keys. Access at all times. T.V. lounge. Full central heating. Open all year. Reductions for senior citizens off peak times.

Single Room per one person B&B		Double Room for two persons B&B		5
MIN £ 7.00	MAX £ 11.00	MIN £ 14.00	MAX £ 22.00	OPEN 1-12

The Links Guest House

20 Beechwood Road, Rhyl, Clwyd,
LL18 3EU.
Tel: (0745) 53291.

A friendly welcome atmosphere awaits you at The Links, only 50 yards to East Parade, and the "Tropical Sun Centre". All bedrooms recently modernised with hot and cold, shaver points, tea makers and full central heating. Highly recommended for good traditional food and hospitality. Special rates for children and senior citizens. Try us with confidence.

	Single Room per one person B&B		Double Room for two persons B&B		8
P ✕	MIN £ 8.50	MAX £ 10.00	MIN £ 15.00	MAX £ 19.00	OPEN 3-11

Rosemount

9-11 Crugan Avenue, Kinmel Bay,
Nr. Rhyl, Clwyd, LL18 5DF.
Tel: (0745) 4273.

L

Detached house of great character near to beach and every amenity. Beamed ceilings, beautiful lounge. Landscaped gardens with ponds and waterfall. Comfortable bedrooms, central heating, colour T.V. and really excellent food. Ideal for seaside holidays and/or touring Snowdonia. Quietly situated yet very near to coast road. Single or double rooms. Family and O.A.P.'s very welcome.

	Single Room per one person B&B		Double Room for two persons B&B		2
P ✕	MIN £ 7.50	MAX £ 8.00	MIN £ 15.00	MAX £ 16.00	OPEN 1-12

Sandy Shores

48, River Street, Rhyl, Clwyd,
LL18 1PY.
Tel: (0745) 51989/ 38242.

A warm welcome awaits you at Sandy Shores. We offer excellent cuisine, clean, comfortable accommodation. Hot drink facilities and T.V. All rooms free use of shower and private car park. Special diets catered for. Adjacent promenade, short walk town, bus/train stations and markets. Ground floor accommodation available. We aim to make your stay a happy one.

	Single Room per one person B&B		Double Room for two persons B&B		9
P ✕	MIN £ 7.50	MAX £ 11.00	MIN £ 15.00	MAX £ 22.00	OPEN 1-12

Seaspray Guest House

14 Beechwood Road, Rhyl, Clwyd,
LL18 3EU.
Tel: (0745) 4177.

A quiet homely guest house with an excellent reputation for genuine home cooking. Situated 50 yards from Rhyl's splendid East Parade and Tropical Sun Centre. Fully centrally heated. Shaver points and tea making facilities in all rooms. Full fire certificate. Reduced rates for children and senior citizens.

	Single Room per one person B&B		Double Room for two persons B&B		5
P ✕	MIN £ 8.50	MAX £ 10.00	MIN £ 15.00	MAX £ 18.00	OPEN 3-10

The Wroxeter

29 Warren Road, Rhyl, Clwyd,
LL18 1DR.
Tel: (0745) 53904.

Situated close to all amenities. Hot and cold, shaver points, colour televisions, radio alarms, baby minding intercoms all bedrooms, own keys. Separate tables. Licensed bar. Television lounge. Good home cooking. Open all year. Fire certificate held. Laundry service available. Wales Tourist Board approved one crown rating. Car collection from coach or train station free.

	Single Room per one person B&B		Double Room for two persons B&B		7
✕	MIN £ 8.00	MAX £ 9.50	MIN £ 16.00	MAX £ 19.00	OPEN 1-12

LLŶN-SNOWDON'S PENINSULA

Llŷn, an emphatic arm of land pointing forcefully into the Irish Sea, has always been out-on-a-limb, a place apart. Its whitewashed farmsteads, wind-tossed hedgerows, severe cliffs, wave-scoped bays and sandy beaches are westward looking by nature, Celtic in character.

Standing between the peninsula and Snowdonia's mountains is Porthmadog, a bustling old harbourside town busy with sailing craft and the little engines of the Ffestiniog Narrow-gauge Railway. Llŷn itself is dotted – whenever the cliffs and headlands will allow – with charming little resorts. There's castle-crowned Criccieth, a Victorian gem. Pwllheli has fine sands, Abersoch a sheltered, boat-filled harbour, Nefyn a superb succession of sandy bays.

Some of Wales's wildest coastline surrounds far-flung Aberdaron. And around Trefor, Yr Eifl mountains take a breathtaking plunge into the sea. Little wonder, then, that Llŷn is another 'Area of Outstanding Natural Beauty'.

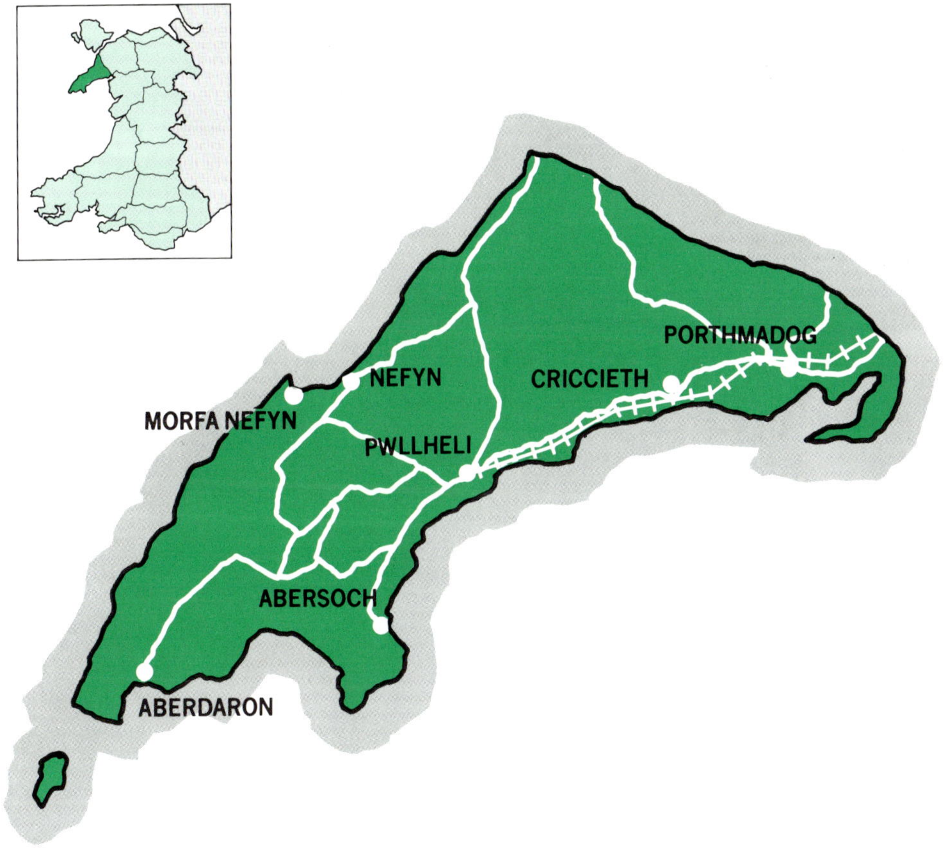

Aberdaron

Map Ref Aa5

Small picturesque village on the tip of the Llŷn Peninsula. Y Gegin Fawr, now a café and souvenir shop, was once a rest house for pilgrims to the nearby Bardsey Island, which you can see across Bardsey Sound.

Hotels

Ship Hotel

Aberdaron, Nr. Pwllheli, Gwynedd, LL53 8BE.
Tel: (075 886) 204. L

Fully licensed family Inn situated in centre of village within yards of beach. Golf, fishing, riding all nearby. Pool, darts in bar, evening meal, bar snacks available as required. Separate residents' bar. Dining room. Lounge with T.V. Children welcome in our cheerful informal atmosphere.

	Single Room per one person B&B		Double Room for two persons B&B		8
	MIN £	MAX £	MIN £	MAX £	OPEN
	12.00	12.00	24.00	24.00	1-12

Guest Houses

Carreg Plâs Guest House

Aberdaron, Pwllheli, Gwynedd, LL53 8LH.
Tel: (075 886) 308.

17th century manor house of historic interest in secluded wooded grounds. Two miles from Aberdaron, close to the famous Whistling Sands Beach. Ideal base for exploring many fine beaches and lovely coastline, largely National Trust owned. Single, double and family rooms available with hot and cold, shaver points, tea making facilities, colour T.V. Children welcome, special reductions given.

P	Single Room per one person B&B		Double Room for two persons B&B		6
	MIN £	MAX £	MIN £	MAX £	OPEN
	10.00	12.00	20.00	24.00	1-12

Abersoch

Map Ref Ac5

Dinghy sailing and windsurfing centre with safe sandy beaches. Superb coastal scenery with easy walks. Pony trekking, golf, fishing and sea trips.

Guest Houses

Angorfa Guest House

AWARD

Abersoch, Gwynedd, LL53 7EB.
Tel: (075 881) 2967.

Village situated, family run friendly guest house. Sea views. Water sports, safe sandy beaches and golf within minutes. Horse riding nearby. Bedrooms high standard, washbasins and shaver points. T.V./video lounge. Central heating. High quality home cooked evening meal (optional) and full English breakfast, both freshly prepared. Fire certificate. Children welcome. For brochure send s.a.e. to Chris Stanworth.

P	Single Room per one person B&B		Double Room for two persons B&B		4
	MIN £	MAX £	MIN £	MAX £	OPEN
			19.00	22.00	2-11

Berwyn

Lôn Golff, Abersoch, Pwllheli, Gwynedd, LL53 7EF.
Tel: (075 881) 2392. L

Ideally situated imposing detached family house in peaceful location within 2 minutes walk of beach, golf course and village centre. Other lovely beaches, walks, fishing and sailing nearby, including Snowdonia. Bedrooms have hot and cold, shaver points, tea/coffee facilities, central heating. T.V. lounge. Home cooking. Parking. A warm welcome awaits you at Berwyn.

P	Single Room per one person B&B		Double Room for two persons B&B		5
	MIN £	MAX £	MIN £	MAX £	OPEN
	10.00	12.00	20.00	22.00	1-12

Craigle

Maesgwyndryn, Abersoch, Gwynedd.
Tel: (075 881) 2613.

Situated in an ideal position in the lovely town of Abersoch. Convenient for the harbour and shops and having the quiet peacefulness of this beautiful house recently converted to a high standard as a guest house, yet maintaining its original character. Superb decor and homely atmosphere will make your stay at Craigle a happy one.

P	Single Room per one person B&B		Double Room for two persons B&B		5
	MIN £	MAX £	MIN £	MAX £	OPEN
	10.00	12.00	20.00	24.00	1-12

Llysfor Guest House

Abersoch, Nr. Pwllheli, Gwynedd, LL53 7AL.
Tel: (075 881) 2248.

Welcome to our small family-run guest house. H & C, kettles, shaver points all bedrooms. Comfortable lounge with T.V. Residential licence. 2 minutes to beach overlooking harbour. Miles of golden sand, safe bathing, skiing, surfing, fishing and golf courses within easy reach. Ideal centre for touring Llŷn Peninsula and Snowdonia National Park. Fire certificate granted. Send s.a.e. for brochure.

P	Single Room per one person B&B		Double Room for two persons B&B		8
	MIN £	MAX £	MIN £	MAX £	OPEN
	10.00	12.00	20.00	24.00	3-10

Pengwern

Lôn Sarn Bach, Abersoch, Gwynedd, LL53 7ER.
Tel: (075 881) 3301. L

Beautifully situated on the edge of Abersoch with sea and mountain views. Peaceful, yet only 10 minutes walk to shops and beach. All rooms have central heating, hot and cold and tea making facilities. Home cooking. Reduced rates for children. Colour T.V. in residents' lounge. Downstairs bedrooms for disabled. Vegetarians welcome. Discounts for groups.

P	Single Room per one person B&B		Double Room for two persons B&B		5
	MIN £	MAX £	MIN £	MAX £	OPEN
	8.00	10.00	16.00	20.00	1-12

Ty Draw Guest House

Abersoch, Pwllheli, Gwynedd, LL53 7EL.
Tel: (075 881) 2647.

A beautiful guest house overlooking Cardigan Bay, set in attractive and restful gardens, in a quieter part of the village. Large private and secure car and boat park. Family rooms with reductions for children. Baby sitting by request. All bedrooms have vanity units. One bedroom en-suite. Comfortable T.V. lounge. Fresh home cooked food of high quality and quantity. Proprietors, Jean & Peter Collins.

P	Single Room per one person B&B		Double Room for two persons B&B		7
	MIN £	MAX £	MIN £	MAX £	OPEN
	9.00		18.00		4-9

Criccieth

Map Ref Ad7

Ideal family resort, safe beach with sea-front hotels. Romantic ruined castle overlooking the sea. Visit Llanystumdwy nearby, the boyhood home of Lloyd George, with an interesting museum of his memorabilia.

Hotels

Bron Rhiw Private Hotel

Caernarfon Road, Criccieth,
Gwynedd, LL52 0AP.
Tel: (076 671) 2257.

Cosy licensed family-run hotel situated in elevated position near centre of village. Five minutes from beach, also within easy reach of tennis, fishing, squash, golf, pony trekking. Bar, lounge, T.V. lounge. Italian, English cuisine. Children welcome. School parties catered for out of season.

	Single Room per one person B&B		Double Room for two persons B&B		12
P	MIN £ 12.00	MAX £ 12.00	MIN £ 24.00	MAX £ 24.00	OPEN 1-12

Caerwylan Hotel

Beach Bank, Criccieth, Gwynedd,
LL52 0HW.
Tel: (076 671) 2547.

AA*/RAC* appointed comfortable family-run hotel superbly situated 30 yds from beach. All bedrooms have radio, intercom and colour television, some bedrooms with bathroom. Lift to all floors. Residential and restaurant licence. Garages and parking. Fire certificate.

	Single Room per one person B&B		Double Room for two persons B&B		29
P	MIN £ 12.00	MAX £ 12.00	MIN £	MAX £	OPEN 3-10

Glyn-y-Coed Hotel

Porthmadog Road, Criccieth,
Gwynedd, LL52 0HL.
Tel: (076 671) 2870.

Lovely Victorian house overlooking sea, mountains and Criccieth castle. AA/RAC listed. Cosy bar. Highly recommended cooking. Catering for all diets. Most bedrooms have en-suite facilities, tea/coffee making facilities. Moderate rates. Children welcome. Pets also. Parking in grounds. Golf, fishing, schools, clubs. Parties catered for. Send s.a.e. for brochure please.

	Single Room per one person B&B		Double Room for two persons B&B		10
P	MIN £ 11.00	MAX £	MIN £ 22.00	MAX £	OPEN 1-12

Min-y-Gaer Hotel

Porthmadog Road, Criccieth,
Gwynedd, LL52 0HP.
Tel: (076 671) 2151.

A comfortable, licensed family-run hotel. Conveniently situated near beach, with delightful views of the Cardigan Bay coastline. Ideal base for touring Snowdonia and the Llŷn Peninsula. Reduced rates for children. Tea/coffee making facilities in all bedrooms. Some en-suite rooms available. Ample car parking on premises. AA/RAC listed. Brochure on request.

	Single Room per one person B&B		Double Room for two persons B&B		10
P	MIN £ 10.00	MAX £ 12.00	MIN £ 20.00	MAX £ 24.00	OPEN 3-10

Neptune and Môr Heli Hotels

Min-y-Mor, Criccieth, Gwynedd,
LL52 0EF.
Tel: (0766 71) 2794/2802.

Well established family-run hotels situated on sea front. Noted for good food and friendly atmosphere. Comfortably furnished throughout with an attractive licensed bar for guests and diners. For brochure and terms contact Mrs. C. Williams. Licensed. Car park. AA listed.

	Single Room per one person B&B		Double Room for two persons B&B		20
P	MIN £ 12.00	MAX £	MIN £ 24.00	MAX £	OPEN 3-10

Guest Houses

The Moelwyn Restaurant

27/29 Mona Terrace, Criccieth,
Gwynedd, LL52 0HG.
Tel: (076 671) 2500.

A pretty Victorian restaurant with six comfortable bedrooms, all with sea and mountain views and tea/coffee making facilities. Situated on the seafront in picturesque Criccieth. A la carte and table d'hôte dinners and bar lunches. Residential and restaurant licence. Fire certificate granted. Recommended for fine food and a warm atmosphere.

	Single Room per one person B&B		Double Room for two persons B&B		6
	MIN £ 10.00	MAX £	MIN £ 20.00	MAX £	OPEN 3-11

Preswylfa Guest House

4 Castle Terrace, Criccieth,
Gwynedd, LL52 0DY.
Tel: (076 671) 2829.

Small guest house facing castle and bay. Offering good food, service, bed and breakfast, dinner optional. Lounge, colour T.V. Hot and cold, shaver points. Fire certificate granted. Convenient for town centre and for touring. Porthmadog only 5 miles. Ideally located for the many sandy beaches of the famous Llŷn Peninsula and North Wales coast. Mastercard, Access and Eurocard taken.

	Single Room per one person B&B		Double Room for two persons B&B		6
P	MIN £ 8.50	MAX £ 10.00	MIN £ 18.00	MAX £ 20.00	OPEN 1-12

The Rhoslyn

8 Marine Terrace, Criccieth,
Gwynedd, LL52 0EF.
Tel: (076 671) 2685.

Seafront family guest house. Home cooked meals, friendly service. Tea and coffee making facilities all bedrooms. Full central heating. Packed lunches available. Guest lounge with colour T.V. Reduced terms senior citizens except high season. All quotations totally inclusive. Children's terms available. Open all year. Brochure on request. Pam and Ken Rose.

	Single Room per one person B&B		Double Room for two persons B&B		7
	MIN £ 9.00	MAX £	MIN £ 18.00	MAX £	OPEN 1-12

Farmhouses

Cefn Meusydd Isaf

Pentrefelin, Criccieth, Gwynedd,
LL52 0RB.
Tel: (076 671) 2378. L

Historic 18th century secluded farmhouse with magnificent views of Tremadog Bay, halfway between Criccieth and Porthmadog. Excellently situated for touring the Llŷn Peninsula and Snowdonia. The farm has many good walks with an abundance of wildlife and excellent birdwatching. All rooms are clean, comfortable and beautifully furnished. Golf, fishing, beach and riding nearby.

	Single Room per one person B&B		Double Room for two persons B&B		2
P	MIN £ 7.50	MAX £ 8.50	MIN £ 15.00	MAX £ 17.00	OPEN 5-9

Trem-yr-Eifl Farm

Rhoslan, Criccieth, Gwynedd,
LL52 0NW.
Tel: (076 671) 2320. L

Come and stay in our comfortable farmhouse in a beautifully converted old stone barn. We are 2½ miles from Criccieth. Comfortable, spacious rooms. 2 doubles, 1 family. All with H/C, also bathroom with shower. Separate tables. Television lounge. Competitive rates are available for weekly bookings.

	Single Room per one person B&B		Double Room for two persons B&B		3
P	MIN £ 10.00	MAX £ 12.00	MIN £ 17.00	MAX £ 20.00	OPEN 3-10

Morfa Nefyn
Map Ref Ab6

Popular Llŷn Peninsula seaside village, with extensive sandy beaches, situated between the little harbour of Porthdinllaen and the resort of Nefyn. Set against the mountainous backdrop of Garn Boduan.

Hotels

Erw Goch Hotel
Morfa Nefyn, Pwllheli, Gwynedd,
LL53 6BW.
Tel: (0758) 720539.

Set in own grounds with benefit of large car park. Ideal centre for touring historic Llŷn Peninsula, Caernarfon, Snowdonia, sandy beaches with water sports predominant. Home cooking at its best. A very warm welcome whether one night, weekend or longer. Licensed bar with bar meals available lunch time or evening. Open all year round. Reduction for children.

Single Room per one person B&B		Double Room for two persons B&B		15
MIN £ 12.00	MAX £	MIN £ 24.00	MAX £	OPEN 1-12

Guest Houses

Llys Olwen
Morfa Nefyn, Gwynedd, LL53 6BT.
Tel: (0758) 720493.

Situated along quiet country lane, close to cliff walk, safe sandy beaches for swimming, sailing, windsurfing. 1 mile to 18 hole golf course. Large garden. Excellent food. Personal service. Award for rural tourism.

Single Room per one person B&B		Double Room for two persons B&B		8
MIN £ 10.00	MAX £ 12.00	MIN £ 20.00	MAX £ 24.00	OPEN 3-10

Nefyn
Map Ref Ab6

Old fishing village on Llŷn Peninsula perched above sweeping bay. Two miles of sand, safe swimming, sailing and fishing.

Hotels

Dolwen House Hotel
Ffordd Dewi Sant, Nefyn, Gwynedd,
LL53 6EA.
Tel: (0758) 720667.

Ideally situated in unspoilt village of Nefyn, LLŷn Peninsula. Close beaches, cliff walks, 18 hole golf course, fishing, Snowdonia, little trains of Wales. Attractive detached hotel. Good food, cleanliness, service and happy informal atmosphere. Licensed residents' bar, separate T.V. lounge. Good Room Award Guest Accommodation 1987. Resident proprietors, Dudley and Paula Mitchell.

Single Room per one person B&B		Double Room for two persons B&B		6
MIN £ 10.00	MAX £ 12.00	MIN £ 20.00	MAX £ 24.00	OPEN 1-11

The Three Herrings
Well Street, Nefyn, Nr. Pwllheli,
Gwynedd, LL53 6HW.
Tel: (0758) 720864.

Llŷn Peninsula close to unspoilt beaches with golf, boating, fishing and windsurfing facilities. Olde worlde licensed hotel with attractive restaurant and bar service. Good food with wide choice of menu. All rooms with hot and cold, shaver points. Single, double and family rooms. Central heating. T.V. lounge. Large car park nearby.

Single Room per one person B&B		Double Room for two persons B&B		3
MIN £ 8.50	MAX £ 10.50	MIN £ 17.00	MAX £ 20.00	OPEN 1-12

Guest Houses

Bodowen
Rhodfa'r Môr Nefyn, Gwynedd,
LL53 6EB.
Tel: (0758) 720627.

Peaceful village with all the splendour of the Llŷn Peninsula. 100 yards from secluded golden beach, golf, fishing, walks. Bodowen offers the highest standards. All bedrooms centrally heated. Washing facilities. Showers. Two T.V./video lounges. Library. Bar. Separate dining room with good home cooking. Full fire certificate. Discounts offered pensioners, children. Weekly rates.

Single Room per one person B&B		Double Room for two persons B&B		7
MIN £ 10.60	MAX £ 11.50	MIN £ 21.00	MAX £ 23.00	OPEN 3-10

The Old Rectory
Boduan, Nr. Pwllheli, Gwynedd,
LL53 6DT.
Tel: (0758) 720923/721363.

Situated on Pwllheli to Nefyn main road, 2 miles from Nefyn. House in own 2 acre grounds. All rooms with private bathroom, colour T.V., radio and telephone. Fully centrally heated. Restaurant open each evening.

Single Room per one person B&B		Double Room for two persons B&B		4
MIN £ 11.50	MAX £ 11.50	MIN £ 23.00	MAX £ 23.00	OPEN 1-12

Porthmadog
Map Ref Ae7

Harbour town and shopping centre, close to Snowdonia and Llŷn Peninsula. Ffestiniog Railway terminus for slate caverns at Blaenau Ffestiniog. Porthmadog pottery, maritime museum. Welsh Highland Railway. Convenient for Portmeirion 'Italianate' village.

Hotels

The Old Rectory Hotel
Maentwrog, Gwynedd, LL41 4HN.
Tel: (076 685) 305.

The Old Rectory dates back to the 16th century and is set in three acres of garden borderd by the Dwyryd river. Plenty of local walks. Ideally situated for touring Mid, North Wales. All rooms en-suite with central heating. Fifty seat restaurant, special diets catered for. Dogs welcome. Reduced rates for weekly stays.

Single Room per one person B&B		Double Room for two persons B&B		8
MIN £ 10.50	MAX £ 12.00	MIN £ 21.00	MAX £ 24.00	OPEN 1-12

Guest Houses

7 Brittania Terrace
Opposite Ffestiniog Railway,
Porthmadog, Gwynedd, LL49 9NB.
Tel: (0766 51) 3073.
L

Situated opposite Narrow Gauge Ffestiniog Railway. Two minutes town centre. Rooms with delightful views of mountains, Ffestiniog Railway, and harbour. Central heating throughout. Rooms comprising H & C, shaver points, free tea/coffee facilities, television. Private colour T.V. lounge. Showers. Single, double, twin, family rooms. Open throughout year. Homely stay guaranteed, with best ever breakfasts.

Single Room per one person B&B		Double Room for two persons B&B		3
MIN £ 8.00	MAX £ 10.00	MIN £ 15.00	MAX £ 16.00	OPEN 1-12

Gwyddfan

8 Ralph Street, Borth-y-gest,
Porthmadog, Gwynedd, LL49 9UR.
Tel: (0766) 512456. L

The house is situated in the village approximately one mile from Porthmadog. We have sandy beaches and country walks. The lounge/dining room has a splendid view of the mountains. We try to make guests feel welcome, offering light refreshments, early morning tea, T.V., central heating. The village has a shop and eating establishments.

	Single Room per one person B&B		Double Room for two persons B&B		3
	MIN £ 7.50	MAX £ 8.50	MIN £ 15.00	MAX £ 17.00	OPEN 4-10

Hendre Wen

Morfa Bychan, Porthmadog,
Gwynedd, LL49 9YU.
Tel: (0766) 513725.

Detached residence of character in large enclosed grounds leading to first tee on local golf course. Double and family rooms with hot and cold, shaver points. Centrally heated. Bathroom, shower and separate toilet. Residents' television lounge. Ample parking space. Within walking distance of sandy beaches. Ideal touring centre for Snowdonia. Full fire certificate.

P	Single Room per one person B&B		Double Room for two persons B&B		3
	MIN £	MAX £	MIN £ 17.00	MAX £ 22.00	OPEN 3-10

49 Madog Street

Porthmadog, Gwynedd, LL49 9BU.
Tel: (0766) 513107 L

Ideally situated for touring Snowdonia, visiting the Ffestiniog railway and local beaches. Within easy reach of the town centre, convenient for buses and railway station. Homely atmosphere, good cooking. Children always welcome. Central heating in all rooms. Ample parking nearby. Open all the year round. Contact Mrs G. Roberts, proprietor.

P	Single Room per one person B&B		Double Room for two persons B&B		4
	MIN £ 8.00	MAX £ 9.00	MIN £ 16.00	MAX £ 18.00	OPEN 1-12

The Oakleys Guest House

The Harbour, Porthmadog, Gwynedd,
LL49 9AS.
Tel: (0766) 512482. L

Situated on the harbour in Porthmadog. Licensed. An excellent base for visiting Snowdonia, Portmeirion and the beaches of Llŷn Peninsula, taking in Pwllheli, Abersoch and Criccieth. Fishing, sea trout, salmon, golf course nearby. Spacious free car park. Comfortable lounge. Informal holiday atmosphere. Two bedrooms with showers, 1 bedroom en-suite. Electric blankets. Contact Mr. & Mrs. A. H. Biddle, proprietors.

P	Single Room per one person B&B		Double Room for two persons B&B		8
	MIN £ 8.00	MAX £ 9.50	MIN £ 16.00	MAX £ 19.00	OPEN 4-11

Treforris

Garth Road, Porthmadog, Gwynedd,
LL49 9BN.
Tel: (0766) 512853.

Large Victorian house with lovely view of mountains and harbour. Five pleasant bedrooms with hot and cold water. Separate sitting room and T.V. lounge. Near sea and Snowdonia countryside. Personal attention.

P	Single Room per one person B&B		Double Room for two persons B&B		5
	MIN £ 9.00	MAX £ 9.00	MIN £ 18.00	MAX £ 18.00	OPEN 1-12

Ty Newydd Guest House

30 Dublin Street, Tremadog,
Porthmadog, Gwynedd, LL49 9RH.
Tel: (0766) 512553.

Small family guest house providing an ideal base for touring Snowdonia and the Llŷn Peninsula. Within easy reach of many sandy beaches. All rooms have hot and cold water and colour T.V. and tea making facilities. Two with private showers. Dining room with separate tables. Private car park.

P	Single Room per one person B&B		Double Room for two persons B&B		4
	MIN £	MAX £	MIN £ 18.00	MAX £ 24.00	OPEN 2-10

Farmhouses

Garreghylldrem

Llanfrothen, Penrhyndeudraeth,
Gwynedd, LL48 6SH.
Tel: (0766) 770566. L

Situated in the Snowdonia National Park within easy distance of beaches, Snowdonia and narrow gauge railways. Family bedroom available. Special rates for children. Pony trekking also available locally.

P	Single Room per one person B&B		Double Room for two persons B&B		3
	MIN £ 8.00	MAX £ 8.50	MIN £ 16.00	MAX £ 17.00	OPEN 4-10

Wern

Llanfrothen, Penrhyndeudraeth,
Gwynedd, LL48 6LX.
Tel: (0766) 770556.

Pat and Tony Bayley offer a warm welcome at "Wern", situated in beautiful countryside at foot of the Moelwyns. Five miles from Porthmadog and marvellous beaches. Central for walking, climbing and pony trekking. Double and family rooms with reduced rates for children. Plentiful home cooked, varied menu including vegetarian dishes. Central heating. T.V. lounge.

P	Single Room per one person B&B		Double Room for two persons B&B		5
	MIN £	MAX £	MIN £ 20.00	MAX £ 24.00	OPEN 1-12

Pwllheli

Map Ref Ac7

Small resort town of Llŷn Peninsula – seaside and promenade, harbour, shopping. River and sea fishing.

Hotels

Miramar

Embankment Road, South Beach,
Pwllheli, Gwynedd, LL53 5AB.
Tel: (0758) 613021.

Comfortable, family-run, six bedroom hotel, offering full central heating with showers and T.V. in bedrooms. Residents' lounge, licensed bar restaurant offering one of the best cuisines in the area. All fresh produce used for cooking, in a friendly atmosphere to make your holiday a happy one in this beautiful part of the Llŷn Peninsula. Situated 50 yards from beach, and near the town centre.

P	Single Room per one person B&B		Double Room for two persons B&B		6
	MIN £ 10.00	MAX £ 12.00	MIN £ 20.00	MAX £ 24.00	OPEN 1-12

Farmhouses

Henllan Farm

Caernarfon Road, Pwllheli, Gwynedd,
LL53 6TT. Tel: (0758) 612077. L

Two double, one family room. Bathroom. Sitting, dining rooms. 5 minutes beach. Central for all amenities, enjoying very good views of sea and mountains. Clean, homely with very good food. Ideally located for touring the Llŷn Peninsula, Snowdonia and the North Wales coast resorts.

P	Single Room per one person B&B		Double Room for two persons B&B		3
	MIN £ 10.00	MAX £	MIN £ 16.00	MAX £	OPEN 4-10

Mathan Uchaf Farm

Boduan, Pwllheli, Gwynedd,
LL53 8TU. Tel: (0758) 720487. L

Dairy farm situated off the Pwllheli to Nefyn main road. Centrally positioned for northern and southern beaches of the Peninsula. Guests can participate in farm activities. Large garden provides safe area for children. One double room and one family room with washbasins, one twin bedded room. Dining room, lounge with T.V. Good food, friendly atmosphere are our aim.

P	Single Room per one person B&B		Double Room for two persons B&B		3
	MIN £ 9.00	MAX £ 10.00	MIN £ 18.00	MAX £ 20.00	OPEN 5-10

Pot Plants Nursery

Tyddyn Berth, Rhosfawr, Pwllheli,
Gwynedd, LL53 6YA. Tel: (0766) 810545. L

Situated centre Llŷn Peninsula. Large lounge and gardens. Special rates for children under 14. Small nursery and camp site, games room. Organic produce from garden. 9 acres, farm animals including donkey. School groups welcome.

P	Single Room per one person B&B		Double Room for two persons B&B		4
	MIN £ 8.00	MAX £ 8.00	MIN £ 16.00	MAX £ 16.00	OPEN 3-10

SNOWDONIA MOUNTAINS AND COASTLINE

This is powerful, big country, with a history to go with it. Wales's most famous, formidable fortress, Caernarfon Castle, watches over Snowdonia, mountain stronghold of the Welsh in medieval times. The boulder-strewn Llanberis and Nant Ffrancon Passes lead upwards from the Menai Strait into these rugged mountains, the highest in southern Britain.

The loftiest of all, Mount Snowdon, gives its name to the spectacular Snowdonia National Park, an 845-square-mile expanse which dominates this area. This is a mountainous parkland of soaring peaks, lakes, rushing rivers, tumbling waterfalls and forests criss-crossed with waymarked walks. Explore this lofty landscape from Llanrwst, Betws-y-Coed, Beddgelert or Llanberis. Follow mountain footpaths – or climb to the summit the easy way on the Snowdon Mountain Railway.

You'll learn all about this once-great industry at Blaenau Ffestiniog's fascinating slate caverns – and see the wealth it created at Penrhyn Castle, a gigantic castellated house near Bangor built by a local slate baron.

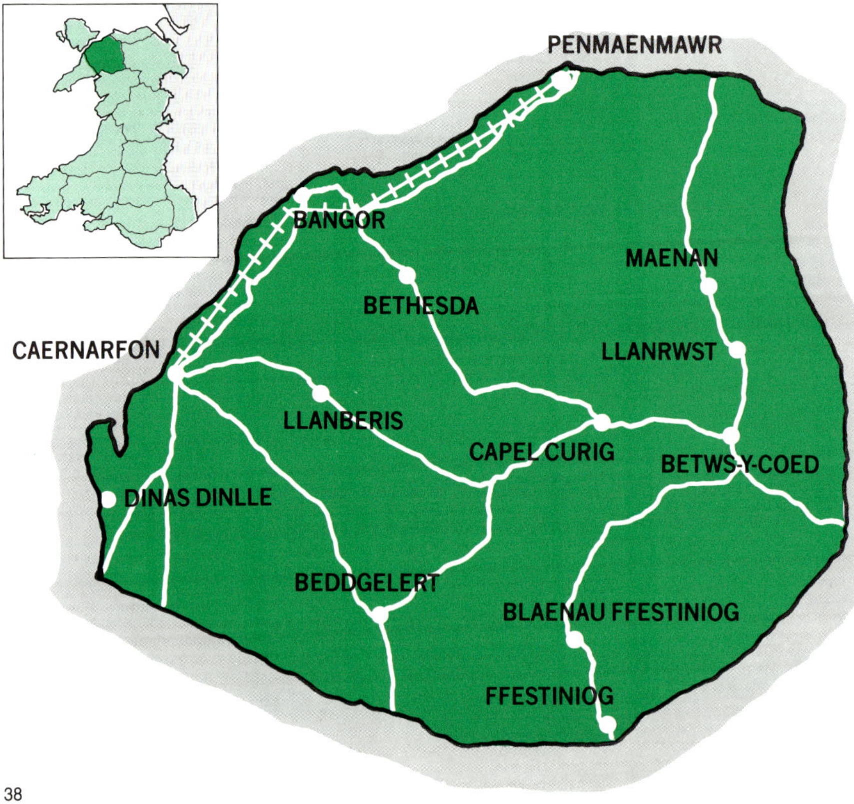

Bangor
Map Ref Ae3

University and holiday city at the eastern entrance to the Menai Strait and gateway to Anglesey and the Ogwen Valley. Town dominated by its cathedral founded in AD 548. Theatr Gwynedd has opera, ballet, drama, pantomime and film. Museum, heated swimming pool. Yachting and fishing.

Guest Houses

Bryn Eglwys
1 Ffordd Caergybi, Bangor,
Gwynedd, LL57 2EG.
Enq. to: Mrs. M.E. Morgan.
Tel: (0248) 362948.

Good value guest house offering 4 bedrooms, of which two are double, two are twin. Special price for children. Situated in Upper Bangor, suitable for touring Anglesey and the North Wales coast. Close to Penrhyn Castle and the mountains of Snowdonia.

Single Room per one person B&B		Double Room for two persons B&B		4
MIN £	MAX £	MIN £	MAX £	OPEN
9.00		18.00		1-12

Dilfan
Garth Road, Bangor, Gwynedd,
LL57 2RT.
Tel: (0248) 353030.

Situated opposite swimming pool, five minutes city centre. On A5 London to Holyhead road. All rooms hot and cold. Car parking space. T.V. lounge. Open all year. Evening meal optional. Two bedrooms with shower.

Single Room per one person B&B		Double Room for two persons B&B		6
MIN £	MAX £	MIN £	MAX £	OPEN
9.00	11.00	18.00	21.00	1-12

Farmhouses

Glasinfryn Farm
Glasinfryn, Bangor, Gwynedd,
LL57 4UE.
Tel: (0248) 353359.

Eighteenth Century country farmhouse on the edge of Snowdonia National Park, within easy distance of city of Bangor, Caernarfon, Anglesey coastline and two famous outdoor pursuit centres. Good wholesome cooking with food produced on our mixed farm. One double room and one family room. Competitive rates for longer stays.

Single Room per one person B&B		Double Room for two persons B&B		3
MIN £	MAX £	MIN £	MAX £	OPEN
10.00		17.00	19.00	3-9

Goetre Isaf Farmhouse
Caernarfon Road, Bangor, Gwynedd,
LL57 4DB.
Tel: (0248) 364541.

Superb country situation with magnificent mountain views. 2 miles from Bangor station, easy access for A5 and A55. Imaginative farmhouse cooking and provision for special diets. Three bedrooms with dial phone facilities. Vegetarians welcome. Stabling by arrangement. Ideal touring centre for Snowdonia and Anglesey.

Single Room per one person B&B		Double Room for two persons B&B		3
MIN £	MAX £	MIN £	MAX £	OPEN
8.50	10.50	17.00	20.00	1-12

Beddgelert
Map Ref Ae6

Small village set amidst glorious mountain scenery. On the doorstep of Snowdonia's most spectacular scenery and the Nant Gwynant valley. The rocky Aberglaslyn Pass guards Beddgelert's southern approach. Wordsworth set off from here on a famous dawn ascent of Mount Snowdon. Marvellous walks in all directions.

Guest Houses

Ael-y-Bryn
Caernarfon Road, Beddgelert,
Gwynedd.
Tel: (076 686) 264.

Detached house of character within 3 minutes walk of village centre. Bedrooms with hot and cold, razor points, some with private shower. Colour T.V. Central heating. Log fire. Enjoys magnificent views across salmon and trout river, Colwyn and Moel Hebog. Golden sands at Black Rock, narrow gauge railways, golf courses, trekking locally. A complete delight.

Single Room per one person B&B		Double Room for two persons B&B		4
MIN £	MAX £	MIN £	MAX £	OPEN
8.50	9.50	17.00	19.00	1-12

Colwyn
Beddgelert, Gwynedd, LL55.
Tel: (0766 86) 276.

18th century riverside guest house (cottage style). Beams, log fire, warm, cosy and friendly. Lovely scenery winter and summer. Miles of unspoiled coast. Walkers welcome. Ideal base for touring. Many scenic drives. Dozens of places to visit, pretty villages, wooded valleys, waterfalls. Stay a few days and enjoy it all. Rooms en-suite. Dinner to prior order.

Single Room per one person B&B		Double Room for two persons B&B		6
MIN £	MAX £	MIN £	MAX £	OPEN
8.50	12.00	17.00	24.00	1-12

Farmhouses

Tŷ Newydd
Nantmor, Caernarfon, Gwynedd,
LL55 4YN.
Tel: (076 686) 226.

AWARD

"As usual very sad to go, how we shall miss those meals!". A typical entry in our visitors book. We offer all the comforts of a small country house to civilised people. Lovely situation, total peace, in heart of National Park. Ideal walkers/naturalists. No children under 14 or pets. Brochure, Mrs. B. Platt.

Single Room per one person B&B		Double Room for two persons B&B		3
MIN £	MAX £	MIN £	MAX £	OPEN
10.00		18.00		4-9

Bethesda
Map Ref Ae4

Busy town 4 miles south-east of Bangor on A5. Penrhyn Quarries open to visitors April–Sept. by arrangement. All around is the magnificent scenery of the Snowdonia National Park.

Guest Houses

Tŷ Pengarreg
1 Pengarreg, Nant Ffrancon,
Bethesda, Gwynedd, LL57 3LX.
Tel: (0248) 600122.

Situated in Nant Ffrancon Valley with magnificent mountain views. A warm welcome and good home cooking awaits. Double and family room available, both with hot and cold and free tea/coffee making facilities. Separate shower room and bathroom. Ideal touring centre for beaches, castles, railways, etc. Superb walking, climbing and mountaineering country. Ample parking.

Single Room per one person B&B		Double Room for two persons B&B		2
MIN £	MAX £	MIN £	MAX £	OPEN
		16.00	19.00	1-12

Yr Ocar
Coed-y-Parc, Nr. Bethesda,
Gwynedd, LL57 4YS.
Tel: (0248) 600812.

Enjoy the contrasting seasons in a beautiful 18th century house set in four acres of gardens and woodlands on the bank of the Galedffrwd. All rooms fitted vanity units, tea making facilities, one with shower en-suite. Magnificent lounge, dining room, log fires, colour T.V. Home cooking, diets catered for. Animals by arrangement.

Single Room per one person B&B		Double Room for two persons B&B		3
MIN £	MAX £	MIN £	MAX £	OPEN
10.00	10.00	20.00	20.00	1-12

Farmhouses

Maes Caradog Farm

Nant Ffrancon, Bethesda, Bangor,
Gwynedd, LL57 3DQ.
Tel: (0248) 600266.

Farmhouse in Snowdonia National Park, one mile off the A5, between Capel Curig and Bethesda. Ideally placed for walking and climbing. Hot and cold, shaving points in both double and family rooms. Good home cooking. Reduced rates for children. Car park on forecourt.

Single Room per one person B&B		Double Room for two persons B&B		2
MIN £	MAX £	MIN £	MAX £	OPEN
8.50	9.00	17.00	18.00	1-12

Betws-y-Coed

Map Ref Bb6

Stone built houses and hotels cling to rocky outcrops in this Snowdonia village. Tumbling rivers and waterfalls emerge from a tangle of treetops. Trout fishing, theatre, craft shops, railway museum. Nature trails nearby – very popular with hikers. Swallow Falls not to be missed.

Hotels

Church Hill Hotel

Vicarage Road, Betws-y-Coed,
Gwynedd, LL24 0AD.
Tel: (069 02) 447.

Situated in slightly elevated position in centre of village convenient for train and bus. Family run licensed hotel with full central heating, dining room lounge, T.V., bar. Nine rooms en-suite, all with tea making facilities. Evening meals optional. Rambling clubs catered for. Open Christmas and New Year. Fire certificate held.

Single Room per one person B&B		Double Room for two persons B&B		12
MIN £	MAX £	MIN £	MAX £	OPEN
8.50	10.50	17.00	21.00	1-12

Fairhaven Hotel

Betws-y-Coed, Gwynedd, LL24 0AY.
Tel: (069 02) 307.

Family hotel and licensed restaurant with home cooking situated in village centre amidst the beauty of Snowdonia. Ideal for golf, fishing, walking, climbing, horse riding and touring. Clean comfortable bedrooms with full central heating, showers, colour television and tea making facilities. Residents lounge with pleasant outlook. Parking available. Children welcomed.

Single Room per one person B&B		Double Room for two persons B&B		9
MIN £	MAX £	MIN £	MAX £	OPEN
10.50	11.50	21.00	23.00	2-11

Mount Garmon Hotel

Holyhead Road, Betws-y-Coed,
Gwynedd, LL24 0AN.
Tel: (069 02) 335.

Small private hotel. Residential licence. Central heating. Most bedrooms en-suite. Lounge with T.V. and cheerful lounge bar. Snacks available 11 a.m. to 11 p.m. Private car park. Public telephone. Evening meals by prior arrangement. Excellent centre for walking, golf, fishing and touring. Short breaks mid-week at good discounts.

Single Room per one person B&B		Double Room for two persons B&B		6
MIN £	MAX £	MIN £	MAX £	OPEN
		21.00	24.00	3-11

Plas Derwen Hotel and Restaurant,

Betws-y-Coed, Gwynedd, North
Wales, LL24 0AY.
Tel: (06902) 388.

Situated in the village centre. Family run, very clean and homely accommodation with an excellent 'value for money' licensed restaurant. Colour television, tea and coffee making facilities amd heating to all rooms. Some rooms en- suite. Ideal base to take advantage of the majestic Snowdonia National Park. Children at reduced rates welcome. Free parking available.

Single Room per one person B&B		Double Room for two persons B&B		8
MIN £	MAX £	MIN £	MAX £	OPEN
		22.00	22.00	1-12

Summer Hill Hotel

Coedcynhelier Road, Betws-y-Coed,
Gwynedd, LL24 0BL.
Tel: (069 02) 306.

Non smokers guest house, delightfully situated in peaceful surroundings overlooking the river. Eight attractive bedrooms with continental quilts, hot and cold water. Comfortable residents lounge, colour T.V. Sunny dining room. Traditional breakfast. Residental licence. Golf, fishing, riding, guided mountain walks available. Numerous forest trails start from our gate.

Single Room per one person B&B		Double Room for two persons B&B		8
MIN £	MAX £	MIN £	MAX £	OPEN
9.50		17.00	20.00	4-10

Guest Houses

Bod Hyfryd Guest House

Holyhead Road, Betws-y-Coed,
Gwynedd, LL24 0BN.
Tel: (069 02) 220.

Attractive house enjoying central position close to River Llugwy with scenic views at front. All rooms centrally heated with tea making facilities. Three with en-suite bathrooms. Comfy sitting room, pretty dining room and a warm welcome awaits you. Special diets catered for on request.

Single Room per one person B&B		Double Room for two persons B&B		7
MIN £	MAX £	MIN £	MAX £	OPEN
8.50	10.50	17.00	21.00	1-12

Bron Celyn

Llanwrst Road, Betws-y-Coed,
Gwynedd, LL24 0HD.
Tel: (069 02) 333.

Quiet elevated position overlooking village. Good food, comfort and a relaxed atmosphere. Centrally heated rooms. Double, twin, family rooms available, tea making facilities, rooms with shower and toilet en-suite. T.V. supplement £1.50 per person. Private car park. Fire certificate held. Ideal touring centre.

Single Room per one person B&B		Double Room for two persons B&B		7
MIN £	MAX £	MIN £	MAX £	OPEN
8.50	10.00	18.00	22.00	3-11

Bryn Afon

Mill Street, Betws-y-Coed, Gwynedd,
LL24 0BB.
Tel: (069 02) 403.

Situated in centre of village overlooking River Llugwy. Ideal situation for fishing, walking and touring. Full central heating. Beverage making facilities in bedrooms. Open all year round. Excellent base for touring Snowdonia and the North Wales coast resorts.

Single Room per one person B&B		Double Room for two persons B&B		7
MIN £	MAX £	MIN £	MAX £	OPEN
9.00	10.50	16.00	19.00	1-12

Bryn Llewelyn

Holyhead Road, Betws-y-Coed,
Gwynedd, LL24 0BN.
Tel: (069 02) 601.

Bryn Llewelyn is situated on the main A5 road near the centre of the village and has a beautiful view of practically all of Betws-y-Coed. Ideal for hiking, climbing and touring. All rooms centrally heated. Hot and cold hand basins. Tea/coffee facilities in bedrooms. Showers. Bath. T.V. lounge. Fire certificate. Shaver points.

Single Room per one person B&B		Double Room for two persons B&B		7
MIN £	MAX £	MIN £	MAX £	OPEN
8.50	8.50	17.00	17.00	1-12

Craig Dinas

Dinas Hill, Betws-y-Coed, Gwynedd,
LL24 0HF.
Tel: (069 02) 254.

Charming country house in 4 acres of secluded wooded grounds. Spectacular views of Lledr valley and forests with mountains beyond. Large rooms with tea/coffee making facilities. Central heating, colour T.V., log fires. Ample parking. Forest walks direct from the house. Ideal touring centre. Close to amenities. Excellent food and a warm welcome.

Single Room per one person B&B		Double Room for two persons B&B		6
MIN £	MAX £	MIN £	MAX £	OPEN
8.50	9.00	17.00	21.00	4-9

Glan Llugwy

Holyhead Road, Betws-y-Coed,
Gwynedd, LL24 0BN.
Tel: (069 02) 592.

Situated on A5 with lovely view across river and forest. Comfortable accommodation, C/H, colour T.V. in rooms. Pleasant guests' lounge. Parking for 5 cars. Good for walking, fishing, 9 hole golf course approximately ½ mile. Evening meal on request. Dogs by arrangement. Open all year.

Single Room per one person B&B		Double Room for two persons B&B		5
MIN £	MAX £	MIN £	MAX £	OPEN
9.00	9.50	18.00	19.00	1-12

Llwyn Onn Guest House

Pentrefoeglas, Nr Betws-y-Coed,
Gwynedd. LL24 0TW.
Tel: (069 05) 678.

Completely secluded, detached seventeenth century country residence of character, standing in three acres of gardens and with panoramic views of Snowdonia. Centrally situated for lakes, forest walks, trout fishing. All rooms are centrally heated and comfortably furnished to a high standard with colour T.V. and tea/coffee making facilities. Some rooms en-suite.

Single Room per one person B&B		Double Room for two persons B&B		7
MIN £	MAX £	MIN £	MAX £	OPEN
8.50	10.00	17.00	24.00	1-12

Tan Dinas

Betws-y-Coed, Gwynedd, LL24 0BL.
Tel: (069 02) 635.

Lovely country home delightfully situated in 3 acres of woodland offering peace and seclusion. Fabulous views. Spacious rooms with H & C, tea/coffee facilities. Large private car park. Log fires. Central heating. Dinners by arrangement. Children all ages welcome, special rates. Forest walks from house. Open all year. Winter breaks. Ideal centre for touring Snowdonia.

Single Room per one person B&B		Double Room for two persons B&B		6
MIN £	MAX £	MIN £	MAX £	OPEN
8.50	10.00	17.00	20.00	1-12

Ty'n-y-Celyn Guest House

Llanrwst Road, Betws-y-Coed,
Gwynedd, LL24 0HD.
Tel: (069 02) 202.

A large Victorian guest house situated in a quiet elevated position in Snowdonia National Park. Beautiful views overlooking the picturesque village of Betws-y-Coed. Ideal touring centre. Nearby golf course. Convenient for fishing, riding, walking. Eight bedrooms centrally heated, all with colour television, en-suite and tea and coffee making facilities. Licensed. Ample parking.

Single Room per one person B&B		Double Room for two persons B&B		8
MIN £	MAX £	MIN £	MAX £	OPEN
12.00		24.00		1-12

Farmhouses

Llys Peiran

15 Llwyn Brith, Betws Road,
Llanrwst, Gwynedd, LL26 0HH.
Tel: (0492) 641673.

Enjoy a homely and friendly welcome with home cooking in a modern bungalow on a small private estate, 150 yards from A470. Llanrwst is a small market town ideally situated to explore Snowdonia and its beauty, or the seashores. 1 double, 1 twin, bathroom/shower/toilet, ideal for the disabled. Children welcome. B & B from £8.

Single Room per one person B&B		Double Room for two persons B&B		2
MIN £	MAX £	MIN £	MAX £	OPEN
		16.00		1-12

Maes Gwyn Farm

Pentrefoelas, Betws-y-Coed,
Gwynedd, LL24 0LR.
Tel: (069 05) 668.

Maes Gwyn is a 17th century farmhouse with oak beams and panelling, inglenook fireplace in lounge with colour T.V. Good breakfasts, home produced beef, lamb, pork served with fresh vegetables. Good centre for touring North Wales. Six miles from famous Betws-y-Coed. Double room and family room. Bathroom with shower.

Single Room per one person B&B		Double Room for two persons B&B		2
MIN £	MAX £	MIN £	MAX £	OPEN
9.00	10.00	17.00	18.00	4-11

Maes-y-Garnedd

Capel Garmon, Llanrwst, Gwynedd,
LL26 0RR.
Enq. to: Mrs. Eluned Jones.
Tel: (069 02) 428.

140 acre mixed farm superbly situated in Capel Garmon (2 miles off A5 road). Beautiful country scenery and excellent walks. Salmon and trout fishing (permit required). Excellent home produced meals served, including Welsh lamb and roast beef. Packed lunches available. One double and one family bedroom. Children welcome. Car essential. Ample parking. Send s.a.e. for brochure. AA listed.

Single Room per one person B&B		Double Room for two persons B&B		2
MIN £	MAX £	MIN £	MAX £	OPEN
9.00		16.00	18.00	4-9

Penrhyn Farm

Penmachno Road, Betws-y-Coed,
Gwynedd, LL24 0PW.
Tel: (069 02) 356.

Penrhyn is a mixed farm of 120 acres situated two miles from Betws-y-Coed on the B4406 in peaceful surroundings. Two double bedrooms with tea/coffee facilities. Separate tables in dining room and colour T.V. in sitting room. An ideal centre for touring Snowdonia and within easy reach of beaches.

Single Room per one person B&B		Double Room for two persons B&B		2
MIN £	MAX £	MIN £	MAX £	OPEN
9.50	10.00	19.00	20.00	4-11

Royal Oak Farmhouse

Betws-y-Coed, Gwynedd, LL24 0AH.
Tel: (069 02) 427/632.

Old water mill set in five acres on a pretty meander of the River Llugwy. Quiet peaceful seclusion but only 3 minutes walk from village centre. Just two pretty bedrooms, bathroom with shower, T.V. lounge with open log fire. Fishing available from grounds. Golf course close by.

Single Room per one person B&B		Double Room for two persons B&B		2
MIN £	MAX £	MIN £	MAX £	OPEN
		17.00	19.00	4-11

Tan-yr-Eglwys Farm

Llanrhychwyn, Llanrwst, Gwynedd,
LL27 0YJ.
Tel: (0492) 640547.

Tan-yr-Eglwys is a modernised farmhouse, walls up to a yard in thickness. H & C in all rooms. Log fires available on chilly evenings. Ideal position for walkers and country lovers. Surrounded by Gwydr forest. Central for mountains of Snowdonia and coast. Good home cooking assured. Some guests return year after year. Betws-y-Coed 4 miles, Trefriw 1 mile, Llandudno 10 miles, Llanrwst 2 miles.

Single Room per one person B&B		Double Room for two persons B&B		3
MIN £	MAX £	MIN £	MAX £	OPEN
9.00	12.00	18.00	24.00	3-10

Ty Coch Farm & Trekking Centre

Penmachno, Betws-y-Coed,
Gwynedd, LL25 0HJ.
Tel: (069 03) 248.

AWARD

In heart of Snowdonia National Park. Very comfortable farmhouse, all rooms private facilities. Central heating. Pony trekking optional. Holiday resort of Betws-y-Coed a short drive away. Very quiet area, car essential. Good base for touring, walking, golfing, fishing, slate mines, castle, etc. Excellent meals served. Friendly. Many recommendations. W.T.B. award. T.V. lounge. Real fire. Video.

Single Room per one person B&B		Double Room for two persons B&B		4
MIN £	MAX £	MIN £	MAX £	OPEN
11.50	12.00	19.00	20.00	2-11

Tyddyn Gethin Farm

Penmachno, Betws-y-Coed,
Gwynedd, LL24 0PS.
Tel: (069 03) 392.

Three bedrooms. H & C in 1 bathroom, shower in bathroom, two toilets. Very central for touring, lovely views. Clean and comfortable. Dining room, two sitting rooms, separate tables. Always a welcome here. 200 yards off B4406, near to Conwy Falls and woollen mill. 3½ miles from Betws-y-Coed.

Single Room per one person B&B		Double Room for two persons B&B		3
MIN £	MAX £	MIN £	MAX £	OPEN
10.00	11.00	17.00	19.00	1-12

Blaenau Ffestiniog
Map Ref Ba7

Centre of the Welsh slate industry in its heyday, now housing the memorable attraction of two cavernous slate quarries, which can be visited and a narrow-gauge railway running from Portmadog on the coast. Marvellous mountain scenery.

Guest Houses

Afallon
Manod Road, Blaenau Ffestiniog,
Gwynedd, LL41 4AE.
Tel: (0766) 830468. L

Situated in Snowdonia National Park. Family-run guest house with good food, clean accommodation, T.V. Central heating all rooms. Separate shower, bathroom, toilet. Slate mines, narrow gauge railway, walks, trekking, fishing, golfing all locally. 13 miles from Black Rocks Sands, historic castles. Dinner by prior arrangement. Dogs by arrangement. Reduced rates for children.

	Single Room per one person B&B		Double Room for two persons B&B		3
P	MIN £	MAX £	MIN £	MAX £	OPEN
	8.00	9.00	16.00	18.00	1-11

Gwynfryn
Gellilydan, Blaenau Ffestiniog,
Gwynedd, LL41 4EA.
Tel: (0766 85) 225. L

Detached house of character in centre of village. Lovely scenery. Plenty of places to visit, ideal base for touring. Two bedrooms with washbasins. Full central heating. Plenty of good food and homely atmosphere. A real Welsh welcome awaits all guests. Children welcome at reduced rate depending on age.

	Single Room per one person B&B		Double Room for two persons B&B		3
P	MIN £	MAX £	MIN £	MAX £	OPEN
	7.00	8.00	16.00	17.00	1-12

Farmhouses

Llainwen
Trawsfynydd, Blaenau Ffestiniog,
Gwynedd, LL41 4TN.
Tel: (076 687) 242. L

A warm Welsh welcome awaits guests on this 41 acre mixed farm, set amidst the magnificent scenery of the Snowdonia National Park. Modernised farmhouse offering 1 family bedroom with 2 double beds and 1 single bed and 1 double bedroom. Convenient for the many sandy beaches of Mid and North Wales and an ideal touring base.

	Single Room per one person B&B		Double Room for two persons B&B		2
P	MIN £	MAX £	MIN £	MAX £	OPEN
	9.00	10.00	17.00	20.00	1-10

Caernarfon
Map Ref Ad4

Site of a magnificent Edwardian Castle, the most famous of Wales's many medieval fortresses, Segontium Roman Fort and Museum. Sailing popular, old harbour, market square. A versatile holiday centre at the gateway of Snowdonia.

Hotels

Alexandra Hotel
North Road, Caernarfon, Gwynedd,
LL55 1BA.
Tel: (0286) 2871.

Situated on the main A487 road close to town centre, Castle, port. Good centre for Snowdonia, fishing, sailing, golf. Good sandy beaches within easy reach. All rooms have heating, H & C, shaving points, tea/coffee facilities. Toilet/bathroom within 4 metres of each room. Accommodation includes full Welsh breakfast. Draught beers. Fire precaution.

	Single Room per one person B&B		Double Room for two persons B&B		3
P	MIN £	MAX £	MIN £	MAX £	OPEN
	9.00	10.50	17.00	21.00	1-12

Menai Bank Hotel
North Road, Caernarfon, Gwynedd,
LL55 1BD.
Tel: (0286) 3297.

Welcome to our licensed hotel overlooking Menai Strait and Isle of Anglesey. Ideally situated to explore Snowdonia and Llŷn Peninsula. Tea/coffee facilities, colour television, central heating all rooms. Family terms, varied menus, bar, lounges, private parking, lawned flower garden. Group discounts, bargain breaks, brochure available. Friendly atmosphere. Service by experienced hoteliers Ian & Deborah Baxter. AA* RAC*.

	Single Room per one person B&B		Double Room for two persons B&B		12
P	MIN £	MAX £	MIN £	MAX £	OPEN
	11.00	12.00	22.00	24.00	1-12

Guest Houses

Cae'r Menai Guest House
15 Church Street, Caernarfon,
Gwynedd, LL55 1SW.
Tel: (0286) 2612.

The AA listed guest house situated within the old town walls and adjoining the harbour and quiet promenade leading to the castle, is approximately 200 yards from the town centre. Comfortable, heated bedrooms with hot and cold water and shaver points. Colour T.V. lounge. Dining room. Solarium. Fire certificate. B & B from £9.00.

	Single Room per one person B&B		Double Room for two persons B&B		7
	MIN £	MAX £	MIN £	MAX £	OPEN
	9.00	9.50	18.00	19.00	3-12

Cae'r Siddi
Llanddeiniolen, Caernarfon,
Gwynedd, LL55 3AD.
Tel: (0248) 670462.

Former Georgian vicarage in peaceful rural setting, surrounded by trees with glorious views to Snowdon, Caernarfon Bay and the Rivals. Ideally located for all attractions in Gwynedd, Caernarfon 4 miles on B4366. Fully modernised, warm spacious accommodation. Colour T.V. lounge. Children specially catered for. Farmhouse breakfast, three course dinner, tea making facilities in bedrooms, no extra charge.

	Single Room per one person B&B		Double Room for two persons B&B		2
P	MIN £	MAX £	MIN £	MAX £	OPEN
	9.00	9.00	18.00	18.00	1-12

Castle View Guest House
23 Segontium Terrace, Caernarfon,
Gwynedd, LL55 2PH.
Tel: (0286) 77407.

Small, friendly guest house in quiet Georgian terrace, overlooking castle, Menai Strait. Two minutes buses, shops. Central heating, H & C basins, shaver points all bedrooms. Separate shower room and bathroom. Home cooked, traditional food. Evening dinner optional. Guests' lounge with colour television. Dining room with separate tables. Reduced rates for children. High chair, cot supplied.

	Single Room per one person B&B		Double Room for two persons B&B		4
	MIN £	MAX £	MIN £	MAX £	OPEN
	10.50	11.50	17.00	20.00	1-12

Chatham Farmhouse
Llandwrog, Caernarfon, Gwynedd,
LL54 5TG.
Tel: (0286) 831257.

Croeso, welcome to our warm friendly guest house. Books, records, T.V., inglenook in lounge. Wholesome meals, home made soups, preserves, bread, delicious desserts, home grown organic vegetables, free range eggs to enjoy during a lazy breakfast. Pretty bedrooms with washbasins, kettles, soft towels, crisp sheets, lovely views. Perfect base for touring, beach three miles.

	Single Room per one person B&B		Double Room for two persons B&B		2
P	MIN £	MAX £	MIN £	MAX £	OPEN
	8.00	8.00	16.00	16.00	4-9

Dingle Nook
Dinas Dinlle, Llandwrog, Caernarfon,
Gwynedd, LL54 5TW.
Tel: (0286) 830457.

Situated 200 yds from very popular beach. Good centre for touring North Wales. Near Caernarfon castle, Snowdon slate mines. Hot and cold, shaver points in all bedrooms. Bath and shower room. Suitable for disabled persons. All rooms on ground level. Single, double, family rooms. Home cooking. Evening meals provided.

	Single Room per one person B&B		Double Room for two persons B&B		3
P	MIN £	MAX £	MIN £	MAX £	OPEN
	9.00		18.00		3-10

Gwynant

Stryd Ganol, Saron, Bethel,
Gwynedd, LL55 1YP.
Tel: (0248) 670029.

Gwynant, in the village of Bethel is beautifully placed as a base from which to enjoy a holiday in Snowdonia, Anglesey and North West Wales. Comfortable accommodation, 2 bedrooms with bathroom en-suite. Adequate parking facilities. Walking, climbing, sailing, canoeing, windsurfing, fishing, birdwatching, castles, museums, craft centres, horse riding all within reasonable distance.

Single Room per one person B&B		Double Room for two persons B&B		4
MIN £ 10.00	MAX £ 12.00	MIN £ 20.00	MAX £ 24.00	OPEN 1-12

Sunnyside

North Road, Caernarfon, Gwynedd,
LL55 1BE.
Tel: (0286) 3860.

Victorian house ⅔ miles from town centre and castle, overlooking Menai Strait 200 yds from waters edge. Hot and cold water in bedrooms, T.V. available. Parking off road. Shower/bathroom available. Caernarfon is central for touring Snowdonia and visiting beaches of Anglesey and the Llŷn Peninsula.

Single Room per one person B&B		Double Room for two persons B&B		2
MIN £ 9.00	MAX £ 10.00	MIN £ 16.00	MAX £ 18.00	OPEN 5-10

Tal Menai

Bangor Road, Caernarfon, Gwynedd,
LL55 1TP.
Tel: (0286) 2160.

In its own ground off A487 Caernarfon to Bangor road. Unobstructed views over Menai Strait and Anglesey. Central heating and T.V. lounge. One bedroom with shower/W.C. en-suite. Tea/coffee making facilities. Evening meal available on request with special diets catered for. RAC listed. Reductions for children and weekly bookings. French and Welsh spoken.

Single Room per one person B&B		Double Room for two persons B&B		5
MIN £ 9.50	MAX £ 10.00	MIN £ 18.00	MAX £ 20.00	OPEN 1-12

Ty'n Llwyn Cottage

Llanllyfni, Caernarfon, Gwynedd,
LL54 6RP.
Tel: (0286) 881526.

Situated on a quiet country road half mile off the A487 Caernarfon to Porthmadog road, seven miles south of Caernarfon, seven miles from Snowdon. Beautiful Welsh stone cottage with attractive garden, good home cooked food, large dining room with open fire, lounge with T.V. Three bedrooms, one en-suite, all with H & C and shaver points.

Single Room per one person B&B		Double Room for two persons B&B		3
MIN £ 9.00	MAX £ 10.00	MIN £ 18.00	MAX £ 20.00	OPEN 1-12

Victoria House

13 Church Street, Caernarfon,
Gwynedd, LL55 1SW.
Tel: (0286) 3133.

Situated within town walls, 250 yards from Caernarfon castle, 2 minutes walk from shops and bus station. Comprehensive breakfast menu, central heating. All rooms have H & C, shaver points, T.V.'s and easy chairs. Tea and coffee available on request. Full fire certificate. Reduced prices for children. Ideal base for touring Snowdonia, Anglesey and the Llŷn Peninsula.

Single Room per one person B&B		Double Room for two persons B&B		7
MIN £ 9.00	MAX £ 9.50	MIN £ 17.00	MAX £ 18.00	OPEN 1-12

Wallasea Guest House

21 Segontium Terrace, Caernarfon,
Gwynedd, LL55 2PH.
Tel: (0286) 3564.

RAC listed Georgian terrace house circa 1828. Two minutes walk from buses. Overlooking River Seiont, castle and Menai Strait. Hot and cold water all bedrooms. Cot, high chair available. Central heating. Lounge with colour television. Fire certificate. Tea/coffee facilities in bedrooms optional. Ideal base for touring Snowdonia, Llŷn Peninsula, Anglesey. Fully modernised throughout.

Single Room per one person B&B		Double Room for two persons B&B		4
MIN £ 10.50	MAX £ 11.50	MIN £ 17.00	MAX £ 20.00	OPEN 1-12

Farmhouses

Pantiau Farm Holidays

Rhosgadfan, Caernarfon, Gwynedd,
LL54 7LD.
Tel: (0286) 830002.

Pantiau enjoys a privileged position overlooking Caernarfon Bay and Anglesey. From here you can see the mountains and also experience living on one. All rooms have washbasins and tea making facilities. Home cooking with emphasis on own and local produce. Children welcome. Kennels available by arrangement. Share our peace and tranquility for a while.

Single Room per one person B&B		Double Room for two persons B&B		3
MIN £ 8.50	MAX £ 9.00	MIN £ 17.00	MAX £ 18.00	OPEN 1-11

Pant-yr-Afallen Farm

Portdinorwic, Gwynedd, LL56 4QN.
Tel: (0248) 670654.

Bed, breakfast, optional evening meal available on 250 acre mixed farm. Close to mountains, sea, trekking, etc. As only two letting bedrooms (double or family) both with washbasins, guests are assured of homely atmosphere and personal attention. Farm fresh produce used for good home cooking. Send s.a.e. please or phone.

Single Room per one person B&B		Double Room for two persons B&B		2
MIN £	MAX £	MIN £	MAX £ 20.00	OPEN 3-11

Pengwern

Saron, Llanwnda, Caernarfon,
Gwynedd, LL54 5UH.
Tel: (0286) 830717.

A 130 acre cattle and sheep breeding farm. Situated in a quiet location with unspoilt views of Snowdonia. The land runs down to the sea shore and is noted for its birdlife. Situated 3 miles from historic town of Caernarfon, 3 miles from Dinas Dinlle beach. Jane, Mrs Jones's daughter, has a cookery diploma and provides all the excellent meals. Wales Tourist Board farmhouse award.

Single Room per one person B&B		Double Room for two persons B&B		3
MIN £ 9.00	MAX £ 10.00	MIN £ 18.00	MAX £ 20.00	OPEN 3-10

Rhyddallt Ganol

Caeathro, Caernarfon, Gwynedd,
LL55 2TH.
Tel: (0286) 2085.

Caernarfon 2½ miles. A warm welcome awaits you at Rhyddallt Ganol midst the peace and quietness of a beautiful garden. 2 double, 1 twin room available. Hot and cold all rooms. Evening meal optional.

Single Room per one person B&B		Double Room for two persons B&B		3
MIN £ 8.50	MAX £	MIN £ 17.00	MAX £	OPEN 4-12

Capel Curig

Map Ref Ba6

Ringed by mountains in Snowdonia, this village offers accommodation and craft shops and is a great favourite with climbers. Good walking and fishing in the area.

Guest Houses

Bryn Derwen

Capel Curig, Betws-y-Coed,
Gwynedd, LL24 0EL.
Tel: (069 04) 312.

Warm welcome in comfortable family home. Centrally situated in Snowdonia by A5 trunk road. Unrivalled views of Moel Siabod, Mymbyr lakes and Snowdon range. Convenient for climbing, walking, fishing, beaches and many centres of interest. Home cooking, central heating, reduced rates for children, ample parking. Tea/coffee making facilities.

Single Room per one person B&B		Double Room for two persons B&B		3
MIN £ 8.50	MAX £ 10.00	MIN £ 17.00	MAX £ 20.00	OPEN 1-12

Llugwy Guest House

Capel Curig, Nr. Betws-y-Coed,
Gwynedd, LL24 0ES.
Tel: (069 04) 218.

Ideally situated, five miles from Snowdon and an excellent centre for enjoying all the North Wales attractions including mountains, seaside resorts, little trains, castles, hill walking, climbing, fishing, artificial ski slope. A warm welcome with home cooking. Two lounges, one with T.V. Beamed dining room and wonderful mountain view from each bedroom.

P	Single Room per one person B&B		Double Room for two persons B&B		7
	MIN £ 9.00	MAX £ 10.00	MIN £ 17.00	MAX £ 18.00	OPEN 1-12

Dinas Dinlle
Map Ref Ac5

Situated 5 miles from Caernarfon, the excellent sands and the views of the Llŷn Peninsula make Dinas Dinlle a popular holiday beach. Caravan park, shops and refreshments are among its amenities, and sea-angling is popular.

Hotels

Hotel Plas Tandinas and Dingles

Dinas Dinlle, Llandwrog, Caernarfon,
Gwynedd, LL54 5TW.
Tel: (0286) 830266.

Situated edge Snowdonia National Park. 2 minutes beach which provides ideal bathing. Cosy bar. Excellent menu. Single, double and family room with reduced rates for children, some free. Country Inn in grounds. Family entertainment in high season. Within easy reach of all North Wales main attractions. Ample parking.

P	Single Room per one person B&B		Double Room for two persons B&B		8
	MIN £ 12.00	MAX £	MIN £ 23.00	MAX £	OPEN 5-9

Ffestiniog
Map Ref Dc1

The village stands on a high bluff looking towards the sea, neighbour of Blaenau Ffestiniog, once slate capital of the world. Explore underground slate caverns or ride the Ffestiniog Narrow Gauge Railway.

Guest Houses

On The Hill Coffee/Antique Shop

17-18 Pen-y-Bryn, Llan Ffestiniog,
Gwynedd, LL41 4LU.
Tel: (076 676) 2782. L

Situated in the centre of the National Park, "On The Hill" provides an excellent base for beaches, Ffestiniog Railway, slate mines, craft centres, castles and outdoor pursuits. All bedrooms, guests sitting room and bathroom have central heating. Full breakfast. Our coffee shop can supply a range of home cooked and vegetarian meals. Warm welcome.

	Single Room per one person B&B		Double Room for two persons B&B		3
	MIN £ 9.50	MAX £ 10.50	MIN £ 19.00	MAX £ 21.00	OPEN 1-12

Llanberis
Map Ref Ae4

The centre for walkers and climbers in Snowdonia. The least difficult walk to Snowdonia's summit, some 3½ miles away at 3,560 ft is from here. There is a lake railway, slate industry museum, Oriel Eryri (The Snowdon Gallery) and Padarn Country Park. The Snowdon Mountain Railway runs from here to the summit.

Hotels

Alpine Lodge Hotel

1 High Street, Llanberis, Caernarfon,
Gwynedd, LL55 4EN.
Tel: (0286) 870294.

Situated at the Caernarfon end of Llanberis village, with views of lake and mountains. Facilities include a large private car park, licensed bar and restaurant, colour television lounge, telephone calls available from your room, full central heating and fire certificate. Canoes, sailboards and mountain bikes are available for hire to guests at half price.

P	Single Room per one person B&B		Double Room for two persons B&B		8
	MIN £ 9.00	MAX £ 11.00	MIN £ 18.00	MAX £ 22.00	OPEN 1-12

Dolafon Hotel

High Street, Llanberis, Gwynedd,
LL55 4SU.
Tel: (0286) 870993.

Detached, licensed hotel in own grounds, close by foot route to Snowdon. Full central heating. T.V. lounge, bar, comfortable rooms with tea making facilities. Evening meal optional. Rambling and climbing groups catered for. Open all year. An ideal base for touring, or enjoy our lakes and local amenities which include lakeside and mountain railways.

P	Single Room per one person B&B		Double Room for two persons B&B		9
	MIN £ 11.00	MAX £ 11.00	MIN £ 20.00	MAX £ 24.00	OPEN 1-12

Glyn Afon Hotel

High Street, Llanberis, Gwynedd,
LL55 4HA.
Tel: (0286) 872528.

Situated near the foot of Mount Snowdon. The Glyn Afon Hotel is a family-run hotel with a high standard of service, complimented with a hearty traditional breakfast. Ideal for walking, climbing or fishing. Excellent accommodation and good home cooked food are our speciality. Tea/coffee making facilities in all rooms. Packed lunches available.

P	Single Room per one person B&B		Double Room for two persons B&B		8
	MIN £ 9.50	MAX £ 12.00	MIN £ 19.00	MAX £ 24.00	OPEN 1-12

Mount Pleasant Hotel

High Street, Llanberis, Gwynedd,
LL55 4HA.
Tel: (0286) 870395.

Friendly, family-run hotel in Snowdonia. Ideal for walking, climbing and touring North Wales. Single, double, twin and family rooms, H & C, shaver points and tea making facilities, some private showers. Central heating. Separate dining room, T.V. lounge and well stocked bar. Evening meals, bar snacks and à la carte menu. Special rates for children and parties.

P	Single Room per one person B&B		Double Room for two persons B&B		7
	MIN £ 9.50	MAX £ 11.50	MIN £ 19.00	MAX £ 23.00	OPEN 1-12

Guest Houses

Beech Bank Guest House

High Street, Llanberis, Gwynedd,
LL55 4EN.
Tel: (0286) 870414. L

Small, homely, family-run guest house with personal friendly service at quiet end of village, overlooking Llyn Padarn and mountains. All bedrooms have hot and cold water, shaver points, easy chairs and central heating. Large dining room with separate tables. Full Welsh breakfast. Private parking. Convenient for buses, shops, restaurants, railways, museums and lake.

P	Single Room per one person B&B		Double Room for two persons B&B		3
	MIN £ 8.00	MAX £ 8.50	MIN £ 16.00	MAX £ 17.00	OPEN 3-10

Hafod y Gwynt

Pen y Gwryd, Nant Gwynant,
Caernarfon, Gwynedd, LL55 4NS.
Tel: (0286) 871057.

Situated in the heart of Snowdonia. Next door to famous climbing Inn. One mile from start of Pyg and miners tracks up Snowdon. Fly fishing in our own lake. One family room en-suite, one twin bedded room. Log fire. Central heating. T.V. room. Good home cooking. Guided walks and climbing by arrangement.

P ✕	Single Room per one person B&B		Double Room for two persons B&B		2
	MIN £	MAX £	MIN £	MAX £	OPEN
	8.50	9.50	17.00	19.00	1-12

Llanrwst
Map Ref Bb6

Chief shopping centre of the Upper Conwy Valley with the crystal clear river rolling in lush meadows. There is a much-photographed river bridge designed by Inigo Jones in 1636. Gwydir Park has bowling, putting and children's playground. Good variety of accommodation available. Bodnant Gardens are 8 miles away.

Hotels

Cornucopia Hotel

Bridge Street, Llanrwst, Gwynedd,
LL26 0ET.
Tel: (0492) 640275.

Cornucopia Hotel originally a 16th century post house which has been converted into a comfortable hotel. All bedrooms centrally heated, hot and cold handbasins. Cornucopia Hotel is surrounded by the beauty of the Conwy valley, whilst the market town of Llanrwst steeped in history of a thousand years offers immense interest for the tourist.

P ✕	Single Room per one person B&B		Double Room for two persons B&B		14
	MIN £	MAX £	MIN £	MAX £	OPEN
	10.00	11.00	18.00	20.00	1-12

Guest Houses

Awelon

Plas Isa, Llanrwst, Gwynedd,
LL26 0EE. Tel: (0492) 640047.

Small family-run guest house on outskirts of the market town of Llanrwst, four miles from Betws-y-Coed. Family, double bedrooms all with H & C, shaver points, and bedside lights. Private parking. Central heating. Large bathroom with shower. Ideal centre for touring, walking Snowdonia. Clean, friendly accommodation. Bed and breakfast or dinner, bed and breakfast. Reduction for children.

P ✕	Single Room per one person B&B		Double Room for two persons B&B		2
	MIN £	MAX £	MIN £	MAX £	OPEN
			16.00	17.00	3-10

Bryn Afon

Nebo Road, Llanrwst, Gwynedd,
LL26 0SD. Tel: (0492) 641679. L

A detached, mid-nineteenth century riverside house standing alone on the edge of open country, a few minutes walk from the historic market town of Llanrwst. The area offers a wide choice of outdoor leisure activities, (mountaineering instruction available by arrangement). Children welcome, (baby sitting service). A wholefood/vegetarian option offered at all meals.

P ✕	Single Room per one person B&B		Double Room for two persons B&B		3
	MIN £	MAX £	MIN £	MAX £	OPEN
	8.00	12.00	16.00	24.00	1-12

Llys Llywelyn

Trefriw, Nr. Llanrwst, Gwynedd,
LL27 0JH. Tel: (0492) 640625.

Snowdonia National Park. Friendly, uncommercialised village setting retaining much original character. Guests warmly welcomed in our stone house of character. Parking. Home comforts. Lounge. E/M optional. C/H. H/C. Tea/coffee facilities. Ideal touring, hiking, fishing, pony trekking. So much to do and see whatever the weather. Non smokers preferred.

P ✕	Single Room per one person B&B		Double Room for two persons B&B		5
	MIN £	MAX £	MIN £	MAX £	OPEN
				19.00	3-11

Farmhouses

Nant Isaf

Crafnant Valley, Trefriw, Gwynedd,
LL27 0JZ. Tel: (0492) 640286.

17th century farmhouse on river bank in beautiful Crafnant Valley, secluded but within easy reach of lakes, castles, mines, etc. One twin room, one double. Tea making facilities, handbasins, and W.C. en-suite. Ideal situation for fishing, climbing, walking or just relaxing. Betws-y-Coed 4 miles, coast 15 miles. A warm welcome always.

P ✕	Single Room per one person B&B		Double Room for two persons B&B		2
	MIN £	MAX £	MIN £	MAX £	OPEN
	9.50	9.50	19.00	19.00	3-10

Maenan
Map Ref Bb5

A village not far from the busy market town of Llanrwst. Suitable for visiting interesting places at both ends of the Conwy valley, such as Conwy Castle in the north and Betws-y-Coed in the south.

Guest Houses

The White Cottage

Maenan (A470) Llanrwst, Gwynedd,
LL26 0UL.
Tel: (0492) 640346. L

Situated in the beautiful Conwy valley two miles north of Llanrwst (A470). All bedrooms have open views, hot and cold and central heating. Ample parking. Colour T.V. Bathroom with shower. Stroll in country or woodland or relax in lovely garden. Good home cooking and warm welcome from Kathleen and Tony Isherwood.

P ✕	Single Room per one person B&B		Double Room for two persons B&B		3
	MIN £	MAX £	MIN £	MAX £	OPEN
			17.00	17.00	1-12

Penmaenmawr
Map Ref Ba4

Small North Wales coast resort offering sailing, water-skiing, safe swimming and golf. On edge of Snowdonia National Park, conveniently situated between Conwy and Bangor, for access to several kinds of attractive venues on this popular coast.

Guest Houses

Cynlas

Fernbrook Road, Penmaenmawr,
Gwynedd, LL34 6ED.
Tel: (0492) 623491.
C/Res: (0492) 53626

Welcome to "Cynlas" comfortable accommodation. All rooms have handbasins and shaving points, free tea/coffee facilities. Reduced rates children sharing parents room and senior citizens. Colour T.V. lounge, separate dining tables. We are noted for cleanliness, good food and friendliness. Enclosed parking. Pleasant gardens. Sea and mountain views.

P ✕	Single Room per one person B&B		Double Room for two persons B&B		3
	MIN £	MAX £	MIN £	MAX £	OPEN
	7.50	8.00	15.00	16.00	3-9

CLWYD COUNTRYSIDE AND HERITAGE

This large slice of landscape encompasses everything from heather-clad moorlands to rolling hill country, mammoth man-made reservoirs to pastoral, sheltered vales. The Vale of Clwyd cuts a grassy swathe through the area, its western slopes rising to the lonely Hiraethog moors, Clocaenog Forest and Llyn Brenig reservoir.

Eastwards, its fertile farmlands blend into the Clwydian Hills, the last upland barrier before the Wales/England border. These fresh, windy hills designated an 'Area of Outstanding Natural Beauty', are traversed by the long-distance Offa's Dyke Path.

Pretty Llangollen, host every year to the famous International Musical Eisteddford, is crowned by a ruined castle. The medieval ancestry of towns such as Denbigh and Ruthin is plain to see. Along the Dee Estuary, there's Flint Castle, Holywell's ancient religious shrine and the Greenfield Valley Heritage Park. And in the Wrexham area, don't miss Erddig, an unusually interesting country house which vividly portrays the 'upstairs, downstairs' way of life.

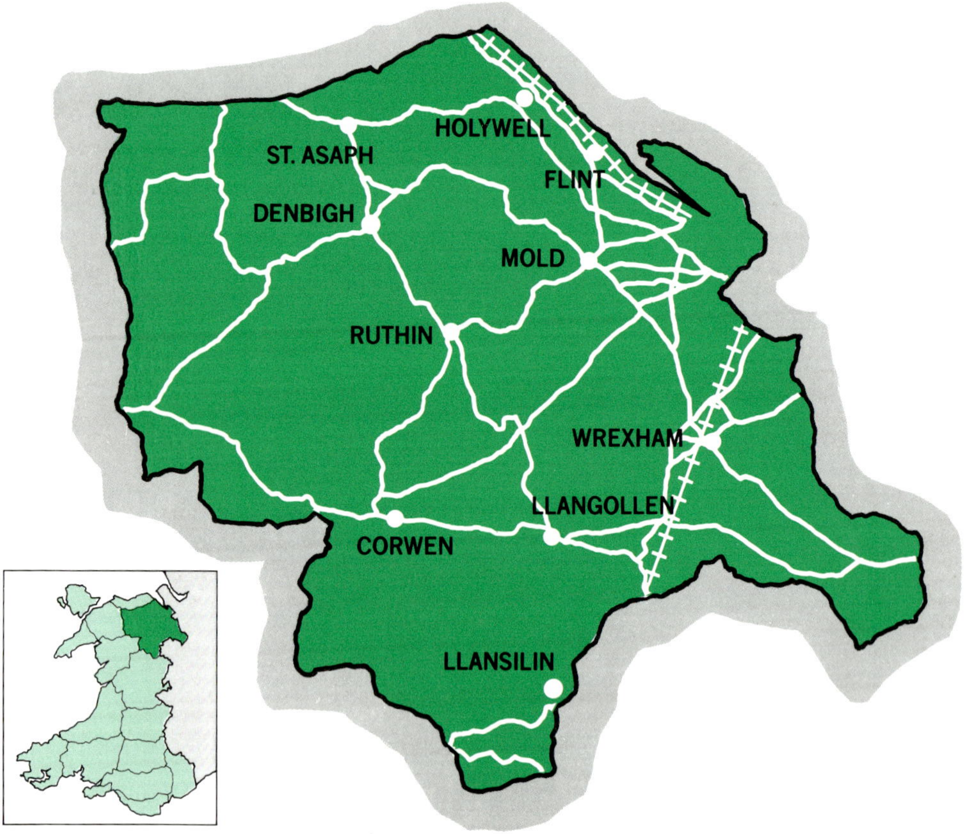

Corwen
Map Ref Be7

Pleasant market town in the Vale of Edeyrnion. Livestock mart held regularly. Fishing on the River Dee, swimming pool with picnic area. Good walks.

Hotels

Corwen Court Private Hotel
London Road, Corwen, Clwyd,
LL21 0DP.
Tel: (0490) 2854.

Situated on the A5. Converted old police station and courthouse. Six prisoner's cells now single bedrooms, hot and cold in each. Double bedrooms have bathroom en-suite. Lounge with colour T.V. and dining room with separate tables where magistrates once presided. Centrally heated. Fire certificate. AA listed. Convenient base for touring North Wales.

Single Room per one person B&B		Double Room for two persons B&B		10
MIN £ 10.00	MAX £ 10.00	MIN £ 20.00	MAX £ 20.00	OPEN 3-12

Guest Houses

Coleg y Groes
Corwen, Clwyd, LL21 0AU.
Tel: (0490) 2169.

18th century stone guest house built as row of almshouses at foot of Berwyn mountains. Convenient for A5 road and facilities of Corwen, yet quiet and secluded with own garden adjacent to woods. Ideal place for touring, walking, relaxing. Washbasins and tea making facilities in all rooms. Comfortable beds with duvets. Four poster. Good home cooking.

Single Room per one person B&B		Double Room for two persons B&B		6
MIN £ 10.00	MAX £ 12.00	MIN £ 20.00	MAX £ 24.00	OPEN 1-12

Powys House
Corwen, Clwyd, LL21 9EG.
Tel: (0490) 2367.
L

Situated in beautiful Dee Valley. Three large bedrooms, one with private bathroom. Guest lounge with television. All rooms centrally heated. Good home cooking. Use of swimming pool and tennis court. Ideal base for touring North Wales. Good walking, fishing, canoeing and riding nearby. Weekend breaks available all year. Reduced rates for children.

Single Room per one person B&B		Double Room for two persons B&B		3
MIN £ 9.00	MAX £ 12.00	MIN £ 18.00	MAX £ 24.00	OPEN 1-12

Farmhouses

Hendre Arddwyfaen
Ty Nant, Corwen, Clwyd, LL21 0RG.
Tel: (049 082) 396.

Historical Welsh 18th century farmhouse. Ideal centre for walking, pony trekking, golf, fishing, sailing, birdwatching and sightseeing. 100 yards off the A5. Betws-y-Coed 9 miles, Bala 7 miles, Llangollen 15 and Ruthin 12. Traditional Welsh farmhouse meals. Lounge and dining room pleasant. Twin, double or family rooms available. 2 rooms with private showers. Write or telephone for brochure.

Single Room per one person B&B		Double Room for two persons B&B		3
MIN £ 10.00	MAX £ 12.00	MIN £ 20.00	MAX £ 24.00	OPEN 3-11

Denbigh
Map Ref Be5

Castled town in the Vale of Clwyd. Much historic interest. Pony trekking, riding, fishing, golf, tennis and bowls. Indoor heated swimming pool. Centrally located for enjoyng the rolling hillsides of Clwyd – a fruitful agricultural area, full of small and attractive villages.

Hotels

Saracen's Head Hotel
Llansannan, nr Denbigh, Clwyd,
LL16 5HH.
Tel: (074 577) 212.

Set in the beautiful countryside of North Wales this 12th century inn provides the holiday maker with an abundance of "olde worlde" comfort and charm. Llansannan, a picturesque village is situated in the peaceful tranquility of the Welsh hills yet within easy reach of the coastal towns of Llandudno, Colwyn Bay, Rhyl and Conwy.

Single Room per one person B&B		Double Room for two persons B&B		5
MIN £ 11.50	MAX £ 11.50	MIN £ 20.00	MAX £ 20.00	OPEN 1-12

Farmhouses

College Farm
Peniel, Denbigh, Clwyd, LL16 4TT.
Tel: (074 570) 276.

Mixed farm of 140 acres near Denbigh (2½ miles) birth place of H.M. Stanley of Livingston fame. Brenig Reservoir just 5 miles away has facilities for sailing, fishing, windsurfing. Bedrooms have washbasins with shaving points. Home cooking, evening meal by arrangement. You are assured of a warm welcome by the bilingual Parry family. Croeso cynnes i chwi.

Single Room per one person B&B		Double Room for two persons B&B		2
MIN £ 8.50	MAX £ 9.00	MIN £ 17.00	MAX £ 18.00	OPEN 4-11

Flint
Map Ref Cb4

Town on Dee Estuary, across from The Wirral. Edwardian castle mentioned in Shakespeare's play, "Richard II".

Farmhouses

Oakenholt Farm
Flint, Clwyd, CH6 5SU.
Tel: (035 26) 3264.
L

Welcome to our former 15th century Welsh hall house. Beams, log fire, cosy, friendly and relaxed atmosphere. Lovely situation, ideal for touring Chester, North Wales. Two doubles, one twin. Tea/coffee facilities. Overlooking large garden. Guest bathroom, T.V. lounge. Good home cooking, local produce. Children welcome. Evening meal by arrangement.

Single Room per one person B&B		Double Room for two persons B&B		3
MIN £ 8.00	MAX £ 9.00	MIN £ 16.00	MAX £ 18.00	OPEN 1-12

Holywell
Map Ref Cb4

A place of pilgrimage for centuries, St Winifred's holy well has been called the Lourdes of Wales. Nearby are the remains of Basingwerk Abbey (1131) and the Grange Caverns Military Museum. New Leisure Centre.

Guest Houses

The Hall
Lygan-y-Wern, Pentre Halkyn,
Holywell, Clwyd, CH8 8BD.
Enq. to: Mrs. James Vernon.
Tel: (0352) 780215.
L

Conveniently situated on the A55, 15 miles Chester, 70 miles Holyhead. Open all year! Self contained, centrally heated accommodation in recently reconstructed 18th century cottages, comprising 5 bedrooms, two bathrooms, dining/T.V. room.

Single Room per one person B&B		Double Room for two persons B&B		5
MIN £ 10.00	MAX £ 11.00	MIN £ 20.00	MAX £ 22.00	OPEN 1-12

Farmhouses

Bryn Glas

Babell, Nr. Holywell, Clwyd, CH8 8PZ.
Tel: (0352) 720493. L

Comfortable farmhouse with views of Clwydian hills, close to A55 and A541 roads. Convenient access for North Wales top ten attractions and Chester. Two large bedrooms with T.V., tea making facilities, central heating. Colour T.V. lounge. Working farm, cattle, sheep, horses. Cooked breakfast. Children welcome, half price when sharing parents room. Infants free. AA listed. Send s.a.e. for reply.

P	Single Room per one person B&B		Double Room for two persons B&B		2
	MIN £ 9.00	MAX £	MIN £ 16.00	MAX £	OPEN 2-11

Garreg Ganol Farm

Lloc, Nr. Holywell, Clwyd, CH8 8SE.
Tel: (0745) 560488.

Garreg Ganol is a working small holding offering you warm hospitality. It is in a secluded rural setting overlooking the Dee Estuary. We have antique furniture, antique linen and a brass bed. We offer home baked bread, free range eggs and fresh fruit in the bedrooms. Country Landowners Perpetual Challenge Cup 1986. AA listed.

P	Single Room per one person B&B		Double Room for two persons B&B		2
	MIN £ 10.00	MAX £ 10.00	MIN £ 20.00	MAX £ 20.00	OPEN 3-10

Greenhill Farm

Bryn Celyn, Holywell, Clwyd,
CH8 7QF.
Tel: (0352) 713270.

Greenhill is a timber framed farmhouse, modernised to include 3 family rooms (one en-suite), twin and double bedrooms. We have an oak beamed lounge and panelled dining room. Also a games/utility room with tea making and washing facilities and snooker table. Children welcome especially to watch the milking, morning and night.

P	Single Room per one person B&B		Double Room for two persons B&B		5
	MIN £	MAX £	MIN £ 18.00	MAX £	OPEN 3-11

Llangollen

Map Ref Ec1

Romantic, famous Llangollen, the home of the International Musical Eisteddfod; competitors from more than 30 countries come annually in July to sing and dance. The town, on the River Dee, offers interesting little shops, a pottery, weavers, a Canal Museum, Plas Newydd (an historic house) and golf course. Two miles away in a magnificent setting is Valle Crucis Abbey. Castell Dinas Brân overlooks the town.

Guest Houses

2 Arfryn Villas

Hill Street, Llangollen, Clwyd,
LL20 8AH.
Tel: (0978) 861197.

Victorian town house with magnificent view of the valley and mountains. Bedrooms with washbasins, central heating. Residents' lounge with colour T.V. Friendly atmosphere. Ideally located for touring the magnificent Clwyd countryside which offers excellent walking, activities and scenery.

	Single Room per one person B&B		Double Room for two persons B&B		2
	MIN £ 9.00	MAX £ 9.00	MIN £ 17.00	MAX £ 17.00	OPEN 3-11

Bryn Hyfryd

School Lane, Llantysilio, Llangollen,
Clwyd, LL20 8BU.
Tel: (0978) 860011. L

Bryn Hyfryd is a magnificently situated villa guest house with breathtaking views over the Dee Valley. Ideal for touring North Wales or walking in some of Wales' most beautiful countryside. All bedrooms have private bathroom and spectacular views.

P	Single Room per one person B&B		Double Room for two persons B&B		3
	MIN £	MAX £ 9.00	MIN £	MAX £ 18.00	OPEN 4-11

Fron Deg

Abbey Road, Llangollen, Clwyd,
LL20 8EF.
Tel: (0978) 860126.

Attractive Regency style detached house in idyllic surroundings. Particularly convenient for walkers, anglers, canoeists and general tourists. 10 minutes walk to Llangollen centre, 100 metres from International Eisteddfod field. All bedrooms modernised with central heating, washbasins, tea and coffee facilities, television, fully inclusive in price. Family room available. Drying facilities. Unique brand of hospitality.

P	Single Room per one person B&B		Double Room for two persons B&B		4
	MIN £ 8.50	MAX £ 8.50	MIN £ 17.00	MAX £ 17.00	OPEN 1-12

Glanafon

Abbey Road, Llangollen, Clwyd,
LL20 8SS.
Tel: (0978) 860725. L

Family-run guest house overlooking River Dee and ten minutes walking distance from Llangollen town centre. Double and twin rooms with hot and cold, tea/coffee making facilities in all rooms. Children's facilities. Beautiful views of Vale of Llangollen. Ideally situated for walking holiday.

P	Single Room per one person B&B		Double Room for two persons B&B		2
	MIN £ 8.00	MAX £	MIN £ 16.00	MAX £	OPEN 1-12

The Grange

Grange Road, Llangollen, Clwyd,
LL20 8AP.
Tel: (0978) 860366. L

Attractive country house of character in large secluded and tranquil gardens offering good clean accommodation. Spacious comfortable twin and double or family bedrooms with washbasins. Luxury guest bathroom. Five minutes walk from town with its many and varied eating places. Ideally located for touring and walking. Parking in grounds. Reductions for children.

P	Single Room per one person B&B		Double Room for two persons B&B		2
	MIN £	MAX £	MIN £ 18.00	MAX £ 18.00	OPEN 1-12

Henllys

Berwyn, Llangollen, Clwyd,
LL20 8AL.
Tel: (0978) 861263. L

Henllys guest house is set in the beautiful Vale of Llangollen. All our rooms have a delightful view across the valley, with easy access to walks in the Berwyn Hills, and the beauty spots of this part of north-east Wales. We are an ideal place for a relaxing break, winter or summer.

P	Single Room per one person B&B		Double Room for two persons B&B		3
	MIN £ 9.00	MAX £ 10.00	MIN £ 18.00	MAX £ 20.00	OPEN 1-12

Hillcrest

Hill Street, Llangollen, Clwyd,
LL20 8EU.
Tel: (0978) 860208.

Centrally situated for walks. 4 minutes from bus station. Situated 200 yards from Plas Newydd leisure centre with swimming pool 4 miles away. Open all year. Hot and cold, shaver points in 3 bedrooms. Double and family rooms available with special rates for children. Good home cooking, evening meals available on request. Television lounge.

P	Single Room per one person B&B		Double Room for two persons B&B		3
	MIN £ 9.00	MAX £ 10.00	MIN £ 18.00	MAX £ 20.00	OPEN 1-12

The Old Vicarage Guest House

Vicarage Road, Llangollen, Clwyd,
LL20 8HF.
Tel: (0978) 861000/860539.

Spacious house set in large gardens, Glorious scenery, walking, touring, trekking. Homely atmosphere. Residents' lounge, colour T.V. Pets welcome. Babysitter. Tea making facilities, hot and cold in bedrooms. Fire certificate. Good food, fresh whenever possible, vegetarian and special diets available. Children's reductions. Leisure centre 4 miles. Golf course 1 mile. Evening meals available.

Single Room per one person B&B		Double Room for two persons B&B		12
MIN £	MAX £	MIN £	MAX £	OPEN
9.00	9.00	18.00	18.00	1-12

Whitegate

Grange Road, Llangollen, Clwyd,
LL20 8AP.
Tel: (0978) 860960.

A perfect base from which to explore Llangollen and North Wales. Whitegate is an attractive Edwardian family house set on the edge of Llangollen, adjacent to Plas Newydd, long renowned as the home of "the ladies of Llangollen". All bedrooms have hot and cold water, central heating. Ample parking. Children welcome. T.V. lounge.

Single Room per one person B&B		Double Room for two persons B&B		3
MIN £	MAX £	MIN £	MAX £	OPEN
9.00	10.00	18.00	20.00	1-12

Farmhouses

Argoed Farm

Gate Road, Froncysyllte, Nr. Llangollen, Clwyd, LL20 7RH.
Tel: (0691) 772367.

Situated in beautiful Vale of Llangollen on Welsh/English border. Modernised farmhouse, centrally heated, oak beams, tasteful furnishings and large gardens overlooking Telford's aqueduct and River Dee. 1 twin with shower room, 1 double with bathroom. Colour T.V. in lounge. Ideal for walking, touring North Wales, Chester, Shrewsbury. Pony riding, tennis, fishing, golf, leisure centre available locally.

Single Room per one person B&B		Double Room for two persons B&B		2
MIN £	MAX £	MIN £	MAX £	OPEN
		19.00	22.00	4-10

Cae Madoc

Llandegla, Nr. Wrexham, Clwyd,
LL11 3BD.
Tel: (097 888) 270. L

Cae Madoc is a working farm with sheep and cattle. The 200 yr old stone/slate house boasts beams, with garden, central heating. Accommodates 6 guests. Situated on Chester/Dolgellau route nestling in hills betwixt Llangollen and Ruthin, car an advantage. Offa's Dyke nearby for walking. Stabling, grazing for riders. Playroom. Central for touring and National Trust properties.

Single Room per one person B&B		Double Room for two persons B&B		3
MIN £	MAX £	MIN £	MAX £	OPEN
9.00	10.50	17.00	21.00	3-12

Cefn-y-Fedw Farmhouse

Garth, Trevor, Llangollen, Clwyd.
Tel: (0978) 823403. L

Completely secluded sixteenth century stone farmhouse nestling in the hills behind Llangollen. Olde worlde beams, log fires, double room, family room. A paradise for birdwatchers, walkers. One mile Offa's Dyke. Golf, pony trekking, leisure centre, country park, fishing close by. W.I. member. (Own horse, dog welcome prior arrangement).

Single Room per one person B&B		Double Room for two persons B&B		2
MIN £	MAX £	MIN £	MAX £	OPEN
10.00		16.00	20.00	5-10

Dinbren House

Dinbren Road, Llangollen, Clwyd,
LL20 8TF.
Tel: (0978) 860593.

Lovely old house in extensive gardens. Beautiful views across the Dee Valley and within easy walking distance of Llangollen centre. Large comfortable bedrooms with washbasins, tea and coffee making facilities and television in all rooms. Guests' own bathroom, W.C. Family room available. 2½ acre garden with play area. Friendly atmosphere and a warm welcome.

Single Room per one person B&B		Double Room for two persons B&B		3
MIN £	MAX £	MIN £	MAX £	OPEN
8.50	9.00	17.00	18.00	1-12

Maes-yr-Ychain Farm

Llantysilio, Llangollen, Clwyd,
LL20 8DB.
Tel: (0978) 861381. L

Pat and John Hammond welcome you to their comfortable centuries old farmhouse in a secluded setting with magnificent views over the Dee Valley and Berwyn mountains. Lounge, dining room, double, twin (with washbasin) and single bedrooms. Luxury guests' bathroom. Good food using own produce, home baked bread. Tastefully decorated and centrally heated throughout.

Single Room per one person B&B		Double Room for two persons B&B		3
MIN £	MAX £	MIN £	MAX £	OPEN
8.50		17.00		4-10

Pen Lan Farm

Llangollen, Clwyd, LL20 7BU.
Tel: (0978) 860745. L

Pen Lan Farm is a mixed sheep and cattle farm overlooking Llangollen and picturesque valley of River Dee. A warm welcome always with good food served. Good area for touring, walking, pony trekking, shooting. Double room with washbasin, family room. Bathroom. Reduced rates for children. Lounge with colour T.V.

Single Room per one person B&B		Double Room for two persons B&B		2
MIN £	MAX £	MIN £	MAX £	OPEN
		16.00	20.00	6-11

Pen-y-Clawdd Farm

Pentredwr, Llangollen, Clwyd,
LL20 8DG. Tel: (0978) 860716. L

350 year old listed farmhouse situated in beautiful mountain setting 2½ miles from Llangollen. Three bedrooms with separate bathroom and shower, lounge with television, all rooms centrally heated. Dogs by arrangement and reduced rates for children. Good home cooking. Evening meal by arrangement. Open all year round.

Single Room per one person B&B		Double Room for two persons B&B		3
MIN £	MAX £	MIN £	MAX £	OPEN
	9.00		17.00	1-12

Saith Daran Farm

Llandegla, Wrexham, Clwyd,
LL11 3BA. Tel: (097 888) 685.

Beautifully situated near the top of the Horseshoe Pass at the junction of the A542 and A5104. Ideal for touring North Wales coast, Snowdonia, Chester, Shropshire. Bedrooms have showers en-suite, tea making facilities, shaver points, electric blankets. Children welcome. Cot, high chair. 85 acre working dairy, beef farm. Home cooking from local produce. Please contact Mrs Pat Thompson.

Single Room per one person B&B		Double Room for two persons B&B		3
MIN £	MAX £	MIN £	MAX £	OPEN
8.50	10.00	17.00	20.00	1-12

Ty'n Celyn

Tyndwr, Llangollen, Clwyd,
LL20 8AR.
Tel: (0978) 861117.

Situated in pleasant countryside surroundings, Ty'n Celyn is an oak beamed farmhouse of character. Double, twin and family rooms with reduced rates for children, cot available. Comfortable television lounge with log fire. Kitchen for tea, coffee and snack making. 1½ miles from centre of Llangollen. Parking on forecourt. All bedrooms heated. Sorry no pets.

Single Room per one person B&B		Double Room for two persons B&B		3
MIN £	MAX £	MIN £	MAX £	OPEN
8.50	8.50	17.00	17.00	1-12

Llansilin

Map Ref Ec2

Pleasant village in hills west of Oswestry. Owain Glyndwr's chief residence was at Sycharth a mile or so to the south. Pony trekking and walking in the Vale of Ceiriog.

Hotels

Wynnstay Inn

Llansilin, Nr. Oswestry, Clwyd,
SY10 7QB. Tel: (069 170) 355.

18th century inn. Comfortable, centrally heated accommodation. Colour T.V. lounge. Log fire. Inglenook. Unspoilt countryside, walking, fishing, pony trekking, birdwatching. Good home cooked food, friendly atmosphere. Many local places of interest to visit. Easily accessible from A5. Only 7 miles from Oswestry on B4580. Send s.a.e. or telephone for further details.

Single Room per one person B&B		Double Room for two persons B&B		4
MIN £	MAX £	MIN £	MAX £	OPEN
8.00	10.00	16.00	17.00	1-12

Farmhouses

Bwlch-y-Rhiw

Llansilin, Oswestry, Shropshire,
SY10 7PT.
Enq. to: Mrs. Brenda M. Jones.
Tel: (0691 70) 261.

Bwlch-y-Rhiw, an 18th century limestone farmhouse having splendid views of the Tanat Valley. The welcome is warm here. Three spacious bedrooms have bathrooms en-suite and tea making facilities. The character filled dining room has inglenook fireplace, old oak furniture. Comfortable lounge with colour T.V. Ideal spot for most country pursuits, touring, ancient monuments, Offa's Dyke, etc.

P	Single Room per one person B&B		Double Room for two persons B&B		3
	MIN £ 12.00	MAX £	MIN £ 20.00	MAX £	OPEN 3-10

Mold

Map Ref Cb5

The county town of Clwyd and administrative centre on the edge of Clywdian Range. Theatr Clwyd offers a wide range of entertainment. Friendly inns, good walking nearby. Open markets Mondays and Fridays.

Farmhouses

Ddol Ucha

Afonwen, Nr. Mold, Clwyd, CH7 5UN.
Enq. to: Mrs. C. Morris.
Tel: (0352) 720217. L

Former farmhouse, attractively situated in two acres of sheltered ground with own pond. Adjacent to nature reserve, with easy access to A541 road. Home cooked food. Large comfortable dining room and lounge with television. Family, double, twin or single rooms with tea making facilities. Surrounding area of great scenic and historical interest. Fishing nearby.

P	Single Room per one person B&B		Double Room for two persons B&B		4
	MIN £ 9.00	MAX £ 9.00	MIN £ 18.00	MAX £ 18.00	OPEN 1-12

Trebeirdd Farm

off Wrexham Road, Mold, Clwyd,
CH7 4HD. Enq. to: Mrs E. Hughes.
Tel: (0352) 3011. L

An eighteenth century farmhouse ten minutes from Mold town centre. Good, comfortable, clean accommodation comprising of one double, two twin. Good home cooking, evening meal by arrangement. Relaxed family atmosphere. Sports centre two minutes walk. Ideally situated for touring Chester, Llangollen, Ruthin and North Wales coast. Children and dogs welcome. Brochure Mrs. E. Hughes.

P	Single Room per one person B&B		Double Room for two persons B&B		3
	MIN £ 8.00	MAX £ 8.00	MIN £ 16.00	MAX £ 16.00	OPEN 1-12

Ruthin

Map Ref Ca6

An attractive and historic market town with notably fine architecture. Hilltop town square, where medieval days are held weekly in season. The ancient St Peter's Church has beautiful gates. The castle is now a hotel which holds medieval banquets. Good range of small shops. Craft centre with workshops. Excellent and interesting base for the Vale of Clwyd.

Guest Houses

Argoed Guest House

Llanfwrog, Ruthin, Clwyd, LL15 1LG.
Tel: (082 42) 3407.

An attractive timbered house, fully centrally heated with ample parking facilities. Single, double, twin bedded and en-suite rooms. Lounge with T.V. Shower and baths available. Friendly personal attention. Situated within easy walking distance of the historic town of Ruthin in the beautiful Vale of Clwyd. Guided tour facilities available upon request, in season.

P	Single Room per one person B&B		Double Room for two persons B&B		3
	MIN £ 8.50	MAX £ 10.00	MIN £ 20.00	MAX £ 20.00	OPEN 1-12

Eyarth Station

AWARD

Llanfair D.C., Ruthin, Clwyd,
LL15 2EE.
Tel: (082 42) 3643.

Former railway station now beautifully converted guest house with outdoor swimming pool, T.V. lounge. Private family suite own bathroom. Four bedrooms, own bathroom/shower. Private parking. 2 minutes drive from medieval banquets at Ruthin Castle. Central for Chester, Snowdonia, Llangollen, North Wales coast resorts. Magnificent views. AA listed. Brittany Ferries recommended. BTA commended country guest house.

P	Single Room per one person B&B		Double Room for two persons B&B		6
	MIN £ 12.00	MAX £ 12.00	MIN £ 24.00	MAX £ 24.00	OPEN 1-12

The Old Rectory

Clocaenog, Nr. Ruthin, Clwyd,
LL15 2AT.
Tel: (082 45) 740.

Beautiful old former rectory, set in the peace and tranquility of the Clocaenog forest, centrally situated for Snowdonia National Park, Chester and North Wales. Centrally heated accommodation offers H & C or en-suite. Tea making facilities, T.V. lounge, dogs by arrangement, reduced rates for children, optional evening meal. Always a warm welcome.

P	Single Room per one person B&B		Double Room for two persons B&B		4
	MIN £ 8.50	MAX £ 12.00	MIN £ 17.00	MAX £ 24.00	OPEN 1-12

The Old Rectory

Cyffylliog, Ruthin, Clwyd.
Tel: (082 46) 605. L

Situated in peaceful rural village with beautiful views and walks. Within easy travelling distance of many interesting places. Quiet friendly atmosphere offering special rates for families. Home grown and local produce used when available. Babysitting service by arrangement. Colour T.V. in guests' sitting room. Central heating. Guests are requested not to smoke in the house.

P	Single Room per one person B&B		Double Room for two persons B&B		2
	MIN £ 9.50	MAX £ 9.50	MIN £ 19.00	MAX £ 19.00	OPEN 1-12

The White House

Rectory Lane, Llanferres, Mold,
Clwyd, CH7 5SR.
Tel: (035 285) 259. L

Seventeenth century family house with double or family rooms. Relaxed atmosphere and good home cooking with evening meal available. Superb views from all rooms with excellent walks including section of Offa's Dyke. Open March to November. Competitive rates with reductions for children.

P	Single Room per one person B&B		Double Room for two persons B&B		3
	MIN £	MAX £	MIN £ 19.00	MAX £ 21.00	OPEN 3-11

Farmhouses

Bodlywydd Fawr Farm

Llanelidan, Ruthin, Clwyd, LL15 2LA.
Tel: (082 45) 383. L

A warm welcome awaits you at this early 18th century oakbeamed farmhouse in the beautiful vale of Clwyd, 5 miles from medieval Ruthin. Ideal for touring/walking. 2 bedrooms, tea/coffee making facilities. Guests' own lounge and dining room. Centrally heated. Good farmhouse cooking using local produce. Families most welcome with child reductions.

P	Single Room per one person B&B		Double Room for two persons B&B		2
	MIN £ 8.50	MAX £ 9.50	MIN £ 17.00	MAX £ 19.00	OPEN 3-10

Maestyddyn Isa

Clawddnewydd, Ruthin, Clwyd,
LL15 2NH.
Tel: (082 45) 289.

Modernised farmhouse 7 miles Ruthin, mixed 365 acre farm on edge Clocaenog forest. Ideal centre touring North Wales. Sheep, beef, horses. Quiet, peaceful. Triple, double, twin bedrooms all with washbasins, central heating, colour T.V. Family atmosphere with farmhouse fare. Personal attention. Tea/coffee facilities in bedrooms. Pony for riding. Real Welsh welcome.

	Single Room per one person B&B		Double Room for two persons B&B		3
	MIN £	MAX £	MIN £	MAX £	OPEN
	11.00	12.00	22.00	24.00	4-11

St. Asaph
Map Ref Be4

City of smallest cathedral in Britain, venue for the annual North Wales Music Festival. A Cathedral Museum offers information. Nearby are some prehistoric caves. An accessible, pleasant town in the verdant Vale of Clwyd.

Farmhouses

Bach-y-Graig

Tremeirchion, St. Asaph, Clwyd,
LL17 0UH.
Tel: (074 574) 627.

A 16th century farmhouse recently modernised but still retaining its old charm. The comfort of our guests are our priority. Log fires, central heating, good food, personal attention, colour T.V. Family bedroom has bathroom en-suite. Twin. H & C, tea and coffee facilities. Reductions for children. Centrally situated for touring North Wales. Lovely walks. Games room. OS ref. no. SJ075713.

P	Single Room per one person B&B		Double Room for two persons B&B		2
	MIN £	MAX £	MIN £	MAX £	OPEN
			16.00	20.00	3-10

Pen-y-Bryn Farm

Bod Erw, St. Asaph, Clwyd,
LL17 0LF.
Tel: (0745) 583213.

A warm welcome awaits you at this working farm, situated 1 mile west of St. Asaph, 200 yards off A55. Centrally located for touring North Wales. H & C in 1 family and double rooms, with additional single room.
2 bathrooms, shower. Central heating throughout. Guests' own T.V. lounge. Full breakfast. Children welcome with reductions. Send s.a.e., Mrs. B. Williams.

P	Single Room per one person B&B		Double Room for two persons B&B		4
	MIN £	MAX £	MIN £	MAX £	OPEN
	8.00	9.00	16.00	18.00	1-12

Rhewl Farm

Waen, St. Asaph, Clwyd, LL17 0DT.
Tel: (0745) 582287.

A warm welcome awaits you at our 180 acre farm, conveniently situated ½ mile from A55 in a peaceful setting with excellent scenery. Double bedroom with en-suite shower room. Twin and family bedrooms with washbasins. Spacious lounge with original inglenook fireplace. Full breakfast using fresh eggs from farm. Ideal touring centre. Reductions for children.

P	Single Room per one person B&B		Double Room for two persons B&B		3
	MIN £	MAX £	MIN £	MAX £	OPEN
	8.00	8.00	16.00	16.00	3-11

Wrexham
Map Ref Cc6

An industrial and commercial centre, gateway to North Wales. St Giles' Church is one of the wonders of Wales. Nearby Erddig House is a National Trust property. Nearby industrial museum at Barsham. Swimming pool.

Guest Houses

Bridge House

Penley, Nr. Wrexham, Clwyd,
LL13 0LY. Tel: (097 873) 763.

Friendly welcome to a comfortable house in rural Brookside, country setting. Near Cheshire/ Shropshire border. Tea making facilities, colour T.V., central heating, towels in all bedrooms. Children under 12 reduced rates. Cot available. B & B. Evening meal optional (by arrangement).

P	Single Room per one person B&B		Double Room for two persons B&B		4
	MIN £	MAX £	MIN £	MAX £	OPEN
	9.50	9.50	19.00	19.00	1-12

Grove Guest House

36 Chester Road, Wrexham, Clwyd,
LL11 2SD. Tel: (0978) 354288.

Small detached Tudor style guest house with five twin bedded rooms and two singles. Fully centrally heated, two bathrooms, two shower rooms, T.V. lounge. Within walking distance of Wrexham town, car park, gardens.

P	Single Room per one person B&B		Double Room for two persons B&B		7
	MIN £	MAX £	MIN £	MAX £	OPEN
	10.00	12.00	20.00	24.00	1-12

Mill House

Higher Wych, Malpas, Cheshire,
SY14 7JR. Tel: (0948 73) 362.

Modernised mill house on Clwyd/Cheshire border in peaceful rural surroundings with a stream running through the garden. The house is centrally heated with a log fire in the lounge. One bedroom has an en-suite shower/W.C. All bedrooms have washbasins, radio and tea making facilities. Children and senior citizen reductions.

P	Single Room per one person B&B		Double Room for two persons B&B		2
	MIN £	MAX £	MIN £	MAX £	OPEN
	9.00	9.00	18.00	18.00	1-12

Rawcliffe Guest House

3 Belmont Road, Wrexham, Clwyd,
LL13 7PW. Tel: (0978) 266451.

Betty and Neville welcome you to our friendly guest house where we offer comfortable accommodation and good food. H & C all bedrooms. Central heating, spacious bathroom with shower. T.V. lounge. Parking facilities. Ideally situated for touring North Wales and border counties. Near motorway network. Open all year. Reasonable terms. Reduction children. Near, Chester, Llangollen, Mold.

P	Single Room per one person B&B		Double Room for two persons B&B		4
	MIN £	MAX £	MIN £	MAX £	OPEN
	9.50	10.50	17.00	20.00	1-12

Farmhouses

Buck Farm Guest House

Hanmer, Clwyd, SY14 7LX.
Tel: (094 874) 339.

Buck Farm on the A525, a warm, welcoming and cosy Tudor farmhouse, is a good touring base for North Wales, Chester, Shropshire, Staffordshire. We provide vegetarian or vegan meals on request, always make our own breads, muesli, granola, hotcakes and wonderful vegetable soups (sans MSG). French spoken. Library, music. Cycle shelter. No smoking. AA listed. Farmhouse award.

P	Single Room per one person B&B		Double Room for two persons B&B		4
	MIN £	MAX £	MIN £	MAX £	OPEN
	10.00	11.00	20.00	22.00	1-12

MID WALES

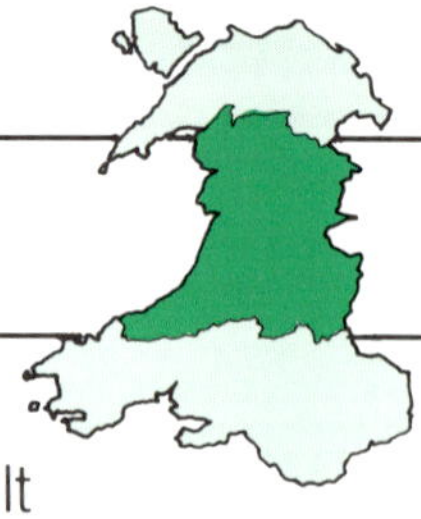

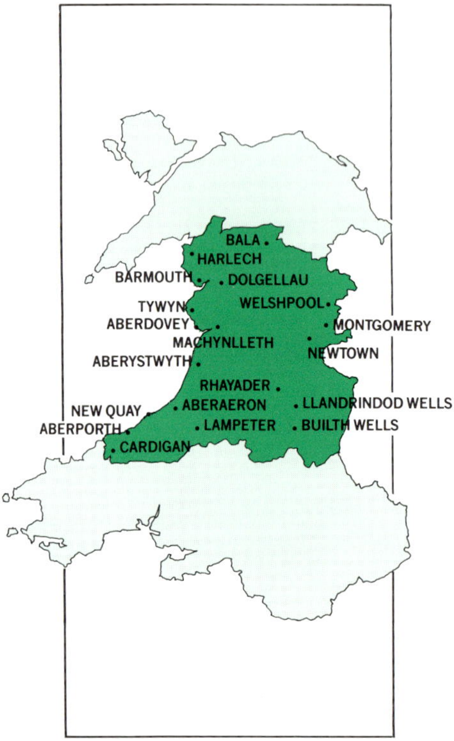

Here, in Wales's quietest holiday region, the atmosphere is traditional, the pace of life restful. Vast stretches of unexplored mountainside fill the horizon. And it's wide open spaces all the way along the great curve of Cardigan Bay.

Mountains sweep down to the sea at two outstandingly lovely estuaries – the luxuriant Mawddach and Dyfi. The Snowdonia National Park might be named after a North Wales peak, but Mid Wales captures most of its area. The massive bulk of Cader Idris, looming above stone-built Dolgellau, guards the park's southern gateway. It opens up onto a patchwork of forests and hill-sheep farmlands stretching away to the bare-flanked mountains above Bala.

Around Welshpool and Newtown, farmlands and lush green hills create a gentler border landscape. High, wild mountains once again reassert themselves across the 'roof of Wales' above Llanidloes and Tregaron. Follow old drovers' routes over this lonely expanse – the domain of the rare kite – to hauntingly beautiful lakelands.

Stay in the heart of the country at a farm or low-beamed inn where stagecoaches once stopped. And help celebrate Mid Wales's 'Festival of the Countryside', an imaginative, summer-long programme of special events.

Everything's also small and friendly along the coast at resorts like Aberystwyth, New Quay, Aberdovey and Barmouth. Wander across cliffs, dunes and beaches unchanged from the heydays of the schooner and windjammer. Go deep-sea fishing or dinghy sailing. Or head for the hills on foot or horseback, where you'll be disturbed only by the chuff of a narrow-gauge steam train.

MEIRIONNYDD

Mountains sweep down to meet the sea all the way along Meirionnydd's majestic coastline. The resorts here – Aberdovey, Barmouth, Fairbourne and Tywyn – are small and pretty. And with so much spectacular countryside just a stone's throw from the sands, they also make marvellous tourist centres.

Almost all of Meirionnydd lies in the Snowdonia National Park. Mountain passes climb past lakes and forested slopes to dizzy viewpoints. Gaze down from the lovely Cregennen Lakes, on the shoulder of towering Cader Idris, to the shining Mawddach Estuary. And from the aptly-named Precipice Walk, you'll have handsome, stone-built Dolgellau and the cool, green Coed y Brenin Forest at your feet.

Bala, besides its mountain-ringed lake, is another fine touring centre. Take a trip along its scenic lakeside narrow-gauge railway. But for the view to end all views, scale the battlements at mighty Harlech, the coastal castle built to command Snowdonia.

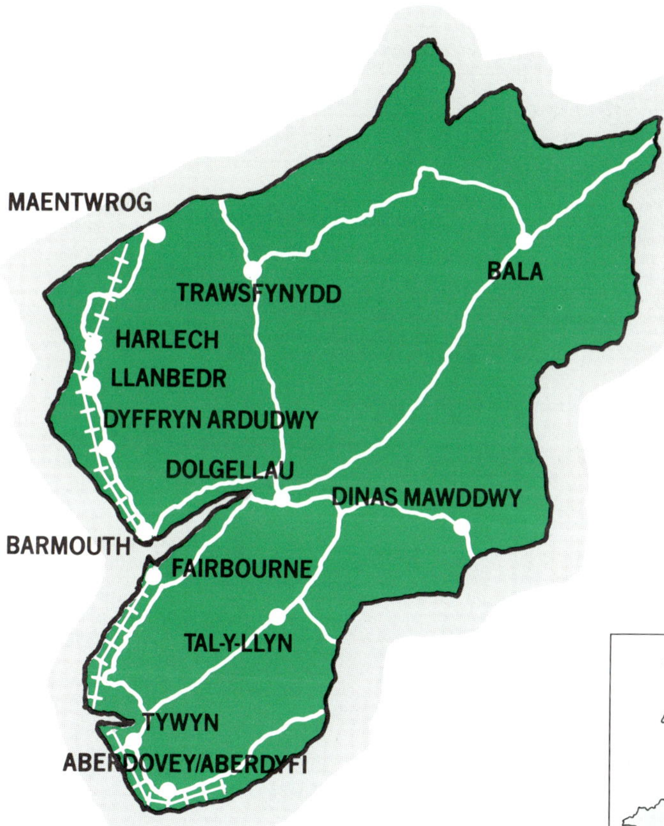

Aberdovey/Aberdyfi
Map Ref Db6

Dinghy sailors' paradise on the Dyfi Estuary. All watersports, thriving yacht club, good inns looking out over the bay and 18-hole golf links. Superb views towards hills and mountains.

Guest Houses

Brodawel Guest House
Tywyn Road, Aberdovey, Gwynedd,
LL35 0SA.
Tel: (065 472) 347.

Brodawel is a detached Edwardian house of great character with lovely views overlooking Cardigan Bay and Aberdovey golf course. Always a friendly atmosphere and we pride ourselves on our substantial breakfasts. Central heating, some en-suite bedrooms, tea/coffee facilities, comfortable lounge. Ideally situated for touring, sailing, golf or relaxing on beach or in garden. AA approved.

P	Single Room per one person B&B		Double Room for two persons B&B		6
	MIN £ 9.50	MAX £ 12.00	MIN £ 19.00	MAX £ 24.00	OPEN 4-10

Plas Dyfi
Pennal, Machynlleth, Powys,
SY20 9LB.
Tel: (0654 75) 688.

On A493 between Machynlleth and Aberdovey. South facing in two acres of grounds with glorious views overlooking Dyfi estuary. All rooms with hot and cold water, razor and electrical points, central heating. Fishing, walking, sailing and golden sands nearby. Children over twelve welcome. Sorry no pets. Plenty of parking space.

P	Single Room per one person B&B		Double Room for two persons B&B		2
	MIN £ 9.50	MAX £ 10.50	MIN £ 19.00	MAX £ 21.00	OPEN 3-10

1 Trefeddian Bank
Aberdovey, Gwynedd, LL35 0RU.
Tel: (065 472) 487.

Small friendly guest house in quiet elevated situation. Panoramic views over golf course, beach and Cardigan Bay. Comfortable lounge, colour T.V., sunbathing terrace, sun porch. All bedrooms have H & C, shaver sockets, tea making facilities. Ideally situated for golf, tennis, all water sports. Beautiful area for walking, birdwatching, touring, etc. Evening meal by arrangement.

P	Single Room per one person B&B		Double Room for two persons B&B		3
	MIN £ 9.00	MAX £ 9.00	MIN £ 18.00	MAX £ 18.00	OPEN 3-10

Farmhouses

Gogarth Hall Farm
Pennal, Machynlleth, Powys,
SY20 9LB.
Tel: (0654 75) 235.

A warm family welcome awaits you at our farm situated 5 miles from Machynlleth, 4 miles from Aberdovey beach. Wonderful views overlooking the Dovey estuary, fishing, shooting, watersports, scenic walks. Ron and Deulwen offer traditional Welsh bed & breakfast & evening meal. Private lounge. Dining room. Bathroom. Bedrooms with washbasins. Children reduced rates. Baby sitting service. Please send for brochure.

P	Single Room per one person B&B		Double Room for two persons B&B		2
	MIN £ 7.50	MAX £ 8.50	MIN £ 15.00	MAX £ 17.00	OPEN 1-12

Tyddyn Rhys Farm
Aberdovey, Gwynedd, LL35 0PG.
Tel: (0654 72) 533.

Tyddyn Rhys is a mixed farm situated half a mile from village of Aberdovey, with outstanding views of Dovey estuary and Cardigan Bay. There is golf, tennis, bowls, pony trekking all within one mile. Comfortable bedrooms with hand washbasins. Bathroom, two toilets. Comfortable sitting room with T.V. Plenty of good food.

P	Single Room per one person B&B		Double Room for two persons B&B		3
	MIN £	MAX £	MIN £ 10.00	MAX £ 18.00	OPEN 3-10

Bala
Map Ref Dd2

A tree-lined street with interesting little shops and charming hotels. There's a lake 4 miles long and a narrow-gauge railway. Golf, sailing and fishing – a natural touring centre for Snowdonia.

Hotels

Frondderw Private Hotel
Stryd-y-Fron, Bala, Gwynedd,
LL23 7YD.
Tel: (0678) 520301.

Frondderw is a charming period mansion set on the hillside overlooking the town of Bala with magnificent views of the Berwyn mountains and Bala Lake. All rooms have hot/cold, central heating, tea and coffee making facilities. Lounge and separate lounge with colour T.V. Ample parking space free of charge. Dinner available.

P	Single Room per one person B&B		Double Room for two persons B&B		8
	MIN £ 9.50	MAX £ 11.50	MIN £ 19.00	MAX £ 23.00	OPEN 1-12

New Inn Hotel
Llangynog, Nr. Bala, Powys,
SY10 0EX.
Tel: (069 174) 229.

Original Inn set in beautiful mountain surround. Ideal for lakes Bala and Vyrnwy. Fishing and pony trekking arranged. Central heating in all rooms. Lounge with television. Some rooms with private bathroom. Licensed bar and restaurant. Meals available all day.
H & C in all bedrooms. Comfortable and friendly atmosphere. Walking parties welcome. Rates apply to 5 bedrooms only.

P	Single Room per one person B&B		Double Room for two persons B&B		8
	MIN £ 12.00	MAX £ 12.00	MIN £ 24.00	MAX £ 24.00	OPEN 1-12

Guest Houses

Maesawelon
Bala, Gwynedd, LL23.
Tel: (0678) 520756. L

Bungalow in a beautiful position ¾ mile from Bala with marvellous views over the town and lake. Bed and breakfast in a comfortable Welsh home. Full central heating, colour T.V. in lounge, homely atmosphere. Parking space.

P	Single Room per one person B&B		Double Room for two persons B&B		4
	MIN £ 7.00	MAX £ 8.00	MIN £ 14.00	MAX £ 15.00	OPEN 1-12

Penisarllan Farm Guest House and Riding Centre
Llanfor, Bala, Gwynedd, LL23 7DW.
Tel: (0678) 520507.

Situated half a mile outside Bala on the A494. An attractive large country house with spacious family accommodation, T.V. lounge, licensed bar, sunbed, sauna, pool table, pony trekking, children's play area. Tea and coffee in all bedrooms, some en-suite with colour T.V. Reduced rates for children. Fire certificate held.

P	Single Room per one person B&B		Double Room for two persons B&B		7
	MIN £ 10.00	MAX £	MIN £ 20.00	MAX £	OPEN 1-12

Farmhouses

Eirianfa Farm
Sarnau, Bala, Gwynedd, LL23 7LH.
Tel: (067 83) 389.

Mixed farm 3 miles from Bala on A494. Family, double, twin bedded rooms, all with washbasins, C/H, tea/coffee facilities. Dining, sitting room with T.V. Bathroom, separate toilet and shower. Good home cooked food served. Private trout lake. Ideal centre for touring North/Mid Wales. Children welcomed.

P	Single Room per one person B&B		Double Room for two persons B&B		3
	MIN £ 9.00	MAX £ 10.00	MIN £ 16.00	MAX £ 18.00	OPEN 3-11

Erw Feurig

Cefnddwysarn, Bala, Gwynedd,
LL23 7LL.
Tel: (067 83) 262.

Beautifully situated facing the Berwyn mountains, this is the ideal centre from which to base your holiday. Extremely comfortable family, double and twin bedrooms available, all with own keys, central heating and tea/coffee making facilities. Excellent breakfasts and dinners served. Fishing available on the farm. Children welcome at reduced rates in family rooms.

Single Room per one person B&B		Double Room for two persons B&B		4
MIN £ 8.50	MAX £ 9.50	MIN £ 17.00	MAX £ 19.00	OPEN 2-12

Rhydydefaid Farm

Frongoch, Bala, Gwynedd,
LL23 7NT.
Tel: (0678) 520456.

Traditional Welsh stone farmhouse, three miles from Bala on A4212 road. One family bedroom, one twin bedroom, both with washbasins, tea/coffee making facilities. Central heating. Separate dining room and sitting room with T.V. Fresh farm produce, good home cooking. Ideal centre for keen anglers, walkers, conoeists, and touring Snowdonia. Children welcome.

Single Room per one person B&B		Double Room for two persons B&B		2
MIN £ 8.00	MAX £ 9.00	MIN £ 16.00	MAX £ 18.00	OPEN 3-10

Barmouth

Map Ref Db4

Golden sands and miles of wonderful mountain and estuary walks near by. Promenade, funfair, pony rides on the beach. Lifeboat house, RNLI Museum and the headquarters of the Merioneth Yacht Club. A thriving holiday town with good shops and inns. Excellent parking on the sea front.

Hotels

Crystal House Hotel

19 Marine Parade, Barmouth,
Gwynedd, LL42 1NA.
Tel: (0341) 280603.

Ideally situated on the seafront. Our lounge, dining room and some bedrooms have magnificent views across Cardigan Bay to the Cader Idris mountain range. Large lounge with colour T.V. Well equipped bedrooms with hot and cold, shaver points, striplights, etc. Fire safety certificate held. Close to all amenities. Cleanliness and home comforts assured.

Single Room per one person B&B		Double Room for two persons B&B		9
MIN £ 8.50	MAX £ 9.50	MIN £ 17.00	MAX £ 19.00	OPEN 4-10

Morwendon Private Hotel

Llanaber, Barmouth, Gwynedd,
LL42 1RR.
Tel: (0341) 280566.

Private hotel set in two acres with superb views over Cardigan Bay. All bedrooms have colour T.V., tea/coffee making facilities and most are with en-suite W.C.'s and showers. Enjoy our home cooked choice of menus. In a peaceful position 1½ miles north of Barmouth on the A496 to Harlech road.

Single Room per one person B&B		Double Room for two persons B&B		6
MIN £ 9.00	MAX £ 10.00	MIN £ 18.00	MAX £ 24.00	OPEN 3-12

Guest Houses

Gwesty Dryll-y-Car

Llanaber, Barmouth, Gwynedd,
LL42 1YY.
Tel: (0341) 280959.

Detached and spacious family home at Llanaber, one mile out of Barmouth, overlooking Cardigan Bay. Delightful bedrooms with vanity units and beverage facilities. Comfortable residents' lounge with colour television. Reduced rates for children. Marvellous centre for sightseeing and activity holidays in North and Mid Wales.

Single Room per one person B&B		Double Room for two persons B&B		2
MIN £	MAX £	MIN £ 22.00	MAX £	OPEN 1-12

Palma

2 Aelfor Terrace, King Edward Street,
Barmouth, Gwynedd, LL42 1PU.
Tel: (0341) 280381.

Centrally situated for railway station, coach station and car parks. Sea and beaches within walking distance. Hot and cold, shaver points, tea making facilities in bedrooms, shower available. Separate tables. T.V. Open all year. Good home cooking. Friendly welcome. For details write to Christine Palmer.

Single Room per one person B&B		Double Room for two persons B&B		3
MIN £ 12.00	MAX £ 12.00	MIN £ 18.00	MAX £ 20.00	OPEN 1-12

Porth Mynach

Llanaber Road, Barmouth, Gwynedd,
LL42 1YG.
Tel: (0341) 280943.

Former coaching house, now converted into guest house and offering modern facilities. Ground floor bedrooms with tea and coffee making facilities, radio alarms, shaver points. Central heating. Showers. Car parking. An ideal base for an enjoyable stay at Barmouth with its sandy beach, and for touring Mid Wales and Snowdonia.

Single Room per one person B&B		Double Room for two persons B&B		3
MIN £ 12.00	MAX £ 12.00	MIN £ 24.00	MAX £ 24.00	OPEN 1-12

The Sandpiper

7 Marine Parade, Barmouth,
Gwynedd, LL42 1NA.
Tel: (0341) 280318.

The Sandpiper is superbly situated on Barmouth seafront. There is free parking outside and we are a short, level walk from the station. Most rooms have en-suite facilities, television and tea/coffee making facilities, including a ground floor bedroom. Super home cooking. Residential licence. Central heating. Brochure from Susan and John Palmer.

Single Room per one person B&B		Double Room for two persons B&B		9
MIN £ 8.50	MAX £ 9.50	MIN £ 17.00	MAX £ 23.00	OPEN 1-12

Farmhouses

Llwyn Dû Farmhouse

Llanaber, Barmouth, Gwynedd,
LL42 1RR. Enq: Paula Thompson.
Tel: (0341) 280144.

Delightful 17th century farmhouse situated north of Barmouth. Magnificent views over Cardigan Bay. Beach ten minutes. Enjoy high quality food all freshly prepared in superb atmosphere of stone, oak and history. Family or double rooms, all with private bathroom, two en-suite. Lounge, colour T.V. Children, vegetarians welcome. A friendly welcome awaits you. Les Routiers recommended. Licensed.

Single Room per one person B&B		Double Room for two persons B&B		4
MIN £ 10.00	MAX £ 12.00	MIN £ 20.00	MAX £ 24.00	OPEN 2-11

Meadow Farm

Dyffryn Ardudwy, Nr. Barmouth,
Gwynedd, LL44 2DY.
Tel: (034 17) 655.

Traditional Welsh stone farmhouse on a small working farm within Snowdonia National Park. Magnificent views of Cardigan Bay. Sandy beaches, walks, trekking. Warm welcome. Lounge, colour T.V. Three bedrooms with showers, all with washbasins, gas central heating. Children welcome.

Single Room per one person B&B		Double Room for two persons B&B		5
MIN £	MAX £ 10.00	MIN £	MAX £ 20.00	OPEN 1-12

Dinas Mawddwy
Map Ref Dd4

Salmon and trout fishing, walking in the beautiful countryside on the edge of the Snowdonia National Park. Visit the Meirion Mill here.

Farmhouses

Bryncelyn Farm

Dinas Mawddwy, Machynlleth,
Powys, SY20 9JA.
Enq to: Mrs E. M. Edwards.
Tel: (065 04) 289.

Bryncelyn Farm is in the peaceful Cywarch Valley just outside Dinas Mawddwy. Log fire in evenings. Good home cooking. Hot and cold in bedrooms, two toilets upstairs. Drink making facilities in each bedroom. Trout fishing for guests on farm. Bryncelyn is a working farm. The Edwards' family offers you a homely holiday in a comfortable farmhouse.

	Single Room per one person B&B		Double Room for two persons B&B		2
	MIN £	MAX £	MIN £	MAX £	OPEN
	9.50	10.00	18.00	20.00	1-12

Bryn Sion Farm

Cwmcywarch, Dinas Mawddwy,
Machynlleth, Powys, SY20 9JG.
Tel: (065 04) 251. L

Breathtaking views of the mountains, set in quiet, secluded woodland 1½ miles from the pretty village of Dinas Mawddwy. Convenient for the coast and the market town of Machynlleth. Idyllic walks in beautiful countryside. Good roads to the farmhouse, car parking. Two double rooms, television lounge. Good value farmhouse fare on this working sheep farm.

P	Single Room per one person B&B		Double Room for two persons B&B		2
	MIN £	MAX £	MIN £	MAX £	OPEN
	8.50	10.00	17.00	20.00	1-12

Dolgellau
Map Ref Dc4

Very Welsh market town set in a wooded valley, centre for routes along Mawddach Estuary. Well situated touring centre in a particularly attractive corner of Wales.

Guest Houses

Dwy Olwyn

Coed-y-Fronallt, Dolgellau, Gwynedd,
LL40 2YG. Tel: (0341) 422822.

A comfortable guest house situated in an acre of landscaped gardens, boasting magnificent views, in a peaceful position yet only 10 minutes walk from the town. Good home cooking. Close to sandy beaches, gold mines, Narrow Gauge Railways, numerous walks, etc. Ample parking. Lounge with colour T.V. Evening meal if desired. Hot and cold all bedrooms.

P	Single Room per one person B&B		Double Room for two persons B&B		3
	MIN £	MAX £	MIN £	MAX £	OPEN
	8.00		16.00		3-11

Floriet

Llanelltyd, Dolgellau, Gwynedd,
LL40 2SO.
Tel: (0341) 422553.

Floriet is situated in its own grounds overlooking the Mawddach Estuary and magnificent view of Cader Idris range, with two double rooms, one twin room, T.V. lounge. Good home cooking. Near the sea and Narrow Gauge Railways. Fishing, pony trekking. Ideal for walking.

P	Single Room per one person B&B		Double Room for two persons B&B		3
	MIN £	MAX £	MIN £	MAX £	OPEN
	8.00		16.00		5-10

Y Goedlan

Brithdir, Dolgellau, Gwynedd,
LL40 2RN.
Tel: (0341) 423131. L

This old vicarage with adjoining farm offers peaceful accommodation in pleasant surroundings. Ideally placed on B4416 road for walks, sea and mountains. Spacious double, twin and family rooms. H & C. Colour T.V. lounge. Central heating. Shower. Two conveniences. Parking. Comfort with homely atmosphere. Hearty breakfast. Separate tables. Tea making facilities. Reductions for children. Dolgellau 2 miles.

P	Single Room per one person B&B		Double Room for two persons B&B		3
	MIN £	MAX £	MIN £	MAX £	OPEN
	8.50	9.50	17.00	19.00	1-11

Herongate

Mawddach Crescent, Arthog,
Gwynedd, LL39 1BJ.
Tel: (0341) 250349.

Herongate is situated at the water's edge of the beautiful Mawddach estuary in what must be one of the loveliest areas in Wales. Especially suitable for adults wanting a quiet holiday. Bedrooms all attractive with hot and cold water and shaving point. Comfortable lounge with colour television. Good breakfast. Ample parking space.

P	Single Room per one person B&B		Double Room for two persons B&B		4
	MIN £	MAX £	MIN £	MAX £	OPEN
	9.50	10.00	18.00	19.00	5-9

Heulwen

Llanfachreth, Dolgellau, Gwynedd,
LL40 2UT.
Tel: (0341 423) 085. L

Heulwen is a large, modern bungalow with beautiful views of the surrounding mountains. We have 2 doubles with H & C and 1 twin bedded room. Bathroom includes shower cubicle and bidet. Separate toilet. Car parking. Patio. C/H. Information leaflets. Varied menu of good home cooking. Dolgellau 4 miles. Precipice walk 1 mile.

P	Single Room per one person B&B		Double Room for two persons B&B		3
	MIN £	MAX £	MIN £	MAX £	OPEN
	8.00	8.50	16.00	17.00	3-10

Ivy House

Finsbury Square, Dolgellau,
Gwynedd, LL40 1RF.
Tel: (0341) 422535.

Country town guest house offering attractive accommodation, a warm welcoming atmosphere and good food. Residential licence for the cellar bar. Lounge with colour T.V., full central heating. All bedrooms tea and coffee facilities. Evening meals or bar snacks available. Perfect touring centre, idyllic walking and climbing area, maps and information available. Sandy beaches 9 miles.

	Single Room per one person B&B		Double Room for two persons B&B		5
	MIN £	MAX £	MIN £	MAX £	OPEN
	12.00		20.00		1-12

Penbryn Croft

Cader Road, Dolgellau, Gwynedd,
LL40 1RN.
Tel: (0341) 422815.

A Georgian guest house situated within two minutes walk of the centre of the old market town, offering a warm and comfortable atmosphere. Reputation for a high standard of catering and excellent varied menu. Separate tables. Five course evening dinner optional. Colour T.V. lounge. H & C all bedrooms. Late night drink included in price.

	Single Room per one person B&B		Double Room for two persons B&B		5
	MIN £	MAX £	MIN £	MAX £	OPEN
	11.00		18.00		1-12

Farmhouses

Cae'r Tyddyn Uchaf

Cross Foxes, Dolgellau, Gwynedd,
LL40 2SH.
Tel: (0341) 423250. L

Situated in pleasant rural surroundings off the A470 Dolgellau to Dinas Mawddwy road. Cae'r Tyddyn Uchaf is an old homely farmhouse on a small hill sheep farm where a warm welcome and good food awaits visitors. One double, one twin bedroom.

P	Single Room per one person B&B		Double Room for two persons B&B		2
	MIN £	MAX £	MIN £	MAX £	OPEN
	8.00		16.00		4-9

Cyfannedd Uchaf

Arthog, Dolgellau, Gwynedd,
LL39 1LX
Tel: (0341) 250526. L

Fantastic views honestly! Renovated farmhouse in foothills of Cader Idris mountain range overlooking Mawddach estuary, Cregennen lakes nearby. Beamed lounge, log fire, central heating. Two double rooms, one twin, each with complimentary tea tray. Excellent for naturalists, walkers, all seeking seclusion. Evening meal optional. Children over 12 welcome. Sorry no pets. Brochure, Mrs Anna Tovey.

P	Single Room per one person B&B		Double Room for two persons B&B		3
	MIN £	MAX £	MIN £	MAX £	OPEN
	8.50	8.50	17.00	17.00	1-12

Fronolau Farm Restaurant

Tabor, Dolgellau, Gwynedd,
LL40 2PS.
Tel: (0341) 422381.

Converted farmhouse and stables on the lower slopes of Cader Idris overlooking the beautiful Mawddach estuary. Quiet and secret, a place of wild beauty. An ideal base for exploring Snowdonia. Single, double, family rooms. T.V., beverages in all rooms. Stable dining room, bar, lounge area with log fire. Golf, fishing, walks, horse riding.

	Single Room per one person B&B		Double Room for two persons B&B		4
P	MIN £ 8.50	MAX £ 10.00	MIN £ 17.00	MAX £ 20.00	OPEN 1-12

Gwanas Farmhouse

Cross Foxes, Dolgellau, Gwynedd,
LL40 2SH.
Tel: (0341) 422624.

Mrs. Evans offers peace and comfort on 1000 acre sheep farm. Spacious farmhouse with homely atmosphere and hearty breakfast. Twin, double, family rooms with H & C. Two bathrooms, showers. Central heating. T.V. Evening refreshments 9.30 p.m. Reductions for children. Ample parking. Situated off A470 road between Dinas Mawddwy and Dolgellau, 400 yards east of Cross Foxes Inn.

	Single Room per one person B&B		Double Room for two persons B&B		3
P	MIN £ 9.00	MAX £	MIN £ 16.50	MAX £ 18.50	OPEN 3-11

Llwyn Talcen

Brithdir, Dolgellau, Gwynedd,
Tel: (0341 41) 276.

Detached house of character within spacious grounds and lovely views. Relaxed atmosphere. 4 miles Dolgellau, easy reach of Cambrian coast. Ideal base for touring Snowdonia National Park. Single, double/family rooms available. Reduced rates for children.

	Single Room per one person B&B		Double Room for two persons B&B		2
P	MIN £ 8.00	MAX £ 10.00	MIN £ 16.00	MAX £ 20.00	OPEN 1-12

Tyddynmawr

Islawrdref, Cadair Road, Dolgellau,
Gwynedd, LL40 1TL.
Tel: (0341) 422331. L

Welcome to Tyddynmawr, 18th century farmhouse. Beams, log fires, warm and friendly. 2 double rooms with mountain views. Good home cooking. We farm the magnificent mountain of Cader Idris. Ideal for walking, climbing. Fishing available on privately owned lake. Spectacular waterfalls, birdwatchers paradise. We offer peace and tranquility. Ideal base for touring.

	Single Room per one person B&B		Double Room for two persons B&B		2
P	MIN £	MAX £	MIN £ 17.00	MAX £ 17.00	OPEN 4-11

Dyffryn Ardudwy

Map Ref Da3

Welsh village set between Barmouth and Harlech.

Farmhouses

Byrdir

AWARD

Dyffryn Ardudwy, Gwynedd,
LL44 2EA. Tel: (034 17) 200.

Traditional, Welsh stone farmhouse, with wood beams, in peaceful national park setting with lovely views. Double and family bedrooms, two with private bathroom, others have own shower and wash basin. Sitting room, colour T.V., separate dining room. Many activities locally, lovely beaches nearby, walks, golf, swimming pool, fishing, riding. Reduced rates for children.

	Single Room per one person B&B		Double Room for two persons B&B		4
P	MIN £ 12.00	MAX £	MIN £ 24.00	MAX £	OPEN 3-10

Llys Bennar

AWARD

Dyffryn Ardudwy, Gwynedd,
LL44 2QX. Tel: (034 17) 316.

Lovely eighteenth century converted farm buildings in a courtyard setting, surrounded by farmland and small stream. Between castle town of Harlech and resort of Barmouth. Ten minutes walk from village and broad sandy beach. Colour television. Attractive bedrooms with private bathroom and tea making facilities. Superb home cooking with friendly and welcoming service.

	Single Room per one person B&B		Double Room for two persons B&B		2
P	MIN £ 9.00	MAX £	MIN £ 18.00	MAX £	OPEN 3-11

Fairbourne

Map Ref Db4

A resort with 2 miles of sand on the south bank of the Mawddach Estuary. Terminus of the narrow gauge Fairbourne Railway.

Guest Houses

Einion Guest House

Fairbourne, Gwynedd, LL38 2NX.
Tel: (0341) 250644.

Enjoy overnight, weekend break, annual holidays. Quiet family-run guest house pleasantly situated over the estuary from Barmouth. Licensed separate dining room, colour T.V. lounge. Close safe sandy beaches, trekking, good touring centre, steam trains, exceptional scenery. W.T.B. two crown accommodation. All amenities. Children welcome. Adventure groups out of season. Group reductions.

	Single Room per one person B&B		Double Room for two persons B&B		5
P	MIN £	MAX £ 9.00	MIN £	MAX £ 18.00	OPEN 2-11

Panteinion Hall

Friog, Fairbourne, Gwynedd,
LL38 2TJ.
Tel: (0341) 250475/250519. L

Snowdonia National Park surrounds this superb accommodation situated in a beautiful secluded valley. Ideal for individuals or family groups for canoeing, climbing, photography, sea and river fishing, pony trekking, miniature railway enthusiasts and ornithology. Drying facilities. Licensed bar in lounge with large open fire. Centrally heated rooms with tea/coffee making facilities. Relaxed atmosphere with friendly staff. Group rates available.

	Single Room per one person B&B		Double Room for two persons B&B		8
P	MIN £ 9.50	MAX £ 10.50	MIN £ 19.00	MAX £ 21.00	OPEN 1-12

Harlech

Map Ref Ae7

A 13th-century castle, its background rich in mythology, overlooking the extensive Morfa dunes is the dominant feature of this small town. Famous 18-hole golf course. Shell beach nearby, theatre and swimming pool.

Hotels

Noddfa Hotel

Lower Road, Harlech, Gwynedd,
LL46 2UB.
Tel: (0766) 780043.

Comfortable AA* hotel overlooking the Royal St. David's golf course with superb views of Snowdon and within bowshot of Harlech castle. Why not go back 700 years and try traditional archery lessons in the hotel grounds. Nearby indoor swimming pool, walking, beach. Owner runs hotel ensuring good food and wine. Six rooms available at rates quoted.

	Single Room per one person B&B		Double Room for two persons B&B		7
P	MIN £ 12.00	MAX £ 12.00	MIN £ 20.00	MAX £ 24.00	OPEN 1-12

Guest Houses

Arundel

High Street, Harlech, Gwynedd,
LL46 2YE.
Tel: (0766) 780637. L

Situated 100 yards above Harlech Castle with beautiful views of golf course, Tremadog Bay and Snowdonia mountains. Central for touring North Wales. Lovely sandy beach. Car parking available. Full central heating. Bathroom with separate shower, separate W.C. Home from home atmosphere.

	Single Room per one person B&B		Double Room for two persons B&B		3
P	MIN £	MAX £	MIN £ 16.00	MAX £ 18.00	OPEN 2-10

Glan-y-Gors Guest House

Llandanwg, Harlech, Gwynedd,
LL46 2SD.
Tel: (034 123) 410.

Detached house 200 yards from sandy beach. Two acres of land. Private access to beach, beautiful Welsh hills surround. Good Welsh home cooking. Separate tables. T.V. lounge. Single, double rooms. Train station within walking distance. One mile swimming pool, golf club, Harlech Castle. Beautiful country lakes, scenery, nature trail walks.

Single Room per one person B&B		Double Room for two persons B&B		3
MIN £ 8.00	MAX £ 8.00	MIN £ 16.00	MAX £ 16.00	OPEN 1-12

Gwrach Ynys Country Guest House

Ynys, Talsarnau, Gwynedd,
LL47 6TS.
Tel: (0766) 780742.

Treat yourself to a relaxing break amongst gloriously peaceful surroundings at our country guest house. Homely and relaxed atmosphere. Six bedrooms en-suite, all with coffee/tea making facilities. Central heating. Fire certificate. Evening meal available. Ideal rambling, birdwatching centre. Golf course, swimming pool, beach 2 miles. Warmest welcome provided by resident proprietors. Brochure sent with pleasure.

Single Room per one person B&B		Double Room for two persons B&B		7
MIN £ 10.00	MAX £ 12.00	MIN £ 20.00	MAX £ 24.00	OPEN 1-12

Farmhouses

Maesyraelfor

Harlech, Gwynedd, LL46 2TH.
Tel: (0766) 780571.

Working farm with Welsh beef and sheep. 1½ miles inland from Harlech, and 2 miles from the beach. Beautiful views of Cardigan Bay and mountains. Two double and one single bedrooms. Lounge with T.V. Dining room. Reduced rates for children and O.A.P.'s. Evening dinner by arrangement.

Single Room per one person B&B		Double Room for two persons B&B		3
MIN £ 8.00	MAX £	MIN £ 16.00	MAX £	OPEN 1-12

Tyddyn Gwynt

Harlech, Gwynedd, LL46 2TH.
Tel: (0766) 780298.

Smallholding situated in Snowdonia National Park. 2½ miles inland from Harlech. Open all year. Hot and cold, shaver points in 3 bedrooms. Sandy beach, many tourist attractions within easy reach with car. Home cooking, separate tables. T.V. lounge. Log fire on chilly evenings. AA listed. Fire certificate held. Electric blankets in winter.

Single Room per one person B&B		Double Room for two persons B&B		3
MIN £ 8.50	MAX £ 9.50	MIN £ 17.00	MAX £ 19.00	OPEN 1-12

Llanbedr
Map Ref Da3

Llanbedr and neighbouring Pensarn form a duo of attractive villages on the Ardudwy coast. At the Maes Artro Craft Village, visitors can watch craftsmen at work and buy their products. Close to Shell Island at Mochras, and slate caverns. The Rhinog Mountains in the background are excellent for walking.

Farmhouses

Hendy Farm

Llanbedr, Gwynedd, LL45 2LT.
Tel: (0341 23) 263.

Situated in beautiful Snowdonia National Park, 500 yards off main A496 coast road overlooking Cardigan Bay. Detached farmhouse with two double and one bunk rooms. Separate bathroom. Colour T.V. lounge. Presenting good home cooking. Nearest beaches ten minutes. Convenient for walks, fishing, trekking, golfing. Evening meal optional. Children under ten reduced rates.

Single Room per one person B&B		Double Room for two persons B&B		3
MIN £ 8.00	MAX £ 9.00	MIN £ 16.00	MAX £	OPEN 5-9

Maentwrog
Map Ref Db1

Characteristic stone houses, attractively designed village, sheltering underneath the imposing Plas Tan y Bwlch, now the venue for residential courses on all aspects of Snowdonia. A pottery in the village and the Ffestiniog Railway nearby. Truly breathtaking scenery of mountains all around.

Guest Houses

Hen Felin (Old Mill)

Rhyd-y-Sarn, Ffestiniog, Gwynedd,
LL41 4NT.
Tel: (076 676) 2409.

A very warm welcome awaits you at our ancient former mill house set in the most beautiful countryside within the Snowdonia National Park. So convenient for many attractions. Evening meals available. When chilly, relax in front of our huge log fire. At the days end, our mill stream will lull you to sleep.

Single Room per one person B&B		Double Room for two persons B&B		4
MIN £ 8.00	MAX £ 10.00	MIN £ 16.00	MAX £ 20.00	OPEN 1-12

Tal-y-Llyn
Map Ref Dc5

Lakeside village below Cader Idris Mountain. Ideally situated for fishing and walking. Talyllyn Narrow Gauge Railway, which runs to a nearby halt, connects with Tywyn.

Farmhouses

Dolffanog Fach

Tal-y-Llyn, Tywyn, Gwynedd,
LL36 9AJ.
Tel: (065 473) 235.

Dolffanog is situated near Tal-y-Llyn lake at the foot of Cader Idris. Bedrooms with hot and cold, razor points, heating. Lounge with colour T.V. Comfort and good home cooking. Fire certificate held. Ample car parking. Ideal centre for touring, walking, activities on the lake or fishing. Contact Mrs. Meirwen Pughe for further details.

Single Room per one person B&B		Double Room for two persons B&B		3
MIN £ 9.00	MAX £ 10.00	MIN £ 18.00	MAX £ 20.00	OPEN 3-10

Trawsfynydd
Map Ref Dc2

In the heartland of Snowdonia National Park, Trawsfynydd stands on the edge of a lake fed by several small streams, tumbling down from the mountains around. The Trawsfynydd Power Station is near the lake. Plenty of hill walking and fishing.

Farmhouses

Bryn Celynog Farm

Cwm Prysor, Trawsfynydd, Gwynedd,
LL41 4TR.
Tel: (076 687) 378.

Situated in beautiful mountain setting. Three miles from village, mountain walks and fishing available. Ideal base for touring Snowdonia National Park. Good food. Two double bedrooms, bathroom, sitting, dining room, T.V. 12 miles from seaside.

Single Room per one person B&B		Double Room for two persons B&B		2
MIN £ 8.00	MAX £ 8.50	MIN £ 16.00	MAX £ 17.00	OPEN 4-10

Tywyn

Map Ref Da5

Cardigan Bay seaside resort. Beach activities, sea and river fishing, and golf course are amongst its notable features. Talyllyn Narrow Gauge Railway heads inland from here and St Cadfan's Stone and Llanegryn Church are important Christian sites. In the hills stands Castell-y-Bere, a native Welsh Castle, and Bird Rock, a haven for birdlife.

Hotels

The Greenfield Private Hotel and Restaurant

Tywyn, Gwynedd, LL36 9AD.
Tel: (0654) 710354.

AA*RAC*. Comfortable, well established family run hotel conveniently situated opposite heated swimming pool and large car park. Bus and railway stations nearby including the popular Tal-y-Llyn narrow gauge railway. Few minutes walk to beach. Central heating throughout. Licensed bar. T.V. lounge. Evening meal available with choice of menu. Reductions for children. Brochure on request.

	Single Room per one person B&B		Double Room for two persons B&B		14
	MIN £ 11.25	MAX £ 11.25	MIN £ 22.50	MAX £ 22.50	OPEN 1-12

Guest Houses

Brynllwyn

Rhoslefain, Tywyn, Gwynedd,
LL36 9NH.
Tel: (0654) 711595/711488.

Brynllwyn is a stone built farmhouse set 5 miles north of Tywyn in the midst of tranquil and beautiful countryside, near the sea. An excellent centre for touring and outdoor activities. Appetizing food, (traditional wholefood or vegetarian), dinner by arrangement. Comfort and seclusion assured. Games room and utility area for guests.

P	Single Room per one person B&B		Double Room for two persons B&B		4
	MIN £ 10.00	MAX £ 11.00	MIN £ 20.00	MAX £ 22.00	OPEN 1-12

Cader View

25 Cambrian Road, Tywyn,
Gwynedd, LL36 0AG.
Tel: (0654) 710809.

Informal homely accommodation. All rooms have hot and cold, shaver points, central heating and tea making facilities. Minutes from beach, shops, swimming pool, cinema. Situated between Tal-y-Llyn narrow gauge railway and main British Rail station. Hot drinks dispenser for bedtime beverages. Ideal touring base for hikers, climbers, little train enthusiasts, etc. S.a.e. appreciated.

P	Single Room per one person B&B		Double Room for two persons B&B		2
	MIN £ 7.50	MAX £	MIN £ 15.00	MAX £	OPEN 3-12

Pant-y-Neuadd Country House

Aberdyfi Road, Tywyn, Gwynedd,
LL36 9HW. Tel: (0654) 711393.

This country house, originally the home of Sir Hayden Jones owner of the famous Tal-y-Llyn railway, has recently been modernised, still retaining character, oak panelling and log fires. All bedrooms have en-suite facilities and heating. Guests' T.V. lounge. Dinner (home grown and cooked) by arrangement. An ideal touring centre surrounded by lovely countryside.

P	Single Room per one person B&B		Double Room for two persons B&B		3
	MIN £ 12.00	MAX £ 12.00	MIN £ 21.00	MAX £ 21.00	OPEN 3-11

Farmhouses

Cynfal Farm

Bryncrug, Tywyn, Gwynedd,
LL36 9RB. Enq to: Mrs Carys Evans.
Tel: (0654) 711703.

Victorian period farmhouse in beautiful setting with Cardigan Bay and Dysynni Estuary in the background. Talyllyn narrow gauge railway is 200 yards from the house. Spacious twin, double and family rooms available with hot/cold, razor points and tea/coffee making facilities. Two private bathrooms with separate W.C. Ideal for walking and most sporting activities.

P	Single Room per one person B&B		Double Room for two persons B&B		3
	MIN £ 8.50	MAX £ 10.00	MIN £ 17.00	MAX £ 20.00	OPEN 4-10

Hendy Farm

Tywyn, Gwynedd, LL36 9RU.
Tel: (0654) 710457.

A stone built farmhouse situated in the Snowdonia National Park with beautiful scenic views, near the town and beach. Talyllyn railway runs nearby. Three spacious double bedrooms have washbasins, tea making facilities, television and radios. Separate dining room and residents' lounge. Relaxed informal atmosphere. Ideal area for walking, golfing and sporting activities.

P	Single Room per one person B&B		Double Room for two persons B&B		3
	MIN £ 9.00	MAX £ 10.00	MIN £ 16.00	MAX £ 18.00	OPEN 4-10

Tanycoed Ucha Farm

Tywyn, Gwynedd, LL36 9UP.
Tel: (065 477) 228.

Tanycoed is situated near Dolgoch falls with Tal-y-Llyn gauge railway running through our land, on the B4405 road from Tywyn to Dolgellau. Central heating. Double, single, twin bedrooms. Dining, sitting room, T.V. Comfort and good home cooking. Reductions for children under 11. Golf, fishing nearby, shooting on farm. Also we have lovely beaches nearby.

P	Single Room per one person B&B		Double Room for two persons B&B		3
	MIN £ 8.00	MAX £ 10.00	MIN £ 16.00	MAX £ 20.00	OPEN 3-12

Tynybryn Farm

Llanfigangel-y-Pennant, Tywyn,
Gwynedd, LL36 9TN.
Tel: (0654 77) 277.

Tynybryn is situated in beautiful picturesque countryside. Two adjoining bedrooms as family bedrooms, both with hot and cold, one with double bed, one with two single beds. Also one double bedroom with hot and cold. All with tea/coffee and bara brith. Two bathrooms with showers. Central heating. Log fires. Sitting and dining room with colour T.V. Near Bera Castle, Cader Idris, Talyllyn railway, trout fishing. Welsh speaking family.

P	Single Room per one person B&B		Double Room for two persons B&B		3
	MIN £ 8.00	MAX £ 12.00	MIN £ 18.00	MAX £ 24.00	OPEN 1-12

CEREDIGION

The salty old quaysides at Aberaeron and New Quay have changed little since bygone times, when they were ports of call for tall-masted schooners. Holiday yachtsmen now sail the waters of this lovely, cliff-backed coast, past sheltered coves and jutting, windy promontories. There's excellent fishing, too, both sea and game – and Ceredigion's green hills are perfect for pony trekking.

Aberystwyth is the premier resort. Nothing has been allowed to diminish its period charm – not even its latest attraction, a Victorian-style Camera Obscura. Lampeter, like Aberystwyth, is an attractive university town. And Cardigan, where the River Teifi meets the sea, is in another pretty setting. These towns are on the doorstep of Ceredigion's brooding, unexplored mountain heights, the haunt of the kestrel and home of the hardy hill-sheep farmer. Lost in their folds are magic places such as Strata Florida Abbey, the falls at Devil's Bridge and the Nant-y-moch lakelands.

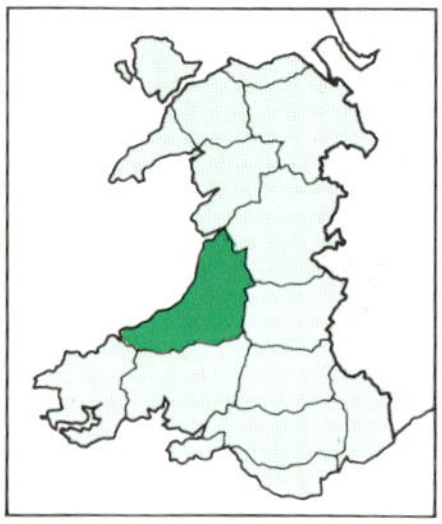

Aberaeron
Map Ref Fc4

Most attractive little town on Cardigan Bay. Pleasant harbour with distinctive Georgian-style architecture. Interesting Marine Aquarium and Coastal Centre. Sailing popular. Good centre for coast and inland.

Guest Houses

Llys Aeron Guest House
Lampeter Road, Aberaeron, Dyfed,
SA46 0ED.
Tel: (0545) 570276. L

A lovely area to spend a relaxed holiday. Aberaeron sits around a charming harbour. Friendly shops. Good pubs. Llys Aeron has cheerful comfortable bedrooms, all with washbasins. Breakfast room overlooking garden. Parking on private forecourt. We welcome you and yours, including well behaved pets.

Single Room per one person B&B		Double Room for two persons B&B		4
MIN £ 10.00	MAX £ 11.00	MIN £ 18.00	MAX £ 20.00	OPEN 1-12

Pier Cottage
Ship Street, Aberaeron, Dyfed,
SA46 0BS.
Tel: (0545) 570132. L

Pier Cottage is a grade II listed building and the oldest house in Aberaeron. It still retains its "old world" charm and character, with many exposed beams, etc. It offers quiet and peaceful accommodation within its own walled gardens, facing the sea and harbour. Pier Cottage is also an old fashioned tearoom offering homemade cooking.

Single Room per one person B&B		Double Room for two persons B&B		3
MIN £ 8.00	MAX £ 10.00	MIN £ 16.00	MAX £ 20.00	OPEN 1-12

Ty Lon Guest House
Ciliau Aeron, Aberaeron, Dyfed,
SA48 8DL.
Tel: (0570) 470726. L

Ty Lon is a family-run guest house set in the beautiful vale of Aeron. $2^1/_2$ miles from Aberaeron within easy reach of Cardigan Bay. Local activities include horse riding, river and sea fishing. All bedrooms have washbasins, shaver points, central heating. Separate bathroom and toilets. Car parking at rear.

Single Room per one person B&B		Double Room for two persons B&B		3
MIN £ 9.00	MAX £ 10.00	MIN £ 18.00	MAX £ 20.00	OPEN 1-12

Farmhouses

Green Grove
Felinfach, Lampeter, Dyfed,
SA48 8AF.
Tel: (0570) 470832. L

Green Grove, a delightful country house in beautiful Aeron Valley dates beyond 1646. Within 5 miles of coast. Children welcome, wooded play area, garden, animals. Residents' T.V. room. Pretty dining room, log fire, beams. Roomy bedrooms. Evening meal optional. Own produce. Pool/darts room, archery, shooting, barbecue. Mrs. Williams.

Single Room per one person B&B		Double Room for two persons B&B		6
MIN £ 8.00	MAX £ 9.00	MIN £ 16.00	MAX £ 18.00	OPEN 3-11

Parc Farm
Derwen Gam (Oakford), Llanarth,
Dyfed, SA47 0RX.
Tel: (0545) 580390. L

Traditional farmhouse quietly secluded midway Aberaeron and New Quay. Ideal for walking, touring, birdwatching, riding. Good home cooking. 3 bedrooms, 2 with washbasin, shaving points. Central heating. Lounge with colour T.V. Dining room with licensed bar. Friendly atmosphere. Clean, level site in unspoilt countryside.

Single Room per one person B&B		Double Room for two persons B&B		3
MIN £ 8.00	MAX £ 10.00	MIN £ 16.00	MAX £ 20.00	OPEN 1-12

Aberporth
Map Ref Fa5

Popular seaside village on Cardigan Bay. Safe swimming from two beaches. Convenient for visiting small coastal villages on Cardigan Bay.

Hotels

Highcliffe Hotel
Aberporth, Cardigan, Dyfed,
SA43 2DA.
Tel: (0239) 810534.

Situated on the west coast of Wales overlooking beautiful Cardigan Bay. Highcliffe is a family-run two star hotel only 200 yards from sandy beaches. All rooms have colour T.V., direct dial telephone, tea/coffee facilities, radio and C/H. We are fully licensed and our restaurant offers good home cooked food and good wines.

Single Room per one person B&B		Double Room for two persons B&B		5
MIN £ 12.00	MAX £ 12.00	MIN £ 24.00	MAX £ 24.00	OPEN 1-12

Guest Houses

Ffynonwen Country Guest House
Aberporth, Cardigan, Dyfed,
SA43 2HT.
Tel: (0239) 810312.

A 300 year old farmhouse brought up to modern standards by the addition of a new bedroom wing and set close to some of the finest unspoilt coastline in Wales. Reduced rates for children and the ideal place for family holidays. It has a nice little bar and offers good traditional meals. Five rooms available at rates quoted.

Single Room per one person B&B		Double Room for two persons B&B		11
MIN £ 12.00	MAX £	MIN £ 24.00	MAX £	OPEN 1-12

Aberystwyth
Map Ref Fe2

Premier resort of the Cardigan Bay coastline. Fine promenade, cliff railway, camera obscura, pier, and many other seaside attractions. University town with good shopping. Start of Vale of Rheidol Narrow Gauge Railway.

Hotels

Glanaber Hotel
7/8 Union Street, Aberystwyth, Dyfed,
SY23 1LG.
Tel: (0970) 617610.

This popular family-run hotel boasts a full à la carte restaurant and bar serving meals and snacks. The bedrooms are centrally heated and have tea/coffee facilities and colour T.V. Families welcome at special rates and good discounts offered for stays over 3 days. Close to all Aberystwyth amenities.

Single Room per one person B&B		Double Room for two persons B&B		15
MIN £ 12.00	MAX £	MIN £ 24.00	MAX £	OPEN 1-12

Llety Gwyn Hotel
Llanbadarn Fawr, Aberystwyth,
Dyfed, SY23 3SX.
Tel: (0970) 3965.

Family-run hotel, 14 bedrooms, 8 en-suite. Ample parking. Known locally for good food. Suitable for disabled. Ideal for touring and walking. T.V. all rooms. Radios, tea making facilities all rooms. T.V. lounge. Licensed. Pool table. $1^1/_2$ miles seafront. Evening dinner. All rooms H & C.

Single Room per one person B&B		Double Room for two persons B&B		14
MIN £ 12.00	MAX £	MIN £ 24.00	MAX £	OPEN 1-12

Marine Hotel

Promenade, Aberystwyth, Dyfed,
SY23 2BX.
Tel: (0970) 612444.

Centrally situated on the promenade, close to shops. Well known for friendly service, good home cooking, excellent cuisine. Dining room, lounge, bars, all on ground floor with sea view. 35 bedrooms, 20 en-suite. Colour T.V., tea making facilities in all rooms. Atlantic ballroom for functions and conferences. Leisure facilities. Car park. Special rate for coaches. Warm welcome.

	Single Room per one person B&B		Double Room for two persons B&B		35
	MIN £	MAX £	MIN £ 22.00	MAX £ 24.00	OPEN 1-12

Windsor Hotel

41 Queen's Road, Aberystwyth,
Dyfed, SY23 2HN.
Tel: (0970) 612134.

Small, friendly hotel close to all amenities. Sea and shops two minutes. In quiet residential area adjacent to local tennis courts, bowls and putting greens. Some rooms with private showers. T.V. and tea/coffee facilities in all rooms. Children and small dogs welcome. Substantial savings on weekly bookings for B & B or half board. Licensed.

	Single Room per one person B&B		Double Room for two persons B&B		9
	MIN £ 9.00	MAX £ 10.50	MIN £ 18.00	MAX £ 21.00	OPEN 1-12

Guest Houses

Bryn-y-Don

36 Bridge Street, Aberystwyth, Dyfed,
SY23 1QB.
Tel: (0970) 612011.

Situated close to station, car park, shopping area and seafront. All bedrooms have hot and cold, shaver points, T.V., tea and coffee making facilities. Evening meals optional. Good home cooking. Separate tables.
Television lounge. Public telephone. Reduced rates children and O.A.P.'s. Off season rates. Cot and high chair, baby sitting service. Homely welcome always.

	Single Room per one person B&B		Double Room for two persons B&B		6
	MIN £ 8.50	MAX £ 9.50	MIN £ 17.00	MAX £ 19.00	OPEN 1-12

Glan-y-Môr

62 Marine Terrace, Aberystwyth,
Dyfed, SY23 2BX.
Tel: (0970) 615312.

Centrally situated on the promenade, close to all amenities. Family-run, friendly service and atmosphere. Full English breakfast. 12 bedrooms, 2 en-suite, central heating, tea/coffee facilities, colour television in all rooms. Children welcome at reduced prices. Tennis and golf nearby. Pony trekking can be arranged. Welcome to all, croeso i bawb.

	Single Room per one person B&B		Double Room for two persons B&B		12
	MIN £ 10.00	MAX £ 12.00	MIN £ 18.00	MAX £ 24.00	OPEN 3-10

Glyn Garth

South Road, Aberystwyth, Dyfed,
SY23 1JS.
Tel: (0970) 615050.

Glyn-Garth is situated adjacent to south promenade, near castle and harbour. All rooms with colour T.V. and tea making facilities. Fully centrally heated, comfortable lounge and cosy basement bar. This family-run guest house is noted for excellent food and service where cleanliness is a high priority.

	Single Room per one person B&B		Double Room for two persons B&B		4
	MIN £ 11.00	MAX £ 12.00	MIN £ 22.00	MAX £ 24.00	OPEN 1-12

Yr Hafod

1 South Marine Terrace,
Aberystwyth, Dyfed, SY23 1JX.
Tel: (0970) 617579.

This comfortable guest house is known for its fine food and hospitality. It is ideally situated on the south promenade adjacent to the castle and overlooking Cardigan Bay. Most bedrooms with panoramic sea view, all with hot and cold, colour T.V., tea/coffee making facilities, etc. Some bedrooms en-suite. Fully centrally heated. A warm welcome always.

	Single Room per one person B&B		Double Room for two persons B&B		5
	MIN £ 10.00	MAX £ 11.00	MIN £ 20.00	MAX £ 22.00	OPEN 1-12

Hemstal Guest House

69 North Parade, Aberystwyth,
Dyfed, SY23 2JN.
Tel: (0970) 624398.

Central position, small, family-run, friendly with good home cooking. All rooms hot and cold, full central heating, shower, bathroom. T.V. lounge. Fire certificate. Our main aim is to make your stay in Aberystwyth a happy one.

	Single Room per one person B&B		Double Room for two persons B&B		6
	MIN £ 10.00	MAX £ 12.00	MIN £ 18.00	MAX £ 20.00	OPEN 1-12

Linkenma

19 Custom House Street,
Aberystwyth, Dyfed, SY23 1JR.
Tel: (0970) 617480.

Linkenma, a small family guest house situated 100 yards from south promenade, castle and harbour, near main shopping centre, rail, bus station. H.C., shaving points all bedrooms. Central heating throughout. T.V. lounge. Early and late tea or coffee served on request. Highly recommended for good food and friendly atmosphere, under personal supervision of proprietress.

	Single Room per one person B&B		Double Room for two persons B&B		3
	MIN £ 8.00	MAX £ 10.00	MIN £ 16.00	MAX £ 20.00	OPEN 1-12

Myrddin

1 Rheidol Terrace, Aberystwyth,
Dyfed, SY23 1JU.
Tel: (0970) 612799.

Comfortable, friendly family-run guest house. Experienced in providing excellent service and good food. 100 yards from south promenade, castle and harbour. All bedrooms have hot and cold, shaver points and central heating. Colour television lounge. Separate dining room. A warm welcome awaits you, why not see for yourselves. Please contact Mrs. Lisa Bumford.

	Single Room per one person B&B		Double Room for two persons B&B		3
	MIN £ 8.00	MAX £ 9.00	MIN £ 16.00	MAX £ 18.00	OPEN 7-9

Myrddin Guest House

6 South Marine Terrace,
Aberystwyth, Dyfed, SY23 1JX.
Tel: (0970) 612031.

This is an ideally situated guest house on the south promenade overlooking Cardigan Bay, adjacent to the castle and harbour. Most rooms have sea views, all with hot and cold, colour T.V., tea making facilities, central heating. Comfortable T.V. lounge. Hair dressing salon. Baby sitting service. Home from home.

	Single Room per one person B&B		Double Room for two persons B&B		4
	MIN £ 10.00	MAX £ 11.00	MIN £ 17.00	MAX £ 19.00	OPEN 1-12

Farmhouses

Erwbarfe Farmhouse

Devil's Bridge, Aberystwyth, Dyfed,
SY23 3JR.
Tel: (097 085) 251.

A warm Welsh welcome awaits guests at Erwbarfe, a 400 acre mixed working farm situated in view of the famous Devil's Bridge falls and Rheidol steam railway. Ideal for fishing, walking or touring. Relax at the farmhouse with its oak beamed ceilings, spacious lounge and bedrooms that have tea and coffee making facilities. Wholesome home cooking with varied menu provided. Rural Tourism Award. AA listed.

	Single Room per one person B&B		Double Room for two persons B&B		2
	MIN £	MAX £	MIN £ 19.00	MAX £ 24.00	OPEN 4-10

Neuadd Parc Farm

Capel Bangor, Aberystwyth, Dyfed,
SY23 3NA.
Tel: (097 084) 260.

Neuadd Parc is a 207 acre farm with pedigree Friesian cows and Welsh Cob show ponies situated in the picturesque Rheidol valley. Victorian style farmhouse with 3 guest bedrooms, toilet, bathroom, dining room and sitting room with colour T.V. Fishing in River Rheidol and private fishing on farms fish pond, farm nature trail, also rough shooting. Tea and coffee facilities in all rooms. Peaceful atmosphere.

	Single Room per one person B&B		Double Room for two persons B&B		3
	MIN £	MAX £	MIN £	MAX £ 15.00	OPEN 3-10

Tycam Farm

Capel Bangor, Aberystwyth, Dyfed, SY23 3NA.
Tel: (097 084) 662. L

Dairy and sheep farm situated in beautiful Rheidol Valley, 7½ miles Aberystwyth, 2 miles off Aberystwyth main A44 road. Home comfort and home cooking is offered here. Ideal for walking, birdwatching, sightseeing, fishing in River Rheidol and nearby lakes. Also pony trekking, golf within easy reach. 1 double, 2 family rooms with central heating, bathroom and toilet. Sitting room and dining room with separate tables (combined). Colour T.V. Ample parking space.

P ✕	Single Room per one person B&B		Double Room for two persons B&B		3
	MIN £	MAX £	MIN £ 17.00	MAX £	OPEN 1-12

Borth

Map Ref Db7

Sandy beaches and fine views to the north across the Dyfi Estuary. Golf links, 2-mile long promenade. A popular holiday village.

Hotels

Golf Hotel

Borth, Dyfed, SY24 5HY.
Tel: (097 081) 362.

Family hotel overlooking sandy beach ideal for bathing. Single, double and family rooms with hot and cold and tea making facilities. Comfortable bar lounge. Restaurant offering a wide range menu. Near golf course. Ideal centre for bird watching. Organised walking holiday parties welcome. Come along and enjoy the friendly atmosphere and home cooking.

P ✕	Single Room per one person B&B		Double Room for two persons B&B		10
	MIN £ 11.50	MAX £ 12.00	MIN £ 23.00	MAX £ 24.00	OPEN 3-12

The Grand Hotel

The Promenade, Borth, Dyfed, SY24 5HY.
Tel: (0970) 81206.

Fully licensed hotel with two bars and restaurant. Eighteen bedrooms some en-suite, all with colour T.V., intercom, radio, baby listening, tea and coffee making facilities. Central heating. Sandy beach three miles long across road from hotel, providing ideal location for sailing, fishing and swimming. Panoramic sea views from most rooms. Walking distance to golf course, shops. Close to railway and riding.

P ✕	Single Room per one person B&B		Double Room for two persons B&B		18
	MIN £ 9.00	MAX £ 12.00	MIN £ 18.00	MAX £ 24.00	OPEN 1-12

Guest Houses

Rock House

Llancynfelin, Machynlleth, Powys, SY20 8PU.
Tel: (097 086) 678.

Situated 3 miles from the popular seaside resort of Borth, overlooking Aberdovey and Cardigan Bay. Open all year. Hot and cold, shaver points all bedrooms and T.V. Two double rooms and one twin, all having washbasins and tea making facilities. Children welcome at reduced rates. Evening meal optional. No pets.

P ✕	Single Room per one person B&B		Double Room for two persons B&B		5
	MIN £ 7.50	MAX £ 9.00	MIN £ 15.00	MAX £ 18.00	OPEN 1-12

Farmhouses

Brynffynnon

Clarach Road, Borth, Dyfed, SY24 5NS.
Tel: (0970) 828720. L

Enjoy a warm Welsh welcome in our modern house on the family dairy farm. Situated on the old coast road 1½ miles from Borth, surrounded by beautiful scenery with the coastal path running through the farm. T.V. lounge, central heating and bathroom with shower for guests's use only. Reduced rates for children, cot available.

P	Single Room per one person B&B		Double Room for two persons B&B		3
	MIN £ 8.00	MAX £ 9.00	MIN £ 16.00	MAX £ 18.00	OPEN 4-10

Cardigan

Map Ref Fa5

Market town close to the Cardigan Bay beaches and resorts. Good shopping facilities, accommodation, inns. Golf and fishing. Base for exploring inland along the wooded Teifi Valley.

Hotels

Butchers Arms

Tegryn, Llanfyrnach, Dyfed, SA35 0BL.
Tel: (023 977) 680. L

Fine village pub set in beautiful Welsh countryside, near Preseli Mountains and National Park. Good area for walking and fishing. Being one of the highest villages in Pembrokeshire, the views from the bar are superb and the garden lovely to sit in. Warm hospitality, good food (evening meals available). Pleasant accommodation assured. Camra listed.

P ✕	Single Room per one person B&B		Double Room for two persons B&B		2
	MIN £ 9.00	MAX £ 11.00	MIN £ 18.00	MAX £ 22.00	OPEN 1-12

Guest Houses

Berwyn

St. Dogmael's, Cardigan, Dyfed, SA43 3HS.
Tel: (0239) 613555.

Have a relaxing holiday. Magnificent views overlooking River Teifi. Situated in two acres delightful grounds. Central to all amenities. Numerous choice of beaches within easy reach. Bedrooms with vanity unit, H & C. You will be assured of a warm welcome and a comfortable stay.

P	Single Room per one person B&B		Double Room for two persons B&B		3
	MIN £ 9.00	MAX £ 12.00	MIN £ 18.00	MAX £ 24.00	OPEN 3-10

Brynhyfryd Guest House

Gwbert Road, Cardigan, Dyfed, SA43 1JH.
Tel: (0239) 612861.

Situated in a pleasant part of Cardigan, two miles from the coast. Ideal centre for touring the inland beauty spots of Ceredigion or relaxing on nearby sandy beaches. Bedrooms have heating, washbasins and tea/coffee making facilities. Comfortable T.V. lounge, payphone. Homely atmosphere. Good food. Parking readily available. AA listed. Nesta and Ieuan Davies.

✕	Single Room per one person B&B		Double Room for two persons B&B		6
	MIN £ 9.00	MAX £ 10.00	MIN £ 18.00	MAX £ 20.00	OPEN 1-12

The Copper Kettle

Penparc, Nr. Cardigan, Dyfed, SA43 1RG.
Tel: (0239) 613610. L

Comfortable, homely accommodation all situated on ground floor. Highly recommended. Hot and cold, shaver points all bedrooms. Full central heating. Attractive lounge with colour T.V. Ample parking. Licensed family restaurant March to October, evening meals available thereafter if required. Good home cooking. Situated three miles north of Cardigan on A487.

P ✕	Single Room per one person B&B		Double Room for two persons B&B		3
	MIN £ 7.50	MAX £ 7.50	MIN £ 15.00	MAX £ 15.00	OPEN 1-12

The Falls Inn

Village of Star, Llanfyrnach, Dyfed, SA35 0AW.
Tel: (023 977) 685.

The Inn is situated in a secluded valley with a trout stream running through pretty gardens and walks nearby. 20 minutes from west coast beaches. 40 minutes from Tenby and south coast. Ideal base for day trips. T.V. lounge. Fire certificate held. Special rates for children.

P ✕	Single Room per one person B&B		Double Room for two persons B&B		3
	MIN £ 9.00	MAX £ 10.00	MIN £ 18.00	MAX £ 20.00	OPEN 1-12

Maes-a-Môr

Gwbert Road, Cardigan, Dyfed,
SA43 1AE.
Tel: (0239) 614929.

Overlooking local park and within 2 minutes walk of market town centre. Nearest beach one mile and numerous sandy beaches within few minutes drive. Yachting, golfing, angling, bowling, tennis, etc. locally. Open all year. Twin, double and family rooms with hot and cold. Separate shower room and bathroom. Full breakfast. T.V. lounge. Homely atmosphere, cordial welcome.

	Single Room per one person B&B		Double Room for two persons B&B		3
P ✕	MIN £ 12.00	MAX £	MIN £ 18.00	MAX £ 24.00	OPEN 1-12

Nant-y-Pele

Feidrfawr, St. Dogmael's, Cardigan,
Dyfed, SA43 3EU.
Tel: (0239) 613590. L

Welcome to our old coastguard house overlooking the Teifi Estuary in riverside village with ancient ruined abbey and working watermill. Near start of Pembrokeshire coastal path, Preseli hills and Poppit Sands. Good centre for walkers, wonderful wild flowers. Comfortable lounge and dining room. Fresh home cooked food. Large interesting garden. Enquiries to Rosemary Antwis.

	Single Room per one person B&B		Double Room for two persons B&B		3
P ✕	MIN £ 8.50	MAX £ 9.50	MIN £ 17.00	MAX £ 19.00	OPEN 3-10

Penwernfach

Ponthirwaun, Nr. Cardigan, Dyfed,
SA43 2RL.
Tel: (0239) 710694. L

Exceptional 18th century farmhouse in 6 acres of glorious countryside. All rooms centrally heated with handbasins, colour T.V. and tea/coffee making facilities. Laundry room. Games room. Adventure play area. Donkey, shetland, goats, ducks to feed. Nearby beaches, pony trekking. Private salmon/trout fishing. Self catering cottages also available. Phone/write for a colour brochure to Mrs. J. Swatton.

	Single Room per one person B&B		Double Room for two persons B&B		3
P	MIN £ 10.00	MAX £ 10.00	MIN £ 20.00	MAX £ 20.00	OPEN 1-12

Tintern House

Llechryd, Nr. Cardigan, Dyfed,
SA43 2QL.
Tel: (023 987) 292.

Stone house of great charm and character, in quiet location with attractive gardens overlooking the River Teifi. The house offers comfortable accommodation, all bedrooms having washbasins and tea/coffee making facilities (two have en-suite bathrooms). Good wholesome home cooking. Tea room/garden open all day for teas, coffee and snacks. Brochure available.

	Single Room per one person B&B		Double Room for two persons B&B		5
P ✕	MIN £ 9.50	MAX £ 9.50	MIN £ 19.00	MAX £ 22.00	OPEN 1-11

Farmhouses

Cwmrhaffau

Sarnau, Llandysul, Dyfed, SA44 6QZ.
Tel: (0239) 811118.

You are assured of a welcome at our licensed farm guest house midway Cardigan/New Quay within walking distance of Penbryn and Tresaith beaches. Children and pets welcome. Cot, high chair available. Surrounded by 17 acres of meadow and woodland rich in wildlife for adults and children to play in. Riding, fishing nearby. Self catering flats available.

	Single Room per one person B&B		Double Room for two persons B&B		4
P ✕	MIN £ 8.50	MAX £ 10.00	MIN £ 17.00	MAX £ 20.00	OPEN 1-12

Hendraws Farm and Rainbow Fountain Restaurant

Rhydlewis, Llandysul, Dyfed,
SA44 5QR.
Tel: (023 975) 345.

Typical Welsh farmhouse built 1832. Family rooms have country views, double beds, bunk beds, H/C, electric heating, shaver point, tea making facilities. Reasonably priced country dishes in licensed à la carte restaurant, inexpensive wines. Colour T.V. room for residents. British farmhouse breakfast served, diets catered for, vegetarian dishes. Play area for children. Central for beaches, walking, fishing.

	Single Room per one person B&B		Double Room for two persons B&B		3
P ✕	MIN £ 9.00	MAX £ 10.00	MIN £ 18.00	MAX £ 20.00	OPEN 1-12

Rosehill Farm

Llangoedmor, Cardigan, Dyfed,
SA43 2LJ.
Tel: (0239) 612019. L

Rosehill is a 15th century farmhouse situated on the banks of the River Teifi. If you enjoy fishing (free), birdwatching or walking this is an ideal venue. There are 5 letting bedrooms one of which is en-suite. T. V. and video are provided. Good home cooking from local produce. Dinner served by arrangement.

	Single Room per one person B&B		Double Room for two persons B&B		5
P ✕	MIN £ 9.50	MAX £ 10.50	MIN £ 18.00	MAX £ 24.00	OPEN 3-10

Devil's Bridge

Map Ref Da2

The Rheidol River meets the Mynach and results in a spectacular series of falls. Beautiful walks, nature trails, picnic sites abound in the area, and a narrow-gauge steam railway run by British Rail is one of the most popular features. Inland from the resort of Aberystwyth.

Guest Houses

Mount Pleasant

Devil's Bridge, Nr. Aberystwyth,
Dyfed, SY23 4QY.
Tel: (097 085) 219.

Family-run guest house set amid beautiful scenic countryside, close to famous waterfalls, Rheidol steam railway and Elan Valley. C/heated. Comfortable bedrooms with T.V., t/facilities, radio/clock alarms, handbasins or en-suite. Licensed dining room, lounge, reception area. 2 nights B & B and 4 course evening dinners £27, en-suite £29 per person. Brochure and full details from Janet and Dave Sherlock.

	Single Room per one person B&B		Double Room for two persons B&B		5
P ✕	MIN £ 8.50	MAX £ 9.50	MIN £ 17.00	MAX £ 19.00	OPEN 1-12

Lampeter

Map Ref Fe5

Farming centre for central Dyfed, close to the picturesque Teifi Valley. St David's College of the University of Wales is here and open to visitors. Concerts and musical events are frequently held in the college. Golf and angling. A bustling commercial centre for surrounding area.

Guest Houses

Min-y-Llan

Llanwenog, Llanybydder, Dyfed,
SA40 9UT.
Tel: (0570) 480378.

Country house in peaceful surroundings with glorious views. Within easy reach of popular resorts and lively market towns. Central heating throughout. Spacious lounge with colour T.V. One double, two twin bedded rooms, washbasins, shaver points. Children welcome. Cot available. Evening meal by arrangement. Traditional Welsh fare. Welcome to a relaxing holiday in lovely Ceredigion.

	Single Room per one person B&B		Double Room for two persons B&B		3
P ✕	MIN £ 9.00	MAX £ 10.00	MIN £ 18.00	MAX £ 20.00	OPEN 4-9

Tal-y-Fan

Cellan, Nr. Lampeter, Dyfed,
SA48 8JA. Tel: (0570) 423158. L

Secluded Edwardian residence 2½ miles from Lampeter. Panoramic views over Teifi valley. Red Kite and Buzzard country. Ideal for visiting coast, mountains, lakes and forests. Good home cooked food. Dining room and lounge with log fires. Hot and cold, shaver points in centrally heated bedrooms. Children welcome at special rates.

	Single Room per one person B&B		Double Room for two persons B&B		3
	MIN £	MAX £	MIN £	MAX £	OPEN
	10.00	10.00	18.00	18.00	1-12

Farmhouses

Abermeurig Mansion

Lampeter, Dyfed, SA48 8PP.
Tel: (0570) 470216.

18th century farmhouse mansion of charm and character in the Vale of Aeron. Holds the B.T.A. & W.T.B. farmhouse awards. This ancestral home with its antiques, is centrally heated and has both canopy and 4 poster beds with shower room en-suite. Tea/coffee making facilities. Private fishing, shooting. Fresh country food whenever possible. Licensed dining room. Open all year excluding Christmas and New Year. Car essential.

	Single Room per one person B&B		Double Room for two persons B&B		3
	MIN £	MAX £	MIN £	MAX £	OPEN
	11.00	12.00	20.00	22.00	1-12

Brynheulog

Mydroilyn, Lampeter, Dyfed,
SA48 7RL. Tel: (0545) 580450. L

Small working farm on edge of lovely valley within easy reach of several safe sandy beaches, pony trekking, clay pigeon shooting, sea/river fishing and golf courses. Good home cooking with own produce. Morning/late night drinks. Electric blankets. T.V. in all rooms. Children playground. 9 hole putting green. Baby sitting. Brochure sent by request.

	Single Room per one person B&B		Double Room for two persons B&B		5
	MIN £	MAX £	MIN £	MAX £	OPEN
	9.50	11.00	19.00	22.00	1-12

Brynog Mansion

Felinfach, Lampeter, Dyfed,
SA48 8AQ.
Tel: (0570) 470266.

Brynog is a 200 year old mansion with a 200 acre farm, situated in the beautiful vale of Aeron midway between Lampeter and the seaside resort of Aberaeron (10 minutes drive), ¾ mile off A482 main road and villages of Felinfach and Ystrad Aeron. Rough shooting, fishing, birdwatching, riverside walks. Modern amenities. En-suite bedroom. W.T.B. farmhouse award. Tea making facilities. Full Welsh breakfast and a warm welcome. Write or phone for brochure to Mrs. S. E. Davies.

	Single Room per one person B&B		Double Room for two persons B&B		5
	MIN £	MAX £	MIN £	MAX £	OPEN
	9.50	10.50	19.00	21.00	1-12

Nantymedd Farm

Llanfair, Lampeter, Dyfed, SA48 8JZ.
Tel: (057 045) 208.

Your ideal country holiday in beautiful surroundings. Free trout and salmon fishing on the River Teifi. Within easy driving distance to the seaside resorts of Aberaeron and New Quay. Pony trekking centre nearby. Good home cooked food. Two double rooms available with special rates for children. Write or telephone or further details.

	Single Room per one person B&B		Double Room for two persons B&B		2
	MIN £	MAX £	MIN £	MAX £	OPEN
			14.00	16.00	5-10

Tangaer Farmhouse

Cellan, Lampeter, Dyfed.
Tel: (0570) 422321. L

A centuries old farmhouse, 3 miles from the university town of Lampeter. Superb views in totally relaxed atmosphere. Full central heating. Good home cooking, evening meal optional. Private fishing and shooting. Pony trekking nearby. Ideally situated for touring. Reduced rates for children.

	Single Room per one person B&B		Double Room for two persons B&B		3
	MIN £	MAX £	MIN £	MAX £	OPEN
	6.00	7.50	12.00	15.00	3-11

Llandysul

Map Ref Fc6

Pleasant Teifi-side village in an area rich with woollen mills which welcome visitors. Salmon fishing very popular on the river, as is canoeing at certain times of the year.

Guest Houses

Min-yr-Afon

Pentrecwrt, Nr. Llandysul, Dyfed,
SA44 5AT.
Tel: (055 932) 2797.

Detached house by a river on the A486 to Llandysul. Large level car park. All bedrooms have washbasin, razor point, tea making facilities, central heating. Ideal touring centre for Cardigan Bay, beaches, Preseli hills, castles, Cenarth falls, Teifi valley steam railway, Henllan falls, country walks.

	Single Room per one person B&B		Double Room for two persons B&B		4
	MIN £	MAX £	MIN £	MAX £	OPEN
	9.50	9.50	19.00	19.00	1-12

Llangrannog

Map Ref Fb4

Popular with children as a safe summer holiday beach, this is an ideal base for touring the Cardigan coast – a typical little seaside village.

Farmhouses

Brynarthen Farm

Glynarthen, Llandysul, Dyfed,
SA44 6TG.
Tel: (023 975) 783.

Charming farmhouse, delightfully situated in a tranquil scenic valley, amidst beautiful unspoilt countryside. Three miles from fine beaches and 10 miles north of Cardigan off the A487. The farmhouse, whilst retaining all its charm, is comfortably furnished and centrally heated. Family-run, personal attention and good home cooking. Families welcome. Also self catering cottage.

	Single Room per one person B&B		Double Room for two persons B&B		3
	MIN £	MAX £	MIN £	MAX £	OPEN
	8.50	11.50	17.00	23.00	1-12

Hendre Farm

Llangrannog, Llandysul, Dyfed,
SA44 6AP.
Tel: (023 978) 342.

100 acre farm in peaceful countryside, 2 miles from Llangrannog on B4321, overlooking Cardigan Bay. Ceredigion's new coastal footpath, sandy beaches nearby. Very comfortable stone built Victorian farmhouse, tastefully furnished, centrally heated. Bedrooms with washbasins. Friendly welcome and excellent home cooking. AA listed. Brochure from Mrs. Bethan Williams.

	Single Room per one person B&B		Double Room for two persons B&B		3
	MIN £	MAX £	MIN £	MAX £	OPEN
	9.00	11.00	18.00	22.00	3-11

Morfa Isaf

Llangrannog, Llandysul, Dyfed,
SA44 6RS.
Tel: (023 978) 282. L

Morfa Isaf is an oak beamed farmhouse built in 1763. Working beef farm. 106 acres with spectacular cliffs and small cove. Good home cooking and relaxed informality ensures a tranquil stay in an area of designated natural and unspoiled beauty. Two double rooms with showers en-suite.

	Single Room per one person B&B		Double Room for two persons B&B		3
	MIN £	MAX £	MIN £	MAX £	OPEN
	10.00	12.00	20.00	24.00	1-12

Penlan Fawr

Plwmp, Llandysul, Dyfed, SA44 6HR.
Tel: (023 975) 205.

Farmhouse just off A487 coast road. Llangrannog beach 4 miles. Ideally situated for touring. A warm welcome, very comfortable accommodation and excellent home cooking awaits you on our 200 acre dairy and shire horse farm. Family, double and single rooms available with washbasins and shaver points.

Single Room per one person B&B		Double Room for two persons B&B		3
MIN £	MAX £	MIN £	MAX £	OPEN
8.50	9.50	17.00	19.00	4-10

Llanybydder

Map Ref Fd5

Market town on the banks of the River Teifi and a centre for the Welsh woollen industry which has now turned from stockings, hats and flannel to fashionable tapestries, car rugs, skirt lengths and shirts. Many mills welcome visitors. The horse fairs at Llanybydder are famous world-wide and are usually held on the last Thursday of the month.

Hotels

Manor Hotel

Maesycrugiau, Pencader, Dyfed,
SA39 9LH.
Tel: (055 935) 224.

Norman style manor house in sylvan setting with excellent oak panelled restaurant, log fires, games room. Enjoys good local trade in friendly atmosphere. Trekking and fishing by arrangement.

Single Room per one person B&B		Double Room for two persons B&B		6
MIN £	MAX £	MIN £	MAX £	OPEN
12.00	12.00	24.00	24.00	3-11

Red Lion Inn

Pencarreg, Nr. Llanybydder, Dyfed,
SA40 9QG.
Tel: (0570) 480018.

The Red Lion Inn welcomes you to their cosy village inn. Two double rooms en-suite, one room W.C./H.C. All with tea/coffee facilities. Enjoy magnificent view, lovely walks, salmon and trout fishing available 35 minutes from coast. Evening meals. Central heating. T.V. lounge. Open all year round. Children welcome. Stay once, you will come again.

Single Room per one person B&B		Double Room for two persons B&B		3
MIN £	MAX £	MIN £	MAX £	OPEN
8.00	12.00	20.00	24.00	1-12

Farmhouses

Penrhiwsych

Llanybydder, Dyfed, SA40 9SA.
Tel: (0570) 480286. L

Penrhiwsych is an eight acre smallholding overlooking the lovely Teifi valley and market town of Llanybydder, famous for its monthly horse marts. Ideally situated for fishing, beautiful country walks. Good home cooking, evening meal by arrangement. Two double, one single bedroom with use of lounge. Comfortable clean accommodation. Friendly welcome.

Single Room per one person B&B		Double Room for two persons B&B		3
MIN £	MAX £	MIN £	MAX £	OPEN
7.50	7.50	15.00	15.00	1-11

Mydroilyn

Map Ref Fd4

Inland from the holiday resort of New Quay, the village is convenient to the many beaches of Cardigan Bay.

Farmhouses

Brynheulog

Mydroilyn, Nr. Lampeter, Dyfed,
SA48 7RL.
Tel: (0545) 580450. L

Farmhouse and annex in 12 acres of lovely countryside, 7 miles sea. 5 bedrooms, single, double and family. Special rates children. Good home cooked food. Tea in bed in morning. 2 bathrooms with showers. Evening meal and lunch if required. Baby sitting. Pets by arrangement. T.V.'s, darts, snooker, sauna, solaria, books, cows, sheep, goats, etc.

Single Room per one person B&B		Double Room for two persons B&B		5
MIN £	MAX £	MIN £	MAX £	OPEN
9.50	11.00	19.00	19.00	1-12

New Quay

Map Ref Fc4

Very pretty holiday and yachting centre on Cardigan Bay popular with campers and caravanners. Boat and fishing trips available. Good base for exploring further along the expansive bay.

Hotels

Cambrian Hotel

New Road, New Quay, Dyfed,
SA45 9SE.
Tel: (0545) 560295.

Small, fully licensed informal hotel under personal supervision of the owner. Hot meals and snacks available all day. Situated about one mile from New Quay town and within a few minutes walk of Llanina and Cei Bach sandy beaches. Ideal centre for touring, cycling and walking. Also, painting and photography. Buses stop right outside. Seven rooms available at rates quoted.

Single Room per one person B&B		Double Room for two persons B&B		8
MIN £	MAX £	MIN £	MAX £	OPEN
10.00	12.00	20.00	24.00	1-12

Guest Houses

Cae'r Llyn Guest House

Gilfachreda, New Quay, Dyfed,
SA45 9SP. Enq to: Mrs. C. Radford.
Tel: (0545) 580121.

Large comfortable cottage in charming valley setting. One and half miles New Quay, ten minutes scenic walk to sandy beaches, safe swimming. Near riding stables. Good position for touring all of Cardigan Bay. Hot and cold in bedrooms. Large lounge. Good food always available. Special rates for children. Separate tables. Baby sitting.

Single Room per one person B&B		Double Room for two persons B&B		3
MIN £	MAX £	MIN £	MAX £	OPEN
8.00	9.00	16.00	18.00	1-12

Neuadd Wen

Llanarth, Dyfed, SA47 0NH.
Tel: (0545) 580316.

Beautiful peaceful bungalow in elevated situation with superb views. No passing traffic. Private woodland walks. Trout fishing. New Quay two miles. Spacious comfortable bedrooms, bathrooms en-suite. Colour T.V., free tea/coffee facilities. Breakfast second to none. Children welcome, some free. Babysitting. Evening meal optional. Paddocks, stables available. Practise pottery making after breakfast N/C. Three crowns. Happy welcome atmosphere. Recommended.

Single Room per one person B&B		Double Room for two persons B&B		2
MIN £	MAX £	MIN £	MAX £	OPEN
10.00	10.00	20.00	20.00	1-12

Farmhouses

Broniwan

Rhydlewis, Llandysul, Dyfed,
SA44 5PF.
Tel: (023 975) 261.

Relax in peaceful surroundings of comfortable farmhouse delightfully situated overlooking fields and stream. Three double bedrooms, one with private shower and W.C. Charming sitting room with wood fire, colour T.V. and separate dining room with lovely views. Home produced milk, eggs, bread. Generous meals imaginatively prepared. Warm welcome. 5 minutes from A487 at Plwmp.

P	Single Room per one person B&B		Double Room for two persons B&B		3
	MIN £ 9.00	MAX £ 10.00	MIN £ 18.00	MAX £ 20.00	OPEN 1-12

Nanternis Farm

Nanternis, New Quay, Dyfed,
SA45 9RP.
Tel: (0545) 560181.

Peaceful village well placed for touring. 2½ miles New Quay, 1½ miles Cwm Tudu. Pleasant views. Comfortable guest lounge with C.T.V. Open wood fire. Separate dining room. Guest bathroom with separate shower and bath. Bedrooms with washbasins and drink making facility. Central heating. Home cooking using organically grown produce from garden. Self catering cottage also available.

P	Single Room per one person B&B		Double Room for two persons B&B		2
	MIN £	MAX £	MIN £ 16.00	MAX £ 20.00	OPEN 4-10

Pontrhydfendigaid

Map Ref Ga3

A large village on the upper reaches of the Teifi in a green and pastoral area full of rivers and small lakes. Strata Florida Abbey is its most famous feature. Annual popular Eisteddfod. Tregaron is the nearest town, with facilities for pony trekking in the nearby remote hills. Fishing available.

Hotels

Black Lion Inn

Pontrhydfendigaid, Dyfed.
Tel: (097 45) 626.

A traditional village inn, offering simply, yet comfortably furnished rooms in adjoining coach house. Each room has en-suite shower and w.c., colour T.V. and tea making. Home cooking, real ales and log fires when necessary in our cosy little bar make this an ideal base for exploring this peaceful part of Wales.

P	Single Room per one person B&B		Double Room for two persons B&B		3
	MIN £	MAX £	MIN £ 20.00	MAX £ 20.00	OPEN 3-10

Talgarreg

Map Ref Fc5

A small and scattered rural village surrounded by agricultural land, near New Quay and Llangrannog, totally Welsh in character. Within easy reach of the Teifi Valley, woollen mills, Cenarth waterfalls.

Farmhouses

Sunny Hill

Pisgah, Talgarreg, Llandysul, Dyfed,
SA44 4ET.
Tel: (054 555) 685. L

Delightful smallholding. Peaceful, open views, very quiet. New ground floor accommodation, family room or unit available. Good farmhouse breakfast to set you up for the day. Trekking, fishing, birdwatching nearby. Only 12 minutes from New Quay and Cardigan Bay. Ideal touring centre.

P	Single Room per one person B&B		Double Room for two persons B&B		2
	MIN £ 8.00	MAX £ 8.00	MIN £ 16.00	MAX £ 16.00	OPEN 1-12

Tregaron

Map Ref Ga3

Small traditional market town offering many pony trekking centres. Also good area for fishing and for naturalists to wander. The Tregaron Bog Nature Reserve is a haven for flora and fauna. Silversmith working in town.

Guest Houses

The Lodge

Dre Isaf, Ystrad Meurig, Dyfed,
SY25 6AA.
Tel: (097 45) 303. L

Quietly situated small family run guest house, combining a warm welcome with good home cooking. Single, family and twin rooms. Separate bathroom with shower. Ample parking space. Overlooking Cors Caron Nature Reserve and within easy reach of Strata Florida Abbey and Devil's Bridge.

P	Single Room per one person B&B		Double Room for two persons B&B		3
	MIN £ 7.50	MAX £	MIN £ 15.00	MAX £	OPEN 1-12

Farmhouses

Hillcroft

Werncoli, Llandewi Brefi, Nr.
Lampeter, Dyfed, SA48 8LH.
Tel: (0570) 45300. L

Situated on the B4343 between Tregaron and Lampeter, Hillcroft is a new house set in 3 acres on the farm. Home cooking. We offer fishing, pony trekking, golf and birdwatching. 9 miles from sea. Large dining room. T.V. lounge. Double, twin, single rooms with magnificent views, tea facilities. Ample car park. Details Mrs. E. Jones.

P	Single Room per one person B&B		Double Room for two persons B&B		4
	MIN £ 8.00	MAX £ 10.00	MIN £ 16.00	MAX £ 20.00	OPEN 1-12

Tresaith

Map Ref Fb5

On a popular stretch of small coves and beaches on the Cardiganshire coast, a little village offering all the pleasures of a small seaside location with pleasant walks.

Guest Houses

Iscoed

Tresaith, Nr. Aberporth, Cardigan,
Dyfed, SA43 2JG.
Tel: (0239) 810030.

Peacefully situated in large grounds on quiet B road, but only 10 minutes walk to sandy beach and waterfall. All food including wholemeal bread is homemade, vegetables from own garden, eggs from own free range hens. All rooms have H & C, tea making facilities. Large lounge with log fire for those chilly evenings.

P	Single Room per one person B&B		Double Room for two persons B&B		4
	MIN £ 9.00	MAX £ 9.00	MIN £ 18.00	MAX £ 18.00	OPEN 3-10

MONTGOMERYSHIRE

Nothing ever seems to change in Montgomeryshire's timeless high plateaux and rolling border country. Its historic market towns are solid and traditional, though there are marked differences in architecture which reflect the two sides of this intriguing part of Wales.

In the east, around Welshpool, Montgomery and Newtown, the lush, hummocky borderlands are dotted with striking 'magpie' – style black-and-white buildings. As the hills become mountains further westwards, Wales shrugs off its cross-border influences in favour of traditional, stone-built farmhouses.

Llanidloes, with its mixture of both styles – the ancient half-timbered market hall here is a gem – has a foot in both camps. It's an ideal touring centre – as is Machynlleth, traditional home of Owain Glyndwr's Welsh parliament. Point yourself in almost any direction and you'll stumble across hidden lakelands, waterfalls and forgotten villages. And be sure to visit opulent Powis Castle, near Welshpool, with its marvellous Clive of India Museum.

Berriew
Map Ref Ec5

Pretty village 5 miles south of Welshpool and bordering the Montgomery Canal. Black-and-white half-timbered houses are a notable feature of the gentle pastoral land around. Convenient for Newtown and Welshpool.

Farmhouses

Lower Luggy
Berriew, Welshpool, Powys,
SY21 8AB.
Tel: (068 685) 389. L

Farmhouse, beautifully situated in Severn Valley on main Welshpool/Newtown road, 2 miles from idyllic village of Berriew. Enjoy pretty walks along River Rhiew and Montgomery canal. Good base for touring. Charming family, double and single rooms all with washbasins and heating. Sitting room with television. Young family providing relaxed, informal atmosphere.

	Single Room per one person B&B		Double Room for two persons B&B		Bedrooms: 3
P	MIN £ 10.00	MAX £ 10.00	MIN £	MAX £ 20.00	OPEN 1-12

Caersws
Map Ref Ea6

Site of Roman fort on a great loop of the Severn. Excellent centre for touring the upper Severn Valley with its black-and-white timbered farms and manors.

Farmhouses

Pinkins Farm
Carno, Caersws, Powys, SY17 5JU.
Tel: (0686) 420289. L

A genuine Welsh farm set in beautiful mountain landscape. The entrance to the farm is off the A470, about midway between Newtown and Machynlleth. Excellent position for touring, being central for coastal and country beauty spots and also the great little steam trains of Mid Wales. Good home cooking.

	Single Room per one person B&B		Double Room for two persons B&B		Bedrooms: 3
P, pets, meals	MIN £ 8.50	MAX £ 9.50	MIN £ 17.00	MAX £ 19.00	OPEN 3-10

Lake Vyrnwy
Map Ref Ea3

One of the huge lakes in the chain of Mid Wales lakelands in a dramatic mountain-locked location. Walking and pony trekking country.

Farmhouses

Tynymaes
Llanwddyn, Powys, SY10 0NN.
Tel: (069 173) 216.

AWARD

A very warm welcome is extended to all guests at Tynymaes. It is situated 2 miles from Lake Vyrnwy and is on the edge of Snowdonia National Park. All bedrooms have washbasins and heating. Good farmhouse fare, dining room and spacious lounge. Homely atmosphere. Children are welcome. AA listed and holder of Wales Farmhouse Award.

	Single Room per one person B&B		Double Room for two persons B&B		Bedrooms: 3
P, meals	MIN £ 10.00	MAX £ 10.00	MIN £ 18.00	MAX £ 19.00	OPEN 5-10

Llanbrynmair
Map Ref De5

A scattered mountain-ringed village on Afon Twymyn, a tributary of the Dyfi. Travel south from here on the B4518 to Llyn Clywedog – an inspiring mountain route.

Guest Houses

Cyfeiliog Guest House
Bont Dolgadfan, Llanbrynmair,
Powys, SY19 7BB.
Tel: (065 03) 231. L

18th century riverside cottage guest house, beams, log fire, cosy and friendly atmosphere. Magnificent scenery. Mountains, rivers, forests, lake, quaint market towns. Centre of excellent touring area, lots to see and do. 4 bedrooms, 2 bathrooms, cot available. Free baby sitting service. Farmhouse style food. Diets catered for. A warm welcome is assured.

	Single Room per one person B&B		Double Room for two persons B&B		Bedrooms: 4
P, pets, meals	MIN £ 9.00	MAX £ 10.50	MIN £ 18.00	MAX £ 21.00	OPEN 1-12

Llanfair Caereinion
Map Ref Fb5

Famous as terminus for the Welshpool and Llanfair Light Railway. Llanfair Caereinion itself is a pleasant town set amidst forests in the lovely Vale of Banwy.

Hotels

Goat Hotel
Llanfair Caereinion, Nr. Welshpool,
Powys, SY21 0QS.
Tel: (0938) 810428.

Take a traditional country inn, a crackling fire, blackened beams, glowing brasses, deep comfy chairs and a choice of real beers and country food. Add some modern amenities, central heating, private bathrooms and tea makers. Put it all together in a glorious location in the heart of Wales. Result: "The Goat" at Llanfair.

	Single Room per one person B&B		Double Room for two persons B&B		Bedrooms: 6
P, pets, meals	MIN £ 11.00	MAX £ 12.00	MIN £ 18.00	MAX £ 22.00	OPEN 1-12

Guest Houses

Old Mill House
Llanfair Caereinion, Welshpool,
Powys, SY21 0SB.
Tel: (0938) 810623. L

A warm welcome to our small friendly guest house on the banks of the delightful River Banwy and the outskirts of a rural village. Excellent centre for touring, walking and fishing. Beautiful scenery, mountains, lakes, rivers and narrow gauge railway. Home cooking. Licensed restaurant. Washbasins and heating in bedrooms.

	Single Room per one person B&B		Double Room for two persons B&B		Bedrooms: 4
P, pets, meals	MIN £ 8.50	MAX £ 8.50	MIN £ 17.00	MAX £ 17.00	OPEN 1-12

Farmhouses

Madog's Wells
Llanfair Caereinion, Welshpool,
Powys, SY21 0DE.
Tel: (0938) 810446. L

Warm welcome and good home cooking await visitors to our small stockrearing hill farm situated in quiet, secluded valley surrounded by plenty of wildlife. Centrally heated farmhouse. Colour T.V. Tea and cake served evenings. Ideal location for touring Mid Wales. Families welcome. Reduced rates for under 12's. Washing facilities.

	Single Room per one person B&B		Double Room for two persons B&B		Bedrooms: 3
P, pets, meals	MIN £	MAX £ 7.50	MIN £	MAX £ 15.00	OPEN 1-12

Tyn-y-Bryn

Llanfair Caereinion, Welshpool,
Powys, SY21 0HB.
Tel: (0938) 810418.

L

A warm welcome awaits you from Roger and Eirlys at Tyn-y-Bryn. A genuine working hill farm situated in peaceful surroundings with unspoilt views from all bedrooms. Ideal for walking and touring. Local activities include light railway, pony trekking, golf, sports centre, Powis castle. Plenty of good home cooking using home produce whenever possible.

	Single Room per one person B&B		Double Room for two persons B&B		3
P (dog) (cutlery)	MIN £	MAX £	MIN £	MAX £	OPEN
		9.00		18.00	4-10

Llanfyllin
Map Ref Eb3

Historic small country town in the rolling Powys farmlands. Lake Vyrnwy and the 240 feet high Pistyll Rhaeadr waterfall are popular beauty spots nearby.

Farmhouses

Delwyn Farm

Delwyn Lane, Llanfyllin, Powys,
SY22 5LB.
Tel: (069 184) 249.

L

Delwyn has one family room with washbasin, twin bedroom with washbasin, double en-suite bedroom. Visitors are welcome to enjoy the beauty and peace of the area, situated three hundred yards down a lane, opposite the southern entrance to Llanfyllin. Ideal for walking, cycling and touring.

	Single Room per one person B&B		Double Room for two persons B&B		3
P (dog)	MIN £	MAX £	MIN £	MAX £	OPEN
	7.75	8.00	15.50	16.00	3-10

Y Gadair Farm

Llanfyllin, Powys, SY22 5LD.
Tel: (069 184) 271.

Gadair Farm is a spacious, 17th century farmhouse on a working farm, set in unspoilt countryside 1 mile from Llanfyllin. Lovely walks. Only a car ride away from the many attractions of Mid Wales, lakes, mountains, waterfalls, castles, etc. Washbasins and heaters in bedrooms. Friendly family welcome. Good home cooking. Children and pets welcome. Wales Tourist Board Farmhouse Award.

	Single Room per one person B&B		Double Room for two persons B&B		3
P (dog) (cutlery)	MIN £	MAX £	MIN £	MAX £	OPEN
		9.00		18.00	4-10

Llangurig
Map Ref Gc1

At 1,000 feet up in the mountains this village is the first on the fledgling River Wye. A few cosy trout fishing hotels, an inn, a craft centre and a 14th-century church make this an interesting place. A good touring centre for the lakes and mountains of Central Wales.

Guest Houses

The Old Vicarage

Llangurig, Nr. Llanidloes, Powys,
SY18 6RN.
Tel: (055 15) 280.

Enjoy the beauty of Mid Wales at our spacious Victorian vicarage guest house 1000ft up in the mountains. Ideal base for walking, birdwatching or touring the lakes and valleys of central Wales. H & C all rooms. Tea making facilities. Two guest lounges, log fires. Home cooking, diets catered for. Evening meal. Warm welcome guaranteed.

	Single Room per one person B&B		Double Room for two persons B&B		5
P (dog) (cutlery)	MIN £	MAX £	MIN £	MAX £	OPEN
	10.50	12.00	21.00	23.00	1-12

Llangynog
Map Ref Ea3

A pretty little village deep in the Berwyn Mountains on the route from the English border to Bala. Breathtaking views. The main holiday activity is pony trekking.

Farmhouses

Glanhafon Ucha

Llangynog, Oswestry, Shropshire,
SY10 0HL.
Tel: (069 174) 236.

L

Set in beautiful mountain scenery about 3/4 mile from Llangynog village. A small, comfortable, cottage style farmhouse with heavy oak beams in living rooom and reception hall. A mountain footpath leads through the farm to famous Llanrhaeadr waterfall. One family, one double room, evening meal by arrangement. Reduced rates for children under 14.

	Single Room per one person B&B		Double Room for two persons B&B		2
P (cutlery)	MIN £	MAX £	MIN £	MAX £	OPEN
	8.00	8.00	16.00	16.00	4-11

Llanidloes
Map Ref Gd1

An historic and attractive market town at the confluence of the Severn and Clywedog Rivers. Llanidloes is an excellent touring centre. There are fine half timbered buildings (especially the old market hall, now a museum), adequate shopping and free car parks. The massive Clywedog dam and lake are a short distance west of the town.

Guest Houses

Gorphwysfa Guest House

Westgate Street, Llanidloes, Powys,
SY18 6HL.
Tel: (055 12) 3356.

Comfortable accommodation in lovely Victorian house within walking distance of town in Mid Wales, area of great natural beauty. Cosy lounge with colour television. Centrally heated. Double and single rooms with hot and cold. Family room available if required. Recreational facilities in the area include golf, fishing, sailing, walking and riding.

	Single Room per one person B&B		Double Room for two persons B&B		5
P (dog) (cutlery)	MIN £	MAX £	MIN £	MAX £	OPEN
	9.00	9.00	18.00	18.00	1-12

Hafod

Llandinam, Powys, SY17 5BA.
Tel: (055 12) 2527.

Secluded country house in large grounds, set in lovely wooded valley, one mile off A470. Five miles old market town of Llanidloes. Single, double and family rooms with washbasins. Panelled dining room/lounge with colour T.V. Vegetarian and special diets. Home cooking. Ground floor bedrooms and facilities. Ideal walking, touring, birdwatching. Children welcome.

	Single Room per one person B&B		Double Room for two persons B&B		5
P (dog) (cutlery)	MIN £	MAX £	MIN £	MAX £	OPEN
	8.00	9.50	16.00	19.00	1-12

Farmhouses

Cwmllwydion Farm

Llandinam, Powys, SY17 5DJ.
Tel: (068 684) 314.

Delightful accommodation overlooking the Severn valley halfway between Newtown and Llanidloes, just off the A470. Home made food, personal attention. Heating, shower, H & C, tea making facilities, separate lounge with colour T.V. and dining room. Ideal fishing, walking, hunting, trekking and golf. Brochure and details from Mrs. G. Rowlands.

	Single Room per one person B&B		Double Room for two persons B&B		2
P (dog) (cutlery)	MIN £	MAX £	MIN £	MAX £	OPEN
	10.00		20.00		1-12

Dol-Llys Farm

Llanidloes, Powys, SY18 6JA.
Tel: (055 12) 2694.

Dol-Llys is a 17th century farmhouse, intriguing because it has so many levels and small staircases. Situated just one mile from the market town of Llanidloes on banks of River Severn. Guests welcome to wander around the 150 acre farm. Wales Tourist Board Farmhouse Award. Fishing and rough shooting available on the farm. Also child's pony.

	Single Room per one person B&B		Double Room for two persons B&B		2
	MIN £ 9.00	MAX £ 10.00	MIN £ 18.00	MAX £ 20.00	OPEN 4-10

Llanrhaeadr ym Mochnant

Map Ref Eb3

A quiet backwater in a valley of peace and beauty where Bishop William Morgan translated the Bible into Welsh in the 1580's. Some small hotels and guest houses, used by local pony trekkers. Three miles away is Wales's highest waterfall – Pistyll Rhaeadr (240 ft) – one of the 'Seven Wonders of Wales'.

Guest Houses

Bron-Heulog

Waterfall Road, Llanrhaeadr ym Mochnant, Clwyd, SY10 0JX.
Tel: (069 189) 521.

Spacious, centrally heated Victorian home set in large gardens situated on edge of picturesque village 4 miles from Pistyll Rhaeadr, highest waterfall in England and Wales. Excellent holiday area for walking, cycling, horse riding, fishing and birdwatching. A warm welcome awaits with good home cooking. Visits available to family rare breeds farm.

P	Single Room per one person B&B		Double Room for two persons B&B		3
	MIN £ 7.50	MAX £ 10.00	MIN £ 15.00	MAX £ 16.00	OPEN 1-12

Machynlleth

Map Ref Dc5

Busy market town on westernmost border of Powys. Owain Glyndwr's Parliament House is now the Tourist Information Centre (a museum and Dyfi Centre located here). Discover the alternative lifestyle at the Centre for Alternative Technology, tucked into the mountains behind Machynlleth. An interesting collection of shops; accommodation. Superb views towards mountains.

Guest Houses

Maenllwyd

Newtown Road, Machynlleth, Powys, SY20 8EY.
Tel: (0654) 2928.

Small family guest house providing warm welcome. Large comfortable rooms with washbasins, central heating and drink making facilities. Pleasant lounge with colour television and piano. Large garden and car park at rear. Ideal for walking, touring, fishing, pony trekking. Golf course nearby. Vegetarians welcome. Wales Tourist Board Guest House Award. Contact Mrs. Vince.

P	Single Room per one person B&B		Double Room for two persons B&B		7
	MIN £	MAX £	MIN £ 18.00	MAX £ 21.00	OPEN 1-12

Rhiw Goch Guest House

Talywern, Machynlleth, Powys, SY20 8NY.
Tel: (0654) 2594.

Seven miles east of Machynlleth in peaceful hills, old farmhouse now comfortable guest house. Easy reach of Snowdonia National Park and beaches. Ideal for walking and cycling. Superb centre for touring. All rooms have washbasins, hot and cold. Full central heating. Log fires. Personal attentive service.

P	Single Room per one person B&B		Double Room for two persons B&B		3
	MIN £ 8.50	MAX £ 9.00	MIN £ 17.00	MAX £ 18.00	OPEN 1-12

Talbont Drain Guest House & Hill Walking Centre

Uwchygarreg, Machynlleth, Powys, SY20 8RR.
Tel: (0654) 2192.

L

Remote and comfortable converted farmhouse offering an ideal base for walkers, birdwatchers, photographers or anyone enjoying the countryside. Small, friendly guest house offering excellent food. Special interest holidays, brochure available. Within easy reach of Snowdonia National Park, Centre for Alternative Technology, sandy beaches, golf and fishing. Four miles from Machynlleth on quiet country lane. Pianola.

P	Single Room per one person B&B		Double Room for two persons B&B		6
	MIN £ 11.00	MAX £ 11.00	MIN £ 22.00	MAX £ 25.00	OPEN 1-12

Farmhouses

Bacheiddon Farm

Machynlleth, Powys, SY20 8SG.
Tel: (0654) 2229.

Situated six miles from the market town of Machynlleth, we are in easy reach of the sea and of the Snowdonia National Park. All rooms in the farmhouse are comfortable. Guests are accommodated in three double bedrooms, each with its own toilet and shower. Lounge has colour T.V. Brochure from Mrs. A. Lewis.

P	Single Room per one person B&B		Double Room for two persons B&B		3
	MIN £ 12.00	MAX £	MIN £ 24.00	MAX £	OPEN 5-10

Cefn

Darowen, Machynlleth, Powys, SY20 8NS.
Tel: (065 02) 336/273.

Lies at end of small peaceful village amidst beautiful hill farming country. Central for touring North and Mid Wales and West coast. Excellent walking from house. Oak beamed lounge/dining room with excellent views, television, log fires. Three bedrooms with washbasins, one family room, one en-suite. Personal attention to comfort.

P	Single Room per one person B&B		Double Room for two persons B&B		3
	MIN £ 8.00	MAX £ 9.00	MIN £ 16.00	MAX £ 18.00	OPEN 1-12

Cefn Coch Uchaf

Cemmaes Road, Machynlleth, Powys, SY20 8LH.
Tel: (065 02) 552.

L

One mile off main road. Beautiful mountain scenery, easy access to Cardigan Bay beaches. Ideal countryside for fishing, horse riding and birdwatching. T.V. lounge provided. Also all home cooking and home comforts.

P	Single Room per one person B&B		Double Room for two persons B&B		3
	MIN £ 7.50	MAX £ 8.00	MIN £ 15.00	MAX £ 16.00	OPEN 4-10

Gwernstablau Farm

Llanwrin, Machynlleth, Powys, SY20 8QH.
Enq. to: Mrs. Mary E. Davies.
Tel: (065 02) 262.

18th century farmhouse in the Dovey Valley. Beams, log fire. Twin, double, 2 singles, all rooms, H & C. Separate W.C., shower, bath. Tea/coffee facilities free 24 hours. Central heating. Ornithologist area 8 miles. Seaside 12 miles.

P	Single Room per one person B&B		Double Room for two persons B&B		4
	MIN £ 9.00	MAX £	MIN £ 18.00	MAX £	OPEN 1-12

Mathafarn

Machynlleth, Powys, SY20 8QJ.
Tel: (065 02) 226.

Originally the home of Dafydd Llwyd, the Welsh poet. Henry VII is reputed to have stayed here en-route to the Battle of Bosworth. Now this 16th century elegant country house is part of a sheep and cattle farm. Inglenook log fires. Peaceful surroundings. Close to Machynlleth and the beautiful coastline at Aberdovey.

P	Single Room per one person B&B		Double Room for two persons B&B		2
	MIN £ 9.50	MAX £ 10.50	MIN £ 17.00	MAX £ 19.00	OPEN 1-12

Montgomery

Map Ref Ec6

Hilltop market town of distinctive Georgian architecture beneath the ruins of a 13th century castle. Offa's Dyke, which once marked the border, runs nearby.

Guest Houses

Glanhafren

Abermule, Montgomery, Powys, SY15 6NA.
Tel: (068 686) 202.

Delightful accommodation in early nineteenth century Georgian hall conveniently set in the Severn valley, midway between the market towns of Newtown and Welshpool. Ideal for river and canal fishing or walking. Spacious, centrally heated family rooms with washbasins, one en-suite, tea/coffee making facilities. Good home cooking. Croeso cynnes.

P	Single Room per one person B&B		Double Room for two persons B&B		3
	MIN £	MAX £	MIN £ 19.00	MAX £ 20.00	OPEN 1-12

Farmhouses

The Drewin Farm

Churchstoke, Montgomery, Powys, SY15 6TW.
Tel: (058 85) 325.

17th century border farmhouse with inglenook fireplace and wealth of oak beams. Panoramic views over most beautiful countryside. Fully centrally heated with washbasins and tea making facilities in bedrooms. The Drewin is a mixed farm consisting of sheep, cattle and corn. Games room with snooker table available. Offa's Dyke footpath runs through the farm.

P	Single Room per one person B&B		Double Room for two persons B&B		2
	MIN £ 8.50	MAX £ 10.00	MIN £ 17.00	MAX £ 20.00	OPEN 4-10

Little Brompton Farm

Montgomery, Powys, SY15 6HY.
Tel: (068 681) 371.

17th century, Wales Tourist Board Award, farmhouse, traditionally furnished. 2 miles from Georgian town of Montgomery. H/C, shaver points, tea trays all rooms. A genuine mixed working farm. We use home grown produce whenever possible. Offa's Dyke crosses our land. Comfort, elegance, personal attention with value for money are our priorities. Brochure on request.

P	Single Room per one person B&B		Double Room for two persons B&B		3
	MIN £ 9.00	MAX £ 10.00	MIN £	MAX £	OPEN 1-12

Newtown

Map Ref Eb6

Busy Severn Valley market town. History of textile industry recounted at small museum. Home of Robert Owen, founder of Co-operative movement. Theatr Hafren.

Guest Houses

Brook Mill

Mochdre, Newtown, Powys, SY16 4JF.
Tel: (0686) 24679.

On the banks of a trout stream in the wooded Mochdre valley, this 180 year old flannel mill has been newly converted to a private house with crayfish ponds. Two twin bedded rooms, hot and cold, tea/coffee facilities, T.V., central heating. Washing machine and cooking facilities by arrangement. Private parking. T.V. and breakfast lounge. £10 per person.

P	Single Room per one person B&B		Double Room for two persons B&B		2
	MIN £	MAX £	MIN £ 20.00	MAX £ 20.00	OPEN 6-11

Fron Haul Country Guest House

Llandinam, Nr. Newtown, Powys, SY17 5DD.
Tel: (068 684) 8928. L

Means "hillside of sun". T.V. lounge. Large family, double and single rooms with heating, hot and cold, tea/coffee and books. Original 19th century elegant decor. Choice of meals, diets arranged. Table licence. Walk aound gardens with lawns (bowls available), shrubs, trees overlooking River Severn, surrounded by mountains and forests. Off the main road.

P	Single Room per one person B&B		Double Room for two persons B&B		8
	MIN £ 9.00	MAX £ 12.00	MIN £ 18.00	MAX £ 24.00	OPEN 1-12

Greenfields

Kerry, Newtown, Powys, SY16 4LH.
Tel: (068 688) 596. L

Situated ¼ of a mile east of the picturesque village of Kerry on the A489 (approx. 3½ miles from Newtown). A warm welcome with home cooking is extended to all guests. All bedrooms have hot and cold and shaving points. Ample parking. T.V. lounge.

P	Single Room per one person B&B		Double Room for two persons B&B		3
	MIN £ 8.00	MAX £ 10.00	MIN £ 16.00	MAX £ 18.00	OPEN 1-12

Farmhouses

Gate Farm

Llandyssil, Montgomery, Powys, SY15 6LN.
Tel: (068 688) 625. L

Stay on working dairy farm set in the Mongomeryshire countryside. Superb views and totally relaxed informal atmosphere. Well placed for excursions and activities to interest all the family. Reduced rates for children. Pets welcome. Double and twin bedrooms. Farmhouse cooking. T.V. lounge. Central heating. Baby sitting service. Evening meal by arrangement. Brochure Mrs. Anwen Lloyd.

P	Single Room per one person B&B		Double Room for two persons B&B		3
	MIN £ 9.00	MAX £ 10.00	MIN £ 18.00	MAX £ 19.00	OPEN 1-12

Lower Gwestydd

Llanllwchaiarn, Newtown, Powys, SY16 3AY.
Tel: (0686) 26718.

Lovely peaceful setting on hillside, 2 miles from Newtown. Lower Gwestydd is a 17th century farmhouse with 200 acres of mixed farm land. Home produced beef, lamb, chicken, fruit and vegetables for the table. All bedrooms have H & C, tea making facilities and shaving points. Separate toilet, shower room. Dining room. Lounge, C.T.V. 2 crowns' farmhouse award. Friendly family atmosphere.

P	Single Room per one person B&B		Double Room for two persons B&B		3
	MIN £ 10.00	MAX £ 10.50	MIN £ 20.00	MAX £ 21.00	OPEN 3-12

Welshpool
Map Ref Ec5

A borderlands market town. Golf and angling. Shopping centre. Powis Castle is an impressive stately home with a new museum featuring Clive of India memorabilia. Ride the Welshpool and Llanfair light railway.

Guest Houses

A Country Manor

Dysserth House, Powis Castle,
Welshpool, Powys, SY21 8RQ.
Tel. (0938) 2153. L

Powis Castle, National Trust, is a short walk from our lovely home set amidst superb, peaceful scenery with views over Severn Valley. Rooms comfortably furnished with antiques. Pretty bedrooms. Two bathrooms. Morning room with colour television. Home farm produce. Light suppers are available, or join us for dinner and be treated as true guests. Brochure.

	Single Room per one person B&B		Double Room for two persons B&B		2
P ✕	MIN £ 12.00	MAX £ 12.00	MIN £ 24.00	MAX £ 24.00	OPEN 3-12

Heath Cottage

Forden, Welshpool, Powys,
SY21 8LX.
Tel: (0938 76) 453. L

18th century cottage on working smallholding. Full central heating, tea making facilities, colour T.V., 2 bathrooms. Excellent food, free range poultry and lovely views. Near Powis and Montgomery castles, narrow gauge railway, riding stable and arboretum. Ideal for exploring Mid Wales and Shropshire borderland.

	Single Room per one person B&B		Double Room for two persons B&B		3
P ✕	MIN £	MAX £	MIN £ 18.00	MAX £ 22.00	OPEN 4-10

Farmhouses

Mount Farm

Berriew, Welshpool, Powys,
SY21 8AR.
Tel: (068 685) 289. L

An 18th century farmhouse situated a few minutes away from Powis Castle and Welshpool/Llanfair light railway. Ideal position for touring the beautiful Mid Wales countryside. Two double and one twin bedded room. Separate shower room and bathroom. Totally relaxed informal atmosphere. Good home cooking. Evening meal optional. Reduced rates for children.

	Single Room per one person B&B		Double Room for two persons B&B		3
P ✕	MIN £	MAX £	MIN £ 16.00	MAX £ 18.00	OPEN 1-12

Plasdwpa

Berriew, Welshpool, Powys,
SY21 8PS.
Tel: (068 685) 298.

AWARD

Situated 1½ miles from the pretty village of Berriew. Working farm, dairy, poultry. Enjoying magnificent views. Modern house, one double, one twin and one family bedroom with hot and cold, tea making facilities. Large lounge, colour T.V. A warm welcome and good food awaits visitors. Ideal for touring, lakes, castles. Brochure on request, Mrs. F. M. Hughes.

	Single Room per one person B&B		Double Room for two persons B&B		3
P ✕	MIN £ 9.00	MAX £ 10.00	MIN £ 18.00	MAX £ 20.00	OPEN 3-10

Tynllwyn Farm

Welshpool, Powys, SY21 9BW.
Tel: (0938) 3175/3054.

AWARD

Although Tynllwyn is a working farm with a fine selection of animals and pets, its high standard of furnishings, decor and general appearance are equivalent to the finest hotel. All bedrooms have tea/coffee making facilities and colour T.V. Meal times are an unforgettable experience with fresh produce and varied menus. Hospitality is second to none from Mrs. Emberton and family. Brochure on request.

	Single Room per one person B&B		Double Room for two persons B&B		5
P ✕	MIN £ 10.50	MAX £ 10.50	MIN £ 21.00	MAX £ 21.00	OPEN 1-12

Upper Brithdir Farm

Welshpool, Powys, SY21 8AP.
Tel: (068 685) 263.

Working family farm, dairy, beef and sheep. Eighteenth century farmhouse with mainly home produce served in dining room with exposed beams overlooking Severn valley. Rooms are large, adaptable to most requirements. Double, twin, single or family. Washbasins and radios in all bedrooms. Bathroom with shower. Willing to meet the main line train in Welshpool.

	Single Room per one person B&B		Double Room for two persons B&B		2
P ✕	MIN £ 9.00	MAX £ 9.00	MIN £ 18.00	MAX £ 20.00	OPEN 1-12

Upper Pandy Farm

Berriew, Welshpool, Powys,
SY21 8PW.
Tel: (068 685) 338.

AWARD

Black and white timbered farmhouse. 140 acres stockrearing farm 1½ miles from the village of Berriew. One double or twin bedded room. One family room with washbasins. Tea making facilities. Good home cooking and a warm welcome to all. Reduced rates for children. Good touring area. Brochure from Mrs. Elizabeth Jones.

	Single Room per one person B&B		Double Room for two persons B&B		2
P ✕	MIN £ 9.00	MAX £ 9.50	MIN £ 18.00	MAX £ 19.00	OPEN 4-10

HEART OF WALES

For once the name says it all. Nowhere in Wales is it greener than in the hills around Rhayader, Llandrindod Wells and Builth Wells. Farming traditions are deeply rooted here – and one event in every farmer's diary is the Royal Welsh Show, which transforms placid Builth into the lively agricultural capital of Wales every July.

Water also has its part to play. In Victorian times, Llandrindod and the other 'Wells' towns here were fashionable spa resorts. Genteel, gracious Llandrindod preserves memories of its *belle époque*. Today, it is also a popular touring centre for the Elan Valley lakelands (call in first at Elan's Visitor Centre), set amid the bulky, bare Cambrian Mountains. Beautifully located Llanwrtyd Wells stages an imaginative series of special events – including a 'Man versus Horse' marathon! There are, though, easier ways to explore these green mountains from this region's excellent selection of pony trekking centres.

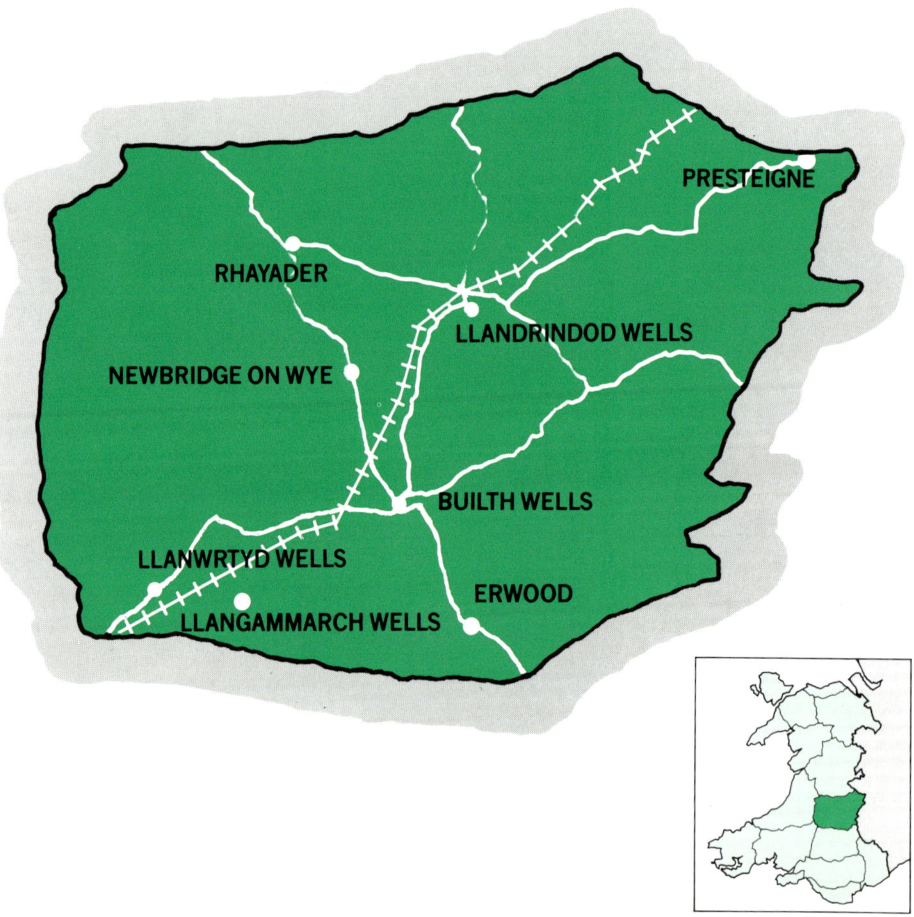

Builth Wells

Map Ref Ge4

The agricultural centre of Wales cradled in a ring of hills. Annual Royal Welsh Agricultural Show in July. Local market for cattle and sheep. Touring centre for Mid Wales hills, good shopping for local product. Wyeside Arts Centre.

Hotels

Erwood Inn

Erwood, Builth Wells, Powys,
LD2 3EZ.
Tel: (098 23) 218. L

Situated on A470 in the centre of the village of Erwood which is in the beautiful Wye Valley. Comfortable, clean accommodation, central heating. Coffee and tea makers in all bedrooms. Two bathrooms and toilets. Dining room. Lounge, T.V. Good wholesome cooking. Fishing, salmon and trout, glorious walks, golf, birdwatching.

Single Room per one person B&B		Double Room for two persons B&B		Bedrooms
				3
MIN £	MAX £	MIN £	MAX £	OPEN
8.50		17.00		1-12

Llanelwedd Arms Hotel

Station Road, Builth Wells, Powys,
LD2 3SR.
Tel: (0982) 553282.

This family-run hotel situated in the beautiful Wye Valley adjacent to the Royal Welsh Showground offers friendly and comfortable accommodation and good home cooked food. Trout and salmon fishing available, golf and riding available locally. All rooms colour T.V. and tea making facilities.

Single Room per one person B&B		Double Room for two persons B&B		Bedrooms
				6
MIN £	MAX £	MIN £	MAX £	OPEN
10.00	12.00	20.00	24.00	1-12

Guest Houses

Bron Wye Guest House

5 Church Street, Builth Wells, Powys,
LD2 3BS.
Tel: (0982) 553587.

Bron Wye licensed guest house overlooking River Wye, central point for hikers, cyclists and tourers. Open all year. Pets and children welcome. Hot and cold. Central heating. T.V. lounge. Dining room. Car parking. Snacks, evening meals, basket meals. Tea and coffee. Radios. Fishing, golf, shooting, pony trekking, walking, canoeing locally. Garage available for cycle parking.

Single Room per one person B&B		Double Room for two persons B&B		Bedrooms
				4
MIN £	MAX £	MIN £	MAX £	OPEN
7.50	8.00	15.00	16.00	1-12

Maendee Guest House

Park Road, Builth Wells, Powys,
LD2 3BA.
Tel: (0982) 552293. L

Situated in town centre with its golf, fishing facilities, sports hall near. Good home cooking. Single, family and double rooms available. Special rates for children. Off season rates. Five bedrooms, all with H & C, tea/coffee. Separate lounge, dining room. Car park. Excellent walking area. Small parties during winter months and otherwise. Central heating. Meals available.

Single Room per one person B&B		Double Room for two persons B&B		Bedrooms
				5
MIN £	MAX £	MIN £	MAX £	OPEN
8.50	9.00	17.00	17.00	1-12

Querida

43 Garth Road, Builth Wells, Powys,
LD2 3AR.
Tel: (0982) 553642.

Querida is within easy reach of the town centre with its golf, fishing facilities, sports hall, etc. Also within reach of Brecon Beacons, Black Mountains, Elan Valley. Friendly homely atmosphere with central heating, T.V., sitting room, bathroom and shower. One twin, two double rooms. Ample parking. Hot and cold in all rooms.

Single Room per one person B&B		Double Room for two persons B&B		Bedrooms
				3
MIN £	MAX £	MIN £	MAX £	OPEN
8.00	8.50	16.00	17.00	1-12

Farmhouses

Caepandy Farm

Builth Wells, Powys, LD2 3NS.
Tel: (0982) 553793. L

We are situated on the A483 Builth/Llandovery road, one mile out of Builth Wells in an excellent position for touring Mid Wales. There are magnificent views of the Irfon and Wye Valleys from the farmhouse which is modernised. Comfortable beds and good food assured. Pets allowed. Ample parking. Garden and lounge for guests' use.

Single Room per one person B&B		Double Room for two persons B&B		Bedrooms
				3
MIN £	MAX £	MIN £	MAX £	OPEN
8.00	8.50	16.00	17.00	1-12

Dollynwydd Farm

Builth Wells, Powys, LD2 3RZ.
Tel: (0982) 553660. L

17th century farmhouse, 200 acres beef and sheep. Home cooking, own produce. Superb area for walking, birdwatching, touring, golf, riding, salmon and trout fishing can be arranged. Also horse riding. Own trout river. Tennis courts, sports hall, bowling all nearby. We are one mile from Builth Wells on the B4520.

Single Room per one person B&B		Double Room for two persons B&B		Bedrooms
				4
MIN £	MAX £	MIN £	MAX £	OPEN
8.00	9.00	16.00	18.00	4-10

Nant-y-Dderw Farm

Cwmbach, Builth Wells, Powys,
LD2 3RU. Enq to: Mrs. Phillips.
Tel: (0982) 553675.

Nant-y-Dderw is convenient to A470, 4 miles north of Builth Wells. Working sheep farm. Homestead situated in centre of 45 acres. Accommodation all one level. Maximum four guests, in twin bedded rooms. Guests bathroom adjacent. Lounge with views towards the Eppynt hills. Special diets. Disabled guests very welcome. Freedom of farm for nature study.

Single Room per one person B&B		Double Room for two persons B&B		Bedrooms
				2
MIN £	MAX £	MIN £	MAX £	OPEN
9.50	10.50	19.00	21.00	5-10

Ty Isaf Farm

Erwood, Builth Wells, Powys, LD2 3SZ.
Tel: (098 23) 607.

Ty-Isaf Farm, just off A470 overlooking Wye Valley near village of Erwood, which has two homely inns. Ideal spot from which to tour Mid Wales. 340 acre farm, full central heating, hot and cold all rooms, two toilets, bath, shower. Guests are welcome to walk round the farm. AA listed. Farmhouse Award. Lounge, dining room, tea & coffee rooms.

Single Room per one person B&B		Double Room for two persons B&B		Bedrooms
				3
MIN £	MAX £	MIN £	MAX £	OPEN
8.00	8.50	16.00	17.00	1-12

Erwood

Map Ref Ha5

Pretty Wyeside village set amongst wooded valley. The idea of 'Punch' magazine conceived at the local inn.

Guest Houses

Old Vicarage

Erwood, Builth Wells, Powys,
LD2 3EX.
Tel: (098 23) 680. L

Situated in 1½ acre grounds south of Erwood in the Wye Valley. Ideally situated for touring Mid Wales, fishing, walking. Three bedrooms, two with H & C. Home grown vegetables, home produced Welsh lamb for meals. Own T.V. lounge, log fire. Less than three minutes walk from two local inns. Young children welcome. We keep sheep. C.H.

Single Room per one person B&B		Double Room for two persons B&B		Bedrooms
				3
MIN £	MAX £	MIN £	MAX £	OPEN
7.00	7.50	14.00	15.00	1-12

Llandrindod Wells

Map Ref Ge3

A Victorian Spa town with spacious streets and impressive architecture. You can still take the waters at Rock Park Gardens. A popular inland resort with lots of entertainment – golf, fishing, bowling, boating, and tennis available. Good selection of hotels. Excellent touring centre for Mid Wales hills and lakes. Annual Victorian Festival in September.

Hotels

Gwystre Inn

Gwystre, A44, Nr. Llandrindod Wells,
Powys, LD1 6RN.
Tel: (0577 87) 650.

18th century coaching inn. Log fires. Central heating all rooms. Home cooking. Riverside gardens. Large car park. Children welcome. Friendly atmosphere. Two bars, coffee lounge, dining room. Beautiful countryside, six miles from Rhayader and lovely Elan Valley, five miles from spa town of Llandrindod Wells. Interesting and varied drives and walks from the Gwystre.

Single Room per one person B&B		Double Room for two persons B&B		4
MIN £ 9.00	MAX £ 11.00	MIN £ 18.00	MAX £ 22.00	OPEN 1-12

Ithondale Country Hotel

Llanbister, Llandrindod Wells, Powys,
LD1 6TN.
Tel: (059 783) 244.

A warm friendly welcome awaits you in our comfortable, well appointed, licensed country hotel. We offer excellent food made from fresh produce, complimented by an interesting selection of wines. Ideally situated for private fishing, buzzard watching, walking, horse riding and touring beautiful quiet Mid Wales. Recommended by "Les Routiers". Access cards welcome.

Single Room per one person B&B		Double Room for two persons B&B		3
MIN £ 11.50	MAX £ 11.50	MIN £ 20.00	MAX £ 23.00	OPEN 2-12

Guest Houses

Bridge Guest House

Howey, Llandrindod Wells, Powys,
LD1 5PT.
Tel: (0597) 4646.

Family-run, licensed guest house situated in quiet village, 1½ miles Llandrindod Wells with shop and inns. Comfortable bedrooms with H & C, some en-suite, T.V., tea making facilities, central heating. Relax in a friendly atmosphere. Enjoy good home cooking, varied menu. Residents' lounge. Car parking. Good base touring, fishing, golf, walking, bowling, trekking.

Single Room per one person B&B		Double Room for two persons B&B		6
MIN £	MAX £	MIN £ 16.00	MAX £ 20.00	OPEN 1-12

Clifton House

Wellington Road, Llandrindod Wells,
Powys, LD1 5NB.
Tel: (0597) 2527.

Clifton House is tastefully decorated throughout. Situated close to all amenities, within 5 minutes walk of town centre. Restaurant with à la carte menu, bar. All bedrooms C.H., H.C., colour T.V. Special rates for children. Bargain breaks available throughout the year, discounts for parties over 10. Ideal for the discerning travellers.

Single Room per one person B&B		Double Room for two persons B&B		8
MIN £ 10.00	MAX £ 12.00	MIN £ 20.00	MAX £ 24.00	OPEN 1-12

Corven Hall

AWARD

Howey, Llandrindod Wells, Powys,
LD1 5RE.
Tel: (0597) 3368. C/Res: (0654) 3101

Victorian house of character in peaceful setting, surrounded by beautiful countryside. The house is licensed, centrally heated, spacious. Good home cooking, large dining room, T.V. lounge, bar. Most bedrooms en-suite, tea/coffee facilities. Ground floor accommodation. Ideal walking, touring, birdwatching, country, fishing. Golf in area. AA listed. W.T.B. Guest House Award. Brochure available.

Single Room per one person B&B		Double Room for two persons B&B		7
MIN £ 9.00	MAX £ 11.00	MIN £ 18.00	MAX £ 22.00	OPEN 1-12

Disserth Farm Guest House

AWARD

Howey, Llandrindod Wells, Powys,
LD1 6NL.
Tel: (059 789) 277.

Nestling in the beautiful Ithon valley, Disserth provides the ideal touring centre. A warm welcome awaits you. Comfort, hospitality, centrally heated throughout, tea making facilities and good home cooking in peaceful surroundings. Oak beams, original stone fireplaces, tastefully furnished rooms, licensed bar, coffee and craft shop. Walking, private trout fishing, in this birdwatcher's paradise.

Single Room per one person B&B		Double Room for two persons B&B		2
MIN £ 9.00	MAX £ 10.00	MIN £ 18.00	MAX £ 20.00	OPEN 1-12

Merlin Guest House

Temple Street, Llandrindod Wells,
Powys, LD1 5HF.
Tel: (0597) 4800.

Centrally situated and close to all amenities. Real home cooking. H & C in all rooms, tea making facilities. Separate shower room. Colour T.V. lounge. Central heating throughout. Special rates for children. Friendly, homely atmosphere from Audrey and John Skinner.

Single Room per one person B&B		Double Room for two persons B&B		3
MIN £ 8.00	MAX £ 8.50	MIN £ 16.00	MAX £ 17.00	OPEN 1-12

Rhydithon

Dyffryn Road, Llandrindod Wells,
Powys, LD1 6AN.
Tel: (0597) 2624.

Small, family guest house in a quiet side road just off the High Street. Hot and cold in rooms. Television lounge. Close to all amenities, public car park, main bus stop and railway station under 200 yards. An ideal location for touring the countryside and reservoirs of Mid Wales.

Single Room per one person B&B		Double Room for two persons B&B		4
MIN £ 8.00	MAX £ 8.00	MIN £ 16.00	MAX £ 16.00	OPEN 1-12

Sunnybank Guest House

Ithon Road, Llandrindod Wells,
Powys, LD1 6AS.
Tel: (0597) 4977.

Relax in comfort at our licensed, family-run guest house adjacent to spa with views over Ithon Valley. Riverside walks nearby, short stroll town centre. Attractive rooms with central heating, colour T.V., tea/coffee making facilities. Good home cooking. Evening dinner £5.50., traditional and vegetarian. Excellent wines. Packed lunches. Indoor swimming by arrangement. Free fishing.

Single Room per one person B&B		Double Room for two persons B&B		4
MIN £ 9.00	MAX £ 10.50	MIN £ 18.00	MAX £ 21.00	OPEN 1-12

Ty Clyd Licensed Guest House

Park Terrace, Llandrindod Wells,
Powys, LD1 6AY.
Tel: (0597) 2122.

Century old building with modern comfort in quiet situation overlooking wooded park. Easy parking. Licensed restaurant open to non-residents for dinner. Varied cuisine including our French selection of food and wine. Central for all sporting activities and town amenities.

Single Room per one person B&B		Double Room for two persons B&B		6
MIN £ 10.00	MAX £ 10.00	MIN £ 20.00	MAX £ 20.00	OPEN 1-12

Farmhouses

Broadheath Farm

Presteigne, Powys, LD8 2HG.
Tel: (0544) 267416.

Welsh border Georgian farmhouse. 1½ miles Presteigne, 20 miles Hereford. Easy reach Offa's Dyke, Elan Valley, Ludlow. Beautiful unspoilt countryside. Tea and coffee, H & C. AA listed.

Single Room per one person B&B		Double Room for two persons B&B		3
MIN £ 10.00	MAX £ 12.00	MIN £ 20.00	MAX £ 24.00	OPEN 4-10

Brynhir Farm

Howey, Llandrindod Wells, Powys, LD1 5PB. Enq. to: Mrs. C. Nixon.
Tel: (0597) 2425.

Situated in beautiful mountain setting 1 mile off the A483 road. 17th century farmhouse, 150 acre working hill farm. Ideal for birdwatching, trout fishing available. Superb views from farm. Walkers welcome. All rooms with H & C, heated, some en-suite, tea/coffee facilities. Log fires. Full Welsh breakfast. Separate tables, evening meals by arrangement. AA listed.

Single Room per one person B&B		Double Room for two persons B&B		Bedrooms: 6
MIN £	MAX £	MIN £	MAX £	OPEN
9.00	9.50	18.00	19.00	3-11

Dolberthog Farm

Llandrindod Wells, Powys. LD1 5PH.
Tel: (0597) 2255. C/Res: (0654) 3101

Enjoy comfort, relaxation and superb meals at our 250 acre farm in quiet countryside, 15 minutes walk from Llandrindod Wells. River fishing, bird watching and ideal walks. A Welsh welcome awaits you and personal service will ensure individual attention to your every comfort. Colour T.V. lounge. Separate dining room. AA listed. Farmhouse award. Brochure and enquiries: Mrs. Evans.

Single Room per one person B&B		Double Room for two persons B&B		Bedrooms: 3
MIN £	MAX £	MIN £	MAX £	OPEN
8.50	9.50	17.00	19.00	4-11

Highbury Farm

Llanyre, Llandrindod Wells, Powys, LD1 6EA.
Tel: (0597) 2716.

A smallholding situated one mile outside Llandrindod Wells on the edge of the village of Llanyre. A warm welcome awaits you. Comfortable, spacious rooms, one double, one family/twin room and one single. Full central heating, colour T.V. in lounge. Separate dining room. Evening meal optional. Farmhouse certificate held. AA listed.

Single Room per one person B&B		Double Room for two persons B&B		Bedrooms: 3
MIN £	MAX £	MIN £	MAX £	OPEN
8.00	9.00	16.00	18.00	4-10

Holly Farm

Howey, Llandrindod Wells, Powys, LD1 5PP.
Tel: (0597) 2402. C/Res: (0654) 3101

Delightfully situated in peaceful position away from traffic, 1½ miles south of Llandrindod Wells and ¼ mile off the A483. Holly Farm, a 70 acre working farm, offers guests a warm and friendly welcome. All bedrooms with hot and cold, some en-suite, tea/coffee making facilities. Lounge with log fire and T.V. Dining room with separate tables offers highly recommended home cooking. Rural Tourism Award for catering farmhouse award. AA listed. Send s.a.e. for brochure to Mrs. Ruth Jones.

Single Room per one person B&B		Double Room for two persons B&B		Bedrooms: 3
MIN £	MAX £	MIN £	MAX £	OPEN
9.00	10.00	18.00	20.00	4-11

Three Wells Farm

Howey, Llandrindod Wells, Powys. LD1 5PB. Tel: (0597) 4427.

Welcome to our licensed farm guest house on 50 acre working farm, overlooking fishing lake in beautiful countryside. 1½ miles from spa town of Llandrindod Wells. Good food. Spacious dining room, lounge, sun lounge, T.V. room, 2 bars. 11 bedrooms, all bath or shower en-suite, tea/coffee makers, centrally heated. AA and RAC. FGH Diploma. Lift. All bedrooms with T.V. Ron and Margaret Bufton.

Single Room per one person B&B		Double Room for two persons B&B		Bedrooms: 12
MIN £	MAX £	MIN £	MAX £	OPEN
9.50	12.00	19.00	24.00	1-12

Llangammarch Wells

Map Ref Gc5

An attractive village 560 ft above sea level, renowned for its excellent trout fishing by the River Irfon. At one time the village had a 'spa' well, its water believed to be efficacious in the cure of gout, heart disease and rheumatism. The disused pumphouse and well are in the groups of the Lake Hotel.

Guest Houses

Mayo Hall

Llangammarch Wells, Powys, LD4 4BS. Tel: (059 12) 469.

Mayo Hall sits in an elevated position overlooking the River Irfon. The Brecon Beacons or the beautiful Elan Valley are within ½ hour drive. Three double bedrooms and one family room. All with hot and cold handbasins and tea making facilities. T.V. lounge. Good home cooking. Ample parking. Reduced rates for children.

Single Room per one person B&B		Double Room for two persons B&B		Bedrooms: 4
MIN £	MAX £	MIN £	MAX £	OPEN
11.00	12.00	22.00	24.00	4-10

Llanwrtyd Wells

Map Ref Gc5

One of the four Mid Wales 'spa' towns. Today a centre for pony trekking, walking and fishing. The Cambrian woollen weaving mill is a popular attraction. For spectacular views explore the nearby Abergwesyn Pass/Llyn Brianne area. Mountain Bike Centre.

Hotels

Carlton Court Hotel

Llanwrtyd Wells, Powys, LD5 4SN.
Tel: (059 13) 248.

Situated in glorious countryside of Mid Wales. All bedrooms centrally heated, hot and cold water, colour T.V., complimentary tea and coffee. Log fire in lounge. An excellent centre for fishing, birdwatching, walking. Reduced green fees at nearby course. Reduction in rates for stay of a week. Bargain breaks throughout the year.

Single Room per one person B&B		Double Room for two persons B&B		Bedrooms: 9
MIN £	MAX £	MIN £	MAX £	OPEN
10.95	12.00	19.90	23.90	1-12

The Stonecroft

Llanwrtyd Wells, Powys, LD5 4RA.
Tel: (059 13) 262.

The Stonecroft is a small friendly pub on the outskirts of the smallest town, bordered by the River Irfon and green fields. We offer good home cooking with the warmth of a family home. Log fire, B/B/Q's and discos. Ideally situated for walking, ornithology, cycling, leisurely holidays. Children and pets welcome. Contact Helen Storey.

Single Room per one person B&B		Double Room for two persons B&B		Bedrooms: 3
MIN £	MAX £	MIN £	MAX £	OPEN
8.00	10.00	16.00	20.00	1-12

Guest Houses

Caeglas

Ffos Road, Llanwrtyd Wells, Powys, LD5 4RS.
Tel: (059 13) 547.

Caeglas, half mile from town, situated in open countryside with views of nearby Eppynt hills, has three guest rooms, bathroom, shower room, colour T.V., log fire in residents' lounge. Home cooking, wholemeal bread, free range eggs, own honey. Ideal centre for touring, walking. Can book pony trekking/riding/ mountain bikes. Red Kite country.

Single Room per one person B&B		Double Room for two persons B&B		Bedrooms: 3
MIN £	MAX £	MIN £	MAX £	OPEN
9.00	9.50	17.00	18.00	1-12

Newbridge on Wye
Map Ref Gd3

Old village on A470 in peaceful pony trekking country. Good base for mountains of central Wales.

Farmhouses

Ty'n Rhos
Newbridge-on-Wye, Llandrindod Wells, Powys, LD1 6ND.
Tel: (0597 89) 425. L

In the hills and vales of the forgotten heart of Wales, Red Kites are flying high with buzzards soaring by. Walk this land of solitude which waits the new explorer's mood. Sit and fish with rod and line where mountain streams and rivers twine. Then, refreshed by farmhouse fare, your adventures you can share.

Single Room per one person B&B		Double Room for two persons B&B		4
MIN £ 8.50	MAX £ 8.50	MIN £ 17.00	MAX £ 17.00	OPEN 1-12

Rhayader
Map Ref Gd2

Convenient for the lakelands (Elan and Claerwen reservoirs), pony trekking and fishing.

Guest Houses

Brynteg
East Street, Rhayader, Powys, LD6 5EA. Tel: (0597) 810052.

Family-run guest house where you can be assured of a very warm welcome and comfortable stay. Central heating, shaving points, hot and cold all rooms. T.V. lounge. 2 bathrooms with showers. Separate tables in dining room. Children half price. 3 miles from beautiful Elan Valley lakes. An ideal centre for touring Mid Wales.

Single Room per one person B&B		Double Room for two persons B&B		3
MIN £	MAX £	MIN £ 14.00	MAX £ 14.00	OPEN 4-10

Glanrhos Private House
East Street, Rhayader, Powys, LD6 5EA.
Tel: (0597) 810536. L

Glanrhos is nicely situated in the centre of Rhayader. This quaint town is close to the beautiful scenery of the Elan Valley with its reservoirs and all that goes with this part of Mid Wales. Glanrhos offers bed and breakfast, colour television lounge, children's activities. Ample car parking. Dogs accepted. Warm welcome to all guests.

Single Room per one person B&B		Double Room for two persons B&B		2
MIN £ 8.00	MAX £	MIN £ 14.00	MAX £	OPEN 3-10

The Mount
East Street, Rhayader, Powys, LD6 5DN.
Tel: (0597) 810585. L

Warm friendly welcome at the Georgian home of Pamela Powell. Tea making, hot and cold water and central heating in all bedrooms. Full cooked traditional breakfast. Beautiful Elan Valley with walking, birdwatching, pony trekking, mountain biking and fishing, three miles out of the market town of Rhayader.

Single Room per one person B&B		Double Room for two persons B&B		3
MIN £ 8.00	MAX £	MIN £ 16.00	MAX £	OPEN 4-10

Wye Lodge
South Street, Rhayader, Powys, LD6 5BH.
Tel: (0597) 810274. L

All the spacious rooms face south, overlooking the Wye alongside the garden, and have washbasins, shaver points and tea/coffee making facilities. Ground floor bedroom for disabled. Children sharing parents' room half price. Cot. Colour television. Traditional home cooking but imaginative vegetarian meals to order. Bath and shower.

Single Room per one person B&B		Double Room for two persons B&B		3
MIN £ 8.00	MAX £ 8.00	MIN £ 16.00	MAX £ 16.00	OPEN 1-12

Farmhouses

Beili Neuadd Farmhouse
AWARD

Rhayader, Powys, LD6 5NS.
Tel: (0597) 810211.

An attractive stone built farmhouse set amidst beautiful countryside in a quiet secluded position. Guests are assured of every comfort with central heating, log fires and spacious accommodation in single, double and twin bedded rooms. Shower and bathrooms. Good wholesome meals using fresh garden and farm produce. Centre for most countryside pursuits.

Single Room per one person B&B		Double Room for two persons B&B		2
MIN £ 9.00	MAX £ 9.50	MIN £ 18.00	MAX £ 19.00	OPEN 1-12

Dolifor
Llanwrthwl, Llandrindod Wells, Powys, LD1 6NU.
Tel: (0597) 810240. L

Stone built oak beamed 17th century farmhouse in quiet situation. The house is centrally heated. Guests have their own shower room and sitting room with T.V. and coffee/tea making facilities. Special diets are catered for. An R.S.P.B. Reserve adjoins the property which is set in 100 acres of farm land overlooking the River Elan.

Single Room per one person B&B		Double Room for two persons B&B		3
MIN £ 7.50	MAX £ 9.00	MIN £ 15.00	MAX £ 18.00	OPEN 3-10

Downfield Farm
Rhayader, Powys, LD6 5PA.
Enq to: Mrs. G. Price.
Tel: (0597) 810394. L

A mixed farm situated one mile east of Rhayader set off the A44 Cross Gates road. Surrounded by hills and lakes, fishing, pony trekking and good walking country nearby. We extend a warm welcome to all our guests. Three double bedrooms, all with hot and cold water. Comfortable lounge with colour television. Bed and breakfast.

Single Room per one person B&B		Double Room for two persons B&B		3
MIN £ 8.50	MAX £	MIN £ 16.00	MAX £ 17.00	OPEN 3-10

Gigrin Farm
Rhayader, Powys, LD6 5BL.
Enq. to: L. M. Powell.
Tel: (0597) 810243. L

Gigrin is a 17th century Welsh long house situated ½ mile south of Rhayader overlooking Wye Valley. Two bedrooms with washbasins, bathroom with shower. Traditional farmhouse cooking. The 200 acre hill farm offers a "farm and nature trail" to residents or anyone visiting the area. A friendly welcome awaits you.

Single Room per one person B&B		Double Room for two persons B&B		2
MIN £ 9.00	MAX £ 10.00	MIN £ 17.00	MAX £ 18.00	OPEN 4-11

SOUTH WALES

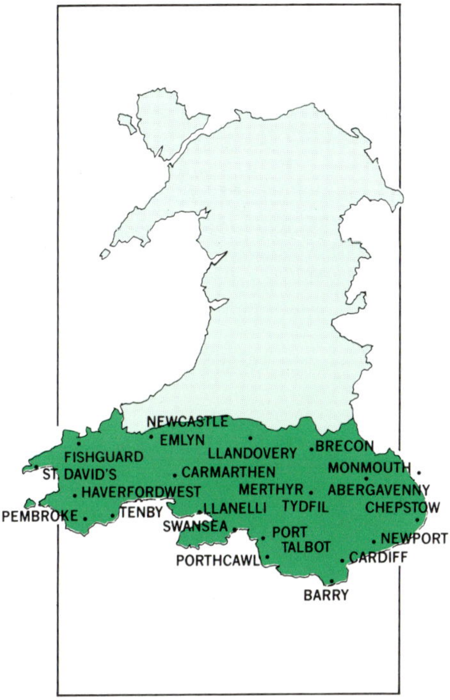

Go west as far as the sea-cliffs of the Pembrokeshire Coast National Park, where the land ends in the most spectacular of fashions. The mountains are fresh, green and graceful in South Wales's second national park – the Brecon Beacons. Rivers such as the Wye, Usk, Teifi and Tywi have carved out for themselves beautiful vales dotted with charming old country towns. And there's more magnificent shoreline stretching from the evocative, silent sands of Carmarthen Bay, around the lovely Gower Peninsula to Glamorgan's impressive Heritage Coast.

South Wales is a holiday area of sharp and unexpected contrasts. Dylan Thomas's sleepy sea town of Laugharne is just down the coast from the pretty, boat-filled harbours at Saundersfoot and Tenby. Tiny St. David's is an hour's drive from the waterfalls, woods, woollen mills and coracles of the Teifi Valley. Cardiff, Wales's capital, and breezy Swansea, two cities by the sea, are on the doorstep of the great outdoors in the Brecon Beacons. And close by are the intriguing Welsh Valleys, birthplace of industry and an area of surprising, dramatic beauty.

Pembrokeshire was described as a 'land of magic and enchantment' way back in medieval times. It's the same today. Mile after mile – 180 in all – of beach, bay, cove and headland, teeming only with seabirds, are protected as Britain's only coastal national park. Gower's superb shoreline and the weaving, wooded Wye Valley are also protected, thanks to their official 'Outstanding Beauty' status. South Wales's attractions are equally outstanding. Visit mysterious prehistoric sites linked with Stonehenge, a unique Roman gold mine, castles by the score, showcaves, wildlife parks – even an old coalmine, now open to visitors.

PEMBROKESHIRE

It's impossible to do justice to this incomparable 180-mile national park coast in a mere 100 words. We can only pick out just some of the highlights. Cliffs and sea-pinnacles rise sheer out the waves at Stack Rocks. Wild surf crashes onto the Dale Penisula's remote shores. The sheltered, still waters of the Milford Haven, with their new marina developments and river cruises, wind their way inland to historic Haverfordwest.

Porthgain, on the undiscovered northern coast, has unusual beauty. Peace settles over the tiny cathedral city of St. David's and the headlands around Fishguard. The sands at Newgale, Broad Haven and away-from-it-all Marloes are superb. Inland, there are the haunting, mysterious Preseli Hills. Pembrokeshire's beauty extends to its stylish main resorts of Tenby – a cliff-top jewel and neighbouring Saundersfoot, a popular water sports centre. And attractions extend inland to nearby Narberth, where the new, action-packed Oakwood Leisure Park has something for everyone.

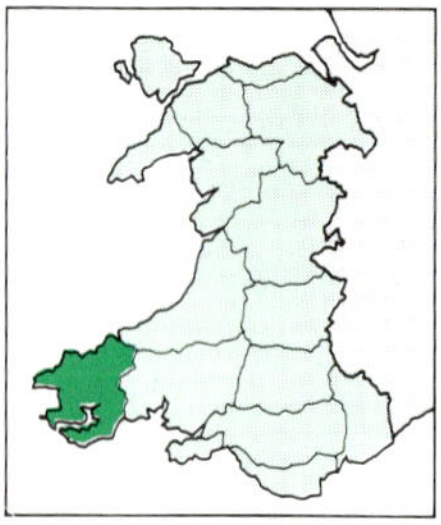

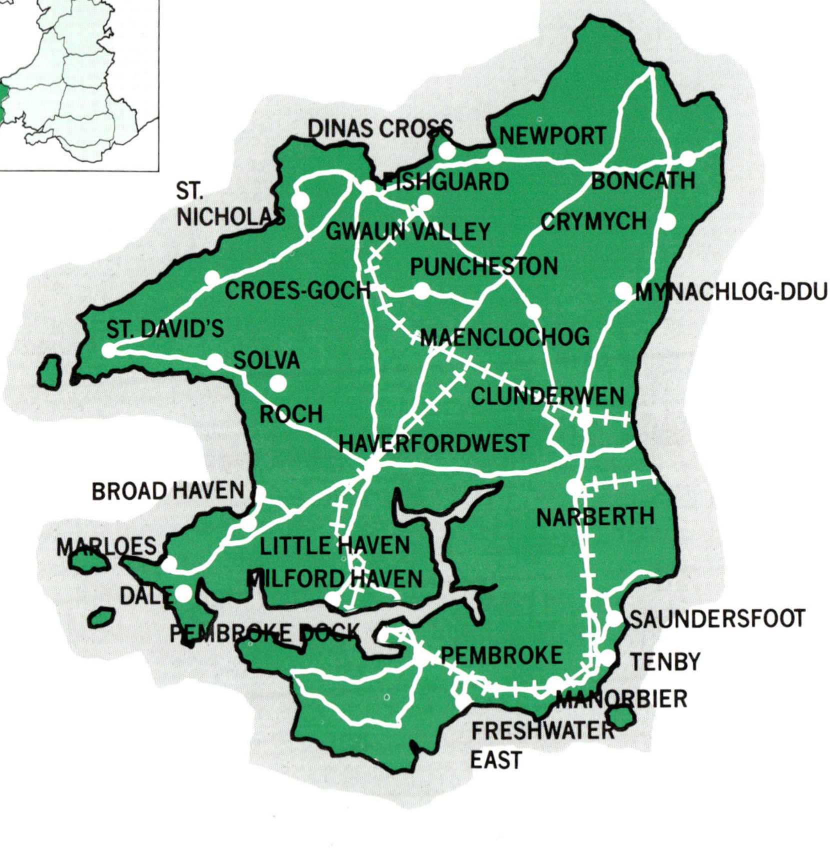

Boncath
Map Ref Fa6

Small village in the foothills of the Preseli Mountains on the edge of the Pembrokeshire Coast National Park.

Guest Houses

Awel-y-Grug
Boncath, Dyfed, SA37 0JP.
Tel: (023 974) 260.

2 crowns W.T.B. award winning rural licensed guest house. Hot and cold in all bedrooms. Storage heaters. Log fire. T.V. lounge. Outdoor badminton. Laundry room. Games room, darts, table tennis, etc. Cots, high chairs. Children welcome. Large garden, mown field. Plentiful home cooking including vegetarian menu. 6 miles Cardigan coast.

P	Single Room per one person B&B		Double Room for two persons B&B		4
	MIN £ 9.50	MAX £ 11.00	MIN £ 19.00	MAX £ 22.00	OPEN 1-12

Maes-yr-Haf
Boncath, Dyfed, SA37 0HR.
Tel: (023 974) 349.

Double or twin bedded rooms with lovely views, two with private cloakrooms. Large quiet gardens. Excellent home cooking, varied, imaginative menus (including vegetarian) using home grown vegetables and locally produced meat and fish whenever possible. Convenient touring centre. Beaches, mountains, rivers, forests, and varied coastline scenery within easy reach. Fishing, riding, etc. nearby.

P	Single Room per one person B&B		Double Room for two persons B&B		5
	MIN £ 9.50	MAX £ 9.50	MIN £ 19.00	MAX £ 19.00	OPEN 1-12

Broad Haven
Map Ref Jb5

Sand and velvet green hills cradle this village in the midst of one of the most beautiful stretches of the Pembrokeshire Coast National Park. Good beach, accommodation, shops.

Hotels

Galleon Inn
35 Enfield Road, Broad Haven,
Nr. Haverfordwest, Dyfed.
Tel: (0437) 781467. L

Situated directly opposite Broad Haven beach. Most rooms have panoramic views of St. Bride's Bay. Set in the heart of a National Park. The area is very popular for underwater pursuits. The coastline is breathtaking. Good cooking and the friendly atmosphere at the Galleon will make it a memorable holiday, for yourself and your family.

P	Single Room per one person B&B		Double Room for two persons B&B		5
	MIN £ 9.50	MAX £ 11.50	MIN £ 18.00	MAX £ 22.00	OPEN 1-12

Guest Houses

Anchor House
Broad Haven, Haverfordwest,
Pembrokeshire, SA62 3JW.
Tel: (0437) 781542. L

Standing alongside a magnificent sandy beach, Anchor House is ideally situated for a holiday in the Pembrokeshire Coast National Park. Three double and three family rooms command superb views of St. Bride's Bay. Ample car parking. Half price for children sharing parents' room. Licensed. Fire certificate held.

P	Single Room per one person B&B		Double Room for two persons B&B		6
	MIN £ 8.00	MAX £ 10.50	MIN £ 16.00	MAX £ 21.00	OPEN 4-10

Cigfran
7 Atlantic Drive, Broad Haven
Haverfordwest, Pembrokeshire,
SA62 3JA.
Tel: (0437) 781460. L

If you like a cosy atmosphere, our home, with a sea view and a lazy cat, may be just right for you. Three pretty guest rooms (one ground floor, next to toilet). Own T.V. and tea things. Wonderful breakfasts. Pot luck suppers, including vegetarian. Come and go as you wish. We ask you not to smoke, please. (Megan Keeler).

P	Single Room per one person B&B		Double Room for two persons B&B		3
	MIN £ 8.00	MAX £ 8.00	MIN £ 16.00	MAX £ 16.00	OPEN 2-11

Glenfield
5 Atlantic Drive, Broad Haven,
Pembrokeshire, SA62 3JA.
Tel: (0437) 781502. L

A warm welcome awaits you at our comfortable guest house, with ample home cooked meals and friendly service. Hot and cold in all bedrooms. Full central heating. Colour television. Own key. 300 yards to beach and coastal path.

P	Single Room per one person B&B		Double Room for two persons B&B		4
	MIN £ 8.00	MAX £ 8.50	MIN £ 16.00	MAX £ 17.00	OPEN 1-12

Clunderwen
Map Ref Je4

Halfway between popular south Pembrokeshire and the north Cardigan coast, and central for the entire Pembrokeshire Coast National Park. The lively town of Haverfordwest is not far away. The Oakwood Leisure Park is nearby.

Farmhouses

Mount Pleasant Farm
Penffordd, Nr. Clunderwen,
Pembrokeshire, SA66 7HY.
Tel: (099 12) 447.

A traditional beamed farmhouse comfortably furnished, where you are assured of a warm welcome and home cooking. Evening meal if required. Mount Pleasant, with views of the Preseli Hills, is centrally situated to enjoy the castles, hill walking, fishing and beaches of Pembrokeshire. Member of Family History Society, and assistance given to searchers.

P	Single Room per one person B&B		Double Room for two persons B&B		2
	MIN £ 9.00	MAX £ 9.00	MIN £ 18.00	MAX £ 18.00	OPEN 1-12

Croes-goch
Map Ref Jb3

Small village, useful spot for touring north and west of the Pembrokeshire Coast National Park and nearby holiday centres of St Davids and Fishguard.

Farmhouses

Trearched Farm Guest House
Croes-goch, Haverfordwest, Dyfed,
SA62 5JP.
Tel: (034 83) 310.

Trearched is a 100 acre arable farm. Guests are accommodated in an old, centrally heated farmhouse. Two single, two twin bedded, three double bedrooms, all with H & C, shaver points. Footpath link to coastal footpath at Tre-fin. AA and RAC listed. Farmhouse Award certificate W.T.B. Spacious grounds. Self catering also available for two. Two crowns.

P	Single Room per one person B&B		Double Room for two persons B&B		7
	MIN £ 10.00	MAX £ 12.00	MIN £ 20.00	MAX £ 22.00	OPEN 2-11

Crymych
Map Ref Fa7

Centre of an upland farming area, good walking and hiking on the gentle slopes of the Preseli Hills. Handy for the sandy bays of north Pembrokeshire and Cardigan Bay.

Guest Houses

Gwelfor Guest House
Blaenffos, Nr. Crymych, Dyfed,
SA37 0DS.
Tel: (0239 73) 599.

Special activities and interests for all within ten miles of Gwelfor, the small country guest house. Excellent traditional/vegetarian breakfast/dinners. C/heating, tea equipment, H & C all rooms. Two rooms shower, toilet en-suite. Situated six miles south of Cardigan on A478 Tenby road looking onto Preseli mountains. Special rates per week including three course dinner.

Single Room per one person B&B		Double Room for two persons B&B		4
MIN £	MAX £	MIN £	MAX £	OPEN
10.00	12.00	20.00	24.00	1-12

Iet-y-Banadl
Glandwr, Hebron, Whitland, Dyfed,
SA34 0XY.
Tel: (099 47) 444. L

Situated in peaceful valley near Preseli Hills, old stone cottage with lovely views. Good food, home grown produce. Evening meal available. Tea/coffee making facilities in bedrooms. Walkers welcome. Ideal base for touring Pembrokeshire and Cardiganshire.

Single Room per one person B&B		Double Room for two persons B&B		3
MIN £	MAX £	MIN £	MAX £	OPEN
6.50		13.00		4-10

Farmhouses

Penlan Uchaf
Crymych, Dyfed, SA41 3RB.
Tel: (023 973) 257. L

We offer personal friendly service to a high standard and very comfortable accommodation on our 150 acre upland farm. 2 bedrooms with tea and coffee making facilities, 1 with H & C. Guest bathroom. Sitting room with beamed ceiling and colour T.V. 3 course E.M. by arrangement. Good home cooking served with style. Riding, beaches nearby.

Single Room per one person B&B		Double Room for two persons B&B		2
MIN £	MAX £	MIN £	MAX £	OPEN
			23.00	4-10

Dale
Map Ref Jb6

Sheltered yachting village. Henry VII landed near here and marched on to take the crown at the Battle of Bosworth Field in 1485. Many good beaches nearby. Skokholm and Skomer Islands just off the coast – both havens for sea birds.

Hotels

The Post House Hotel
Dale, Haverfordwest, Dyfed,
SA62 3RE.
Tel: (064 65) 201.

Licensed family-run hotel, one hundred yards from bay in National Park. Seven letting rooms, three with en-suite facilities, showers in most of the others. Residents' television lounge, large conservatory. Restaurant serving local crab, sewin, salmon and lobster in season. Ideal for walking, birdwatching, sailing, windsurfing, visiting the islands of Skomer and Skokholm. Closed in February.

Single Room per one person B&B		Double Room for two persons B&B		7
MIN £	MAX £	MIN £	MAX £	OPEN
11.00	11.00	20.00	24.00	1-12

Dinas Cross
Map Ref Jd2

A small village on the coast road down to Fishguard, with lovely coastal and hill surroundings. Within the Pembrokeshire National Park boundaries and not far from the Pentre Ifan stone age cromlech.

Farmhouses

Cilwenen Hill
Dinas Cross, Pembrokeshire,
SA42 0XU.
Tel: (034 86) 239.

Just off main road with superb views overlooking beach and woodland. Footpath down to beach to link up Pembrokeshire National Park coastal path. Guests welcome all year. Tea, coffee all rooms. Ideally placed for touring. Dining room with separate tables, lounge with colour T.V. Children welcome. Ample parking.

Single Room per one person B&B		Double Room for two persons B&B		2
MIN £	MAX £	MIN £	MAX £	OPEN
10.00		20.00		1-12

Fishguard
Map Ref Jc2

Lower Fishguard is a cluster of old wharfs and cottages about a beautiful harbour. 'Under Milk Wood' with Richard Burton was filmed here in 1971. Good shopping in Fishguard town. Good walks along the Pembrokeshire coastal path and in the country. Nearby Goodwick is the Irish ferry terminal with a direct rail link to London. Excellent range of craft workshops in the area.

Guest Houses

Coach House Cottage
Glendower Square, Goodwick,
Fishguard, Dyfed, SA64 0DH.
Tel: (0348) 873660. L

Charming stone cottage overlooking Fishguard Bay. 5 minutes walk from ferry. Colour T.V., central heating. Ideal base for touring and quiet holidays. Walkers welcome, convenient for coastal path. Good home cooking, evening meal by arrangement. Special diets catered for, vegetarian food a speciality. Painting and calligraphy lessons available. Always a warm welcome.

Single Room per one person B&B		Double Room for two persons B&B		2
MIN £	MAX £	MIN £	MAX £	OPEN
9.00		18.00		1-12

Hamilton Guest House
Hamilton Street, Fishguard, Dyfed,
SA65 9HL.
Tel: (0348) 873834. L

Centrally situated in Fishguard within one hundred yards of Pembrokeshire coastal path. Hot and cold in all bedrooms. Bathroom with separate shower. Single, double and family rooms with speical rates for children under twelve sharing family room. Lounge with colour television. Central heating, babysitting available. Supper licence. Late night ferry bookings accepted.

Single Room per one person B&B		Double Room for two persons B&B		5
MIN £	MAX £	MIN £	MAX £	OPEN
10.00	10.50	18.00	19.50	1-12

High Fields Guest House
48 St. David's Road, Letterston,
Dyfed, SA62 5SJ.
Tel: (0348) 840461. L

Detached house set in an ideal spot for touring the West Wales coast. Close to lovely Fishguard Bay with its adjoining beaches, and near Irish ferry. Haverfordwest only 10 miles away. Central heating. Large car parking area. Colour television lounge. Hot and cold in all rooms.

Single Room per one person B&B		Double Room for two persons B&B		3
MIN £	MAX £	MIN £	MAX £	OPEN
9.00	10.00	18.00	20.00	1-12

Hillside

Bryn Henllan, Dinas Cross, Dyfed,
SA42 0SE.
Tel: (034 86) 467. L

Overlooking Dinas Island, Fishguard and Newport Bays, just 800m from the safe and secluded beach of Pwll Gwaelod. Fully centrally heated detached house of character and grounds. Lounge with colour T.V., tea making facilities. All bedrooms have hidden vanity units. Walkers and ferry travellers welcome. Good and sensible cooking in a relaxed and welcome atmosphere.

	Single Room per one person B&B		Double Room for two persons B&B		4
	MIN £ 8.50	MAX £ 10.00	MIN £ 17.00	MAX £ 20.00	OPEN 1-12

Llys Mair Guest House

High Street, Fishguard, Dyfed,
SA65 9AU.
Tel: (0348) 874515.

Ideal centre for North Pembrokeshire. Spacious accommodation in former Georgian vicarage. Residential licence, evening meals, T.V. lounge, drying facilities for walkers, private off street parking.

	Single Room per one person B&B		Double Room for two persons B&B		4
	MIN £ 10.00	MAX £ 11.00	MIN £ 20.00	MAX £ 22.00	OPEN 1-12

55 West Street

Fishguard, Dyfed, SA65 9NG.
Tel: (0384) 873592. L

Town house close to centre of Fishguard. Large car park to rear. Television lounge. Hot and cold in all rooms. Near ferry port, late night arrivals welcome. Reductions for children. Large comfortable rooms all C.H. Golf, fishing, sea and river, riding, excellent sailing facilities and spectacular walks.

	Single Room per one person B&B		Double Room for two persons B&B		3
	MIN £ 8.50	MAX £ 9.00	MIN £ 17.00	MAX £ 18.00	OPEN 1-12

Farmhouses

Erw-Lon Farm

Pontfaen, Fishguard, Dyfed,
SA65 9TS.
Tel: (034 882) 297.

A comfortable working farm of beef and sheep at foot of Preseli Hills overlooking the Gwaun Valley. Central for touring, visiting historical places, coastal path, walking. All bedrooms with hot and cold and shaver points. Dining room with separate tables. Colour T.V. in lounge. Bathroom with separate shower. Good home cooking. Homely atmosphere.

	Single Room per one person B&B		Double Room for two persons B&B		3
	MIN £ 9.00	MAX £ 12.00	MIN £ 18.00	MAX £ 24.00	OPEN 3-10

Gilfach Goch Farmhouse

AWARD

Fishguard, Dyfed, SA65 9SR.
Tel: (0348) 873871.

Attractive smallholding 2 miles Fishguard. National Park situation with magnificent views of sea and countryside. Stone farmhouse with interesting books/antiques, set in lawns/gardens. Pretty bedrooms (hot and cold), tea/coffee, some T.V.'s. Residential licence. Fire certificate. Farmhouse Award. Grid ref. SM982373. Contact June Devonald for colour brochure and details.

	Single Room per one person B&B		Double Room for two persons B&B		5
	MIN £ 8.50	MAX £ 10.00	MIN £ 17.00	MAX £ 20.00	OPEN 1-12

Freshwater East

Map Ref Jd6

Sheltered sandy bay backed by dunes.

Guest Houses

Seahorses

Freshwater East, Pembroke, Dyfed,
SA71 5LA. Tel: (0646) 672405.

Ideal touring centre within Pembrokeshire National Park, close to many sandy beaches, overlooking the sea and close to the famous coastal footpath. The guest house is centrally heated with a colour television lounge and good home cooking. Friendly service. Car park. The popular resort of Tenby is only 8 miles away and Pembroke 3 miles.

	Single Room per one person B&B		Double Room for two persons B&B		3
	MIN £	MAX £	MIN £ 17.00	MAX £ 24.00	OPEN 3-11

Gwaun Vallev (Nr. Fishguard)

Map Ref Jd3

In the Pembrokeshire Coast National Park, it runs through the hills, between the coastal towns of Fishguard and Newport.

Hotels

Gellifawr Country House

Pontfaen, Fishguard, Dyfed,
SA65 9TX. Tel: (0239) 820343. L

Nestling at foot of Preseli Hills, overlooking the famous Gwaun Valley in the Pembrokeshire National Park. Small family-run hotel with licensed bar and restaurant. Single, double and family rooms with special rates for children. Heated swimming pool. Seasonal bargain breaks available. Ideally situated for walking, fishing, trekking, golf and beaches. Also self-catering units.

	Single Room per one person B&B		Double Room for two persons B&B		9
	MIN £ 11.00	MAX £ 12.00	MIN £ 22.00	MAX £ 24.00	OPEN 1-12

Farmhouses

Tregynon Farmhouse

AWARD

Pontfaen, Nr. Fishguard, Dyfed,
SA65 9TU. Tel: (0239) 820531.

Comfortable beamed 16th century farmhouse in foothills of Preseli mountains in Pembrokeshire Coast National Park. Magnificent views, ancient oaken forest, abundant wildlife, nearby coastal path offers paradise. Renowed cuisine, own trout, wholefood and vegetarian specialities. Licensed. Central heating, log fires. Joint winner Wales Farm Holiday Guide award. International vegetarian handbook 3 star award. AA listed. RAC "acclaimed". 4 rooms available at rate quoted.

	Single Room per one person B&B		Double Room for two persons B&B		6
	MIN £ 12.00	MAX £	MIN £ 24.00	MAX £	OPEN 1-12

Haverfordwest

Map Ref Jc5

Ideal base for exploring the Pembrokeshire Coast Natioonal Park, this town is the main administrative and shopping centre for the area. Medieval churches and narrow streets. Graham Sutherland collection in Picton Castle, a few miles east. Art galleries in the town.

Hotels

Portfield Hotel

Hawthorn Rise, Haverfordwest,
Dyfed, SA61 2BA. Tel: (0437) 3257.

Licensed hotel with breathtaking views. Convenient for sea, British Ferries Sealink/B&I to and from Eire. Ideal for family holidays and suitable for disabled. Substantial discounts for university field study groups, coach parties and other outdoor pursuits. Small children sharing parents' room have free accommodation. Convenient for shops and town centre. For colour brochure contact proprietress: Mrs. Gwenda Griffiths on (0437) 3257.

	Single Room per one person B&B		Double Room for two persons B&B		15
	MIN £ 9.50	MAX £ 9.50	MIN £ 19.00	MAX £ 19.00	OPEN 1-12

Guest Houses

Abbots Leigh

Chapel Road, Keeston, Nr.
Haverfordwest, Dyfed, SA62 6HL.
Tel: (0437) 710556. L

Small friendly establishment with beautiful views of Preseli Hills. Swimming, surfing, lovely beaches and the coastal path are nearby. Guests have their own bathroom. There is colour T.V. and central heating. Special terms for children. Babysitting undertaken. Home grown and home cooked evening meals. One family and one single room.

	Single Room per one person B&B		Double Room for two persons B&B		2
	MIN £ 7.00	MAX £ 7.00	MIN £ 14.00	MAX £ 14.00	OPEN 1-12

Ashdale House

Llangwm, Haverfordwest, Dyfed,
SA62 4NX.
Tel: (0646) 601587.

Ashdale is a 16th century former hunting lodge set in 3 acres of wooded countryside. 3 double, 1 single bedrooms, 1 en-suite, 2 with vanity units/shaver points, tea/coffee making facilities. Lounge with colour T.V./video. Separate dining room. Friendly, informal amosphere. Good home cooking using fresh local produce. Car advisable. Large car park. 10 minutes walk to River Cleddau.

P	Single Room per one person B&B		Double Room for two persons B&B		3
	MIN £	MAX £	MIN £	MAX £	OPEN
	8.00	9.00	16.00	18.00	1-12

College Guest House

St. Thomas Green, Haverfordwest,
Dyfed, SA61 1QX.
Tel: (0437) 3710.

Family-run guest house. Central heating, T.V. all rooms. Car park opposite. Situated top of town. Central for touring Pembrokeshire and coastal paths etc.

P	Single Room per one person B&B		Double Room for two persons B&B		5
	MIN £	MAX £	MIN £	MAX £	OPEN
	10.00	11.00	20.00	24.00	1-12

North Headborough

Dale Road, Walwyn's Castle,
Haverfordwest, Dyfed, SA62 3AE.
Tel: (0437) 781585.

Non smoking, comfortable farm guest house in lovely surroundings, centrally situated for touring Pembrokeshire. We have three spotless bedrooms with washbasins and shaver points. There are two new shower rooms for guests. Our large guest lounge has a colour television and is beautifully furnished. Excellent home cooking and friendly service. Reductions for weekly bookings.

P	Single Room per one person B&B		Double Room for two persons B&B		3
	MIN £	MAX £	MIN £	MAX £	OPEN
	12.00	12.00	21.00	24.00	1-12

Farmhouses

Cuckoo Mill Farm

Pelcomb Bridge, Haverfordwest,
Dyfed, SA62 6EA.
Tel: (0437) 2139. L

Situated peacefully in central Pembrokeshire. Two miles out of Haverfordwest. Six miles coastline walks, beaches. Mixed livestock working farm. Two comfortable bedrooms each with night storage heater, toilet, bathroom. Lounge with T.V. and open fire. Personal attention. Good home cooking using home produce. Evening meal at short notice. Children welcome.

P	Single Room per one person B&B		Double Room for two persons B&B		2
	MIN £	MAX £	MIN £	MAX £	OPEN
	8.00	9.00	16.00	18.00	1-12

Dreenhill Farm

Dale Road, Haverfordwest, Dyfed,
SA62 3XG.
Enq. to: Mrs. G. M. Warren.
Tel: (0437) 4494. L

Small dairy farm 100 yards off B4327, conveniently situated 2 miles Haverfordwest and 3 miles Pembrokeshire Coast National Park. Three comfortable bedrooms, one with twin beds, two with single beds (additional folding bed available). Guests' bathroom with W.C. Central heating. Non smokers. Tea/coffee facilities. Wide choice of breakfast. Reduction for over 3 nights.

P	Single Room per one person B&B		Double Room for two persons B&B		3
	MIN £	MAX £	MIN £	MAX £	OPEN
			10.00	20.00	1-12

Little Haven

Map Ref Jb5

With Broad Haven over the headland, the villages form a complete family seaside holiday centre in the Pembrokeshire Coast National Park. The houses here tumble down to a pretty sandy beach which runs non-stop to Broad Haven. Sailing, swimming and surfing popular here.

Guest Houses

Valley View

Strawberry Hill, Little Haven, Nr.
Haverfordwest, Dyfed, SA62 3UT.
Tel: (0437) 781227. L

Comfortable, peaceful bungalow with quiet relaxed atmosphere and views over wooded country. Two twin bedrooms, H/C, shaver points, central heating. Large living room, colour T.V. Substantial breakfasts. Tea/coffee always available. Easy access to renowned scenic coastal path, minutes walk from picturesque fishing village with sandy beaches. Three excellent hostelries, bistro and shops.

P	Single Room per one person B&B		Double Room for two persons B&B		2
	MIN £	MAX £	MIN £	MAX £	OPEN
			18.00	20.00	3-12

Maenclochog

Map Ref Je3

Typical Pembrokeshire village south of Preseli Hills. Llys-y-Fran Reservoir with its nature trails and sailing are close at hand and the area offers much opportunity for gentle hill-walking.

Farmhouses

Llandilo Isaf

Maenclochog, Clunderwen, Dyfed,
SA66 7XS.
Tel: (099 13) 488.

Pleasantly situated in peaceful wooded valley, our recently refurbished farmhouse is ideally located for beaches and many leisure pursuits including fishing, walking and golf. Four comfortable bedrooms all offer central heating, double glazing, H & C and colour television, most have en-suites. Laundry facilities and tea/coffee available. A warm welcome and good wholesome food awaits visitors. Brochures from Ian and Sylvia Mackean.

P	Single Room per one person B&B		Double Room for two persons B&B		4
	MIN £	MAX £	MIN £	MAX £	OPEN
	10.00		19.00	22.00	4-10

Manorbier

Map Ref Jd6

Manorbier was described as the 'most delightful part of Pembroke' 800 years ago. Today, it is still an unspoilt village centred around an imposing Norman castle on the coast of south Pembrokeshire. A pleasant sandy bay adds to its appeal.

Guest Houses

Y Glŷder

Manorbier, Nr. Tenby, Dyfed,
SA70 7TE.
Tel: (0834 82) 318. L

Ring us! Leave your name and address, we'll do the rest.

P	Single Room per one person B&B		Double Room for two persons B&B		7
	MIN £	MAX £	MIN £	MAX £	OPEN
	10.00	10.00	20.00	20.00	3-11

Marloes
Map Ref Jb5

A remote, sandy stretch of Pembrokeshire Coast National Park. Safe for surfing and swimming. Coast overlooking the island of Skomer, haven for puffins and other seabirds, which can be visited.

Guest Houses

Foxdale
Glebe Lane, Marloes, Haverfordwest, Dyfed, SA62 3AX.
Tel: (064 65) 527 & 243.

Family-run guest house. H.H.H. commended. Situated in National Trust country, miles coastal footpaths, boat trips to Grassholm/Skomer Island bird sanctuaries. Rooms have country views, hot and cold, washbasins, central heating. T.V. lounge. Bed and breakfast, complimentary tea facilities. Separate dining tables. Parking. Children and pets welcome. Located down first right turn by Marloes Church.

Single Room per one person B&B		Double Room for two persons B&B		Bedrooms 3
MIN £ 9.00	MAX £ 11.00	MIN £ 18.00	MAX £ 22.00	OPEN 1-12

Farmhouses

East Hook Farm
Marloes, Haverfordwest, Dyfed, SA62 3BJ.
Tel: (064 65) 291.

East Hook is a 90 acre mixed farm situated in the picturesque Pembrokeshire National Park and has a panoramic sea view. It has coastal walks and is within walking distance of many sandy beaches and only a short boat trip from Skomer Island, noted for its interesting bird life. Plenty of good food. Children welcomed.

Single Room per one person B&B		Double Room for two persons B&B		Bedrooms 4
MIN £ 9.50	MAX £ 10.50	MIN £ 19.00	MAX £ 21.00	OPEN 3-10

Milford Haven
Map Ref Jc6

Important port on the edge of the Pembrokeshire Coast National Park. Torch Theatre. Excellent touring base.

Hotels

Ferry Inn
Llanstadwell, Neyland, Milford Haven, Dyfed, SA73 1EG.
Tel: (0646) 600270.

Situated on the water's edge, enjoying fine views of the Cleddau estuary and on route of the Pembrokeshire coastal path. Our family-run inn has seven bedrooms, dining room, T.V. lounge, two licensed bars and games room. Children welcome. River front patio/garden. Close to new Neyland marina. Ideal base for touring. Car parking facilities.

Single Room per one person B&B		Double Room for two persons B&B		Bedrooms 7
MIN £ 12.00	MAX £ 12.00	MIN £ 24.00	MAX £ 24.00	OPEN 1-12

Farmhouses

Woodson Farm
Lower Thornton, Milford Haven, Dyfed, SA73 3UQ.
Tel: (0437) 890358.

AWARD

L

A warm welcome is extended to our 200 acre working farm. Good food from local produce, also special diets catered for. All rooms with hot and cold and tea making facilities. Near many lovely beaches and places of historical interest. 4 miles from the Coastal Path. Special rates for children and O.A.P.s.

Single Room per one person B&B		Double Room for two persons B&B		Bedrooms 4
MIN £ 8.00	MAX £ 8.00	MIN £ 16.00	MAX £ 16.00	OPEN 1-12

Mynachlog-ddu
Map Ref Je3

On southern approach to the Preseli Hills. Prehistoric stone circle nearby. Centrally located village for visiting rugged north Pembrokeshire coast and beaches of the south.

Guest Houses

Trefach Guest House
Mynachlog-ddu, Clunderwen, Dyfed, SA66 7RU.
Tel: (099 47) 457/565.

L

Guest house situated in beautiful Preseli hills, off Cardigan/Tenby road. Lounge, T.V. room, licensed bar, separate dining room. Five bedrooms with hot and cold, single, double and family rooms available. Family-run, providing good home cooking and a warm welcome. Fire certificate held. Own stables, riding, trekking available.

Single Room per one person B&B		Double Room for two persons B&B		Bedrooms 5
MIN £ 9.00	MAX £ 10.00	MIN £ 18.00	MAX £ 20.00	OPEN 1-12

Narberth
Map Ref Je5

Small market town, ancient castle. Convenient to the beaches of Carmarthen Bay and resorts of Tenby and Saundersfoot. Pleasant and extremely accessible little town. Nearby is the multi-activity Oakwood Leisure Park.

Hotels

Blaenmarlais Country House Hotel
Redstone Cross, Narberth, Dyfed, SA67 7ES.
Tel: (0834) 860326.

Welcome to our licensed, country house hotel, 2½ acre gardens, lovely views of countryside. 6 bedrooms en-suite, ground floor suite of 2 bedrooms/bathroom for wheelchair users. Imaginative wholesome food using fresh produce. Relax in our bar or T.V. lounge. Ideal base for touring Pembrokeshire's beautiful coastline, National Park and Preseli Hills.

Single Room per one person B&B		Double Room for two persons B&B		Bedrooms 11
MIN £ 10.00	MAX £ 11.50	MIN £ 20.00	MAX £ 21.50	OPEN 1-11

Guest Houses

Traethgwyn Guest House

Robeston Wathen, Narberth, Dyfed,
SA67 8EN.
Tel: (0834) 860598. L

Small family-run guest house, centrally situated for touring Pembrokeshire. Home cooking, home grown vegetables when available. H & C all rooms, tea/coffee making facilities, colour T.V. lounge, central heating, separate tables. Beach 8 miles. Children welcome. Send s.a.e. for terms to Mrs. Eileen Cranmer.

P	Single Room per one person B&B		Double Room for two persons B&B		3
	MIN £	MAX £	MIN £	MAX £	OPEN
	7.50	8.50	15.00	17.00	2-11

Farmhouses

Highland Grange Farm Guest House

Robeston Wathen, Narberth, Dyfed,
SA67 8EP.
Tel: (0834) 860952.

220 acre farm where all ages are welcome. Set amidst lovely countryside. Centrally situated, superior, modern farmhouse. Delicious home cooking, excellent varied menu, 4 course dinner. Morning tea, evening beverages. Lounge, colour T.V., log fires. Central heating. Ideal for families. Babysitting. Country inn 200 yards. Beach 8 miles. Adventure and leisure complex 2 miles. Fishing nearby. Brochure, enclose stamp please.

P	Single Room per one person B&B		Double Room for two persons B&B		5
	MIN £	MAX £	MIN £	MAX £	OPEN
	10.00	12.00	20.00	24.00	1-12

Newport

Map Ref Jd2

Ancient castled village on Pembrokeshire coast. Fine beaches – bas and sea trout fishing. Pentre Ifan Cromlech, burial chamber, is an impressive site, not far away. Accommodation and restaurants. Backed by the heather clad Preseli Hills.

Guest Houses

Brohedydd

Upper St. Mary's Street, Newport,
Dyfed, SA42 0PS.
Tel: (0239) 820525. L

A relaxed, well appointed family home in quiet location in centre of this attractive resort. Comfortable residents' T.V. lounge with wood burning stove. Facilities for making hot drinks etc., at all times. H & C to most bedrooms. Excellent breakfast menu. Bara lawr a speciality. Fresh ground coffee. Good pubs and restaurants close by.

	Single Room per one person B&B		Double Room for two persons B&B		3
	MIN £	MAX £	MIN £	MAX £	OPEN
	8.50	9.00	17.00	18.00	4-10

Hafan Deg

Long Street, Newport, Dyfed,
SA42 0TN.
Tel: (0239) 820301.

Hafan Deg is a very well appointed, large, modern, centrally heated private house situated in town but only a short stroll from the estuary and famous coastal path. All rooms have H & C and tea/coffee making facilities and there are 2 bathrooms. Nearby pubs and restaurants offer a wide choice of eating places.

P	Single Room per one person B&B		Double Room for two persons B&B		3
	MIN £	MAX £	MIN £	MAX £	OPEN
	9.00		18.00		1-12

Pontymeddyg

Dinas Cross, Newport, Dyfed,
SA43 0XL.
Tel: (034 86) 247.

Small guest house set in 8 acres of unspoilt coast with a path through the garden to a secluded beach. Superbly cooked dinner using home produced and local food. 3 double rooms, 1 en-suite, all facing the sea. We offer peace, quiet, stunning views and a reminder of the taste of good food.

P	Single Room per one person B&B		Double Room for two persons B&B		3
	MIN £	MAX £	MIN £	MAX £	OPEN
			11.00	22.00	4-10

"White Berries"

Long Street, Newport, Dyfed,
SA42 0TJ.
Tel: (0239) 820458. L

Spacious private house situated close to Pembrokeshire Coast Path and beach, but also near Newport's attractive town centre. Ideal for walking, birdwatching, boating, swimming, golf, tennis, fishing and riding. Buses, shops, tourist information, pubs and restaurants all nearby. Large lounge, T.V., central heating, open fire. Children welcome. Excellent evening meals available in the town.

P	Single Room per one person B&B		Double Room for two persons B&B		2
	MIN £	MAX £	MIN £	MAX £	OPEN
	8.50	10.00	17.00	18.00	1-12

Farmhouses

Argoed

Felindre Farchog, Nr. Crymych,
Dyfed, SA41 3XG.
Tel: (0239) 820768. L

Farmhouse bed and breakfast. Situated in North Pembrokeshire National Park. Beach approximately 3 miles. Families with children welcomed and catered for. Family bedroom, twin bedroom. Own bathroom and sitting room. Babysitting by arrangement. Packed lunches. Weekly or daily terms. Telephone (0239) 820768.

P	Single Room per one person B&B		Double Room for two persons B&B		2
	MIN £	MAX £	MIN £	MAX £	OPEN
	9.00	9.00	18.00	18.00	1-12

Pembroke

Map Ref Jd6

Ancient borough built around Pembroke Castle. Fascinating Museum of Gypsies. Sandy bays, yachting, fishing – all the coastal activities associated with estuaries. Plenty of things to see and do in the area around.

Guest Houses

High Noon Guest House

Lower Lamphey Road, Pembroke,
Dyfed, SA71 4AB.
Tel: (0646) 683736/681232.

Enjoy the relaxed friendly atmosphere of our family-run guest house. Easy reach castle, Pembrokeshire coastal path, beautiful beaches of Barafundle, Broad Haven, Manorbier. Family, twin, double, single rooms have hot and cold, central heating, shaver points. Ground floor room. Ample shower/toilet facilities. Child reductions. Quality home cooking. Licensed. Complimentary evening drinks served. AA listed. Brochure.

P	Single Room per one person B&B		Double Room for two persons B&B		8
	MIN £	MAX £	MIN £	MAX £	OPEN
	8.95	9.50	17.90	19.00	1-12

The Old Rectory

Cosheston, Pembroke, Dyfed,
SA72 4ST.
Tel: (0646) 684960. L

Set in two acre garden, believed to date from Norman times, The Old Rectory has tastefully furnished bedrooms, spacious lounge with colour T.V., separate dining room where home cooked food is served at times to suit. Ideal touring base, National Park, beaches and castles. Village walks. Farmyard animals to feed. Special rates for children.

P	Single Room per one person B&B		Double Room for two persons B&B		4
	MIN £	MAX £	MIN £	MAX £	OPEN
	9.00	10.00	18.00	20.00	4-10

West Farm House

Cosheston, Pembroke, Dyfed,
SA72 4UN.
Tel: (0646) 683626. L

Welcome to our listed 17th century farmhouse full of character. Situated 3 miles from Pembroke, 15 minutes from nearest beach. Centrally heated house. Beamed bedrooms, hot and cold basins, shaver points. Own comfortable lounge, colour T.V. Children especially welcome. Pets by arrangement. Parking. Very friendly attentive service to you by all the Davies family.

P	Single Room per one person B&B		Double Room for two persons B&B		3
	MIN £	MAX £	MIN £	MAX £	OPEN
	8.50	9.50	17.00	19.00	1-12

Farmhouses

Gupton Farm

Castlemartin, Pembroke, Dyfed,
SA71 5HW.
Tel: (064 681) 268. L

Pembrokeshire working dairy farm near Freshwater West beach. Comfortable friendly atmosphere. Plenty of good home cooked food. All rooms tea/coffee facilities. Two rooms have washbasins. Children welcome, half price. Guests welcome to see milking, feed calves. Situated six miles west of Pembroke, surrounded by beautiful safe sandy beaches, Broad Haven, Angle, Barafundle. Climbing at Bosherston.

Single Room per one person B&B		Double Room for two persons B&B		3
MIN £	MAX £	MIN £	MAX £	OPEN
7.50	8.50	15.00	17.00	1-12

Home Farm

Stackpole, Pembroke, Dyfed,
SA71 5DQ.
Tel: (064 681) 244. L

Friendly farmhouse offers warmth, good food, spacious family rooms with all mod cons, tea making facilities, handbasins provided in bedrooms. Sitting room with colour television. Situated 5 miles south of Pembroke on Bosherston Road, coastal path route very near beautiful sandy beaches. Special rates for children.

Single Room per one person B&B		Double Room for two persons B&B		2
MIN £	MAX £	MIN £	MAX £	OPEN
		17.00	19.00	3-10

West Farm

Castlemartin, Pembroke, Dyfed,
SA71 5HW.
Tel: (064 681) 234. L

Large dairy farm S.W.of Pembroke. Comfortable farmhouse, spacious rooms. Single, double and twin bedded rooms. Tea/coffee making facilities. Friendly relaxed atmosphere. Colour T.V. Good home cooking using fresh food. Sea 3 minutes, local beauty spots nearby. Excellent sandy beaches. Good walking, particularly on the coastal path. Children welcome at reduced rates.

Single Room per one person B&B		Double Room for two persons B&B		4
MIN £	MAX £	MIN £	MAX £	OPEN
8.00	9.00	16.00	18.00	4-9

Pembroke Dock

Map Ref Jc6

Former Naval Dockyard on Milford Haven. Pembroke Castle nearby. Ideal for fishing, sailing and walking Pembrokeshire National Park Coastal path. Cruises on River Cleddau from Hobbs Point.

Guest Houses

Roxana Guest House

Victoria Road, Pembroke Dock,
Dyfed, SA72 6XU.
Tel: (0646) 682722.

Friendly family-run guest house. H & C, centrally heated rooms with hot drinks facilities T.V. lounge. Separate dining room. Single, twin, double and family rooms. Reductions for children. Close to all amenities, including beaches, sports centre, golf course, coastal paths, coaches, trains and ferry terminal. Parking available.

Single Room per one person B&B		Double Room for two persons B&B		4
MIN £	MAX £	MIN £	MAX £	OPEN
8.00	10.00	15.00	19.00	1-12

Roch

Map Ref Jb4

Roch is a small village in mid Pembrokeshire, based around a castle (not open to the public). Near beaches, surfing at Newgale.

Guest Houses

Trefran Cottage

Roch, Haverfordwest,
Pembrokeshire, SA62 6EB.
Tel: (0437) 710503. L

A warm welcome awaits you at our comfortable, peaceful Pembrokeshire cottage. 2 minutes walk Pembrokeshire coastal path and Newgale beach. 1 mile from village. T.V. lounge/dining room and 2 double bedrooms. 1 acre gardens with panoramic views of countryside. Wonderful base for touring the county. Nearby pubs and restaurants for evening meals.

Single Room per one person B&B		Double Room for two persons B&B		2
MIN £	MAX £	MIN £	MAX £	OPEN
7.50	8.00	15.00	16.00	1-12

Saundersfoot

Map Ref Je6

Popular resort on south Pembrokeshire coast offering holiday activities – swimming, sailing, sea angling and birdwatching. Pembrokeshire Coast National Park.

Hotels

Rhodewood Lodge

St. Bride's Hill, Saundersfoot, Dyfed,
SA69 9NU.
Tel: (0834) 812922.

Friendly informal family-run hotel overlooking Carmarthen Bay, within easy walking distance village and beach. Double, single, family rooms. Teasmades, hot and cold, shaver points in all rooms. Private shower, bath if required. Comfortable lounge, colour T.V. Car parking in grounds. Dining room, separate tables. Licensed. Reductions for children. Fire certificate granted.

Single Room per one person B&B		Double Room for two persons B&B		8
MIN £	MAX £	MIN £	MAX £	OPEN
10.00	11.50	20.00	23.00	2-11

Guest Houses

Ashcroft

The Glen, Saundersfoot, Dyfed,
SA69 9NR.
Tel: (0834) 813908. L

Detached Victorian house set in quiet area overlooking woods. 5 minutes walk to beaches and shops. Large bedrooms with view of sea. Ideal base for exploring the lovely coastline, water sports or just a lazy holiday. Families welcome.

Single Room per one person B&B		Double Room for two persons B&B		2
MIN £	MAX £	MIN £	MAX £	OPEN
		16.00	18.00	4-10

Caldey Glimpse

Templebar Road, Kilgetty, Dyfed,
SA68 0RA.
Tel: (0834) 813819. L

Graham and Roberta Pickersgill extend a warm welcome to you at Caldey Glimpse guest house, which is set in pleasant surroundings close to Tenby and Saundersfoot's sandy beaches. Personal attention is assured. Twin, double, family rooms. Hot and cold all rooms. All day access. T.V. lounge. Licensed. Children welcome. Home cooking. Fire certificate.

Single Room per one person B&B		Double Room for two persons B&B		8
MIN £	MAX £	MIN £	MAX £	OPEN
8.50	8.50	17.00	17.00	1-12

Pleasant Valley Guest House

Stepaside, Nr. Saundersfoot, Dyfed,
SA67 8NY.
Tel: (0834) 813607. L

Situated 500 yards from Wiseman's Bridge beach in a beautiful wooded valley. Ample parking. Licensed bar and 32' X 16' swimming pool. Thirty minutes coastal walk into Saundersfoot. All bedrooms have H/C, bedside lights, shaving points with lighted mirrors. There are eight bedrooms and three bathrooms, large residents' lounge, dining room with separate tables. Home cooking.

	Single Room per one person B&B		Double Room for two persons B&B		8
	MIN £	MAX £	MIN £	MAX £	OPEN
	7.00	9.00	14.00	18.00	4-10

Sandy Hill Guest House

Tenby Road, Saundersfoot, Dyfed,
SA69 9DR.
Tel: (0834) 813165.

Comfortable accommodation. Guest rooms all with tea/coffee facilities and colour television. Own car park. Swimming pool. Licensed bar. AA/RAC listed. Fire certificate. Home cooking. Country aspect but only three minutes drive to Saundersfoot beach. Five minutes drive to Tenby. Personal service. Solely run by proprietors Peggy and David Edwards offering warm welcome.

	Single Room per one person B&B		Double Room for two persons B&B		5
	MIN £	MAX £	MIN £	MAX £	OPEN
	9.00	10.50	18.00	21.00	3-10

Springfield Guest House

St. Bride's Hill, Saundersfoot, Dyfed,
SA69 9NP.
Tel: (0834) 813518.

Small guest house overlooking Carmarthen Bay. 5 minutes walk to beach, shops, harbour. All rooms H/C, some en-suite, all with shaver points, central heating. Colour T.V. lounge. Quiet lounge. Parking. Tea making facilities. Children welcome, reduction for children sharing rooms. Assured of a warm friendly welcome. Good home cooking. Full fire certificate held. Residential licence.

	Single Room per one person B&B		Double Room for two persons B&B		5
	MIN £	MAX £	MIN £	MAX £	OPEN
	8.50	9.50	17.00	19.00	4-10

Farmhouses

Carne Mountain Farm

Reynalton, Kilgetty, Dyfed,
SA68 0PD.
Tel: (0834) 860546. L

Warm welcome. 3½ miles from beautiful Saundersfoot beach and harbour. Good farmhouse food, evening meal by arrangement. Comfortable lounge. Tea making facilities. Pretty south facing bedrooms, with hot and cold. Ample car parking. Ideally situated for touring Pembrokeshire National Park, magnificent coastal path and lovely Preseli hills.

	Single Room per one person B&B		Double Room for two persons B&B		2
	MIN £	MAX £	MIN £	MAX £	OPEN
	6.50	7.00	13.00	14.00	3-10

Heatherton Farm

Devonshire Drive, Saundersfoot,
Dyfed, SA69 9EE.
Tel: (0834) 813343.

Spacious new bungalow situated on dairy farm 2½ miles Saundersfoot, 4 miles Tenby. Riding stables and country pub nearby. Good home cooking. Single, double and family room available, H & C in most rooms. Lounge and separate T.V. lounge. Dining room with separate tables. Full size snooker table for guests' use. Special rates for children.

	Single Room per one person B&B		Double Room for two persons B&B		3
	MIN £	MAX £	MIN £	MAX £	OPEN
	8.00	9.00	16.00	18.00	6-10

Little Newton Farm

Kilgetty, Dyfed, SA68 0YD.
Tel: (0834) 312306.

7 acre smallholding situated 5 miles from Tenby, 2½ miles Saundersfoot. Hot and cold in all bedrooms with heaters and shaving points. 2 bathrooms, 2 shower rooms. Excellent meals. Licensed club nearby. Also cricket 50 yards. Bus stop 200 yards. AA listed.

	Single Room per one person B&B		Double Room for two persons B&B		9
	MIN £	MAX £	MIN £	MAX £	OPEN
	8.50	9.50	17.00	19.00	4-9

Vine Farm

The Ridgeway, Saundersfoot, Dyfed,
SA69 9LA.
Tel: (0834) 813543.

Robert and Mary Maxwell invite you to their lovely old farmhouse, peacefully situated on the outskirts of Saundersfoot, just ½ mile from the village centre and beaches. As ex-restauranteurs our food is our great pride, using fresh local produce. En-suite rooms available with colour T.V. Safe secure car parking. Central heating. Summer house in large lawn area with fish pond.

	Single Room per one person B&B		Double Room for two persons B&B		6
	MIN £	MAX £	MIN £	MAX £	OPEN
	11.00	12.00	22.00	24.00	3-11

Solva
Map Ref Jb4

Pembrokeshire coast village with small attractive harbour and good craft shops. Pembrokeshire Coast Path offers good walking. Exotic butterflies at Nectarium.

Farmhouses

Llanddinog Old Farmhouse

Solva, Haverfordwest, Dyfed,
SA62 6NA.
Tel: (034 83) 224.

Peaceful 16th century farmstead. Ideal base for beaches, fishing, riding, walking. Close to St. David's and Preseli Hills. Homely atmosphere (log fires). Substantial meals using mainly home produced foodstuffs. Children's reductions. 3 family, 1 single, washbasins. Central heating, colour television, dining room, 2 lounges. Picnics. Dogs accepted. Washing, drying facilities. High chair, cot. Parking. Play area. Small animals and birds.

	Single Room per one person B&B		Double Room for two persons B&B		4
	MIN £	MAX £	MIN £	MAX £	OPEN
	9.00	9.50	18.00	19.00	1-12

Upper Vanley Farm

AWARD

Solva, Haverfordwest,
Pembrokeshire, SA62 6LJ.
Tel: (034 83) 418/7728.

Upper Vanley is a 150 acre dairy farm situated centre of St. David's Peninsula, 2½ miles Newgale Sands, 4 miles from Solva harbour. The award winning, centrally heated farmhouse has 8 spacious bedrooms with colour T.V., tea making facilities, electric blankets, hot and cold. 4 rooms with private bathrooms. Traditional farmhouse cooking with choice of meals. Chidren welcome with earlier meals if required. Brochure and literature available. RAC/AA listed.

	Single Room per one person B&B		Double Room for two persons B&B		8
	MIN £	MAX £	MIN £	MAX £	OPEN
	8.00	10.00	16.00	20.00	1-12

St. David's
Map Ref Ja4

Smallest cathedral city in Britain, shrine of Wales's patron saint. Ruined Bishop's Palace beside cathedral. Fine beaches in the surrounding area along the Pembrokeshire Coast National Park. Walking, birdwatching, painting courses are popular pastimes. Range of accommodation. A village with great character.

Guest Houses

Alandale Guest House
43 Nun Street, St. David's, Dyfed,
SA62 6NU.
Tel: (0437) 720333.

RAC/AA. Victorian guest house situated within St. David's, close to the cathedral, beaches and beauty spots. Hot and cold, 2 showers, 2 toilets, 1 bathroom, shaver points, central heating. Tea facilities in all bedrooms. T.V. lounge. Coastal view from bedrooms. Home cooking at its best. Dining room with original beams. Weekly rates available.

	Single Room per one person B&B		Double Room for two persons B&B		6
	MIN £	MAX £	MIN £	MAX £	OPEN
	10.00		20.00		1-12

Cwmwdig Water Guest House
Berea, St. David's, Dyfed,
SA62 6DW.
Tel: (034 83) 434.

A beautiful converted farmhouse and barn in superb country position overlooking Aber Eiddi Bay. Beamed restaurant, bar and large lounge, open fires, television lounge, guest kitchen. All rooms with hot drinks facilities, washbasins, etc. and heating. Many with sea view, some showers. Relaxed atmoshpere and high quality food. Credit cards accepted. Child reductions. Brochure on request.

P	Single Room per one person B&B		Double Room for two persons B&B		10
	MIN £	MAX £	MIN £	MAX £	OPEN
	10.00		20.00		3-10

Y Glennydd Guest House
51 Nun Street, St. David's, Dyfed,
SA62 6NU.
Tel: (0437) 720576.

AA, RAC, Routier recommended. Ten spacious rooms, many with splendid view, all with H & C, tea making facilities and centrally heated. Licensed. Old fashioned style and hospitality. Modern creature comforts. Special shower facilities.

	Single Room per one person B&B		Double Room for two persons B&B		10
	MIN £	MAX £	MIN £	MAX £	OPEN
	10.00		20.00		3-10

Ramsey Guest House
Lower Moor, St. David's, Dyfed.
SA62 6PR.
Tel: (0437) 720321.

Comfortable licensed guest house providing warm welcome, personal service and imaginative Welsh cooking. Close to St. David's Cathedral and Pembrokeshire coast path. Ideal base for touring in all seasons; helpful advice on places to visit. All rooms have hot and cold, shaver points, complimentary tea/coffee facilities. Walkers and dogs welcome. Weekend packages October/March, also Christmas.

P	Single Room per one person B&B		Double Room for two persons B&B		7
	MIN £	MAX £	MIN £	MAX £	OPEN
	12.00		24.00		1-12

Redcliffe House
17 New Street, St. David's, Dyfed,
SA62 6SW.
Tel: (0437) 720389.

A comfortable house with 5 rooms. Tea/coffee making facilities, hot and cold, shaver points, colour T.V. Separate tables in dining room. Lounge. Some parking space. AA/RAC listed. Member of Guestaccom good room award. Highly recommended personal service.

P	Single Room per one person B&B		Double Room for two persons B&B		5
	MIN £	MAX £	MIN £	MAX £	OPEN
			20.00	22.00	3-10

Farmhouses

Olmarch Farm
Llandeloy, Haverfordwest, Dyfed,
SA62 6NB.
Tel: (034 83) 247. L

Modernised, centrally heated stone farmhouse. Bedrooms comfortable, one en-suite shower, washbasin. Good home cooking, and evening meal by arrangement. Comfortable lounge with colour T.V. and video. Situated 10 minutes drive from many beautiful sandy beaches. 6 miles St. David's and 10 miles Fishguard. Children welcome.

P	Single Room per one person B&B		Double Room for two persons B&B		3
	MIN £	MAX £	MIN £	MAX £	OPEN
	10.00	12.00	16.00	18.00	4-10

Torbant Farm Guest House
Croes-goch, Haverfordwest, Dyfed,
SA62 5JN.
Tel: (034 83) 276.

Comfortable friendly farmhouse with good home cooking, near St. David's and coast. All bedrooms have central heating and H & C. Colour T.V. lounge. Spacious bar and dining room. Children welcome with reduced rates and early suppers if wanted. Useful utility room for picnic preparation, washing, tea/coffee making. AA/RAC listed. British Relais Routier. S.a.e. please: Mrs. B. B. Charles.

P	Single Room per one person B&B		Double Room for two persons B&B		7
	MIN £	MAX £	MIN £	MAX £	OPEN
	10.00	11.50	20.00	23.00	3-10

Trevaccoon Farm
St. David's, Haverfordwest,
Pembrokeshire, SA62 6DP.
Tel: (034 83) 438.

AWARD

Trevaccoon is a working dairy farm. 17th century modernised farmhouse situated on the coast, north of St. Davids's between Aber Eiddi Bay and Porthgain. Spacious rooms have private bathrooms, heating and breathtaking coastal views. T.V. lounge. Annex for tea and coffee making. Ideal for walking and touring the Peninsula. Free golf. Children welcome. Farmhouse Award.

P	Single Room per one person B&B		Double Room for two persons B&B		5
	MIN £	MAX £	MIN £	MAX £	OPEN
	10.00	10.00	20.00	20.00	1-12

Upper Eweston Farmhouse
Roch, Haverfordwest, Dyfed,
SA62 6JY.
Tel: (0437) 710109.

Away from main road but close to miles of unspoilt coastline with Newgale beach, the Coastal Path (National Park) and the bird sanctuary island of Skomer. Friendly relaxed atmosphere with good home cooking (home baked bread and free range eggs). Lounge with log fires. Evening meal. All bedrooms with H & C and shaver points. Brochure.

P	Single Room per one person B&B		Double Room for two persons B&B		3
	MIN £	MAX £	MIN £	MAX £	OPEN
			17.00	18.00	1-12

St. Nicholas
Map Ref Jc3

Pembrokeshire village on northern coast, a land of many hidden beaches. Near interesting old town of Fishguard, and the coastal path for walking and enjoying the distinctive landscape.

Farmhouses

New Mill
Tregwynt, Nr. St. Nicholas,
Letterston, Haverfordwest, Dyfed,
SA62 5UX.
Tel: (034 85) 637.

AWARD

A small traditional farm set in peaceful valley amidst stream and woodlands, off the A487 Fishguard/St. David's road. Half mile walk or drive from unspoilt beaches of Abermawr, Aberbach and coastal footpath. H & C each bedroom. Central heating. Colour T.V. lounge. Car parking. Excellent cuisine, home organic grown produce, free range eggs, meat. Special diets. Evening meals.

P	Single Room per one person B&B		Double Room for two persons B&B		3
	MIN £	MAX £	MIN £	MAX £	OPEN
			24.00		3-11

Tenby
Map Ref Je6

Popular South Pembrokeshire resort with two wide beaches. Fishing trips are arranged from the attractive Georgian harbour. Also boat trips to nearby Caldy Island. The medieval walled town has fine Tudor buildings. Several art galleries, pottery, museum, bowls, putting, golf. Regatta and Carnival in August.

Hotels

Ashby House
Victoria Street, Tenby,
Pembrokeshire, Dyfed, SA70 7DY.
Tel: (0834) 2867.

Superbly situated 60 yards from South Beach and approximately 150 yards from town centre. All bedrooms have the usual amenities, including tea/coffee makers and free heating. Double, twin, single and family rooms available, some with private facilities and sea view. Please write or telephone for free colour brochure and tariff: Mr. and Mrs. R. Sarrionandia.

Single Room per one person B&B		Double Room for two persons B&B		10
MIN £ 8.50	MAX £ 12.00	MIN £ 17.00	MAX £ 24.00	OPEN 4-10

The Croyland Hotel
10 Deer Park, Tenby, Dyfed,
SA70 7LE.
Tel: (0834) 3880. L

A comfortable, homely hotel 300 yards from town centre and beaches. T.V., video. Tea and coffee in all bedrooms. Good home cooking. Quiet lounge. Friendly bar. Excellent golf course within walking distance. Reduced rates for children. Evening meal by arrangement. Full fire certificate. A warm welcome awaits you from Tony and Marcia Theobald.

Single Room per one person B&B		Double Room for two persons B&B		9
MIN £ 8.00	MAX £ 9.00	MIN £ 16.00	MAX £ 18.00	OPEN 1-12

Paragon Hotel
The Paragon, Tenby, Dyfed,
SA70 7HL.
Tel: (0834) 3022.

Within town walls on seafront. Magnificent views over Carmarthen Bay, Caldy Island and Saint Catherine's Island. Steps to the beach 20 yards from hotel. Gardens opposite. Our own car park. Licensed. Children welcome. Tea making facilities. Some rooms en-suite. Home cooking. Find us at bottom of St. Mary's Street which is opposite back gate of St. Marys's Church.

Single Room per one person B&B		Double Room for two persons B&B		8
MIN £ 9.00	MAX £ 12.00	MIN £ 18.00	MAX £ 23.00	OPEN 1-11

Ripley St. Mary's Hotel
St. Mary's Street, Tenby,
Pembrokeshire, SA70 7HN.
Tel: (0834) 2837.

Highly recommended hotel in quiet floral street in centre of Tenby, 75 yards seafront and Paragon Gardens. Lounge, bar lounge, attractive bedrooms, all with colour T.V., tea makers, six with private bathrooms. Reductions for children and senior citizens. AA listed. RAC acclaimed. Personal supervision by Alan and Kath Mace. Our aim:- to make your holiday an enjoyable and memorable one.

Single Room per one person B&B		Double Room for two persons B&B		14
MIN £ 11.50	MAX £ 12.00	MIN £ 23.00	MAX £ 24.00	OPEN 3-10

Strathmore Hotel
Victoria Street, Tenby, Dyfed,
SA70 7DY.
Tel: (0834) 2323.

The Strathmore Hotel – a small comfortable relaxing hotel, specially for people who enjoy good food. Standard rooms and rooms with private facilities and T.V., some with sea views. Central heating. All rooms have radio, intercom/baby listening service and tea making facilities.

Single Room per one person B&B		Double Room for two persons B&B		11
MIN £ 8.00	MAX £ 12.00	MIN £ 16.00	MAX £ 24.00	OPEN 1-12

Tralee Hotel
Paragon, Tenby, Dyfed, SA70 7HL.
Tel: (0834) 2237.

The Tralee has a magnificent south facing clifftop location, overlooking Tenby South Beach and Caldy Island. Steps to beach adjacent. Children catered for at reduced rates. All bedrooms fitted and furnished for your personal comfort; most with private bathroom. Central heating. Tea making facilities. Free parking in hotel grounds. Licensed. Send s.a.e. for brochure.

Single Room per one person B&B		Double Room for two persons B&B		8
MIN £ 8.00	MAX £ 10.00	MIN £ 16.00	MAX £ 20.00	OPEN 2-11

Guest Houses

Ashford Villa Guest House
Picton Road, Tenby, Dyfed,
SA70 7DP.
Tel: (0834) 3519. L

Two minutes from beach and town, close all car parks. Open all year. Hot and cold all bedrooms. Family, double, twin bedrooms. Special rates children and O.A.P.'s. Good home cooking. T.V. lounge. Babysitting by arrangement. Full fire certificate.

Single Room per one person B&B		Double Room for two persons B&B		5
MIN £	MAX £	MIN £ 15.00	MAX £ 17.0	OPEN 1-12

Clement Dale
South Cliff Gardens, Tenby, Dyfed,
SA70 7DS.
Tel: (0834) 3165.

Superbly situated within a minute's walk of south beach and town centre, overlooking bowling green and gardens. Parking close by. Colour T.V. lounge. Separate dining room, table licence. Noted for good food. Single, double and family rooms. No petty restrictions. No pets. Reductions early and late season, O.A.P.'s. Send s.a.e. for brochure: Mrs. Rosalind Wood.

Single Room per one person B&B		Double Room for two persons B&B		7
MIN £ 8.50	MAX £ 10.50	MIN £ 17.00	MAX £ 21.00	OPEN 4-10

The Coach Guest House
11 Deer Park, Tenby, Dyfed,
SA70 7LE.
Tel: (0834) 2210.

Above average family-run guest house. Central for beaches, shops, car/coach parks, railway station. Nine bedrooms, some en-suite, shaver points, tea/coffee making facilities, colour T.V., central heating, with access at all times. Comfortable lounge. Enjoy a warm welcome, friendly atmosphere and good food in our licensed restaurant and bar.

Single Room per one person B&B		Double Room for two persons B&B		9
MIN £ 10.00	MAX £ 12.00	MIN £ 18.00	MAX £ 24.00	OPEN 1-12

Fairway
The Golf Links, Tenby, Dyfed,
SA70 7EL.
Tel: (0834) 2141.

Delightful house located in a private road only 300 yards from Tenby's South Beach. Literally on the doorstep of the coastal path and Tenby's 18 hole championship golf course. En-suite bedrooms with tea/coffee making facilities. Out of season breaks available. Regret no children or pets.

Single Room per one person B&B		Double Room for two persons B&B		4
MIN £ 8.00	MAX £ 9.00	MIN £ 18.00	MAX £ 22.00	OPEN 1-12

Flemish Court
St. Florence, Tenby, Dyfed,
SA70 8LS.
Tel: (0834) 82413.

A small attractive house with beautifully appointed bedrooms, all with colour T.V. and tea making facilities. Set in pretty courtyard opposite small village pub in the village of St. Florence. Renowned for its prettiness and friendliness to visitors. We would like to invite you to write or telephone for our brochure to see real value for money.

Single Room per one person B&B		Double Room for two persons B&B		4
MIN £ 7.50	MAX £ 9.95	MIN £ 14.50	MAX £ 18.50	OPEN 2-12

High Seas

The Norton, Tenby, Dyfed,
SA70 8AA.
Tel: (0834) 3611.

Situated on the seafront overlooking the North Beach and harbour, close to town centre. Convenient for buses and trains. Many rooms with magnificent sea views across Carmarthen Bay. All bedrooms have colour T.V., H & C, shaver points and tea making facilities. Reductions for children sharing parents' room and for weekly bookings. Evening meal optional.

Single Room per one person B&B		Double Room for two persons B&B		7
MIN £ 10.00	MAX £ 12.00	MIN £ 20.00	MAX £ 24.00	OPEN 3-10

Ivy Bank Guest House

Harding Street, Tenby,
Pembrokeshire, SA70 7LL.
Tel: (0834) 2311.

Sally and Trevor Cromack offer you a warm welcome to our licensed guest house situated in the town of Tenby. Single, double, twin, family rooms all with heating, H & C, shaver points, tea/coffee making facilities, duvets on all beds, electric blankets at no extra charge. Full fire certificate. Write or telephone for free brochure.

Single Room per one person B&B		Double Room for two persons B&B		8
MIN £ 7.50	MAX £ 9.50	MIN £ 15.00	MAX £ 19.00	OPEN 1-12

Lyndale Guest House

Warren Street, Tenby, Dyfed,
SA70 7JX.
Tel: (0834) 2836. L

Situated 2 minutes walk from north beach and town centre, close to railway station, coach station and car parks. Open all year. Full central heating. Lounge, colour television, separate tables in dining room. Hot and cold and own keys to bedrooms and main entrance. Come and go as you please. Evening meal by arrangement.

Single Room per one person B&B		Double Room for two persons B&B		5
MIN £ 8.00	MAX £ 9.00	MIN £ 16.00	MAX £ 18.00	OPEN 1-12

Redlands

2 St. Florence Parade, Tenby,
South Pembrokeshire, SA70 7DT.
Tel: (0834) 2097.

A fine Victorian house tastefully decorated and furnished to compliment the Victorian era. Situated only 20 yards from the seafront. Individually designed bedrooms are comfortably furnished, including chandeliers, and many have sea views, tea and coffee making, and en-suite facilities. Renowned for our high standard of catering and cleanliness, e.g. fresh towels daily. AA and RAC listed.

Single Room per one person B&B		Double Room for two persons B&B		9
MIN £ 8.00	MAX £ 10.00	MIN £ 15.00	MAX £ 20.00	OPEN 3-10

Sutherlands

3 Picton Road, Tenby, Dyfed,
SA70 7DP.
Tel: (0834) 2522.

A small family guest house within easy reach of beaches, shops, car parks, golf course, putting and bowling greens. Shower room. H & C in all rooms. Colour T.V. Home cooking and a varied menu. Friendly, informal atmosphere. Children specially catered for. Full fire certificate. Open all the year.

Single Room per one person B&B		Double Room for two persons B&B		6
MIN £ 7.50	MAX £ 9.50	MIN £ 15.00	MAX £ 19.00	OPEN 1-12

Tides Reach

St. Julian Street, Tenby, Dyfed,
SA70 7BD.
Tel: (0834) 2614.

Lovely Georgian house overlooking castle and South Beach, with private steps onto beach. Large family bedrooms with showers and sea views. Spacious lounge with colour T.V. and patio overlooking Caldy Island. Harbour 50 yards away. Fire certificate held.

Single Room per one person B&B		Double Room for two persons B&B		4
MIN £ 9.00	MAX £ 11.00	MIN £ 18.00	MAX £ 22.00	OPEN 3-10

Victoria

32 Victoria Street, Tenby, Dyfed,
SA70 7DY.
Tel: (0834) 2191.

Victoria is situated within 1 minute's walk of Tenby's lovely South Beach and in close proximity to the bowling green, putting course, golf links and principle shopping centre. All bedrooms have hot and cold water, shaver points plus tea making facilities. We have a large comfortable lounge with colour T.V., separate tables in dining room.

Single Room per one person B&B		Double Room for two persons B&B		9
MIN £ 7.50	MAX £ 9.00	MIN £ 15.00	MAX £ 18.00	OPEN 3-10

Warburton House

Southcliffe Gardens, Tenby, Dyfed,
SA70 7DS.
Tel: (0834) 3373. L

Visit our small guest house and enjoy a relaxing holiday in this beautiful resort. We are 100 yards from South Beach, close to town centre and overlooking bowling green. T.V. lounge. Tea and coffee making facilities in all rooms. Table licence.

Single Room per one person B&B		Double Room for two persons B&B		7
MIN £ 8.00	MAX £ 9.50	MIN £ 16.00	MAX £ 19.00	OPEN 4-10

THE VALES OF DYFED

Some of Wales's best-kept secrets are locked away in these beguiling vales. The meandering Tywi loops languidly through a traditional landscape dotted with whitewashed farms and staunchly Welsh market towns. Meet the locals during Llandovery's livestock sales, held beneath the old town's castle ruins. Wander Llandeilo's steep streets or the busy marketplace at Carmarthen, the legendary 'Merlin's Fort'.

The Tâf flows into the sea near timeless Laugharne, where Dylan Thomas 'got off the bus and forgot to get on again'. Nearby are the sweeping sands and pine forests of the Pembrey Country Park and Kidwelly's well-preserved medieval castle. Traditions live on at the Museum of the Welsh Woollen Industry near Newcastle Emlyn. And there are other sites, so evocative of the spirit of Wales – silent Talley Abbey, for example, and the spectacular 'eagle's nest' castle of Carreg Cennen.

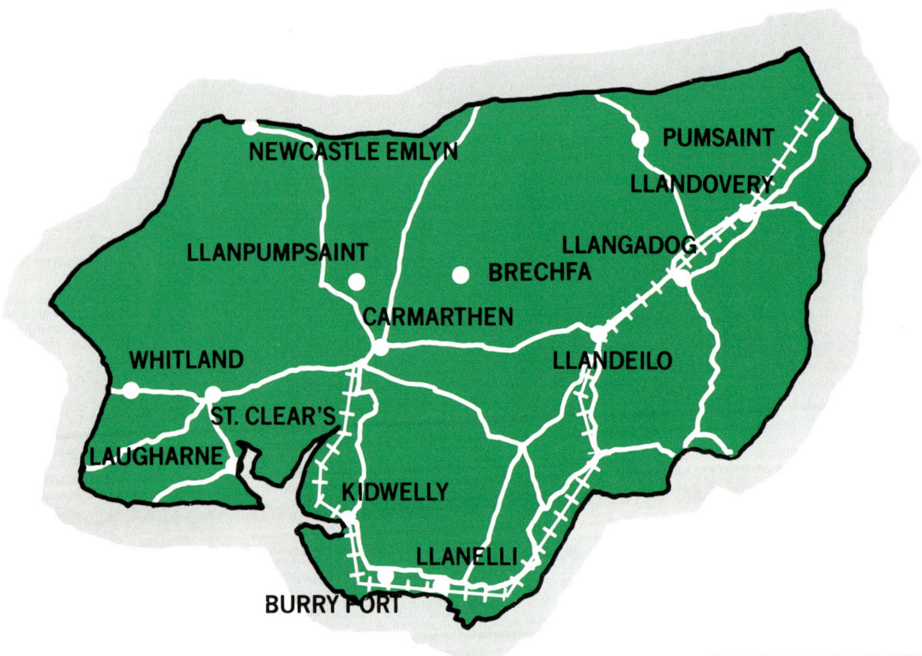

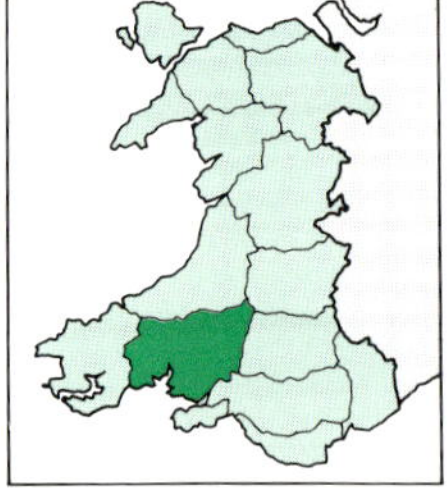

Brechfa
Map Ref Fd7

Quiet secluded farming village in the Cothi Valley surrounded by mountainous Brechfa Forest. Angling and pony trekking area. Good food in local establishments.

Farmhouses

Cae'r Blaidd
Brechfa, Dyfed, SA32 7BS.
Tel: (026 789) 315. L

Attractive character farmhouse on sheep farm. Spacious rooms with mountain views. Situated above Brechfa village and the beautiful Cothi Valley, with wonderful views of the Cambrian mountains and Brechfa Forest. Centrally situated for places of interest and beaches, fishing and trekking locally. Quality meals available, competitive rates for longer stays. Dogs by arrangement.

Facilities	Single Room per one person B&B		Double Room for two persons B&B		Bedrooms: 3
P, dogs, meals	MIN £ 8.50	MAX £ 8.50	MIN £ 17.00	MAX £ 17.00	OPEN 1-12

Burry Port
Map Ref Kd4

One-time harbour now used solely for pleasure craft. The harbour borders Cefn Sidan Sands and Pembrey Country Park. Golf at the Ashburnham Links.

Guest Houses

Adeline Guest House
5 Randell Square, Pembrey, Llanelli,
Dyfed, SA16 0TY.
Tel: (055 46) 2407. ♛♛

Family-run guest house situated in Pembrey village square, approximately one mile from Burry Port. Three family bedrooms fully en-suite, twin room with private bathroom. Television lounge. Fully centrally heated. Evening meal by prior arrangement. Close to all amenities, Cefn Sidan beach, country park, motorsport centre, golf course, pony trekking, yachting and fishing.

Facilities	Single Room per one person B&B		Double Room for two persons B&B		Bedrooms: 4
meals	MIN £ 11.50	MAX £	MIN £ 23.00	MAX £	OPEN 1-12

Tywyn Guest House
42 New Street, Burry Port, Llanelli,
Dyfed, SA16 0RT.
Tel: (055 46) 2649. L

Situated four hundred yards from town centre, harbour and beach. Comfortable licensed private house accommodation with good home cooking. Television lounge. Double and family rooms with vanity units, free tea/coffee facilities. Separate shower and bathroom. Ideal centre for Pembrey Country Park, Welsh Motorsport Centre and seven miles of Cefn Sidan beach.

Facilities	Single Room per one person B&B		Double Room for two persons B&B		Bedrooms: 4
P, meals	MIN £ 9.50	MAX £ 9.50	MIN £ 17.00	MAX £ 19.00	OPEN 1-12

Carmarthen
Map Ref Kc2

County town of Dyfed, markets and shops, livestock mart. Carmarthen Castle was an important residence of the Welsh Princes but only the gateway and towers remain. Museum, golf, fishing and tennis and a well equipped Leisure Centre. Remains of a Roman amphitheatre. Coracle fishing still to be seen on the Tywi, meandering widely through the lush countryside around.

Guest Houses

Cwm Iago
Whitemill, Carmarthen, Dyfed,
SA32 7HH.
Tel: (0267 84) 637. L

Converted cottage set in three acres with lovely views and only six miles from Carmarthen. Comfortable rooms with separate shower room for guests. Friendly and informal, family-run and helped by dogs, cats and horses.

Facilities	Single Room per one person B&B		Double Room for two persons B&B		Bedrooms: 2
P, dogs, meals	MIN £	MAX £	MIN £ 16.00	MAX £ 20.00	OPEN 4-10

Gardde-y-Rebecca Guest House
High Street, St. Clear's, Carmarthen,
Dyfed, SA33 4DY.
Tel: (0994) 230617. L

Seventeenth century country house four miles from Carmarthen Bay and Dylan's "sunhoneyed" Laugharne. Spacious rooms with washbasins, teamaking trolley, television and central heating. Ample parking. Fishing, rambling, trekking, wildlife nearby. Garden fresh food. Once the home of Horniman who dealt in butter and then tea, then Huw Williams the Chartist and Rebecca Figurehead.

Facilities	Single Room per one person B&B		Double Room for two persons B&B		Bedrooms: 7
P, meals	MIN £ 8.50	MAX £ 8.50	MIN £ 17.00	MAX £ 17.00	OPEN 1-12

The Laurels Guest House
St. Clear's Road, Johnstown,
Carmarthen, Dyfed, SA31 3HH.
Tel: (0267) 237066. ♛

Detached house of character within five minutes walk of town centre. Bedrooms with hot and cold, central heating. T.V. lounge. Tea and coffee facilities in lounge. Separate tables in dining room. Ideal base for touring. Half hour run to fine, sandy beaches. Small, friendly three bedroom guest house. Fishing, pony trekking, golf in area.

Facilities	Single Room per one person B&B		Double Room for two persons B&B		Bedrooms: 3
P	MIN £ 10.00	MAX £ 11.50	MIN £ 18.00	MAX £ 20.00	OPEN 4-11

Magnolia Guest House
20 Wellfield Road, Carmarthen,
Dyfed, SA31 1DS.
Tel: (0267) 237562. L

Detached, residential house in own grounds. Five minutes walk to town centre. All bedrooms on first floor plus bathroom, shower. Separate toilet first floor, ground floor. Television lounge, grand piano. Dining room. Cloak room, separate toilet. Parking space for several cars. Central heating. Large rooms. Homely atmosphere. Golfing, fishing, riding available nearby.

Facilities	Single Room per one person B&B		Double Room for two persons B&B		Bedrooms: 3
P, dogs, meals	MIN £ 8.50	MAX £ 9.00	MIN £ 17.00	MAX £ 17.00	OPEN 1-12

Tynygrug
7 Francis Terrace, Carmarthen,
Dyfed, SA31 1EY.
Tel: (0267) 236893. L

A small guest house in town centre. Family run by Mrs Rees who offers a warm Welsh welcome. Comfortable television room. Dining room separate from lounge. All bedrooms fitted with locks and keys. Near shops and town facilities. Good pubs and eating places nearby. Ideally situated for touring south-west Wales. Walking distance trains, buses.

Facilities	Single Room per one person B&B		Double Room for two persons B&B		Bedrooms: 3
	MIN £ 8.50	MAX £ 9.00	MIN £ 17.00	MAX £ 18.00	OPEN 1-12

Ystrad Farmhouse
Llansteffan Road, Johnstown,
Carmarthen, Dyfed, SA31 3PE.
Tel: (0267) 235073. L

One mile from the centre of Carmarthen, 2 minutes leisure centre. Golf, riding, fishing, markets, country parks, castles, etc. 6 miles to lovely sandy beach with castle. A warm welcome to a cosy "ye olde worlde" former farmhouse. Quiet position. Comfortable bedrooms, 1 family and 1 twin. Central heating. Shower in bathroom. Cot available.

Facilities	Single Room per one person B&B		Double Room for two persons B&B		Bedrooms: 2
P, dogs	MIN £	MAX £	MIN £ 16.00	MAX £ 16.00	OPEN 4-10

Farmhouses

Cefnmaes Farm

Alltwalis, Carmarthen, Dyfed.,
SA32 7EG. Tel: (055934) 367.

Our family dairy farm 9 miles from Carmarthen is ideally situated for touring Dyfed and the beaches of Carmarthen and Cardigan Bays. Riding, trekking, fishing, wollen mills and pottery all locally. Hot and cold and shaver points in all rooms, bathroom and shower room. Home cooking from farm produce. Lounge with colour TV.

Single Room per one person B&B		Double Room for two persons B&B		3
MIN £ 10.00	MAX £ 12.00	MIN £ 16.00	MAX £ 20.00	OPEN 4-10

Cwmdwyfran Farm

Cwmdwyfran, Bronwydd Arms,
Carmarthen, Dyfed, SA33 6JF.
Tel: (026 787) 419.

A 25 acre farm overlooking the beautiful Gwili Valley. Central for Cardigan, Brecon Beacons, Pembrokeshire National Park and beaches. Farmhouse built around 1700. Two double rooms, one with adjoining children's room, washbasins, T.V.'s, tea making facilities. Free range eggs, home grown vegetables (seasonal). Golf, fishing, trekking, beautiful walks, birdwatching, Gwili railway nearby.

Single Room per one person B&B		Double Room for two persons B&B		2
MIN £ 8.50	MAX £ 9.00	MIN £ 17.00	MAX £ 18.00	OPEN 1-11

Cwmtwrch Farm Hotel and Four Seasons Restaurant

Nantgaredig, Carmarthen, Dyfed,
SA32 7NY.
Tel: (026 788) 238.

You will enjoy staying at our 30 acre mixed farm in Carmarthen's countryside. Stay in one of our six warm and pretty bedrooms and choose from the country and Italian specialities in our licensed restaurant. AA listed. Wales Tourist Board Farmhouse Award. Apply Jenny Willmott.

Single Room per one person B&B		Double Room for two persons B&B		6
MIN £	MAX £	MIN £ 24.00	MAX £	OPEN 1-12

Pant Farm

Meidrim, Carmarthen, Dyfed,
SA33 5QY.
Tel: (0994) 230252.

Traditional Welsh farmhouse situated in magnificent countryside, spectacular views. Five bedrooms including three en-suite. Working dairy farm, all visitors welcome to partake in a variety of seasonal activities. Private fishing, fascinating fossil quarry, close to beaches and within easy reach of historic market town of Carmarthen. Residential licence. Warm Welsh welcome and hospitality.

Single Room per one person B&B		Double Room for two persons B&B		5
MIN £ 11.00	MAX £ 12.00	MIN £ 22.00	MAX £ 24.00	OPEN 1-12

Plasnewydd

Blaen-y-Coed Road, Carmarthen,
Dyfed, SA33 6EX.
Tel: (0267) 87368.

Plasnewydd is centrally situated for north, south and west coasts of Dyfed. Open all year. Single, double, family rooms available with special rates for children. Superb farmhouse cooking. Many guests return, including family from Scotland 14 times. Take A484 to Cynwyl Elfed, turn left in village, s.p. Blaen-y-Coed. Turn right in Blaen-y-Coed. Farmhouse 1 mile.

Single Room per one person B&B		Double Room for two persons B&B		3
MIN £ 9.00	MAX £ 11.00	MIN £ 18.00	MAX £ 22.00	OPEN 1-12

Trefynys Farm

Peniel Road, Carmarthen, Dyfed,
SA32 7HU. Enq. to: Enid Evans.
Tel: (0267) 237093.

Trefynys, a mixed 200 acre farm with dairy cattle, beef and sheep. Situated 4 miles from the market town of Carmarthen. Trout and Sewin fishing available to guests on the River Gwili. Unheated swimming pool in garden. Enjoy good home cooking with food produced on the farm. An ideal base for touring West Wales.

Single Room per one person B&B		Double Room for two persons B&B		3
MIN £ 10.00	MAX £ 12.00	MIN £ 20.00	MAX £ 24.00	OPEN 1-12

Troedyryrfa Farm

Rhydargaeau, Carmarthen, Dyfed,
SA32 7JA.
Tel: (0267 84) 279.

110 acre working farm, beef and sheep. South facing, centrally heated farmhouse in beautiful setting. Five miles from market town of Carmarthen. Comfortable single, double and family rooms. Television lounge/dining room. Good home cooked food. Pottery, steam railway, trekking, golf, fishing all nearby. Ideal for touring West and Mid Wales. Easy reach various beaches.

Single Room per one person B&B		Double Room for two persons B&B		3
MIN £ 6.50	MAX £ 8.00	MIN £ 13.00	MAX £ 16.00	OPEN 3-10

Kidwelly

Map Ref Kc3

An ancient town which received its first charter from Henry I, lies 9 miles south of Carmarthen. The 14th century bridge and great castle, once unsuccessfully stormed by Princess Gwenllian, plus an ancient church, give this town a perfect medieval air. Fascinating industrial museum on outskirts. Situated at the tip of the Gwendraeth Fach Estuary, Kidwelly is also close to the beaches of the Carmarthenshire coast at Cefn Sidan.

Guest Houses

Upper Mill Guest House and Restaurant

Kidwelly, Dyfed, SA17 4LN.
Tel: (0554) 890431.

Four star comfort in this delightful modern guest house on the outskirts of Kidwelly, suitable for Carmarthen, touring West Wales and the Gower. Private fishing on grounds and golf arranged. Enjoy the peace and tranquility of the setting and the high standards of the bedrooms at Upper Mill. A warm welcome from Mrs. Phillips.

Single Room per one person B&B		Double Room for two persons B&B		4
MIN £ 9.50	MAX £ 12.00	MIN £ 19.00	MAX £ 24.00	OPEN 1-12

Farmhouses

Pen-y-Bac Farm

Mynyddygarreg, Kidwelly, Dyfed,
SA17 4LR.
Tel: (0554) 891200.

Seventeenth century farmhouse in quiet beautiful location. Near castle, industrial museums, beaches, country park, private fishing. South of Carmarthen. Lovely country walks. Convenient touring base. Inglenook fireplace, exposed beams, log fires. Home cooking. Friendly informal atmoshpere. Pets welcome.

Single Room per one person B&B		Double Room for two persons B&B		3
MIN £ 9.00	MAX £ 10.00	MIN £ 16.00	MAX £ 18.00	OPEN 1-12

Laugharne

Map Ref Kb3

The village which provided the model for Dylan Thomas's classic radio play for voices 'Under Milk Wood'. Dylan's Boat House is now a museum dedicated to his memory. Laugharne Castle was built in the 12th century and Henry II stayed there. Interesting little shops, pottery and eating places combine to make Laugharne a lovely place to spend some time, and to enjoy the extensive estuary views.

Farmhouses

Brook House Farm

Pendine Road, Laugharne, Dyfed,
SA33 4NX.
Tel: (099 421) 239. L

Situated in quaint wooded hamlet of Brook, midway between Laugharne and Pendine. The farmhouse occupies a sheltered position with splendid open views – the perfect base for enjoyable family holidays. Hot and cold in bedrooms. Central heating. Log fire in lounge. Residential and restaurant licence. Also self-catering cottage. Free brochure for full details.

P	Single Room per one person B&B		Double Room for two persons B&B		4
	MIN £ 8.50	MAX £ 9.50	MIN £ 17.00	MAX £ 19.00	OPEN 1-12

Llandeilo

Map Ref Ga7

Farming centre at an important crossing of the Tywi River, this town is a handy touring centre for Dinefwr, Dryslwyn and Carreg Cennen Castles. Gelli Aur Country Park nearby has 90 acres including a nature trail, arboretum and deer herd.

Guest Houses

Bryn-y-Wawr Guest House

Pen-y-Banc, Llandeilo, Dyfed,
SA19 7SU.
Tel: (0558) 822419. L

Situated in the village of Pen-y-Banc, one and a half miles from the town of Llandeilo. A small family-run guest house. Excellent views of mountains. Good food. H & C in bedrooms. Ample parking. Fire certificate. Ideal for touring. Open all year. Two double rooms, one family, one single.

P	Single Room per one person B&B		Double Room for two persons B&B		4
	MIN £ 8.50	MAX £ 9.00	MIN £ 17.00	MAX £ 18.00	OPEN 1-12

Llwyndewi Farm Guest House

Trapp, Llandeilo, Dyfed, SA19 6TT.
Tel: (0269) 850362. L

Situated in the Brecon Beacons National Park and close to Carreg Cennen Castle, our guest house is an ideal centre for walking or touring. Full central heating. Log fires. Residential liquor licence. AA listed. Close to the Trapp Craft Centre.

P	Single Room per one person B&B		Double Room for two persons B&B		4
	MIN £ 8.75	MAX £ 9.25	MIN £ 17.50	MAX £ 18.50	OPEN 1-12

Farmhouses

Gorsfelen Farm

Manordeilo, Nr. Llandeilo, Dyfed,
SA19 7AY.
Tel: (0558) 822305. L

19th century spacious farmhouse, peacefully situated within our own fields. Convenient for Gower and Pembrokeshire coasts, Brecon Beacons, castles and reservoirs. Locally excellent fishing. Paradise for ramblers. Bedrooms have panoramic views over Towy valley and Brecon Beacons. Lounge with colour T.V. Home produced food, relaxed homely atmosphere. Help on farm. Send s.a.e. for details.

P	Single Room per one person B&B		Double Room for two persons B&B		3
	MIN £ 9.00	MAX £ 9.50	MIN £ 18.00	MAX £ 19.00	OPEN 4-10

Llandovery

Map Ref Gb6

An important market town with a ruined castle. On the A40 – its Welsh name Llanymddyfri means 'The Church amongst the Waters'. Nearby is the cave of Twm Sion Cati – the Welsh Robin Hood. Good touring centre for Brecon Beacons and Llyn Brianne area.

Hotels

The Feathers Inn

Llanwrda, Llandovery, Dyfed,
SA19 8AY.
Tel: (0550) 777207. L

18th century drovers inn in the picturesque Towy valley, surrounded by afforested hills and clearwater rivers. Two bars, restaurant with excellent home cooking. A mile of fishing rights set among spectacular scenery, castles, nature reserves. Convenient for Brecon Beacons and pretty west coast bays. Ideal centre for fishing, pony trekking and other outdoor pursuits.

P	Single Room per one person B&B		Double Room for two persons B&B		2
	MIN £ 11.00	MAX £ 11.00	MIN £ 18.00	MAX £ 18.00	OPEN 1-11

The Plough Inn

Myddfai, Llandovery, Dyfed,
SA20 0NZ.
Tel: (0550) 20643.

200 year old stone built inn situated in peaceful village in Brecon Beacons. Central heating, log fires. Good home cooking, imaginative dishes for vegetarians. Good area for fishing, walking, birdwatching. Dogs welcome. Two double, three single bedrooms.

P	Single Room per one person B&B		Double Room for two persons B&B		5
	MIN £	MAX £ 10.00	MIN £	MAX £ 20.00	OPEN 1-12

Guest Houses

Llwyncelyn Guest House

Llandovery, Dyfed, SA20 0EP.
Tel: (0550) 20566.

AA/RAC listed. Delightful riverside setting. Town centre 10 minutes walk. Full central heating. Homely atmosphere. Good food. Licensed. Ample parking. Within 60 mile radius of Llwyncelyn visitors would have almost complete coverage of Mid and South Wales, or you could relax on our lawn or laze beside our stretch of the River Tywi.

P	Single Room per one person B&B		Double Room for two persons B&B		6
	MIN £ 13.00	MAX £ 13.00	MIN £ 22.00	MAX £ 24.00	OPEN 1-12

Y Neuadd

Pentre Ty Gwyn, Llandovery, Dyfed,
SA20 0RN.
Tel: (0550) 20603.

Traditional country house in lovely secluded valley. Most bedrooms en-suite, tea/coffee facilities, radios. Log fires. T.V. lounge. Beautiful walks. Fresh home made produce. Cream teas available. Llandovery three miles away. Caves, coast, mountains, bird sanctuary within easy reach.

P	Single Room per one person B&B		Double Room for two persons B&B		5
	MIN £ 12.00	MAX £	MIN £ 23.50	MAX £	OPEN 3-10

Farmhouses

Cwmgwyn Farm

Llangadog Road, Llandovery, Dyfed,
SA20 0EQ.
Tel: (0550) 20410. L

Welcome to our 17th century modernised farmhouse overlooking the River Towy which provides a picturesque view of the Towy valley. Peaceful, ideal for walking. A working livestock farm two miles from Llandovery market town on A4069 road. Ideal centre for touring. One family room and one double room. T.V. lounge and dining room.

P	Single Room per one person B&B		Double Room for two persons B&B		2
	MIN £ 8.50	MAX £ 10.00	MIN £ 17.00	MAX £ 20.00	OPEN 4-9

Galltybere Farm
Rhandirmwyn, Llandovery, Dyfed,
SA20 0PH.
Tel: (05506) 218. L

Farmhouse situated in beautiful Upper Towy Valley, 9 miles from Llandovery. This is an area of outstanding natural beauty. Waterfalls, nature and bird reserves and Llyn Brianne Dam. Ideal centre for touring Mid and South Wales. Many lovely, peaceful walks. 2 double bedrooms with H & C, 1 family room (1 double & 1 single), 1 single room. Bathroom, shower, 2 toilets.

P	Single Room per one person B&B		Double Room for two persons B&B		Beds 4
	MIN £	MAX £ 10.00	MIN £	MAX £ 20.00	OPEN 4-11

Penrhiwfach Farm
Rhandirmwyn, Nr. Llandovery, Dyfed,
SA20 0NH.
Tel: (055 06) 234.

Situated in an Area of Outstanding Natural Beauty, Penrhiwfach affords fine views of the surrounding area. A small traditional farmhouse, positioned off the road and about five miles north of Llandovery (A40). You are assured of a quiet stay. Two comfortable bedrooms. Lounge/dining room, open fire. Good home cooking.

P	Single Room per one person B&B		Double Room for two persons B&B		Beds 2
	MIN £ 9.00	MAX £	MIN £ 18.00	MAX £	OPEN 1-12

Llanelli
Map Ref Kd4

A bustling town with good shopping and covered market, first class rugby in season. Pembrey Country Park adjoins 9 miles of sandy beach. Pembrey is also the home of the Welsh Motor Sports Centre, nearby. Kidwelly Castle and Industrial Museum are worth a visit.

Guest Houses

Awel y Môr Private Guest House
86 Queen Victoria Road, Llanelli,
Dyfed. SA15 2TH.
Tel: (0554) 755357.

Warm, friendly, family-run. Bedrooms with hot and cold, some with shower or en-suite. Central heating. Car park. Colour T.V. lounge. Licensed. Evening meals. Home cooking. Payphone. Reduced rates for children. Cot provided. Convenient for Swansea, beautiful Gower coast beaches and Pembrey Country Park. Five minutes walk to the beach, swimming pool and parks.

P ✕	Single Room per one person B&B		Double Room for two persons B&B		Beds 13
	MIN £ 9.00	MAX £ 12.00	MIN £ 18.00	MAX £ 24.00	OPEN 1-12

Llangadog
Map Ref Ga7

A small market town set on two tributaries of the nearby Tywi. Convenient for walking and touring the Black Mountain and Carmarthenshire. Bethlehem, 2 miles south, is distinguished by a famous Christmas postmark. The route over the Black Mountain to Brynaman is one of the most scenic in South Wales.

Guest Houses

Cefn Cilgwyn AWARD
Llangadog, Dyfed, SA19 9LF.
Tel: (0550) 777493.

Cefn Cilgwyn, which once formed part of the Cilgwyn estate, is now used as a small country guest house. Situated in the beautiful wooded Ydw Valley between Llangadog and Llandovery, and bordering the Brecon Beacons National Park. Two rooms with private bathrooms, shaver points, tea/coffee making facilities. W.T.B. Guest House award. Also self catering cottage. Brochure.

P ✕	Single Room per one person B&B		Double Room for two persons B&B		Beds 3
	MIN £ 10.00	MAX £ 11.00	MIN £ 20.00	MAX £ 22.00	OPEN 4-10

Llanpumpsaint
Map Ref Fc7

Small village off the main Carmarthen-Lampeter (A485) road nestling in a quiet valley between Cwmduad and the western edge of Brechfa Forest.

Farmhouses

Fferm-y-Felin
Llanpumpsaint,. Carmarthen, Dyfed.
SA33 6DA.
Tel: (0267 84) 498.

An eighteenth century farmhouse seven miles from Carmarthen with four double bedrooms. Oak beams, central heating, log fire. Bedrooms with hot and cold, tea making facilities, shower or bathroom available. Enjoy magnificent views over lake and mountains. Excellent home cooking. Totally relaxed atmosphere. Ideal for the discerning traveller. Reduced rates for children. A delight.

P ✕	Single Room per one person B&B		Double Room for two persons B&B		Beds 4
	MIN £ 8.00	MAX £ 10.00	MIN £ 20.00	MAX £ 24.00	OPEN 1-12

Newcastle Emlyn
Map Ref Fb6

Busy market town on the Teifi River. Fine fishing, still done by coracle at Cenarth. Felin Geri Mill for stoneground products nearby. Attractive base for touring north Pembrokeshire and the Teifi Valley, surrounded by rolling farmland.

Hotels

Pelican Inn
Sycamore Street, Newcastle Emlyn
Dyfed, SA38 9AP.
Tel: (0239) 710606. L

A 16th century inn. All rooms have magnificent views of the Teifi river and valley. An ideal base for touring or beach. Away from it all breaks. Central heating, log fire. Good home cooking including our famous "dragon pie".

P ✕	Single Room per one person B&B		Double Room for two persons B&B		Beds 2
	MIN £ 8.50	MAX £ 10.50	MIN £ 17.00	MAX £ 21.00	OPEN 1-12

Guest Houses

Aberceri
Cwm Cou, Newcastle Emlyn, Dyfed,
SA38 9NZ.
Tel: (0239) 710250. L

Aberceri is a beautiful Georgian mansion set in 5 acres of gardens and woodland on the banks of the River Teifi. Private salmon fishing for guests. Superb coastal scenery six miles. Trevor and Valerie Green are both artists and this is reflected in the tasteful and exciting interior decor. A warm welcome is assured.

P	Single Room per one person B&B		Double Room for two persons B&B		Beds 3
	MIN £ 11.00	MAX £ 12.00	MIN £ 22.00	MAX £ 24.00	OPEN 4-10

Farmhouses

Ffynnon Fair Farm
Henllan, Llandysul, Dyfed, SA44 5LJ.
Tel: (023 975) 231. L

250 acre working farm situated alongside the beautiful Teifi valley countryside and only a few miles from the safe sandy beaches of Cardigan coast and market towns. Generous, good home cooking, separate dining room. Sitting room with colour television. Complimentary tea on arrival. Storage heaters in bedrooms. Children welcome. Farm walks.

P ✕	Single Room per one person B&B		Double Room for two persons B&B		Beds 3
	MIN £ 8.00	MAX £ 8.00	MIN £ 15.00	MAX £ 15.00	OPEN 3-10

Llain Farm

Velindre, Llandysul, Dyfed,
SA44 5XT.
Tel: (0559) 370683. L

Beautiful views surround our working dairy farm situated midway between Carmarthen and Cardigan. Ideal for touring South and West coast. Dining room, lounge, T.V., central heating. Within easy reach of the many beautiful sandy beaches of the Cardigan Bay coastline. Many attractions locally.

	Single Room per one person B&B		Double Room for two persons B&B		2
	MIN £	MAX £	MIN £	MAX £	OPEN
	7.50	8.00	15.00	16.00	3-10

Pumsaint

Map Ref Ga5

Near the Caeo Forest on the Cothi River, Pumsaint has always been famous as a site of the Roman Gold mines, a National Trust site open to visitors. Plenty of nature trails to enjoy and not far away, the ruins of Talley Abbey.

Farmhouses

Llystroiddyn Home Farm

Pumsaint, Lampeter, Dyfed,
SA19 8YU.
Tel: (055 85) 482. L

Llystroiddyn Home Farm offers bed and breakfast with a friendly and personal touch. All rooms with handbasins. Central heating. Breakfast room. Sitting room. Packed lunches. Pony trekking, fishing, Roman gold mines nearby. Local pubs. Splendid scenic forestry and hill walks abound in the area. All made welcome and nothing too much trouble.

	Single Room per one person B&B		Double Room for two persons B&B		3
	MIN £	MAX £	MIN £	MAX £	OPEN
	9.00	9.50	16.00	17.00	1-12

St. Clear's

Map Ref Kb2

Agricultural centre, near Carmarthen and close to Dylan Thomas's Boathouse, Laugharne, set in pastoral landscape.

Farmhouses

Castell Gorfod

Llangynin, St. Clear's, Dyfed,
SA33 4JU.
Tel: (0994) 230835.

Country house set in its own beautiful secluded valley, 200 acres in which to walk, shoot or ride, also private trout fishing. The farm has pedigree sheep, beef cattle, free range hens, peacocks, etc. Ideal centre for touring West Wales. Approximately 10 miles from the sea with Tenby and Saundersfoot within easy reach.

	Single Room per one person B&B		Double Room for two persons B&B		3
	MIN £	MAX £	MIN £	MAX £	OPEN
			24.00	24.00	1-12

Whitland

Map Ref Ka2

Market town. Remains of 12th century abbey. Handy touring base for the Pembrokeshire Coast National Park. Canolfan Hywel Dda (Hywel the Good) information centre named after the Welsh king famous for Wales' first legal code.

Farmhouses

Maencochyrwyn Farm

Login, Whitland, Dyfed, SA34 0TN.
Tel: (099 47) 283. L

Welcome to our attractive, well situated farm located in a quiet rural area, within two and a half miles of the village of Llanboidy. 80 acre working diary farm. Good home cooking. Dining room, lounge, colour T.V. One double, one single and one family room. Bathroom, toilet. Part central heating. AA listed.

	Single Room per one person B&B		Double Room for two persons B&B		3
	MIN £	MAX £	MIN £	MAX £	OPEN
	9.00	10.00	18.00	20.00	4-10

BRECON AND THE BEACONS

Wales's great outdoors spread themselves out beneath the razor-edged summit of Pen-y-Fan, at 2,907 ft. the highest peak in South Wales. These are the green hills and open mountainsides of the Brecon Beacons National Park, a superlative 519-square-mile landscape in which the views seem to go on forever – and which offers some of the best terrain in Britain for walking and pony trekking.

Part-medieval, part-Georgian Brecon, in the middle of the park, is an obvious touring centre (it's at its liveliest during the summer Jazz Festival). Or, just like the stagecoaches used to do, stop at Crickhowell, a pretty riverside town faithful to its olde worlde character. The same can be said for traditional Talgarth and Hay-on-Wye, now a famous second-hand book 'capital'. Walk the Beacons' fresh, grassy ridges. Go cruising on the Monmouthshire and Brecon Canal. There's underground spectacle too, at the vast Dan-yr-Ogof Showcaves.

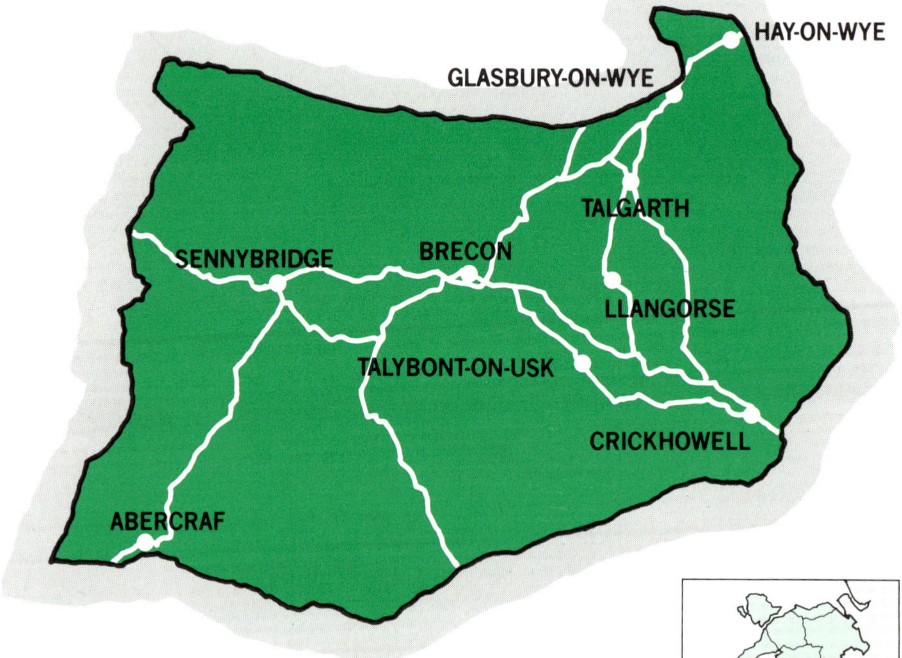

Brecon

Map Ref Ge6

Main touring centre for the 519 square miles of the Brecon Beacons National Park. Castle, priory, museum and shopping centre. Wide range of inns, guest houses and hotels. Centre for riding and pony trekking. Golf and canal cruising available. Popular summer jazz festival.

Hotels

Morning Star Inn & Restaurant

Bwlch, Brecon, Powys, LD3 7HQ.
Tel: (0874) 730080.

Eighteenth century coaching Inn between Black Mountains and Brecon Beacons with superb views down Usk Valley. Renowned locally for good food and value. First in Powys to receive Heartbeat Wales Award for healthy eating and clean establishment. Centrally heated double and family room with handbasins, guest bathroom and toilets. Children welcome. Phone for brochure.

Single Room per one person B&B		Double Room for two persons B&B		2
MIN £ 10.00	MAX £ 12.00	MIN £ 20.00	MAX £ 20.00	OPEN 1-12

Old Castle Farm Hotel

Llanfaes, Brecon, Powys, LD3 8DL.
Tel: (0874) 2120.

A 17th century farmhouse with all modern facilities, west of the market town of Brecon. Half a mile from the town centre, within easy reach of Brecon Beacons. The hotel caters for 26 persons. Most bedrooms en-suite, T.V., radio, tea/coffee making facilities. Licensed bar, lounge. Private car park. Access to hotel at all times. Fire certificate held.

Single Room per one person B&B		Double Room for two persons B&B		11
MIN £	MAX £	MIN £	MAX £ 24.00	OPEN 2-11

Guest Houses

The Beacons Guest House

16 Bridge Street, Brecon, Powys,
LD3 8AH.
Tel: (0874) 3339.

Friendly Georgian guest house situated 100 yards from River Usk and close to town centre. Family owned and run with home cooked food. All rooms have own washbasins and some rooms have en-suite facilities. Small licensed bar and separate dining room and television lounge. Private car park. School parties welcomed and groups catered for.

Single Room per one person B&B		Double Room for two persons B&B		12
MIN £ 8.50	MAX £ 11.50	MIN £ 17.00	MAX £ 23.00	OPEN 1-12

Dolycoed

Talyllyn, Nr. Brecon, Powys,
LD3 7SY.
Tel: (0874 84) 666.

Friendly family home in a sheltered position in the beautiful Brecon Beacons National Park, midway between Brecon and Llangorse Lake. Two double bedrooms with H & C, one also has a shower. Full central heating. Sitting room with colour T.V., log fire in cold weather. Good centre for touring. Further details on request from Mary Cole.

Single Room per one person B&B		Double Room for two persons B&B		2
MIN £ 8.00	MAX £ 8.50	MIN £ 16.00	MAX £ 17.00	OPEN 4-10

Flag & Castle Guest House

11 Orchard Street, Llanfaes, Brecon,
Powys, LD3 8AN.
Tel: (0874) 5860.

Comfortable, homely, family-run former coaching inn within short walk of town centre, opposite Christ College. Lounge with log fire, central heating, colour T.V. Single, twin, double and family bedrooms all with heating. Sunken bath and shower in spacious bathroom. Traditional, Welsh, wholefood and vegetarian cooking. Special activity holidays and weekends can be arranged.

Single Room per one person B&B		Double Room for two persons B&B		5
MIN £ 10.00	MAX £ 10.00	MIN £ 18.00	MAX £ 18.00	OPEN 1-12

The Old Greyhound Guest House

47 The Struet, Brecon, Powys.
LD3 7LW.
Tel: (0874) 4818.

Small guest house near Cathedral. Bed and breakfast from £8.50 per person. Guest lounge with colour T.V. Hot and cold, heating in all rooms. Evening meals extra. No children. An excellent base for touring the Brecon Beacons National Park, Mid Wales lakelands and South Wales valleys. Walking, fishing, golf, pony trekking all available locally.

Single Room per one person B&B		Double Room for two persons B&B		2
MIN £ 8.50	MAX £ 10.50	MIN £ 17.00	MAX £ 17.00	OPEN 1-12

The Old Rectory

Aberyscir, Brecon, Powys, LD3 9NP.
Tel: (0874) 3457.

The Old Rectory is situated just 2¾ miles from Brecon. It has glorious views of the Brecon Beacons and stands in 5½ acres of its own grounds and gardens. All rooms have handbasins, shaver points and are centrally heated. Private lounge. Colour T.V. Home cooking, diets catered for. Golf, trekking, fishing nearby.

Single Room per one person B&B		Double Room for two persons B&B		3
MIN £ 9.00	MAX £ 9.00	MIN £ 18.00	MAX £ 18.00	OPEN 1-12

The Old Rectory

Llanddew, Nr. Brecon, Powys,
LD3 9SS. Tel: (0874) 2058.

Situated 1½ miles from Brecon, magnificent views of Brecon Beacons. Large stone house opposite 13th century church. H & C in all rooms. Good traditional cooking, home produced vegetables, special menus catered for. Private lounge and colour television. Centrally heated. Golf course, pony trekking and country walks nearby. Ample parking.

Single Room per one person B&B		Double Room for two persons B&B		3
MIN £ 10.00	MAX £ 10.00	MIN £ 20.00	MAX £ 20.00	OPEN 1-12

Penpentre House

Llanfihangel, Talyllyn, Brecon,
Powys, LD3 7TG.
Tel: (0874 84) 263. L

Comfortable, traditionally furnished Victorian former farmhouse, one mile from Llangorse Lake with lovely views of the Black Mountains. Twin, double, family room and guests' own bathroom in separate wing of the house. Reduced rates for children. Good home cooking. 20ft sun room with colour television. Friendly atmosphere.

Single Room per one person B&B		Double Room for two persons B&B		3
MIN £ 9.00	MAX £ 10.00	MIN £ 17.00	MAX £ 18.00	OPEN 1-12

Peterstone Court Country Guest House

Llanhamlach, Brecon, Powys,
LD3 7YB.
Tel: (087 486) 666.

AWARD

Charming 18th century country house in beautiful Usk Valley. Brecon Beacons National Park. Secluded setting. 3 miles Brecon. Warm welcome. Comfortable accommodation. H/C, shaver points, tea/coffee making in bedrooms. Some rooms en-suite. Central heating. Separate lounge. Dining room, separate tables. Heated outdoor pool. Evening meals. Residential licence. Beautiful views. Ideal walking. Ample parking.

Single Room per one person B&B		Double Room for two persons B&B		7
MIN £ 10.00	MAX £ 12.00	MIN £ 20.00	MAX £ 24.00	OPEN 2-11

Farmhouses

Brynfedwen Farm

Trallong Common, Sennybridge,
Brecon, Powys, LD3 8HW.
Tel: (087 482) 505.

Brynfedwen is 118 acre livestock farm with lovely views over the Usk Valley and Brecon Beacons. Excellent walking, fishing, pony trekking and golf nearby. Modernised C/H farmhouse, T.V. lounge with log fire. 2 family bedrooms share private bathroom. 1 twin bedded room en-suite, equipped for disabled person. Tea making facilities. Cot/highchair. Good home fare.

Single Room per one person B&B		Double Room for two persons B&B		3
MIN £ 10.00	MAX £	MIN £ 20.00	MAX £	OPEN 4-10

Cefncoedbach Farm

Sarnau, Brecon, Powys, LD3 9PT.
Tel: (0874) 3548.

A mixed farm of 130 acres, four miles from cathedral town of Brecon. Excellent base for touring Beacons, caves, dams or walking, pony trekking. One double, one twin bedded. Washbasins, H & C, central heating. Children welcome. Babysitting. Tea making facilities. Car essential.

P	Single Room per one person B&B		Double Room for two persons B&B		2
	MIN £ 10.00	MAX £ 10.00	MIN £ 20.00	MAX £ 20.00	OPEN 1-12

Llanbrynean Farm

Llanfrynach, Brecon, Powys,
LD3 7BQ.
Tel: (087 486) 222.

Quiet country situation in relaxed and informal farmhouse, working farm. 3 miles from the county town of Brecon, at foothills of the Brecon Beacons. Ideally located for Beacons, River Usk, Brecon, Monmouth Canal and Llangorse Lake. 2 double bedrooms, (one en-suite), 2 twin bedrooms, 1 single. Competitive rates for five day visit or more.

P	Single Room per one person B&B		Double Room for two persons B&B		5
	MIN £ 8.00	MAX £ 8.00	MIN £ 16.00	MAX £ 19.00	OPEN 1-12

Trehenry Farm

AWARD

Felinfach, Brecon, Powys, LD3 0UN.
Tel: (0874 85) 312.

Welcome to Trehenry Farm situated 7 miles east of Brecon in beautiful countryside. Large dining room, lounge with T.V. and log fire. Double, twin and family rooms with hot and cold, shaver points. Central heating all rooms. Tea making facilities. Good home cooking. Dinner by arrangement. Reduced rates for children. Farmhouse Award winner.

P	Single Room per one person B&B		Double Room for two persons B&B		3
	MIN £ 10.00	MAX £ 12.00	MIN £ 20.00	MAX £ 24.00	OPEN 3-11

Crickhowell

Map Ref Hb7

A small country town on the River Usk. Fishing, pony trekking and riding facilities. Norman castle remains and 14th century Tretower Court and earlier castle worth a visit.

Hotels

Dragon House Hotel

High Street, Crickhowell, Powys,
NP8 1BE.
Tel: (0873) 810362.

Beautifully situated in the Brecon Beacons National Park. Ideal for all outdoor pursuits. En-suite rooms with T.V., hair dryers, tea/coffee facilities and telephone.

P	Single Room per one person B&B		Double Room for two persons B&B		8
	MIN £ 12.00	MAX £	MIN £ 23.00	MAX £	OPEN 1-12

Guest Houses

Carlton Guest House

25 High Street, Crickhowell, Powys,
NP8 1BE.
Tel: (0873) 810507.

Character house in centre of town, within Brecon National Park. Close Sugar Loaf and Tabletop Mountains. River fishing, pony trekking, excellent walking. Central heating throughout. Hot and cold, handbasins, power points all double rooms. Single, double and family. Duvets and teamaking facilities all rooms. T.V. lounge. Separate tables. Fire certificate held. Rear parking.

P	Single Room per one person B&B		Double Room for two persons B&B		8
	MIN £ 10.00	MAX £ 12.00	MIN £ 20.00	MAX £ 24.00	OPEN 1-12

Glan-Nant

Brecon Road, Crickhowell, Powys,
NP8 1DL.
Tel: (0873) 810631.

Regency house with large garden and view of Usk Valley and mountains. Peaceful, quiet, off A40 road. Three twin rooms with H & C, fires, tea/coffee available. One with private bathroom. Ideal area for touring, walking, pony trekking, castles. Good local hotels/pubs in Crickhowell for evening meals.

P	Single Room per one person B&B		Double Room for two persons B&B		3
	MIN £ 11.00	MAX £	MIN £ 20.00	MAX £	OPEN 4-10

Farmhouses

Dolfawr Farm

Cwmdu, Crickhowell, Powys,
NP8 1RT.
Tel: (0874) 730684.

The farm is set in delightful rural surroundings in the Brecon Beacons National Park, just a few minutes drive or short walk from the Black Mountains or Myndd Troed. The old market towns of Abergavenny, Crickhowell and Brecon are within easy reach by car. Pony trekking, swimming, sailing, hang gliding, leisure centre are all nearby.

	Single Room per one person B&B		Double Room for two persons B&B		3
	MIN £ 8.00	MAX £	MIN £ 16.00	MAX £	OPEN 4-10

Glasbury-on-Wye

Map Ref Ha5

Three miles from Hay, Glasbury is the haunt of fishermen and farmers. Pony trekking popular in this area.

Guest Houses

The Forge

Glasbury, Nr. Hay-on-Wye, Powys,
HR3 5LN.
Tel: (049 74) 237.

Comfortable 17th century Welsh longhouse. T.V., hot drinks facilities, electric blankets, radio, hot & cold available in bedrooms. Canoeing, pony trekking, gliding, caving arranged. Ideal centre for birdwatching, walking Black Mountains, Brecon Beacons, River Wye beach nearby. 3½ miles Hay-on-Wye bookshops. Quiet village location. Safe car park. Drying facilities. Diets catered for.

P	Single Room per one person B&B		Double Room for two persons B&B		3
	MIN £ 8.00	MAX £ 10.00	MIN £ 16.00	MAX £ 20.00	OPEN 3-10

Hay-on-Wye
Map Ref Hb5

Sited on the Offa's Dyke path, which provides an ancient border between England and Wales, this small market town nestles below the heights of the Black Mountains on a picturesque stretch of the River Wye. Famous as a centre for second-hand bookshops, to be found throughout the town.

Guest Houses

La Fosse
Oxford Road, Hay-on-Wye,
Herefordshire, HR3 5AJ.
Tel: (0497) 820613. L

Situated in Hay-on-Wye, town of books, convenient for all amenities. 160yr old residence. Oak beamed ceilings. Friendly atmosphere. Children welcome. Traditional and wholefood breakfasts. T.V. in all rooms. Centrally heated. Tea, coffee free. The River Wye meanders alongside the quaint town, surrounded by the Brecon Beacons and Black Mountains, Offa's Dyke footpath.

Single Room per one person B&B		Double Room for two persons B&B		3
MIN £	MAX £	MIN £	MAX £	OPEN
12.00		18.00	20.00	1-12

York House
Hardwick Road, Cusop, Hay-on-Wye,
Powys HR3 5QX
Tel: (0497) 820705.

Peter and Olwen Roberts welcome you to their traditional Victorian guest house, quietly situated in beautiful gardens at the edge of Hay. Sunny mountain views enjoyed by all the well equipped, comfortably furnished rooms. All home cooking with special diets on request. Complimentary hot evening drink. Plenty of private parking. AA listed.

Single Room per one person B&B		Double Room for two persons B&B		6
MIN £	MAX £	MIN £	MAX £	OPEN
9.50	10.00	19.00	20.00	1-12

Llangorse
Map Ref Ha6

At the Northern end of Llangorse Lake beneath Mynydd Tan-Troed, this village is set in the beautiful Brecon Beacons and is much used by climbers, pony trekkers, walkers and sailors. Caravans and activity holidays available.

Guest Houses

Lake View Guest House
Llangorse, Nr. Brecon, Powys,
LD3 7UG.
Tel: (087 484) 223. L

Licensed cosy establishment with friendly relaxed atmosphere overlooking beautiful Llangorse Lake and Brecon Beacons. On edge of picturesque village with charming pubs. Delightful bedrooms with tea/coffee, H & C. Lounge with T.V., piano, log fire. Dining room facing Black Mountains. Vegetable garden, orchard, lawns. Parking. Excellent for many varied outdoor pursuits or simply relaxing.

Single Room per one person B&B		Double Room for two persons B&B		5
MIN £	MAX £	MIN £	MAX £	OPEN
8.00	12.00	16.00	24.00	1-12

Farmhouses

Trewalter Farm
Llangorse, Brecon, Powys, LD3 0PS.
Tel: (087 484) 662.

Family-run farm in the eastern part of Brecon Beacons National Park, peacefully situated with panoramic views. Farmhouse is comfortably furnished. Home made meals are personally prepared using home produced meat and vegetables. The area is a paradise for walkers, naturalists, birdwatchers, artists, pony trekkers and water sports on Llangorse Lake. Children welcome, reduced rates.

Single Room per one person B&B		Double Room for two persons B&B		4
MIN £	MAX £	MIN £	MAX £	OPEN
9.00	11.00	18.00	22.00	2-12

Talgarth
Map Ref Ha6

Small market town between Brecon and Hay-on-Wye, on foothills of the Black Mountains. Centre for walkers, pony trekkers, and anglers.

Farmhouses

Pentwyn Farm
Pengenffordd, Talgarth, Nr. Brecon,
Powys.
Tel: (0874) 711468. L

Farm guest house and riding centre with 15 horses should you enjoy riding. Our home is your home during your stay with us. Oak beamed farmhouse, log fires, central heating. Evening meal available. Wash basins in all rooms. Bathroom plus shower room. Recommendations from this country and overseas.

Single Room per one person B&B		Double Room for two persons B&B		3
MIN £	MAX £	MIN £	MAX £	OPEN
9.00	9.00	18.00	18.00	1-12

Penyrheol Farm
Pengenffordd, Talgarth, Powys,
LD3 0EY.
Tel: (0874) 711409. L

Penyrheol is a hill farm of 140 acres in the Brecon Beacons National Park between the Black Mountains and Llangorse Lake, 2½ miles from Talgarth off the A479 road. All bedrooms have washbasins. Travellers Britain listed. We have a T.V., cot and children's pony for guests. Enquiries to Mrs. Ann Powell. S.a.e. please.

Single Room per one person B&B		Double Room for two persons B&B		2
MIN £	MAX £	MIN £	MAX £	OPEN
7.50		15.00		3-10

Upper Trewalkin Farm
Pengenffordd, Talgarth, Nr. Brecon,
Powys, LD3 0HA.
Tel: (0874) 711349.

Upper Trewalkin is a family-run sheep and cattle farm near the Black Mountains in the Brecon Beacons National Park. A comfortable and cosy farmhouse with lovely views over traditional Welsh farmland. Separate brochure will gladly be sent on request illustrating what is on offer in our part of Wales, equidistant Crickhowell, Hay-on-Wye, Brecon.

Single Room per one person B&B		Double Room for two persons B&B		2
MIN £	MAX £	MIN £	MAX £	OPEN
		22.00	22.00	4-10

Talybont on Usk

Map Ref Ge7

Village on banks of River Usk and Monmouthshire/Brecon Canal and within the Brecon Beacons National Park – walking and pony trekking country.

Guest Houses

Abercynafon Lodge

Abercynafon, Nr. Talybont on Usk,
Brecon, Powys, LD3 7UT.
Tel: (0874 87) 342. L

Abercynafon Lodge is situated 5 miles from Talybont on Usk in the Brecon Beacon National Park. Ideal for touring, walking, fishing, pony trekking and birdwatching. Mrs. Jill Carr extends a warm welcome with home cooked food and home produced vegetables (according to season). Packed lunches available on request. Reduced rates for chidren under 12 years.

	Single Room per one person B&B		Double Room for two persons B&B		3
	MIN £ 9.00	MAX £ 9.00	MIN £ 18.00	MAX £ 18.00	OPEN 1-12

Farmhouses

Llanddetty Hall Farm

Talybont on Usk, Brecon, Powys,
LD3 7YR.
Tel: (087 487) 267. AWARD

170 acres family farm between River Usk and Brecon canal in National Park. Accessible to Brecon Beacons and Black Mountains. On bus route. Villages walking distance. O.S. maps available. Use of canoe on canal. Colour T.V. Mrs. Marjorie Morris welcomes you with good food and comfortable accommodation in 17th century farmhouse. Brochure available. S.a.e.

P	Single Room per one person B&B		Double Room for two persons B&B		3
	MIN £	MAX £	MIN £ 17.00	MAX £ 19.00	OPEN 4-10

EVENTFUL '88

Want to visit a major music or cultural festival? Would you like to sample something of the rural life at an agricultural show, sheepdog trial or livestock sale? You can dip into the past at medieval pageants held in the castles of Wales, or enjoy Victorian festivals in period settings. There's also jazz in the streets of a market town and a most entertaining programme of countryside-based events held throughout Mid Wales. We've listed a small selection here to give you a flavour of the multitude of events taking place in Wales throughout 1988.

MARCH

24 Mar-30 Oct: 'Gerald of Wales' Exhibition, Cardiff, National Museum of Wales; similar exhibitions also planned for St. David's and Criccieth.

APRIL

29 April-1 May: Fram International Car Rally, Cardiff.
29 April-2 May: Welsh National Showjumping Championships, Builth Wells.

MAY

1-3 May: Llandudno Victorian Extravaganza.
2 May: Welsh Rugby Union Pro-Am Golf Tournament, St. Pierre Golf and
7 May: Schweppes Rugby Cup Final, National Stadium, Cardiff.
Country Club, Chepstow, Gwent.
27 May-4 June: St. David's Cathedral Bach Festival, St. David's.
28 May: Montgommery Agricultural Show, Welshpool.

JUNE

1-5 June: Beaumaris Festival.
11 June: Aberystwyth Agricultural Show.
16-19 June: Mumbles Victorian Weekend.
18 June-12 July: Margam Festival, Margam Country Park.

JULY

1-3 July: Midsummer Night's Dream Tour by Wales Actors Company at various South Wales castles.
5-10 July: Llangollen International Musical Eisteddfod.
15-30 July: Islwyn/Australian Bicentennial Festival.
16 July: International Snowdon Race, Llanberis.
18-21 July: Royal Welsh Show, Builth Wells.
18-30 July: Gower Festival.
23 July-7 Aug: Aberystwth Summer Festival.
30 July-13 Aug: Menai Strait Regatta.
30 July-6 Aug: Royal National Eisteddfod of Wales, Newport (Gwent).
31 July-28 Aug: Beaumaris Medieval Fayre, Beaumaris Castle.

AUGUST

3 Aug: Vale of Llangollen Sheep Dog Trials, Llangollen.
4 Aug: Gower Show.
9-10 Aug: Anglesey Show, Mona, Nr. Llangefni.
11-12 Aug: United Counties Show, Carmarthen.
16-18 Aug: Pembrokeshire County Show, Withybush, Haverfordwest.
19-21 Aug: Pontardawe International Music Festival.
20 Aug: Cilgerran Coracle and Aquatic Sports, Cilgerran.

SEPTEMBER

10-18 Sept: Llandrindod Wells Victorian Festival.
24 Sept: Battle of Britain at Home Day, RAF St. Athan, Nr. Barry.
26 Sept-22 Oct: Swansea Festival.
30 Sept-1 Oct: Gwyl Werin Caernarfon Folk Festival.

OCTOBER

7-29 Oct: Swansea Festival Fringe.

For a complete list of 1988 events, please contact Wales Tourist Board, P.O. Box 1, Cardiff, CF1 2XN.

SWANSEA, MUMBLES AND GOWER

Swansea, a bright and airy city, stands on the sweeping, sandy curve of Swansea Bay. Once a busy seafaring centre, the city has recently renewed its links with the ocean by transforming the old waterfront into a magnificent new marina and Maritime Quarter. Wales's second largest city also preserves its homely, traditional side – especially in the superb market stocked with local specialities such as cockles and laverbread (a kind of puréed seaweed!) And it's a place packed with entertainment, especially during the prestigious Swansea Festival held each autumn.

Swansea's sandy bay curves all the way around to The Mumbles, a pretty sailing and watersports centre guarding the Gower Peninsula. Gower's renowned coastal splendour – an 'Area of Outstanding Natural Beauty' – starts here. And goes on and on, across sheer limestone cliffs, past crescent-shaped bays at Caswell, Oxwich and Port-Eynon, to a spectacular, abrupt land's end at Rhosili and breezy Worm's Head.

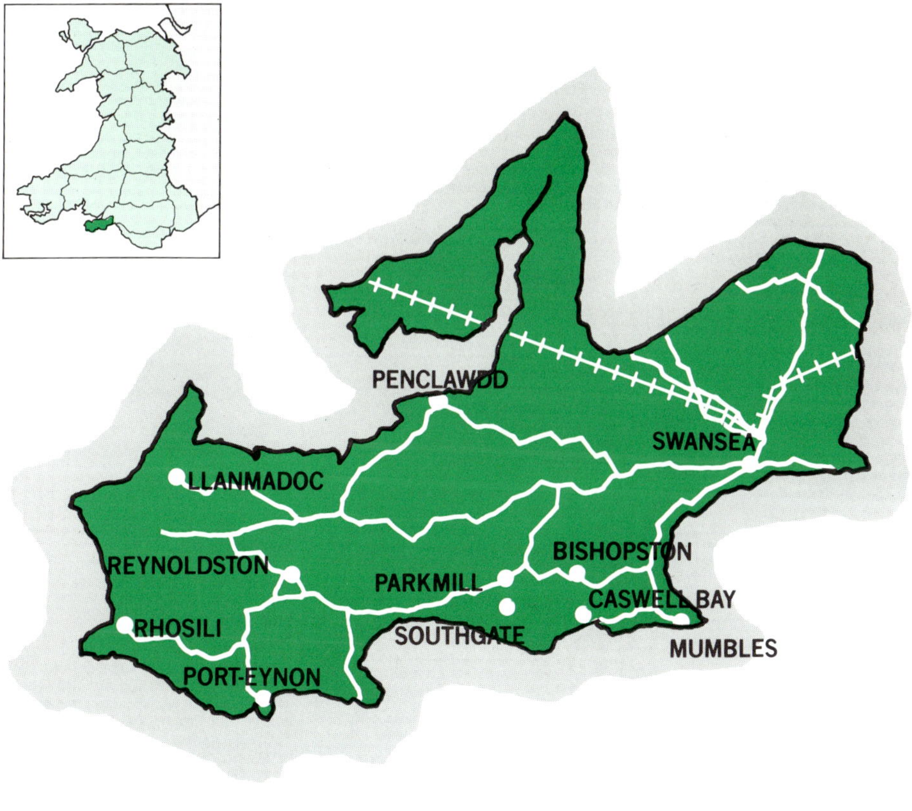

Bishopston
Map Ref Ke5

Gower village that merges with Murton, Newton and The Mumbles – 1½ miles from the sands of Caswell and Pwll-du Bays.

Guest Houses

Kerensa
31 Headland Road, Bishopston,
Swansea, West Glam, SA3 3HD.
Tel: (044 128) 4676. L

Small and friendly. Quietly situated in pleasant village. Ideal position for touring beautiful Gower Peninsula. Only minutes from sandy beaches, coastal and rural footpaths. Comfortable ground floor double bedroom. Hot and cold, private toilet, clock radio, tea making facilities, central heating. T.V. lounge. Access all times. Perfect for walking, golf, birdwatching.

	Single Room per one person B&B		Double Room for two persons B&B		1
P	MIN £	MAX £	MIN £	MAX £	OPEN
			16.00	16.00	1-12

Llanmadoc
Map Ref Kd5

A village on the north-west coast of the Gower Peninsula. Easy access to beaches.

Guest Houses

Riverside Guest House
Cheriton, Gower, West Glamorgan,
SA3 1DA.
Tel: (044 127) 601.
C/Res: (0792) 474308 L

Beamed cottage in peaceful coastal village surrounded by beautiful countryside with golden sandy beaches. Ideally situated for swimming, surfing, horse riding, walking and birdwatching. Large garden with superb views overlooking Whiteford Burrows. Comfortable T.V. lounge with woodburning stove. Children and pets welcome. Free babysitting. Special rates for children. Open all year. Centrally heated.

	Single Room per one person B&B		Double Room for two persons B&B		3
P	MIN £	MAX £	MIN £	MAX £	OPEN
	10.00	10.50	16.00	17.00	1-12

Mumbles
Map Ref La4

Resort on Swansea Bay with attractive waterfront. Centre for most water sports and sailing. Easy access to Gower Peninsula.

Hotels

Brynteg Hotel
Langland Corner, Langland,
Mumbles, Swansea, West Glam,
SA3 4NS.
Tel: (0792) 366820.

Family-run hotel within minutes walk of beautiful sandy beaches, golf course (reduced fees), tennis courts, spectacular cliff walks and picturesque village of Mumbles. All bedrooms have H & C, central heating, tea/coffee making facilities, some en-suite. All amenities expected of AA/RAC listed hotel, including residents' lounge, T.V., friendly bar and private car park.

	Single Room per one person B&B		Double Room for two persons B&B		11
P	MIN £	MAX £	MIN £	MAX £	OPEN
	11.00	12.00	22.00	24.00	1-12

The Mumbles Hotel and Restaurant
650 Mumbles Road, Mumbles,
Swansea, West Glam, SA3 4EA.
Tel: (0792) 367147. L

Family-run hotel centrally situated on seafront overlooking Swansea Bay. Full central heating with most bedrooms en-suite. Licensed. Public restaurant. Spacious sea view lounge. Late breakfast if required. Credit cards accepted. AA listed.

	Single Room per one person B&B		Double Room for two persons B&B		10
	MIN £	MAX £	MIN £	MAX £	OPEN
	12.00	12.00	20.00	24.00	1-12

Guest Houses

80 Overland Road
Mumbles, Swansea,
West Glamorgan.
Tel: (0792) 360485. L

Victorian house with views of sea or woods from each room. A short walk through the charming streets of "Old Mumbles" fishing village to seafront, tennis courts, shops, restaurant, pubs. Glorious local beaches. Open all year. Family rooms available. Meals by arrangement. Snacks always available. Basic cooking facilities by arrangement. Central heating.

	Single Room per one person B&B		Double Room for two persons B&B		4
	MIN £	MAX £	MIN £	MAX £	OPEN
	12.00		17.00	18.00	1-12

Tides Reach Guest House
388 Mumbles Road, Mumbles,
Swansea, West Glamorgan,
SA3 5TN.
Tel: (0792) 404877.

We offer a warm welcome and super food in our conveniently situated seafront guest house. Enjoy a pleasant stay surrounded by antiques and an air of old world charm. All bedrooms centrally heated with tea making facilities, some with showers. Rooms with sea views available. Exceptionally well situated for those wishing to travel by public transport.

	Single Room per one person B&B		Double Room for two persons B&B		7
	MIN £	MAX £	MIN £	MAX £	OPEN
	12.00	12.00	22.00	22.00	4-10

Parkmill
Map Ref Ke5

Gower Peninsula village, easy access to beaches and Swansea.

Farmhouses

Lunnon Farm
Parkmill, Swansea, West Glamorgan,
SA3 2EJ.
Tel: (0792) 371205. L

Situated in central Gower. Convenient for all beaches. 2 double rooms, central heating, shower, shaving points. Parking. Fresh farm produce. 1 public bathroom, separate toilet. 300 year old modernised farmhouse. Pony trekking near and lovely walks. Home cooking.

	Single Room per one person B&B		Double Room for two persons B&B		2
P	MIN £	MAX £	MIN £	MAX £	OPEN
			16.00	18.00	3-9

Reynoldston
Map Ref Kd5

Gower Peninsula village near sandy beaches. Good walking. Near Swansea.

Farmhouses

Greenways Hills Farm
Reynoldston, Gower,
West Glamorgan, SA3 1AE.
Tel: (0792) 390125. L

In beautiful countryside near main road, central to all Gower bays. Working farm with home cooking and own produce. Evening meal by arrangement. Pets by arrangement. Car park. Send s.a.e. please.

	Single Room per one person B&B		Double Room for two persons B&B		3
P	MIN £	MAX £	MIN £	MAX £	OPEN
	9.00	11.00	18.00	22.00	3-10

Rhosili

Map Ref Kc5

Gower Peninsula village, on 3 miles of beach. Good surfing, hang gliding. Worms Head.

Guest Houses

Sunnyside

Rhosili, Gower, West Glamorgan,
SA3 1PL.
Tel: (0792) 390596.

Small guest house near sandy beaches and with sea views. Dining room with separate tables. Good home cooking. Special diets by arrangement. Handbasins and teamaking facilities in bedrooms. T.V. lounge. Parking space. Pets welcome. Access to rooms at all times. Ideally situated for surfing, hang gliding, coastal walks.

P	Single Room per one person B&B		Double Room for two persons B&B		3
	MIN £	MAX £	MIN £	MAX £	OPEN
	8.00	8.00	16.00	18.00	4-10

Southgate

Map Ref Ke5

Gower Peninsula village, fine beaches at Three Cliffs and Oxwich. Swansea (Leisure Centre, marina, museums, shopping centre) nearby.

Guest Houses

Heatherlands

1 Hael Lane, Southgate, Gower,
Swansea, West Glamorgan,
SA3 2AP.
Tel: (044 128) 3256. L

Delightful situation. Heatherlands is a modern residence standing in its own secluded garden, near National Trust land. Cliff walk to beautiful beaches. Three double bedrooms with hot and cold and shaver points. Spacious television lounge. Separate tables in dining room. Ideal base for rest of Gower. Glorious walks. Parking. Bed and breakfast. Send s.a.e. please.

P	Single Room per one person B&B		Double Room for two persons B&B		3
	MIN £	MAX £	MIN £	MAX £	OPEN
	9.50	10.50	18.00	20.00	3-9

Swansea

Map Ref La4

Commercial and shopping centre, also holiday resort for Gower area. Superb new marina complex and Maritime Quarter – leisure centre, Industrial and Maritime Museum nearby. Art galleries. Fine covered market. Swansea Festival and 'Fringe' Festival in October. Theatres and cinemas, restaurants and wine bars.

Hotels

Mansel Hotel

67 Mansel Street, Swansea,
West Glamorgan, SA1 5TN.
Tel: (0792) 52818.

Situated city centre. All rooms have central heating, colour T.V. and showers. Twin rooms have private toilet and shower. Private hotel with personal service from proprietor Mr. Gerald Rees.

	Single Room per one person B&B		Double Room for two persons B&B		9
	MIN £	MAX £	MIN £	MAX £	OPEN
	12.00	12.00	24.00	24.00	1-12

Guest Houses

Belmont Guest House

2 Mirador Crescent, Uplands,
Swansea, West Glamorgan,
SA2 0QX.
Tel: (0792) 466812.

A small friendly guest house with own adjoining private car park. Situated just off the main road, within minutes of all amenities. Good food, homely atmosphere. Fully centrally heated rooms. Bedrooms equipped with washbasins, clock radios, colour television, tea/coffee facilities, razor points. Beautiful residents' lounge. Full fire certificate. Public pay phone.

P	Single Room per one person B&B		Double Room for two persons B&B		6
	MIN £	MAX £	MIN £	MAX £	OPEN
	10.00	12.00	19.00	22.00	1-12

The Coast House

708 Mumbles Road, Mumbles,
Swansea, West Glamorgan,
SA3 4EH.
Tel: (0792) 368702.

First class guest house with a high standard of accommodation. Five bedrooms, one with en-suite facilities. Seafront location. Sea views all rooms, with colour T.V. Snacks available. Child reductions. Unrestricted pets welcome.

	Single Room per one person B&B		Double Room for two persons B&B		5
	MIN £	MAX £	MIN £	MAX £	OPEN
	10.00	11.00	18.00	20.00	1-12

Crescent Guest House

132 Eaton Crescent, Uplands,
Swansea, West Glamorgan,
SA1 4QR.
Tel: (0792) 466814.

A small friendly guest house with a big reputation for comfort and courtesy. Situated in a residential crescent near the city, with easy access to the delightful bays and countryside of Gower. All bedrooms have T.V., clock radios, tea making facilities, H & C, some private showers. Full central heating. Lounge. Separate dining room. Car park.

P	Single Room per one person B&B		Double Room for two persons B&B		8
	MIN £	MAX £	MIN £	MAX £	OPEN
	11.00	12.00	22.00	24.00	1-12

Grosvenor House

Mirador Crescent, Uplands,
Swansea, West Glamorgan,
SA2 1QX.
Tel: (0792) 461522.

Business or pleasure, Pat and Brian will make your stay an enjoyable one. Easy parking and quietly situated. Centrally heated. Colour television lounge. Separate dining room. All bedrooms with hot and cold, clock radio, television and welcome tray. Convenient for Gower and city centre. Evening meal optional. Your comfort is our priority.

	Single Room per one person B&B		Double Room for two persons B&B		8
	MIN £	MAX £	MIN £	MAX £	OPEN
	12.00		22.00		1-12

The Guest House

4 Bryn Road, Brynmill, Swansea,
West Glamorgan, SA2 0AR.
Tel: (0792) 466947.

Licensed family-run guest house at gateway to the Gower, situated opposite Glamorgan County cricket ground. Serving evening meals and bar snacks. Single or twin, centrally heated rooms with modern facilities. Children over 12 welcome. On street parking. 3 minutes beach, walking distance city centre, leisure centre, marina, parks, University and Guildhall.

	Single Room per one person B&B		Double Room for two persons B&B		7
	MIN £	MAX £	MIN £	MAX £	OPEN
	8.50	9.00	16.00	17.00	1-12

Harlton Guest House

89 King Edward Road, Swansea,
West Glamorgan, SA1 4LU.
Tel: (0792) 466938.

Friendly family-run guest house. Within 500 yards of beach, parks, St. Helen's cricket and rugby ground. Easy access to city centre, marina, leisure centre and Gower coast. Centrally heated throughout. Hot and cold all rooms, plus T.V. and tea making facilities. Residents' colour T.V. lounge. Separate tables. Pay phone for guests. Fire certificate.

P	Single Room per one person B&B		Double Room for two persons B&B		7
	MIN £	MAX £	MIN £	MAX £	OPEN
	8.00	9.00	16.00	18.00	1-12

The Hollies

Horton, Gower, Swansea, West Glamorgan, SA3 1LQ.
Tel: (0792) 390423.

The ideal spot for a family holiday. Large garden adjoining beach. Relais Routier recommended. A high standard of traditional home cooking, but speciality diets also catered for. Full central heating. Separate television lounge. Licensed bar. Friendly relaxed atmosphere. In the heart of Gower. Officially designated as Outstanding Natural Beauty. Group reductions offered.

P	Single Room per one person B&B		Double Room for two persons B&B		8
	MIN £ 10.00	MAX £ 12.00	MIN £ 20.00	MAX £ 24.00	OPEN 1-12

Little Haven Guest House

Oxwich, Gower, Swansea, West Glamorgan, SA3 1LS.
Tel: (0792) 390940. L

Situated in Oxwich village, family-run. Located near beach which is ideal for most water sports. Evening meal offered weekends only. Reduction for long stay bookings, children and senior citizens. No pets allowed.

P	Single Room per one person B&B		Double Room for two persons B&B		3
	MIN £	MAX £ 8.50	MIN £	MAX £ 17.00	OPEN 3-10

Malbork Guest House

2 Bonville Terrace, Uplands, Swansea, West Glamorgan, SA1 4QS.
Tel: (0792) 473420.

Situated quiet residential area. Each room with hot and cold water, clock radio, T.V., tea or coffee making facilities. Separate dining tables, English breakfast, personal attention. Convenient for shopping, leisure centre, marina, beaches. Colour television lounge. Cot, highchair available. Choice of shower cubicle or bath. Evening meal by arrangement. Welcome home from home.

P	Single Room per one person B&B		Double Room for two persons B&B		3
	MIN £ 8.00	MAX £ 9.00	MIN £ 15.00	MAX £ 17.00	OPEN 1-12

Mirador Guest House

14 Mirador Crescent, Uplands, Swansea, West Glamorgan, SA2 0QX.
Tel: (0792) 466976.

Comfortable, homely, close to city centre. Easy access to parks, leisure centre, Mumbles, Gower coast. Evening meal optional. Heating, hot and cold, all bedrooms. Razor points. Residents' colour T.V. lounge. Access to rooms at all times. Fire certificate. Weekly rates on application to Beryl and Stan Smith. "Enjoyable holiday, excellent food, everything perfect".

P	Single Room per one person B&B		Double Room for two persons B&B		7
	MIN £ 9.00	MAX £	MIN £ 18.00	MAX £	OPEN 1-12

Stevonia Guest House

57 Bryn Road, Brynmill, Swansea, West Glamorgan, SA2 0AP.
Tel: (0792) 466948.

A well established guest house offering excellent food and service. Family-run, personal attention. Central heating, colour T.V., lounge, pool room, residential licence, bar. Within walking distance of town centre with excellent shopping and leisure centre complex. Close to bus stop. For further deatails contact Sonia Goss.

P	Single Room per one person B&B		Double Room for two persons B&B		7
	MIN £ 9.00	MAX £ 9.00	MIN £ 18.00	MAX £ 18.00	OPEN 1-12

Farmhouses

Coynant Farm

Felindre, Swansea, West Glamorgan, SA5 7PU.
Tel: (0269) 5640/2064.

Near Gower's beaches. Cosy 17th century farmhouse in idyllic setting. Inglenook log fires, fresh home produce, good food, homely atmosphere, absolute peace and magnificent views. Working livestock farm with riding, fishing, tennis court, snooker room and beautiful walks. Most bedrooms have private bathrooms. All have colour T.V., video, radio, tea/coffee. Residential licence. AA/RAC recommended.

P	Single Room per one person B&B		Double Room for two persons B&B		5
	MIN £ 12.00	MAX £ 12.00	MIN £ 24.00	MAX £ 24.00	OPEN 1-12

CARDIFF AND THE SOUTH WALES COAST

Cardiff, Wales's capital, is a city of surprises. Right in the centre there's a huge castle, a unique three-in-one historic site combining Roman remains, a medieval keep and quite fantastic Victorian reconstruction work. The elegant Civic Centre, an architectural masterpiece finished in dazzling white stone, stands nearby. There's a cosmopolitan new shopping complex, the superb St. David's Concert Hall, Victorian arcades, brand new ice rink and all kinds of entertainment – not forgetting, of course, the city's world-famous rugby stadium.

Rural Wales lives on at the Welsh Fork Museum, St. Fagans, in the pastoral Vale of Glamorgan. Green fields meet the sea along Glamorgan's Heritage Coast. The cliffs here give way only to popular, versatile resorts at Porthcawl and Barry Island with all the fun of the fair, fine beaches and attractive surroundings. Aberavon, too, has an excellent beach and seafront Afan Lido, a major sports and entertainment centre. In complete contrast, the mood is Victorian at pretty Penarth, especially along its ornate pier.

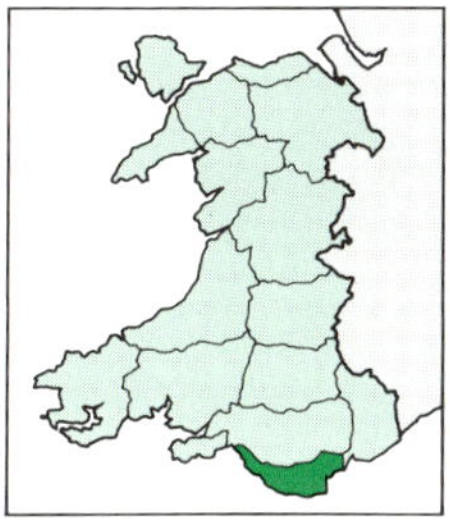

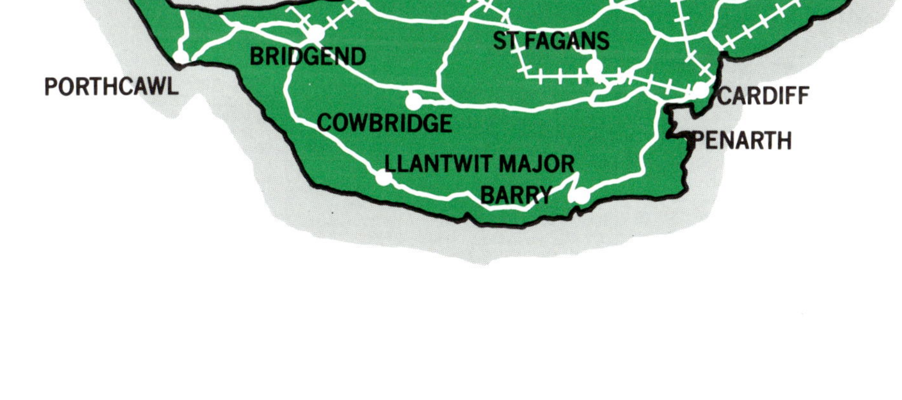

Bridgend
Map Ref Ld5

Bustling industrial and market town in the rural Vale of Glamorgan. Lively resorts and bays nearby. Ewenny Priory said to be one of the best examples of church architecture in Wales. Three Norman castles in the area – Coity, Newcastle and Ogmore.

Guest Houses

St. Andrews
21 West Farm Road, Ogmore-by-Sea, Nr. Bridgend, Mid Glamorgan.
Tel: (0656) 880183. L

Situated on heritage coast in elevated position overlooking sea. Family, double and single bedrooms all centrally heated, with handbasins and shaving points plus tea/coffee making facilities. Dining room, T.V. lounge. Reduced rates for children. Competative rates for groups and visits of one week or more. Will cater during winter months if required.

	Single Room per one person B&B		Double Room for two persons B&B		3
P	MIN £ 8.50	MAX £ 9.50	MIN £ 18.00	MAX £ 19.00	OPEN 1-12

Cardiff
Map Ref Mb5

Capital of Wales, business and trade centre. Splendid civic centre, modern pedestrianised shopping centre, good restaurants, theatres, cinemas, clubs and sports facilities, including ice rink. Visit St David's Hall for top-class entertainment. The National Museum of Wales has a fine collection of Impressionist and Post-Impressionist paintings. The castle right in the city centre is an impressive sight. Home of Welsh rugby. Wide range of accommodation at all prices. Llandaff Cathedral close by and Welsh National Folk Museum at St Fagan's.

Hotels

Cardiff Y.M.C.A. Housing Association
The Walk, Roath, Cardiff, South Glamorgan, CF2 3AG.
Tel: (0222) 497044.

Cardiff Y.M.C.A. is a modern residential centre close to the city centre, consisting of 72 single study bedrooms with a limited number of double rooms. Accommodation is available to male and female for long and short stays. Enquiries from groups welcome. Children welcome.

	Single Room per one person B&B		Double Room for two persons B&B		72
P	MIN £ 8.25	MAX £	MIN £ 14.50	MAX £	OPEN 1-12

Guest Houses

Acorn Lodge Guest House
182 Cathedral Road, Cardiff, South Glamorgan, CF1 9JE.
Tel: (0222) 21373. L

A fine Victorian house of character located centrally in Cardiff's prime conservation area. Central all attractions and within a few minutes walk of city centre. Full central heating. Car park. On main bus route. Fire certificate. All rooms tea and coffee and colour television. Friendly personal service. Choice of diners and restaurants close by.

	Single Room per one person B&B		Double Room for two persons B&B		7
P	MIN £ 12.00	MAX £	MIN £ 22.00	MAX £	OPEN 1-12

Amberley Guest House
22 Plasturton Gardens, Pontcanna, Cardiff, South Glamorgan, CF1 9HF.
Tel: (0222) 374936.

The house is situated within easy reach of the city centre and all amenities, such as shops, theatres, Cardiff castle, new ice rink and National Sports Centre for Wales. A warm friendly atmosphere is provided for guests who are made as comfortable as possible in rooms that have C/H, T.V., tea/coffee making facilities.

	Single Room per one person B&B		Double Room for two persons B&B		3
P	MIN £ 9.00	MAX £ 9.00	MIN £ 18.00	MAX £ 18.00	OPEN 1-12

Arosa Guest House
24 Plasturton Gardens, Pontcanna, Cardiff, South Glamorgan, CF1 9HF.
Tel: (0222) 395342.

Small family-run guest house with central heating, T.V. lounge with tea and coffee making facilities. Also car parking at rear. Within ten minutes of all amenities including castle, museum, town centre, national sports centre, bus and rail station, etc. Clean and reasonably priced with good breakfast.

	Single Room per one person B&B		Double Room for two persons B&B		3
P	MIN £ 8.50	MAX £ 9.00	MIN £ 17.00	MAX £ 18.00	OPEN 1-12

Austins Guest House,
11, Coldstream Terrace, City Centre, Cardiff, South Glamorgan, CF1 8LJ.
Tel: (0222) 377148. L

Situated in the centre of Cardiff, 300 yards from the Castle; 7 single and 6 twin bedrooms all with hot and cold; shaver points; fixed heating; tea and coffee; colour T V on request. T V Lounge. Evening meals by arrangement. Full English breakfast included. 10 minutes from bus and train stations. Fire Certificate held. Rates quoted apply to 10 rooms.

	Single Room per one person B&B		Double Room for two persons B&B		13
	MIN £ 11.50	MAX £	MIN £ 20.00	MAX £	OPEN 1-12

69 Beulah Road
Rhiwbina, Cardiff, South Glamorgan, CF4 6LW.
Tel: (0222) 623543.

In pleasant suburb but only 1 mile from M4. Comfortable private house accommodation. Good home cooking, evening meal optional. Double room. Television lounge. Large pleasant garden and patio. Within walking distance of buses, trains and new sports centre. Ideal touring and sight seeing centre.

	Single Room per one person B&B		Double Room for two persons B&B		1
P	MIN £ 8.50	MAX £ 8.50	MIN £ 17.00	MAX £ 17.00	OPEN 1-12

Bon Maison
39 Plasturton Gardens, (off Cathedral Road), Pontcanna, Cardiff, South Glamorgan, CF1 9HG.
Tel: (0222) 383660.

Ideally situated on edge of city, walking distance to many tourist attractions, e.g. castle, civic centre, parks, shops, bus and railway stations. A warm, family-run house. All rooms have hot and cold, radios, heating. Evening meal optional. All home cooking. Tea and coffee facilities in bedrooms. T.V. lounge. Pass keys. B.B.Q. optional, weather permitting. Child reductions.

	Single Room per one person B&B		Double Room for two persons B&B		3
	MIN £ 10.00	MAX £ 12.00	MIN £ 20.00	MAX £ 24.00	OPEN 1-12

Coniston Guest House
11 Dyfrig Street, (off Cathedral Road), Cardiff, South Glamorgan, CF1 9LR.
Tel: (0222) 32249.

Homely friendly atmosphere. Colour T.V. lounge. Full breakfast. Tea and coffee making facilities in all rooms. Within walking distance of city centre and shops. Central to all tourist attractions, Castle and museums. Also on main bus route. Proprietor Mrs. Freda Heron.

	Single Room per one person B&B		Double Room for two persons B&B		4
P	MIN £ 8.50	MAX £ 9.50	MIN £ 17.00	MAX £ 18.00	OPEN 1-12

Domus Guest House
201 Newport Road, Cardiff, South Glamorgan, CF2 1AJ.
Tel: (0222) 495785.

Small family-run guest house close to city and civic centre. Radio/telephone in each room, also tea/coffee making facilities. Two family rooms en-suite, four with private showers. Large comfortable T.V. lounge. Evening meals.

	Single Room per one person B&B		Double Room for two persons B&B		10
P	MIN £ 12.00	MAX £	MIN £ 22.00	MAX £	OPEN 1-12

Glan-y-Dwr
157 Lake Road West, Cardiff, South Glamorgan, CF2 5PL.
Tel: (0222) 758126. L

Glan-y-Dwr means "water's edge". Friendly welcome in Edwardian family house overlooking Roath Park lake. Rooms have gas fires, washbasins, T.V., tea and coffee making facilities, fresh fruit, biscuits. Special rates for huge family room sleeping five. Full British breakfast. Pleasant walks around park. French, Spanish, German, Welsh spoken. No parking problems. Very convenient bus.

	Single Room per one person B&B		Double Room for two persons B&B		2
P	MIN £ 10.00	MAX £ 11.00	MIN £ 18.00	MAX £ 20.00	OPEN 1-12

57 Ninian Road
Roath Park, Cardiff, South Glamorgan, CF2 5EJ.
Tel: (0222) 481001. L

Comfortable accommodation offered in lovely Victorian house of character overlooking park. Minutes from the centre of Cardiff. Welsh speaking family will guide you to the best in and around Wales' capital city. Small dogs accepted by arrangement. On street parking. Double or family rooms. Superb evening meals by arrangement. T.V., tea making facilities.

	Single Room per one person B&B		Double Room for two persons B&B		3
	MIN £	MAX £	MIN £ 18.00	MAX £ 24.00	OPEN 1-12

Plas-y-Bryn
93 Fairwater Road, Llandaff, Cardiff, South Glamorgan, CF5 2LG.
Tel: (0222) 561717/495825. L

Home from home is what we offer. Comfortable house set in quiet part of Cardiff, within walking distance of buses, train halt, and the pretty shopping area of Llandaff with its cathedral and choice of inns and restaurants. All the comforts of home at Plas-y-Bryn, central heating, colour T.V. lounge and good service.

	Single Room per one person B&B		Double Room for two persons B&B		3
P	MIN £ 10.00	MAX £ 12.00	MIN £ 18.00	MAX £ 20.00	OPEN 1-12

The Preste Gaarden
181 Cathedral Road, Cardiff, South Glamorgan, CF1 9PN.
Tel: (0222) 28607.

Situated in conservation area close to town centre, within walking distance, sports centre, national rugby stadium. Family-run, we offer comfortable accommodation, centrally heated. All rooms have hot and cold water, shaver points, bed lights. Each room has T.V., tea/coffee facilities. Some rooms en-suite. Fire certificate held.

	Single Room per one person B&B		Double Room for two persons B&B		9
	MIN £ 12.00	MAX £ 12.00	MIN £ 21.00	MAX £ 24.00	OPEN 1-12

Rydalmere
151 Lake Road West, Roath Park, Cardiff, South Glamorgan, CF2 5PJ.
Tel: (0222) 754663.

Probably the most beautiful outlook in Cardiff, directly opposite Roath Park Lake. Rydalmere is an elegant family house with superb decor and one room en-suite, one four poster bedroom. Quality furniture throughout. The house to make you enjoy your stay with us. Televisions in all rooms. Central heating and car parking. Close to town centre.

	Single Room per one person B&B		Double Room for two persons B&B		5
P	MIN £ 11.00	MAX £ 12.00	MIN £ 19.00	MAX £ 22.00	OPEN 1-12

Sant-y-Nyll House
St. Brides Super Ely, South Glamorgan, CF1 6EZ.
Tel: (0446) 760209.

Wonderful position looking over Glamorgan Vale. Cardiff only six miles. Close to Welsh Folk Museum at St. Fagans and M4 junction 33. Lovely country house with huge grounds and garden. Centrally heated. Licensed. T.V., coffee/tea making in all rooms. Personal supervision, resident owners Paul and Monica Renwick.

	Single Room per one person B&B		Double Room for two persons B&B		6
P	MIN £ 12.00	MAX £ 12.00	MIN £ 24.00	MAX £ 24.00	OPEN 1-12

Whitebarn House
Rhydlafar Farm, St. Fagans, Cardiff, South Glamorgan, CF5 6JH.
Enq. to: Mrs. M. Pugsley.
Tel: (0222) 843152. L

Charming oak beamed converted barn adjacent farmland on A4119, only four miles from Cardiff. An ideal base for touring South Wales. Separate lounge. Pretty bedrooms with tea/coffee making facilities. Central heating. Colour T.V. 3 bedrooms, 2 bathrooms. Excellent breakfast. Family room available.

	Single Room per one person B&B		Double Room for two persons B&B		3
P	MIN £ 10.00	MAX £ 10.00	MIN £ 19.00	MAX £ 19.00	OPEN 1-12

Cowbridge
Map Ref Le6

A picturesque town with wide main road and pretty houses. Fine old inns and country-ware shops.

Guest Houses

Stembridge Farm Guest House
Stembridge, Nr. Llandow, Cowbridge, South Glamorgan, CF7 7NT.
Tel: (0656 79) 389.

A warm welcome and relaxing atmosphere await you at this centuries old farmhouse in the beautiful Vale of Glamorgan. Splendid open views, close to Heritage Coast and charming old market town of Cowbridge. Oak beamed dining room and comfortable lounges. Three well appointed double bedrooms, all with colour T.V. Three bathrooms, one en-suite.

	Single Room per one person B&B		Double Room for two persons B&B		3
P	MIN £ 10.00	MAX £ 12.00	MIN £ 20.00	MAX £ 24.00	OPEN 1-12

Llantwit Major
Map Ref Ld6

A mile from the sea, Llantwit Major was the site of a Christian settlement in the 5th century where St David and St Teilo studied. The small Col-huw beach has a caravan site, car parking and a shop. Nearby is St Donat's Castle now the International Atlantic College.

Farmhouses

Downs Farmhouse
Wick Road, Llantwit Major, South Glamorgan, CF6 9YU.
Tel: (04465) 4252.

Affording beautiful views across the Bristol Channel and Vale of Glamorgan. This 18th century listed stone built farmhouse offers a high standard of accommodation and cuisine. Colour television, direct dial telephones, electric blankets, central heating, all add to the comfort and convenience of Downs Farmhouse. Large duck pond. Safe car parking. Rhoose Airport 6 miles, beach 3 miles.

	Single Room per one person B&B		Double Room for two persons B&B		3
P	MIN £ 10.00	MAX £ 12.00	MIN £ 20.00	MAX £ 24.00	OPEN 1-12

Penarth
Map Ref Mb6

Small resort near Cardiff offering boating, yachting, fishing, water-skiing and cliff walks. Victorian pier and promenade.

Guest Houses

Alandale Guest House
17 Plymouth Road, Penarth, South Glamorgan, CF6 2DA.
Tel: (0222) 709226. L

The guest house is 5 minutes from seafront, railway station 2 minutes away. Large bedrooms with colour T.V., full central heating, hot and cold, shaver points. Car park. Reduced rates for weekly bookings. Evening meal if required. Cardiff 10 minutes away by car or train, St. Fagans castle 15 minutes away. Spoil yourself with a holiday with good food and accommodation.

	Single Room per one person B&B		Double Room for two persons B&B		4
P	MIN £ 11.00	MAX £ 12.00	MIN £ 22.00	MAX £ 24.00	OPEN 1-12

Starcross Guest House

1 Archer Road, Penarth, Nr. Cardiff, South Glamorgan, CF6 2HW.
Tel: (0222) 702718. L

Attractive Victorian house set in quiet residential area near town centre and railway station, and within walking distance of beach and Cosmeston Country Park. Single, double and family rooms with special rates for children. Lounge with colour television. Full central heating. Standard and vegetarian meals available, home made bread. Welcoming and friendly atmosphere.

P	Single Room per one person B&B		Double Room for two persons B&B		3
	MIN £	MAX £	MIN £	MAX £	OPEN
	9.00		18.00		1-12

Trelawne

4 Albert Crescent, Penarth, South Glamorgan, CF6 1DA.
Tel: (0222) 709184. L

Situated 2 minutes from town centre, this small guest house overlooks a park and bowling green. Ideally placed for beaches/medieval site/country park and lakes, yet only 4 miles from Cardiff.

P	Single Room per one person B&B		Double Room for two persons B&B		3
	MIN £	MAX £	MIN £	MAX £	OPEN
	9.00	9.00			1-12

Port Talbot

Map Ref Lb4

Extensive sands of Aberavon beach – bathing and surfing. Afan Lido sports centre. Margam Country Park is the home of deer herd and sculpture park. Afan Argoed Country Park has the fascinating Welsh Miners' Museum.

Guest Houses

Ty'n-y-Caeau

Margam, Port Talbot, West Glamorgan, SA13 2NW.
Tel: (0639) 883897.

Country guest house in own fields and gardens. Close to junction 38 M4, Margam Park and South Wales coast. Ample parking. Central heating. Large comfortable T.V. lounge and dining room. Fresh home cooked food with garden produce in season. Double and family rooms. Children's play area. Warm welcome assured from Mrs. Rhiannon Gaen.

P	Single Room per one person B&B		Double Room for two persons B&B		3
	MIN £	MAX £	MIN £	MAX £	OPEN
	12.00		20.00	24.00	2-11

Porthcawl

Map Ref Lc6

Traditional seaside resort – beaches, fun fair, promenade, golf. Summer entertainment at the Grand Pavilion. Sailing and windsurfing on the long beaches. Porthcawl is convenient for visiting the Vale of Glamorgan with its lovely thatched-roof cottages and many appealing attractions.

Hotels

Minerva Hotel

Esplanade Avenue, Porthcawl, Mid Glamorgan, CF36 3YU.
Tel: (0656 71) 2428.

A comfortable, licensed, AA listed hotel run personally by the owners, Rosemarie and Tony Giblett. Occupying a central position close to the promenade and shops. All rooms are centrally heated, have tea and coffee making facilities and colour televisions. Some have bathroom en-suite. Children under 12 charged half price.

	Single Room per one person B&B		Double Room for two persons B&B		8
	MIN £	MAX £	MIN £	MAX £	OPEN
	9.00	9.00	18.00	18.00	1-12

Penoyre Private Hotel

29 Mary Street, Porthcawl, Mid Glamorgan, CF36 3YN.
Tel: (0656 71) 4550.

Situated in the heart of Porthcawl within 100 yards of main shopping centre and beach, this small private hotel offers excellent home cooking, with public car park opposite. Bar facilities, colour television lounge are provided for residents' pleasure. Ann and Jim Ormiston extend a warm welcome and personal attention is assured. Evening meals optional.

	Single Room per one person B&B		Double Room for two persons B&B		4
	MIN £	MAX £	MIN £	MAX £	OPEN
	9.00	10.00	18.00	20.00	1-12

Guest Houses

Kenrhos

22 Esplanade Avenue, Porthcawl, Mid Glamorgan, CF36 3YU.
Tel: (0656 71) 4428.

Situated 200 yards from the promenade and close to the town centre. This family-run guest house offers a warm friendly welcome to all. Four rooms all centrally heated with hot and cold water and shaver points. T.V. lounge available to all guests.

	Single Room per one person B&B		Double Room for two persons B&B		4
	MIN £	MAX £	MIN £	MAX £	OPEN
	9.00	12.00	18.00	24.00	1-12

Rockybank Guest House

15 De Breos Drive, Porthcawl, Mid Glamorgan, CF36 3JP.
Tel: (0656 71) 5823.
C/Res: (0792) 474308

Within walking distance of town, beaches, restaurants, funfair, country walks, bus station, children's park 50 yards away. Situated between two excellent golf courses. Ample parking. Colour T.V. Babysitting. Teasmades. Family room en-suite with balcony. Double and twin room, hot and cold, razor point. Separate dining room. Central heating. Special rates for children.

P	Single Room per one person B&B		Double Room for two persons B&B		3
	MIN £	MAX £	MIN £	MAX £	OPEN
			19.90	23.90	1-12

Villa Guest House

27 Mary Street, Porthcawl, Mid Glamorgan, CF36 3YN.
Tel: (0656 71) 5074.

Situated 50 yards from promenade, beaches and town centre. 7 large and well maintained letting bedrooms. Family, double and singles available. All have colour T.V., tea and coffee, H & C. full C/H. Also available, comfortable T.V. lounge and separate dining room. Good home cooking and friendly atmosphere, plus much more. RAC diploma. Fire certificate held.

P	Single Room per one person B&B		Double Room for two persons B&B		7
	MIN £	MAX £	MIN £	MAX £	OPEN
	7.50	8.50	15.00	17.00	1-12

Winchester Guest House

31 Mary Street, Porthcawl, Mid Glamorgan, CF36 3YN.
Tel: (0656) 771807.

Olde worlde family-run guest house with modern facilities. Duvets, hot and cold, full central heating, tea making facilities all rooms, some rooms T.V. Bathroom with shower each floor. Comfortable T.V. lounge. Within walking distance of seafront, shops, disco, bars and amusement park.

P	Single Room per one person B&B		Double Room for two persons B&B		7
	MIN £	MAX £	MIN £	MAX £	OPEN
	8.50	9.00	17.00	18.00	1-12

VALE OF USK AND WYE VALLEY

Wales meets the English border country along these sylvan vales, carved out by two rivers both famed for their fishing. The ebb and flow of history has also swept across these borderlands. The Usk meanders through a patchwork of rivermeadows to the Roman base at Caerleon, near the gateway city of Newport. As well as setting up camp here, the Romans also built an amphitheatre and large bath-house leisure complex to entertain the troops. Caerleon offers visitors a complete Roman experience, for the town also has a new museum which exhibits many exciting finds.

The Wye winds sinuously through shady glades in its thickly wooded vale. Wordsworth was one of the first to spread the word of its beauty when he wrote of the riverside abbey ruins at Tintern. There's so much history here – from Henry V's Monmouth to Chepstow, home of Britain's first stone-built castle, from delightful Penhow Castle to the grandeur of Newport's Tredegar House.

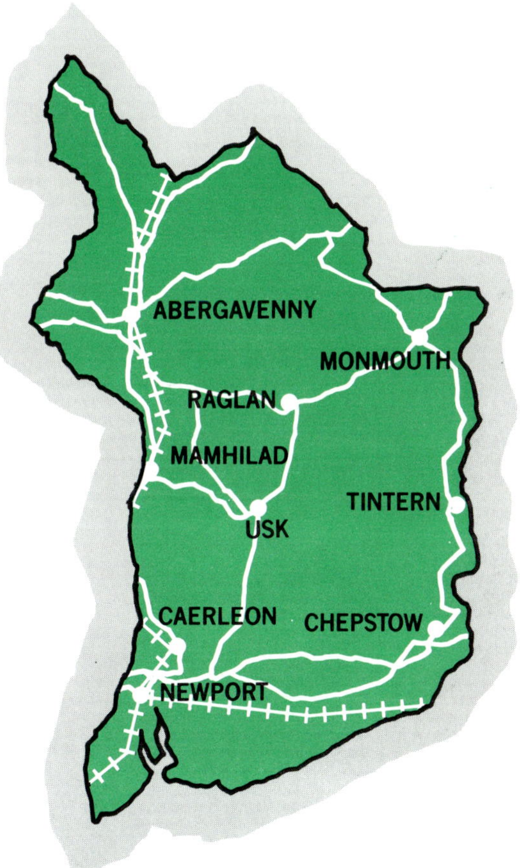

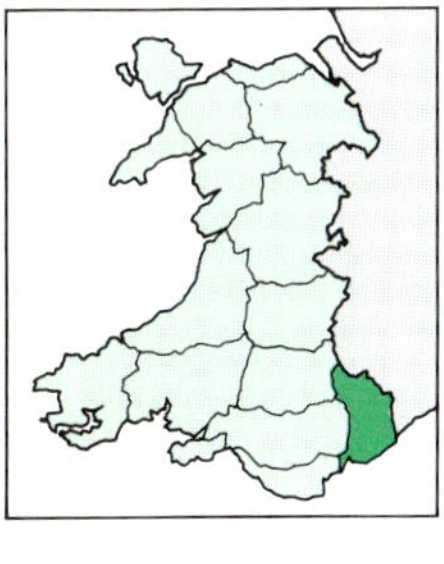

Abergavenny
Map Ref Mc2

Flourishing market town with backdrop of mountains. Leisure Centre. Pony trekking in nearby Black Mountains. Castle with museum. Excellent touring base for the Usk and Wye Valleys.

Hotels

Dragons Head Inn
Llangenny, Nr. Crickhowell, Powys,
NP7 9NG.
Tel: (0873) 810350. L

Old country inn, 4 miles from Abergavenny with a delightful riverside setting, providing real ales, real food, real welcome. Ideally situated for walking, pony trekking, caving, fishing. Excellent choice of meals using local fresh produce aimed at value for money. Local characters and the landlord's real ales complete the perfect atmosphere for country lovers.

Single Room per one person B&B		Double Room for two persons B&B		Rooms 3
MIN £	MAX £	MIN £	MAX £	OPEN
9.00	12.00	17.00	19.00	1-12

The Great George Hotel
Cross Street, Abergavenny, Gwent,
NP7 5EU.
Tel: (0873) 4230.

High standard family-run, town centre free house "within the old town wall". Comfortable bedrooms have coffee/tea facilities, colour T.V., central heating, vanity units, H & C, shaver points. 15th century inn ideally situated for business or pleasure. Close to motorway, golf, boating, fishing, castles, museums, riding, climbing and National Park. Excellent home cooked food.

Single Room per one person B&B		Double Room for two persons B&B		Rooms 4
MIN £	MAX £	MIN £	MAX £	OPEN
			24.00	1-12

Hobby Horse Inn
30 Greenland Road, Brynmawr,
Gwent, NP3 4DT.
Tel: (0495) 310996. L

Colour T.V. in every room. Friendly atmosphere in a country pub on the edge of town. Recommended in Good Beer Guide. Excellent value for money. Bar meals, including steaks and home made specialities. Also full à la carte restaurant. A welcome is assured from Roy and Joan who will make your stay a memorable one.

Single Room per one person B&B		Double Room for two persons B&B		Rooms 3
MIN £	MAX £	MIN £	MAX £	OPEN
7.00	10.00	14.00	18.00	1-12

Park Hotel and Restaurant
Pandy, Nr. Abergavenny, Gwent,
NP7 8DS.
Tel: (0873) 890271.

Ken and Kath Bond welcome you to the Park, formerly a manor house set in three acres. Bedrooms have showers, teasmades, colour T.V. Home cooked food served in our beautiful dining room, fully licensed. Central for Offa's Dyke, Black, Skirrid, Blorange Mountains. Good area for pony trekking, fishing, golf. Central heating. Fire certificate held.

Single Room per one person B&B		Double Room for two persons B&B		Rooms 7
MIN £	MAX £	MIN £	MAX £	OPEN
10.00	12.00	20.00	24.00	1-12

Guest Houses

Ambleside
8 Monmouth Road, Abergavenny,
Gwent, NP7 5HH.
Tel: (0873) 3823. L

Family-run, offering single, twin, double and family rooms. T.V. lounge, with T.V. available in rooms and teamaking facilities as required. H & C all rooms. Good food, friendly home. Central for touring, walking through picturesque Usk, Wye Valleys and surrounding countryside. Close all amenities, Beacons, mountains, railway, leisure centre, historic sites. Come and stay.

Single Room per one person B&B		Double Room for two persons B&B		Rooms 4
MIN £	MAX £	MIN £	MAX £	OPEN
8.00	10.00	16.00	20.00	1-12

Belchamps Guest House
1 Holywell Road, Abergavenny,
Gwent, NP7 5LP.
Tel: (0873) 3204.

Worldwide recommendations for comfort, good food, personal attention. All rooms tastefully furnished, hot and cold, vanity basins, tea/coffee making facilities, power and razor points. Guests' T.V. lounge. Bathroom and toilet, separate shower room and toilet. Access at all times. Guestaccom good room award. AA approved. Fire certificate. Excellent touring centre for historic and beautiful countryside.

Single Room per one person B&B		Double Room for two persons B&B		Rooms 5
MIN £	MAX £	MIN £	MAX £	OPEN
10.00	12.00	20.00	24.00	1-12

Ingleside
61 Monmouth Road, Abergavenny,
Gwent, NP7 5HR.
Tel: (0873) 5262.

Victorian house of character within three minutes walk of town centre. Convenient for train and bus stations. Three double bedrooms with tea and coffee making facilities. Television lounge. Very comfortable accommodation and good food. Car park. Ideal base for tourists and walkers.

Single Room per one person B&B		Double Room for two persons B&B		Rooms 3
MIN £	MAX £	MIN £	MAX £	OPEN
		19.00	20.00	4-10

Pentre Cottage
Brecon Road, Llanwenarth,
Abergavenny, Gwent, NP7 7EW.
Tel: (0873) 3435. L

Small, pretty country house on the turning to the Sugar Loaf mountain. Plenty of parking space, lovely gardens. Bathroom and separate shower room for guests. Sitting room also with television. Pony trekking and lovely walks, River Usk just a short walk down lane.

Single Room per one person B&B		Double Room for two persons B&B		Rooms 2
MIN £	MAX £	MIN £	MAX £	OPEN
12.00	12.00	18.00	19.00	1-12

Farmhouses

Gelli-Llwyd Farm
Llanvetherine, Abergavenny, Gwent,
NP7 8RP.
Tel: (087 386) 243. L

Welcome to our comfortable farmhouse. 120 acre working farm with milking cows, sheep and horses. Delightful surroundings near Skirrid Mountain and Offa's Dyke path and two country local pubs. 3 miles from Abergavenny town. Good home cooking, own dining room, T.V. lounge. Ideal place for children. Warm welcome to all.

Single Room per one person B&B		Double Room for two persons B&B		Rooms 2
MIN £	MAX £	MIN £	MAX £	OPEN
8.00	9.00	16.00	18.00	4-10

Great Llwynfranc Farm
Llanvihangel Crucorney, Nr.
Abergavenny, Gwent, NP7 8EN.
Tel: (0873) 890418.

Comfortable Georgian farmhouse. Good home cooked food. Central heating, log fires, T.V. lounge. Radio, tea/coffee facilities, H & C all bedrooms. Panoramic views of Llantony Valley and Black Mountains. Children welcome. 3 miles from busy market town Abergavenny, with easy access to River Usk, Sugar Loaf Mountain, Wye Valley, Forest of Dean, Brecon Beacons. AA approved.

Single Room per one person B&B		Double Room for two persons B&B		Rooms 3
MIN £	MAX £	MIN £	MAX £	OPEN
10.00	11.00	20.00	22.00	3-11

Great Tre-Rhew Farm
Llanvetherine, Abergavenny, Gwent,
NP7 8RA.
Tel: (0873 86) 268. L

Warm welcome to a Welsh family working farm. 165 acres with cattle, sheep, dogs, ponies and poultry. Good home cooking of local produce. Within easy reach of Wye valley, Black Mountains and Brecon Beacons, castles, walking, pony trekking and canal boating, beautiful countryside. The medieval White Castle lies at the top of the farm fields.

Single Room per one person B&B		Double Room for two persons B&B		Rooms 2
MIN £	MAX £	MIN £	MAX £	OPEN
10.00	12.00	18.00	24.00	3-10

Highfields Farm

Goytre, Nr. Pontypool, Gwent, NP4
Tel: (0873) 880030. L

Attractive farmhouse set in countryside with views of the Usk Valley and Brecon Beacons National Park. The house has a welcoming atmosphere and there is a large, secluded garden to relax in. Easily reached by the major routes into Gwent. Large choice of local restaurants and three pubs within walking distance. Single, double and family rooms.

P	Single Room per one person B&B		Double Room for two persons B&B		3
	MIN £ 10.00	MAX £	MIN £ 20.00	MAX £	OPEN 1-12

The Lawns Farm

Grosmont, Abergavenny, Gwent,
NP7 8ES.
Tel: (0981) 240298. L

Comfortable 17th century farmhouse in unspoilt off the beaten track country, situated almost central to Abergavenny, Monmouth, Hereford, Ross-on-Wye. Ideal for walking, touring. Lovely views. Many local castles, one on farm grounds. Good home cooking from own farm produce. One bedroom antique 4 poster bed.

P	Single Room per one person B&B		Double Room for two persons B&B		4
	MIN £ 9.00	MAX £	MIN £ 18.00	MAX £	OPEN 4-10

Little Treadam

Llantilio Crossenny, Abergavenny,
Gwent, NP7 8TA.
Tel: (0600 85) 326.

Olde worlde character farmhouse with lattice windows and oak beams set in picturesque gardens. H & C all rooms. Traditional Welsh farmhouse food. Fully licensed. Within walking distance of White Castle and Offa's Dyke path. Located on B4233. Les Routiers and AA approved.

P	Single Room per one person B&B		Double Room for two persons B&B		4
	MIN £ 10.00	MAX £ 12.00	MIN £ 20.00	MAX £ 24.00	OPEN 1-12

Upper Goytre Farm

Pandy, Abergavenny, Gwent,
NP7 8EE.
Tel: (0873) 890204. L

This 224 acre stock and arable farm is situated on high ground overlooking the Black Mountains. On approaching the farm the spectacular views include the Skirrid, Sugar Loaf and Malvern Hills. Central for Symonds Yat, Hay-on-Wye, Brecon and many castles. Full cooked breakfast and evening meals are provided in this comfortable, long established farmhouse.

P	Single Room per one person B&B		Double Room for two persons B&B		2
	MIN £ 8.00	MAX £ 10.00	MIN £ 16.00	MAX £ 20.00	OPEN 1-12

Caerleon

Map Ref Mc4

At one time the chief fortress of the second Augustan Legion of Rome. A fort established in AD 74 held about 6,000 troops. Amphitheatre and remains still worth a visit as is the Legionary Museum. Recently the Roman Baths have been opened to the public.

Guest Houses

Great House

Isca Road, Old Village, Caerleon,
Gwent, NP6 1QG.
Tel: (0633) 420216/420312. L

Charming 17th century listed building on banks of River Usk, close to Caerleon village, Roman fortification, museum, Roman baths. Lovely furnishings, beamed rooms, woodburners, warm welcome awaiting you. Beautiful garden, countryside walks, fishing, shooting, golf. ¼ mile M4 to Cardiff, London, Bristol. Excellent pubs nearby. Radios, T.V. 2 double, 1 single. Elegant drawing room. Pretty dining room. 2 bathrooms.

P	Single Room per one person B&B		Double Room for two persons B&B		3
	MIN £ 10.00	MAX £ 12.00	MIN £ 20.00	MAX £ 24.00	OPEN 1-12

Farmhouses

Clawdd Farm

Bulmore Road, Caerleon, Nr.
Newport, Gwent, NP6 1QQ.
Tel: (0633) 423250. L

A small woodland farm secluded near the River Usk, yet only minutes from junctions 24–25 off the M4. Close to the recently renovated Legionnairs Roman baths and museum in Caerleon (Isca). Relax in an informal early Edwardian house full of odd objects including Janet's variety of cooking and the vast activities Gwent has to offer.

P	Single Room per one person B&B		Double Room for two persons B&B		5
	MIN £ 10.00	MAX £ 12.00	MIN £ 20.00	MAX £ 24.00	OPEN 1-12

Chepstow

Map Ref Me4

Home of the first stone-built castle in Britain, this attractive town still has a fortified gate and walls. Excellent shopping, fine walls, fine racecourse, ideal for touring the picturesque Wye Valley.

Guest Houses

Bridge House

Pwllmeyric, Chepstow, Gwent,
NP6 6LF.
Tel: (029 12) 2567. L

Ideal for touring Wye Valley, close to Chepstow town and race course, St. Pierre golf course. We offer one family room, one double room, television lounge, central heating. Evening meal on request. Telephone. Car parking. Situated 1½ miles from Chepstow on A48 Newport road. Near Caldicot Castle for medieval banquets.

P	Single Room per one person B&B		Double Room for two persons B&B		2
	MIN £ 10.50	MAX £ 12.00	MIN £ 19.00	MAX £ 21.00	OPEN 1-12

Hazelhurst Guest House

Gloucester Road, Tutshill, Chepstow,
Gwent, NP6 7DB.
Tel: (029 12) 2266.

Situated close to the Wye Valley and Forest of Dean. A family guest house with central heating, spacious bedrooms with hot and cold water. Located easily on the A48 and only a few minutes walk from Offa's Dyke. All home cooking. Guests' lounge with open fire. Separate dining room. Ample parking.

P	Single Room per one person B&B		Double Room for two persons B&B		4
	MIN £ 8.00	MAX £ 9.00	MIN £ 16.00	MAX £ 18.00	OPEN 1-12

The Old Rectory

Tintern, Chepstow, Gwent, NP6 6SG.
Tel: (029 18) 519. L

A free and easy atmosphere awaits the visitor in this 18/19th century house. Accommodation is in 5 bedrooms, 3 overlooking the River Wye with hot and cold, handbasins. Lounge with stone fireplace and dining room serving good home cooked food. Situated on the border between England and Wales, it makes a perfect base for touring.

P	Single Room per one person B&B		Double Room for two persons B&B		5
	MIN £ 9.00	MAX £ 9.00	MIN £ 18.00	MAX £ 18.00	OPEN 1-12

Orchard Lea

Sedbury Lane, Upper Sedbury,
Chepstow, Gwent, NP6 7HN.
Tel: (029 12) 4574. L

Quiet country bungalow situated two miles from Chepstow. Close to M4 for touring, ¼ mile from Offa's Dyke. Family room with one double bed plus bunk beds, H & C, shaver point, T.V. and tea/coffee making facilities. Central heating. Reduced rates for children. Cot available. Open all year. Evening meal optional. Brochure on request.

P	Single Room per one person B&B		Double Room for two persons B&B		1
	MIN £ 9.00	MAX £ 10.50	MIN £ 18.00	MAX £ 19.00	OPEN 1-12

Roseland

Beachley Road, Tutshill, Chepstow,
Gwent, NP6 7EG.
Tel: (029 12) 3370. L

Detached, centrally heated house overlooking Chepstow on Gloucestershire side of River Wye. Turn right towards Beachley at first crossroads at top of hill. Situated on quiet 'B' road adjacent to grass verge just below first junction on left hand side of road. Cot or extra bed available if required.

P	Single Room per one person B&B		Double Room for two persons B&B		1
	MIN £ 8.00	MAX £ 8.00	MIN £ 15.00	MAX £ 15.00	OPEN 1-12

Lancroft

71, St. Kingsmark Avenue,
Chepstow, Gwent, NP6 5SM
Tel: (029 12) 5569. L

3 minutes from town centre, comfortable C.H. private house accommodation. Good home cooking. Double room with H & C, twin room and single room all with tea/coffee making facilities. Bathroom with power shower. Ideal for start of Wye Valley and Offa's Dyke walks. Good motor touring centre. Home from home comforts.

P	Single Room per one person B&B		Double Room for two persons B&B		3
	MIN £ 8.50	MAX £ 9.00	MIN £ 18.00	MAX £ 20.00	OPEN 1-12

Wansbeck Guest House

28, Bridge Street, Chepstow, Gwent,
NP6 5EZ.
Tel: (029 12) 70158.

Situated on the banks of the River Wye between the old Wye bridge and Chepstow Castle. Centrally heated, tea and coffee facilities and colour television in all rooms. The house has been completely renovated and is 250 years old. Good home cooking including vegetarian food by request. Hot and cold water in all rooms.

	Single Room per one person B&B		Double Room for two persons B&B		3
	MIN £ 9.00	MAX £ 12.00	MIN £ 18.00	MAX £ 24.00	OPEN 1-12

Farmhouses

Cribau

The Cwm, Llanvair Discoed, Nr.
Chepstow, Gwent, NP6 6RD.
Tel: (029 17) 528.

Six miles south of Severn Bridge, two miles from A48. 16th century modernised farmhouse with comfortable facilities in traditional settings. 2 rooms, one double bedded, one twin bedded with own patio. Both have shower room en-suite. Very quiet position, no traffic. Beautiful countryside. Variety of animals kept.

P	Single Room per one person B&B		Double Room for two persons B&B		2
	MIN £ 11.00	MAX £ 11.00	MIN £ 20.00	MAX £ 20.00	OPEN 11-12

Great Llanmelyn Farm

Llanvair Discoed, Nr. Chepstow,
Gwent, NP6 6LU.
Tel: (029 17) 210.

Welcome to our large historical farmhouse. Working farm of 200 acres. Spacious bedrooms, tea/coffee making, centrally heated, hot/cold. Spacious bathroom. Dining room/T.V. lounge. Some antique furniture. Peaceful setting in beautiful countryside. Ideal touring Wye Valley, Caldicot mediaeval banquets, near St. Pierre Golf/Country Club. 6 miles junction 22 Severn Bridge, 1 mile A48. Pub food nearby. AA listed.

P	Single Room per one person B&B		Double Room for two persons B&B		2
	MIN £ 10.00	MAX £ 10.00	MIN £ 20.00	MAX £ 20.00	OPEN 4-10

Parsons Grove

Earlswood, Nr. Chepstow, Gwent,
NP6 6RD.
Tel: (029 17) 382.

Set in 17 acres of peaceful countryside. Magnificent views across Wentwood forest, close to Chepstow and M4. Swimming pool. Vineyard bordered by trout stream. Ideally situated for nature walks and within easy reach of Wye Valley and famous St. Pierre golf course. Some family rooms. Some rooms en-suite facilities and colour T.V. WTB Farmhouse Award, AA Listed.

P	Single Room per one person B&B		Double Room for two persons B&B		4
	MIN £	MAX £	MIN £ 20.00	MAX £ 24.00	OPEN 1-12

Mamhilad

Map Ref Mc3

The village is near Pontypool on the route of the Monmouthshire and Brecon Canal. Although on the edge of an area of tremendous and fascinating industrial heritage commemorated by the Big Pit, Blaenavon and the Valley Inheritance Centre, Pontypool, is nevertheless a very rural village.

Farmhouses

Ty'r Ywen Fach Farm

Mamhilad, Nr. Pontypool, Gwent,
NP4 8TT.
Tel: (049 528) 200.

A remote sixteenth century longhouse, high on the Gwent ridgeway in the Brecon Beacons National Park, with oak beams and panelling, inglenook fire places, four poster beds and luxury en-suite bathrooms. An ideal centre for walking, birdwatching, etc., yet not too distant from tourist attractions. Specialising in home cooking using, as far as possible, own produce.

P	Single Room per one person B&B		Double Room for two persons B&B		2
	MIN £	MAX £	MIN £ 24.00	MAX £	OPEN 1-12

Monmouth

Map Ref Me1

Historic market town – birthplace of Henry V and Charles Rolls (Rolls-Royce). Interesting local history museum with collection of Nelson memorabilia. Castle built in the 12th century. Monmouth is situated in a verdant corner of Gwent on the River Wye, still protected by the fortified gateway spanning the Monnow.

Guest Houses

Burton House

St. James Square, Monmouth,
Gwent, NP5 3DN.
Tel: (0600) 4958. L

Situated in the historic town of Monmouth, we offer you good comfortable clean accommodation. All rooms with hot/cold handbasins, tea making facilities and T.V. Evening meal by arrangement. Use of hairdryers, iron and ironing board. On premises parking.

P	Single Room per one person B&B		Double Room for two persons B&B		3
	MIN £ 12.00	MAX £ 12.00	MIN £ 18.00	MAX £ 18.00	OPEN 1-12

Cypress Rise Guest House

Llandogo, Monmouth, Gwent,
Tel: (0594) 530651. L

Superb accommodation overlooking the Wye with beautiful views. Extensive lounge with T.V. Flexibility and hospitality are our key notes. Full central heating ensures total comfort. Llandogo, between Chepstow and Monmouth, is ideal for golfers (St. Pierre, Rolls and Coleford courses), fishing (coarse and game) and walkers (Wye Valley and Forest of Dean).

	Single Room per one person B&B		Double Room for two persons B&B		3
P	MIN £	MAX £	MIN £	MAX £	OPEN
			22.00		1-12

Lugano

Llandogo, Monmouth, Gwent,
NP5 4TL.
Tel: (0594) 530496.

Lugano, set in pleasant gardens off the main A466 halfway betwen Monmouth and Chepstow in the picturesque village of Llandogo. Ideal touring centre, a walkers paradise. Single, double (one with en-suite bathroom), family/twin bedded rooms, all with hot and cold, tea and coffee making facilities and colour T.V. sets. Access to bedrooms and garden at all times. Brochure available.

	Single Room per one person B&B		Double Room for two persons B&B		3
P	MIN £	MAX £	MIN £	MAX £	OPEN
	10.00		19.00	24.00	2-11

Southview Guest House

Dixton Road, Monmouth, Gwent,
NP5 3PP.
Tel: (0600) 2001.

Comfortable, centrally heated licensed guest house ideally situated for exploring the beautiful Wye Valley and Forest of Dean. Within easy reach of the Brecon Beacons and Black Mountains. Rooms have tea/coffee making facilities and H & C water. Residents' lounge with colour T.V.

	Single Room per one person B&B		Double Room for two persons B&B		5
P	MIN £	MAX £	MIN £	MAX £	OPEN
	11.50	11.50	23.00	23.00	1-12

Tudor Farm

Clearwell, Nr. Coleford,
Gloucestershire, GL16 8JS.
Tel: (0594) 33046.

Seven nicely decorated bedrooms, five with en-suite shower/W.C. A 13th century house in a charming village in the Royal Forest of Dean. Log fires, oak beams and original wood panelling. Comfortable, centrally heated rooms. Traditional English cuisine from fresh local produce and breakfast at a civilised hour. Attractive grounds and excellent walking.

	Single Room per one person B&B		Double Room for two persons B&B		7
P	MIN £	MAX £	MIN £	MAX £	OPEN
			23.00	23.00	2-12

Walnut Tree Cottage

Symonds Yat West, Ross-on-Wye,
Herefordshire, HR9 6BN.
Tel: (0600) 890828.

Combination of good food and comfort in a relaxing and friendly atmosphere set high on the banks of the River Wye. Enjoying panoramic Alpine style views. Excellent river and woodland walks. Set in own grounds with ample parking. Access at all times. Early morning tea. Late night supper. Drinks. Licensed dining room. Two lounges.

	Single Room per one person B&B		Double Room for two persons B&B		7
P	MIN £	MAX £	MIN £	MAX £	OPEN
	10.50	11.50	20.00	22.00	1-12

Wye Avon

Dixton Road, Monmouth, Gwent,
NP5 3PR.
Tel: (0600) 3322.

Spacious Victorian house with lovely views and within easy walking distance of Monmouth town centre. Excellent walking country close by. Ideal touring centre for the Wye Valley, Forest of Dean, Welsh border castles, Cardiff, Hereford and Gloucester. Washbasin and shaver point in all rooms. Central heating. Choice of breakfast.

	Single Room per one person B&B		Double Room for two persons B&B		3
P	MIN £	MAX £	MIN £	MAX £	OPEN
	9.00	9.00	18.00	18.00	1-12

Farmhouses

White House Farm

Penallt, Monmouth, Gwent,
NP5 4AH.
Tel: (0600) 3266. L

Welcome to our 16th century farmhouse and working dairy farm lying at 800 feet above the Wye valley, overlooking the Royal Forest of Dean. 1 single room, 1 double room or family room, children very welcome. Evening meals a speciality, country cooking with home produced products.

	Single Room per one person B&B		Double Room for two persons B&B		2
P	MIN £	MAX £	MIN £	MAX £	OPEN
	9.00	12.00	18.00	24.00	4-10

Newport

Map Ref Mc4

Busy industrial, commercial centre. Interesting murals in the main hall of the civic centre. Newport Museum and Art Gallery in John Frost Square and new Leisure Centre with wave machine. On the outskirts, magnificently restored Tredegar House with extensive country park.

Hotels

Anderley Lodge Hotel

216 Stow Hill, Newport, Gwent,
NPT 4HA.
Tel: (0633) 66781.

This family owned hotel combines warm welcome with Victorian elegance and comfortable facilities. Pleasant decor, showers en-suite, colour television, central heating, radio alarm, residents' lounge, free car parking, tea and telephone making facilities. Dining room overlooks a pleasant secluded garden. Evening meals by prior arrangement. Near M4 junction 27. Tourist advice available.

	Single Room per one person B&B		Double Room for two persons B&B		4
P	MIN £	MAX £	MIN £	MAX £	OPEN
	10.00	12.00	20.00	24.00	1-12

Guest Houses

Widecombe

Old Chepstow Road, Langstone,
Newport, Gwent, NP6 2ND.
Tel: (0633) 413311. L

Small, friendly family home in half acre pleasant garden. Comfortable accommodation in two twin bedded rooms with tea making facilities, clock radio, shaver points, hot and cold. Good home cooking. Lounge. Sun lounge. Ideal base for touring. Just off A48, ¾ mile junction 24, M4 and A449 3½ miles east Newport town centre.

	Single Room per one person B&B		Double Room for two persons B&B		2
P	MIN £	MAX £	MIN £	MAX £	OPEN
	9.50	10.50	19.00	21.00	1-12

Raglan
Map Ref Md2

Historic village dominated by Raglan Castle, noted for its impressive Great Tower of Gwent. Convenient for touring the Usk and Wye Valleys, situated in pleasant rural area.

Guest Houses

Hill House
Monmouth Road, Raglan, Gwent,
NP5 2ET.
Tel: (0291) 690214.

Detached country house of character set in spacious gardens with tennis court. Well appointed bedrooms with commanding views of the Vale of Gwent. Own colour television. Three minutes walk Raglan village, good shopping facilities and pubs, half mile historic Raglan Castle. Easy reach Black Mountains and Wye Valley.

Single Room per one person B&B		Double Room for two persons B&B		3
MIN £ 10.00	MAX £ 12.00	MIN £ 20.00	MAX £ 24.00	OPEN 4-10

Farmhouses

Brooklands Farm
Chepstow Road, Raglan, Gwent,
NP5 2EP.
Tel: (0291) 690782.

Peacefully situated near village amenities. Historic farmhouse with charming beams and arch, bedrooms have hot and cold, shaver points, free tea/coffee making facilities. T.V. lounge, reading lounge. Large garden. Small family-run farm with variety of animals, this spacious relaxed home is often revisited by satisfied customers.

Single Room per one person B&B		Double Room for two persons B&B		2
MIN £	MAX £	MIN £ 20.00	MAX £ 22.00	OPEN 1-12

Tintern
Map Ref Me2

Village on River Wye in particularly lovely stretch of the valley. Tintern Abbey is an impressive site. Forest walks, picnic sites and good fishing.

Guest Houses

Cross Keys Cottage
East Street, St. Briavels, Nr. Lydney,
Glos., GL15 6TQ.
Tel: (0594) 530456.

Cottage annex on edge of historic village in Wye Valley, close to Welsh border. Complete privacy. Family bedroom with double bed and bunks, en-suite facilities. Sitting room and small kitchen for tea and coffee preparation. Good home cooking. Evening meals by arrangement. Special rates for families with young children. Sorry no pets.

Single Room per one person B&B		Double Room for two persons B&B		1
MIN £ 12.00	MAX £ 12.00	MIN £ 18.00	MAX £ 18.00	OPEN 1-12

The Smithy
Trellech Grange, Llanishen,
Chepstow, Gwent, NP6 6QN.
Tel: (0600) 860027.

Ideal touring centre for castles, Wye Valley, Brecon Beacons, Bath within one hour. Recently renovated blacksmith's/carpenter's workshop. Small comfortable rooms, most with hot and cold. Set in small farming community. All rooms tea/coffee facilities. Reductions and packed lunches for extended stays. Warm relaxed family atmosphere. Good imaginative home cooking. Television and telephone available.

Single Room per one person B&B		Double Room for two persons B&B		4
MIN £ 11.00	MAX £ 11.50	MIN £ 17.00	MAX £ 18.00	OPEN 1-12

Stowe Court
Stowe, Nr St. Briavel's, Lydney, Glos.
GL15 6QH.
Tel: (0594) 530214.

A secluded 17th century country house standing in own grounds of 4 acres. Comfortable accommodation in three attractive beamed bedrooms, two with en-suite facilities, each having T.V., tea making facilities and electric blankets. Good food. Friendly atmosphere. Lovely countryside. Central heating. E.T.B. 3 crowns. AA listed. Antiques/collectors shop on premises. Guided antique tours.

Single Room per one person B&B		Double Room for two persons B&B		3
MIN £	MAX £	MIN £ 20.00	MAX £	OPEN 1-12

Tanglewood
Tintern Post Office, Tintern,
Chepstow, Gwent, NP6 6SE.
Tel: (029 18) 242.

Situated ½ mile from Tintern Abbey in the centre of this delightful Wye Valley village. Superb countryside and Abbey views from the residents' 1st floor T.V. lounge. Tanglewood offers comfort and friendly service. H & C, tea and coffee making facilities and razor points in bedrooms.

Single Room per one person B&B		Double Room for two persons B&B		3
MIN £	MAX £ 9.50	MIN £	MAX £ 21.00	OPEN 1-12

Wye Barn
The Quay, Tintern, Nr Chepstow,
Gwent, NP6 6SZ.
Tel: (029 18) 456.

Enjoy a peaceful holiday at this 400 year old converted bark house, accommodating 5 guests, situated by the River Wye less than 200 yards from Tintern Abbey. Comfort with style, good food and a friendly welcome is offered. An ideal location for walking or touring yet only ten minutes drive from the Severn Bridge. Rates quoted apply to 2 rooms.

Single Room per one person B&B		Double Room for two persons B&B		3
MIN £ 10.50	MAX £	MIN £ 21.00	MAX £	OPEN 1-12

Farmhouses

The Meads Farmhouse
Trelleck Grange, Chepstow, Gwent,
NP6 6QW.
Tel: (029 18) 211.

An old stone built farmhouse on a working family farm in the beautiful Wye valley area. Maintains its rural charm with oak beams, inglenook fireplaces and traditional bedrooms. Guests have their own dining room, sitting room and bathroom. One double and one twin bedded room with tea/coffee making facilities. Children welcome.

Single Room per one person B&B		Double Room for two persons B&B		2
MIN £ 9.00	MAX £ 10.00	MIN £ 18.00	MAX £ 20.00	OPEN 1-12

Panta Farm
Devauden, Chepstow, Gwent,
NP6 6PS.
Tel: (029 15) 593.

Comfortable and spacious 17th century farmhouse on 360 acre family farm, enjoying seclusion and extensive views over attractive countryside and woodland. Only 2 miles from Tintern. Family and double room with tea/coffee making facilities. Lounge with colour T.V. Reduced rates for children. Cot and highchair. Contact Mrs. Irene Brooke.

Single Room per one person B&B		Double Room for two persons B&B		2
MIN £ 9.50	MAX £	MIN £ 19.00	MAX £	OPEN 4-10

Sylvia Farm

Brockweir Common, Gwent,
NP6 7NS.
Tel: (029 18) 514.

Comfortable, renovated 16th century farmhouse on small farm with glorious views over Wye valley, 3 miles Tintern. Spacious lounge with beamed ceiling and wood burning stove. Separate dining room, good home cooking. Double, twin and family bedrooms all with washbasins. Large sunny terrace, pleasant gardens. Wales Tourist Board Farmhouse Award winner.

P	Single Room per one person B&B		Double Room for two persons B&B		3
	MIN £	MAX £	MIN £ 24.00	MAX £ 24.00	OPEN 3-12

Usk
Map Ref Md3

Ancient borough on River Usk. Excellent salmon fishing. Five miles north stands the great castle of Raglan. The Model Farm Folk Museum at Wolvesnewton exhibits all manner of crafts. Sailing available on the nearby Llandegfedd Reservoir. A good central location for visiting the county of Gwent.

Guest Houses

Crown House

2 Maryport Street, Usk, Gwent,
NP5 1AB.
Tel: (029 13) 2388.

Relax in our small family-run guest house. Jean and Bill Thompson offer you friendly personal service, good food, every comfort. Centrally situated in Usk, "floral town of Wales". Ideal for exploring Vale of Usk, Wye Valley, Brecon Beacons, border castles, industrial heritage, superb countryside. 20 minutes from M4 and Severn Bridge. Children welcome.

P	Single Room per one person B&B		Double Room for two persons B&B		3
	MIN £	MAX £ 11.00	MIN £ 19.00	MAX £	OPEN 1-12

Farmhouses

Pentwyn Farm

Little Mill, Pontypool, Gwent,
NP4 0HQ.
Tel: (049 528) 249.

A warm welcome awaits you at Pentwyn the home of Stuart and Ann Bradley. It is a working farm of 120 acres. Easily accessible from M4 and M5, yet set in the lovely hills of Gwent. The 16th century longhouse stands in a ½ acre garden with its own swimming pool. AA. Best Family Holiday Wales 1984. Licensed.

P	Single Room per one person B&B		Double Room for two persons B&B		4
	MIN £ 9.50	MAX £ 10.00	MIN £ 19.00	MAX £ 20.00	OPEN 3-11

Ty-Gwyn Farm

Gwehelog, Usk, Gwent, NP5 1RG.
Tel: (029 13) 2878.

Ty-Gwyn is a large modernised farmhouse situated 2 miles from Usk. 15 minutes from junction 24 off M4. Good home produced food. Secluded lawns and fish ponds. H & C in bedrooms, central heating. AA listed. Wales Tourist Board Farmhouse Award winner.

P	Single Room per one person B&B		Double Room for two persons B&B		2
	MIN £	MAX £	MIN £ 18.00	MAX £ 19.00	OPEN 3-10

SOUTH WALES VALLEYS

No visit to South Wales is complete without a trip into the valleys. Contrary to popular opinion, this unique area has a dramatic, compelling beauty – and is rich in attractions, some of the best in Wales. At Cwmcarn, for example, there's a scenic forest drive. Pontypool has a marvellous dry ski slope, Penscynor a Wildlife Park, Merthyr Tydfil a narrow-gauge railway.

Bryngarw, with its woodlands and riverbanks, is the latest addition to this area's many country parks. In the Vale of Neath, there are canalside and riverbank walks leading to forests and waterfalls. And the valley towns are fascinating, friendly places. Many preserve memories of the tumultuous Industrial Revolution. Visit Merthyr Tydfil's Cyfarthfa Castle, home of the all-powerful ironmasters, Afan Argoed's Welsh Miners' Museum and Blaenavon's Big Pit, now open for underground tours.

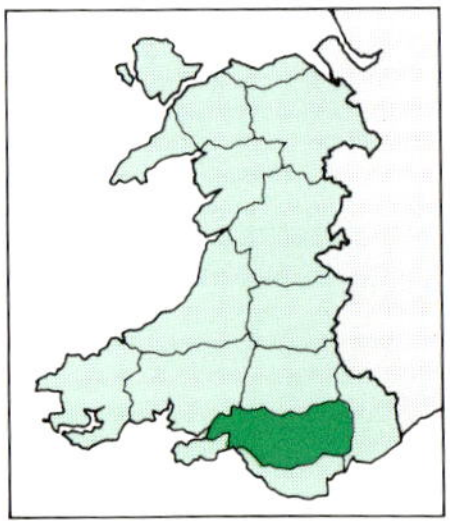

Blackwood
Map Ref Mb3

Gwent valleys town now surrounded by pine-clad cwms rising to mountain tops. Visit Penyfan Ponds, a country park 2½ miles north.

Hotels

Argoed Arms Hotel
Argoed, Blackwood, Gwent, NP2 0HG.
Tel: (0495) 223222. L

2 miles Blackwood, rural setting. Restaurant. Colour television, teasmades in all rooms. Central heating. Children and senior citizens at reduced rates. Open all year round. Small family-run hotel.

P	Single Room per one person B&B		Double Room for two persons B&B		3
	MIN £ 10.50	MAX £ 10.50	MIN £ 20.00	MAX £ 20.00	OPEN 1-12

Caerphilly
Map Ref Ma4

Seven miles north of the capital Cardiff. Huge, 13th century castle with a famous leaning tower – the result of some gunpowder work by the Roundheads. Golf course and shopping centre. Excellent centre for exploring the Valleys and for visiting Cardiff. Caerphilly Mountain offers pleasant walks and excellent views.

Guest Houses

The Cottage
Pwllypant, Caerphilly, Mid Glamorgan, CF8 3HW.
Tel: (0222) 869160.

Three hundred year old large cottage within easy walking distance of Caerphilly and its magnificent Norman Castle. Ideal touring centre for coast, Cardiff, hills and valleys. Bedroom shaver points, H & C. T.V. lounge, central heating. Parking. Numerous recommended restaurants in town. Owner, an official Wales tour guide provides touring service for guests. Croeso.

P	Single Room per one person B&B		Double Room for two persons B&B		3
	MIN £ 10.00	MAX £ 12.00	MIN £ 20.00	MAX £ 24.00	OPEN 1-12

Y Fron Guest House
Pwll-y-Pant, Caerphilly, Mid Glamorgan, CF8 3HW.
Tel: (0222) 882896.

Situated 1½ miles north of Caerphilly town centre on the A469. Former shooting lodge of the Marquis of Bute. Good area for fishing, golf, horse riding, hiking. T.V.'s, teasmades, central heating all rooms. Fire certificate held. Car park.

P	Single Room per one person B&B		Double Room for two persons B&B		6
	MIN £ 10.00	MAX £ 10.00	MIN £ 20.00	MAX £ 20.00	OPEN 1-12

1 Tai Cae Bryn
Groeswen, Caerphilly, Mid Glamorgan, CF4 7UQ.
Tel: (0222) 868213.

Close to Cardiff and magnificent Caerphilly Castle, Castell Coch, St. Fagans Folk Museum, Cardiff centre 8 miles away. Ideal for touring South Wales. Centrally heated. Hot and cold, tea/coffee making facilities. T.V. lounge, dining room. 1 double bedroom, 2 twin bedded rooms, 2 with own showers. Country location with lovely view.

P	Single Room per one person B&B		Double Room for two persons B&B		3
	MIN £ 12.00	MAX £	MIN £ 21.00	MAX £	OPEN 3-10

Cwmbran
Map Ref Mc4

A 'new town' and administrative centre of Gwent. Good sports and leisure facilities. Shopping precinct and sports centre. Theatre and cinema. Good touring centre for the Usk and Wye Valleys.

Guest Houses

Springfields Guest House
371 Llantarnam Road, Llantarnam, Cwmbran, Gwent, NP44.
Tel: (063 33) 2509.

Family-run, in pleasant valley of Llantarnam 1 mile to Cwmbran, 4 miles M4. Good touring area for Wye Valley, Beacons, Cardiff, etc. 1 double en-suite, 1 double, 2 family, 2 twin, 2 single, all with H & C, T.V. Established 15 years. We enjoy our home and work and feel sure you will enjoy your stay. Thank you. Reg, Joan, Graham, Cwmbran 2509.

P	Single Room per one person B&B		Double Room for two persons B&B		8
	MIN £ 10.25	MAX £ 10.25	MIN £ 20.00	MAX £ 24.00	OPEN 1-12

Farmhouses

The Glebe Farm
Croes-y-Ceiliog, Cwmbran, Gwent, NP44 2DE.
Tel: (0633 49) 251/242. L

Enjoy a peaceful stay overlooking a secluded rural valley, yet only 10 minutes drive from M4, Junction 26, A4042 Cwmbran 2 miles, on a 100 acre farm run by my family for over 30 years. A warm Welsh welcome awaits you in my comfortable home. W.T.B. Farmhouse Award. AA listed.

P	Single Room per one person B&B		Double Room for two persons B&B		3
	MIN £ 9.50	MAX £ 10.50	MIN £ 19.00	MAX £ 21.00	OPEN 1-12

Llantrisant
Map Ref Le5

An attractive town, set on a hill in the lower reaches of the Ely Valley and 8 miles from Cardiff. This is the site of the Royal Mint and the home of Dr William Price, the Victorian eccentric.

Hotels

Miskin Arms
Miskin Village, Pontyclun, Mid Glamorgan, CF7 8JQ.
Tel: (0443) 224346.

Homely village pub 10 miles from Cardiff, near ancient town of Llantrisant and Vale of Glamorgan, easy access to coast. Private bathrooms. Tea making facilities. T.V. (Les Routiers) Good food guide recommended. Families welcome. Ample parking.

P	Single Room per one person B&B		Double Room for two persons B&B		4
	MIN £ 12.00	MAX £	MIN £ 24.00	MAX £	OPEN 1-12

Farmhouses

Llwynau Farm Riding/Pony Trekking Centre
Castellau, Llantrisant, Mid Glamorgan, CF7 8LP.
Tel: (0443) 229021/403891. L

Welcome to one of the few remaining 600 year old Welsh longhouse farmhouses, tastefully modernised to include colour T.V. in every room, central heating. Retaining many original features, inglenook fireplaces, oak beams, etc. Riding lessons and trekking available. Longer stays by arrangement. Brochure available. Ideally situated for Cardiff, seaside, mountain, riding, walking. P.T.R.S.W. approved.

P	Single Room per one person B&B		Double Room for two persons B&B		3
	MIN £ 12.00	MAX £ 12.00	MIN £ 24.00	MAX £ 24.00	OPEN 1-12

Merthyr Tydfil
Map Ref Le2

Once a town of tremendous industrial importance, producing iron and steel. Cyfarthfa Castle, an imposing mansion built by a local ironmaster, now houses a fascinating museum. The narrow-gauge Brecon Mountain Railway makes the most of the town's location on the doorstep of the Brecon Becons National Park. Excellent road link direct to Cardiff.

Farmhouses

Tyncoedcae Farm
Swansea Road, Merthyr Tydfil, Mid Glamorgan, CF48 1PB.
Tel: (0685) 77855.

Welsh hill farm situated in 100 acres on the edge of Brecon Beacons National Park. Ideal base for exploring both coastal and mountain scenery. Enjoy the on site wildlife with walks along the hillside stream. Two double rooms, one family all with washbasins. Separate bathroom. Television lounge. Come join us down on the farm.

P ✕	Single Room per one person B&B		Double Room for two persons B&B		🛏 3
	MIN £ 9.00	MAX £ 9.00	MIN £ 18.00	MAX £ 18.00	OPEN 1-12

Neath
Map Ref Lb3

Busy town, now emerging as a tourist centre. The Vale of Neath features a wide variety of tourist attractions including an abbey, Penscynor Wildlife Park and the Aberdulais Canal Basin. Superbly located for a choice of activities – surrounded by forests.

Guest Houses

Europa Hotel
32/34 Victoria Gardens, Neath, West Glamorgan, SA11 3BH.
Tel: (0639) 55094. 👑👑

Situated 5 minutes from town centre, bus and rail stations, overlooking central gardens. Clean, comfortable accommodation with relaxed atmosphere. Good home cooking, dinner by arrangement. Full English breakfast. Tea/coffee facilities. Licensed bar. All bedrooms hot and cold, handbasins. 10 minutes M4. Close to all local tourist attractions, beaches and beautiful countryside.

P ✕	Single Room per one person B&B		Double Room for two persons B&B		🛏 12
	MIN £ 12.00	MAX £ 12.00	MIN £ 22.00	MAX £ 22.00	OPEN 1-12

3 Main Road
Cadoxton, Neath, West Glamorgan, SA10 8AP. Enq: Mrs. B. Lang
Tel: (0639) 59423. L

Three small Welsh cottages charmingly converted into unique accommodation. Family run B & B. Guest sitting room, dining room. T.V., tea/coffee facilities. Two twin bedrooms, one single. Central heating. One mile Penscynor Wildlife Park and Aberdulais Falls and canal basin. Convenient town centre. Next to excellent tavern and restuarant. Children welcome, half price.

P	Single Room per one person B&B		Double Room for two persons B&B		🛏 3
	MIN £ 8.50	MAX £ 8.50	MIN £ 17.00	MAX £ 17.00	OPEN 1-12

Pontardawe
Map Ref Lb3

A town situated on a crossroads in the wooded hill area around the Crynant Forest, south of the Black Mountain. Within easy reach of the Brecon Beacons, the waterfalls of Ystradfellte, Penscynor Wildlife Park and the city of Swansea. Folk festival annually in August.

Guest Houses

Bryn Haul Farm
Rhiwfawr, Swansea Valley, West Glamorgan, SA9 2RY.
Tel: (0639) 830259. 👑👑

Luxury traditional famhouse set in six acres with scenic views, ideal walking country. Riding, golf, fishing by arrangement. Easy reach Gower, Brecon Beacons and West Wales. Cordon bleu cooking using home and local produce. 4 bedrooms all hot and cold, tea/coffee making facilities. T.V. room. Heated outdoor pool.

P 🐕 ✕	Single Room per one person B&B		Double Room for two persons B&B		🛏 4
	MIN £ 11.00	MAX £ 12.00	MIN £ 20.00	MAX £ 24.00	OPEN 2-11

MAPS OF WALES

The maps which follow divide Wales into twelve sections, each with a slight overlap. The grid overlaying each map will help you find the town or village of your choice for against the entry of each of them in this book is a reference number indicating the section of map and grid square. Simply turn up the appropriate map sheet, look for the grid square quoted in the code and pick out the place itself in that square. The maps are at 5 miles or 8 kilometres to one inch scale.

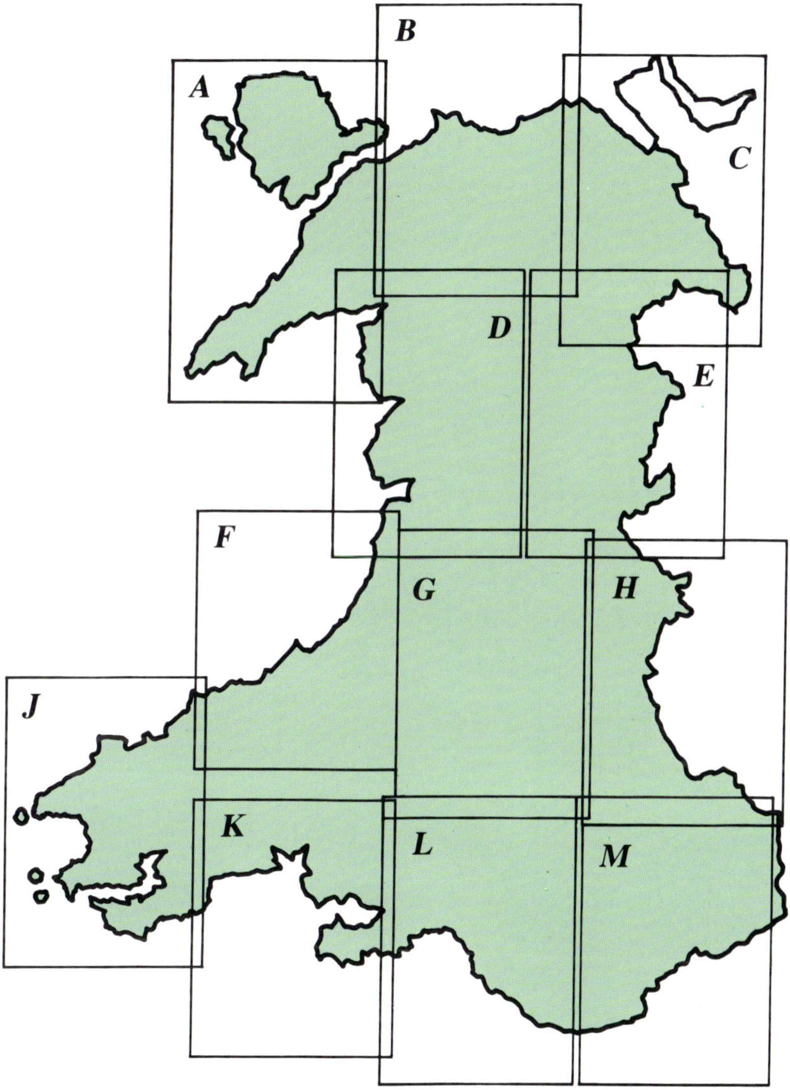

Map A

Miles 0 1 2 3 4 5
Kilometres 0 1 2 3 4 5 6 7 8
N
a
b
c
d
e
1
2
3
4
5
6
7
The Skerries
Carmel Hd.
Hen Borth
Cemlyn Bay
WYLFA NUCLEAR POWER STATION
Bull Bay
Cemaes Bay
Amlwch
Point Lynas
Llaneilian
Tregele
Llanfair-ynghornwy
Llanfechell
Bodewryd
Rhosgoch
Penysarn
Ynys Dulas
Parys Mountain
Traeth-yr-ora
Dulas Bay
Rhydwen
Llanrhuddlad
Church Bay
Llanfaethlu
Traeth Lligwy
Moelfre
Porth Trefadog
Porth Tywyn-mawr
Dublin
Llanddeusant
Llanbabo
VISITOR CENTRE
Llandyfrydog
LLIGWY CROMLECH
Traeth Bychan
Llanerchymedd
Llanfwrog
N.Stack
Holyhead Mount 720ft.
S. Stack
Caergybi
Holyhead
Llanfachraeth
Llanfawr
Traeth-y-gribin
Llyn Alaw
Llanfihangel Tre'r-Beirdd
Benllech
Brynteg
Red Wharf Bay
Traeth Coch
Penmon
Bodedern
Trefor
Llangwyllog
Llanbedr-goch
Llanddona
Llangoed
Dyffryn Valley
Pentraeth
Mynydd Llwydiarth
Llanfaes
y Island
Caer-geiliog
Llanfaes
Porthdafarch
Porth-y-post
Trearddur Bay
Four Mile Br.
Bryngwran
Bodffordd
AIRFIELD
Rhos-meirch
Talwrn
Beaumaris
Rhoscolyn
R.A.F.
Gwalchmai
Heneglwys
Llangefni
Llansadwrn
Penmynydd
Llandegfan
Traeth Lafan
Cymyran Bay
Groeslon
Cerrigceinwen
Porthaethwy
Menai Bridge
Garth
Rhosneigr
Llanfaelog
Ty Croes
Pentre-berw
Llanfair PG
CATHEDRAL
PENRHYN CASTLE
Porth Nobla
BARCLODIAD Y GAWRES
Porth Trecastell
Gaerwen
BRYN CELLI DDU
Bangor
Tal-y-bont
Bodorgan
Llanddaniel Fab
PLAS NEWYDD
Llanllechid
Aberffraw
Llangadwaladr
Glasinfryn
Rachub
Hermon
Malltraeth
Llangaffo
BODOWYR
Newborough
Niwbwrch
Forest
Bryn siencyn
Y Felinheli
Port Dinorwic
Seion
Pentir
Rhiwlas
Llanddeiniolen
Bethel
Penisa'r waen
PENRHYN SLATE QUARRIES
Dwyran
Caernarfon
Aber Menai Pt.
SEGONTIUM
BRYN BRAS
Llanrug
Deiniolen
Cwm-y-glo
LLANBERIS LAKE RAILWAY
Caeathro
Llanddwyn I.
DINORWIG PUMPED STORAGE SCHEME
Llanberis
Y Garn 3104ft.
Nant Peris
Ty-hen
Porth-oer
Methlem
Rhoshirwaun
Llandygwnning
Mynydd Rhiw 999ft.
Llangian
Mynytho
Abersoch
Botwnnog
PLAS YN RHIW
Rhiw
Mynydd Anelog 628ft.
Aberdaron
Llanfaelrhys
Porth Neigwl (Hell's Mouth)
Llanengan
Porth Ceiriad
Pen-y-cil
Trwyn Cilan
Bont-newydd
Llanfaglan
Foryd Bay
Waunfawr
Moel Eilio 2382ft.
Betws Garmon
SNOWDON MOUNTAIN RAILWAY
LLANBERIS PASS
Glyder Fawr
AIRFIELD
Llanwnda
Dinas Dinlle
Rhostryfan
Llandwrog
Groeslon
Carmel
Mynydd Mawr 2290ft.
Yr. 3560ft.
Yr Wyddfa
SNOWDON
Glynllifon
Nantlle
Penygroes
Tal-y-sarn
Y Garn 2080ft.
Rhyd-ddu
Yr Aran 2451ft.
Pontllyfni
Llanllyfni
Nebo
Nazareth
Aberdesach
Garnedd goch 2301ft.
Beddgelert
Clynnog Fawr
1984ft.
1996ft.
Forest
FOREST PARK CENTRE
ABERGLASLYN PASS
Beddgelert
Pant-glas
2566ft. Moel Hebog
Bwlch Mawr 1670ft.
1712ft. Gyrn Ddu
Nantmor
Trefor
Cnicht 2265ft.
Mynydd Cenin 859ft.
Bryncir
Yr Eifl 1850ft.
TRE'R CEIRI
Llanaelhaearn
Nant Gwrtheyrn
Garndolbenmaen
Llithfaen
Moel Ddu 1811ft.
Tan-lan
Dolbenmaen
Garreg
FFYNNON GYBI
Llangybi
Penmorfa
Tremadog
WELSH HIGHLAND RLY.
Porthdinllaen
Nefyn
Garn Boduan 918ft.
PENINSULA
Pentre-felin
Edern
Morfa Nefyn
Y Ffôr
Criccieth
Porthmadog
VALE
Minffordd
Chwilog
Llanystumdwy
Morfa Bychan
Borth-y-gest
Penrhyndeudraeth
Porth Ysgadan
Boduan
Llannor
Abererch
Portmeirion
Traeth Bach
Talsarnau
Porth Ychen
Traeth Penllech
Tudweiliog
Dinas
Efail-newydd
BUTLIN'S HOLIDAY CAMP
Black Rock Sands
Llanfihangel-y-traethau
Carn Fadryn 1217ft.
Rhyd-y-clafdy
Pwllheli
Penychain
Penllech
Llaniestyn
Penrhos
South Beach
Morfa Harlech
Eisingrug
Porth Colmon
Llangwnnadl
LLYN
TREMADOG BAY
Harlech
Sarn
Bryncroes
Botwnnog
Llanbedrog
Ty-hen
Mynytho
SLATE CAVERNS
Llanfair

Map B

N
Miles 0 1 2 3 4 5
Kilometres 0 1 2 3 4 5 6 7 8
a
b
c
d
e
1
2
3
4
5
6
7
Point of A
Gt. Ormes Hd.
GT. ORME TRAMWAY
CABIN LIFT
North Shore
Toll
Little Ormes Hd.
Penrhyn Bay
Llandudno
West Shore
NORTH WALES G.C.
Llandrillo -yn-rhos
Rhos on Sea
Colwyn Bay
CONWY BAY
Deganwy
MAESDU G.C.
Morfa Conwy
Llandudno Junc.
ZOO
Conwy
Penmaenmawr
Old Colwyn
Llysfaen
Rhyd-y-foel
Llanddulas
Pensarn
Abergele
Towyn
Kinmel Bay
SUN CENTRE
Rhyl
Meliden
Prestatyn
Gronant
Gwespyr
Llanasa
Trelawnyd
Trelogan
BODRHYDDAN HALL
Dyserth
Rhuddlan
Marian
Gorsedd
Bodelwyddan
St George
Rhuallt
St. Asaph
Caerwys
Tremeirchion
VALE OF CLWYD
Capelulo
Moel-llys
Gyffin
Llansantffraid Glan Conwy
Llanelian -yn-Rhos
Dolwen
Llanfairfechan
Moelfre 1423ft.
Llangelynnin
Tal-y-fan 2001ft.
Tyn-y-groes
Pentre-felin
BODNANT GARDENS
Betws -yn-rhos
Moelfre -isaf
1038ft.
Wern-fach
Cefn Meiriadog
CAVES
Llannefydd
Aber
Carreg Fawr
ROMAN
Graig
Ro-wen
Tal-y-cafn
Moel Gyffylog
Mynydd Bran
1299ft.
Moelfre -uchaf
Trefnant
Bodfari
Moel Wnion 1903ft.
Drum 2529ft.
Aber Falls
Caerhun
Eglwys Bach
Llanbedr-y Cennin
Llanfair Talhaearn
Henllan
Green
Waen
Y. Drosgl 2484ft.
Foel Fras 3092ft.
2876ft.
Yr Aryg
Tal-y-Bont
Dolgarrog
Pentre
Llangernyw
Pen-y-mwdwl 1178ft.
Bryn-rhyd-yr-arian
FRIARY
Dinbych
Denbigh
TOWN WALLS
Llandyrnog
Waen
Llyn Dulyn
Pont Dolgarrog
Llyn Eigiau
Foel Grach
3485ft.
Carnedd Llywelyn
Carnedd Dafydd 3424ft.
VALE OF CONWY
Llanddoged
Pandy-Tudur
Llansannan
Groes
Llanrhaeadr-yng-Nghinmeirch
Prion
Llanynys
Trefriw
Pentre Tafarn-y-fedw
Llanrwst
Gwytherin
Bylchau
Waen
Nantglyn
Pentre Saron
1128ft.
Rhewl
CRAFT CENTRE
Llyn Ogwen
Capel Curig
GWYDYR UCHAF FOREST VISITOR CENTRE
SWALLOW FALLS
1696ft.
Llyn Brenig
Brenig Reservoir
Cyffylliog
Bontuchel
3010ft.
Glyder Fach
Pen-y-Gwryd
Ty-hyll
Betws-y-coed
RAILWAY MUSEUM
Nebo
Cefn Rhyd
Moel Seisiog 1534ft.
Llyn Aled
Mynydd Hiraethog
1703ft.
Clocaenog
Forest
PINCYN LLYS
Clocaenog
Efenechtyd
Pwllglas
Moel Siabod 2861ft.
Pont-y-pant
CAIRN
Capel Garmon
Llyn Alwen
1742ft.
CRONFA ALWEN
FOREST VISITOR CENTRE
1557ft.
LLYN BRENIG VISITOR CENTRE
Clawdd Newydd
Pentre
Gwydyr Forest
PENMACHNO WOOLLEN MILL
Pentrefoelas
Pont Alwen
BOD PETRUAL FOREST VISITOR CENTRE
Pont Petryal
Derwen
Dolwyddelan
TY MAWR
Penmachno
Ro-Wen 1961ft.
Y Foel
Rhydlydan
Glasfryn
Cefn-brith
Llanfihangel Glyn Myfyr
Bryn Saith Marchog
1083ft.
Ysbyty Ifan
Garn Prys 1747ft.
Cerrigydrudion
Melin-y-wig
1274ft.
Gwyddelwern
GLODDFA GANOL
LLECHWEDD SLATE CAVERNS
Mwdwl Eithin 1543ft.
Betws Gwerfil Goch
STWLAN DAM
Moelwyn Mawr 2527ft.
Blaenau Ffestiniog
Gylchedd 2059ft.
Cader Benllyn
2194ft.
Carnedd-y-Filiast
Llangwm
Maerdy
Tyn-y-cefn
Corwen
Moelwyn Bach 2331ft.
Bethania
Dduallt
Ffestiniog
Migneint
Arennig Fach
Foel Goch 2004ft.
Four Crosses
Dwyryd
Glan-

Map C

N

Miles 0 1 2 3 4 5
Kilometres 0 1 2 3 4 5 6 7 8

a b c d e

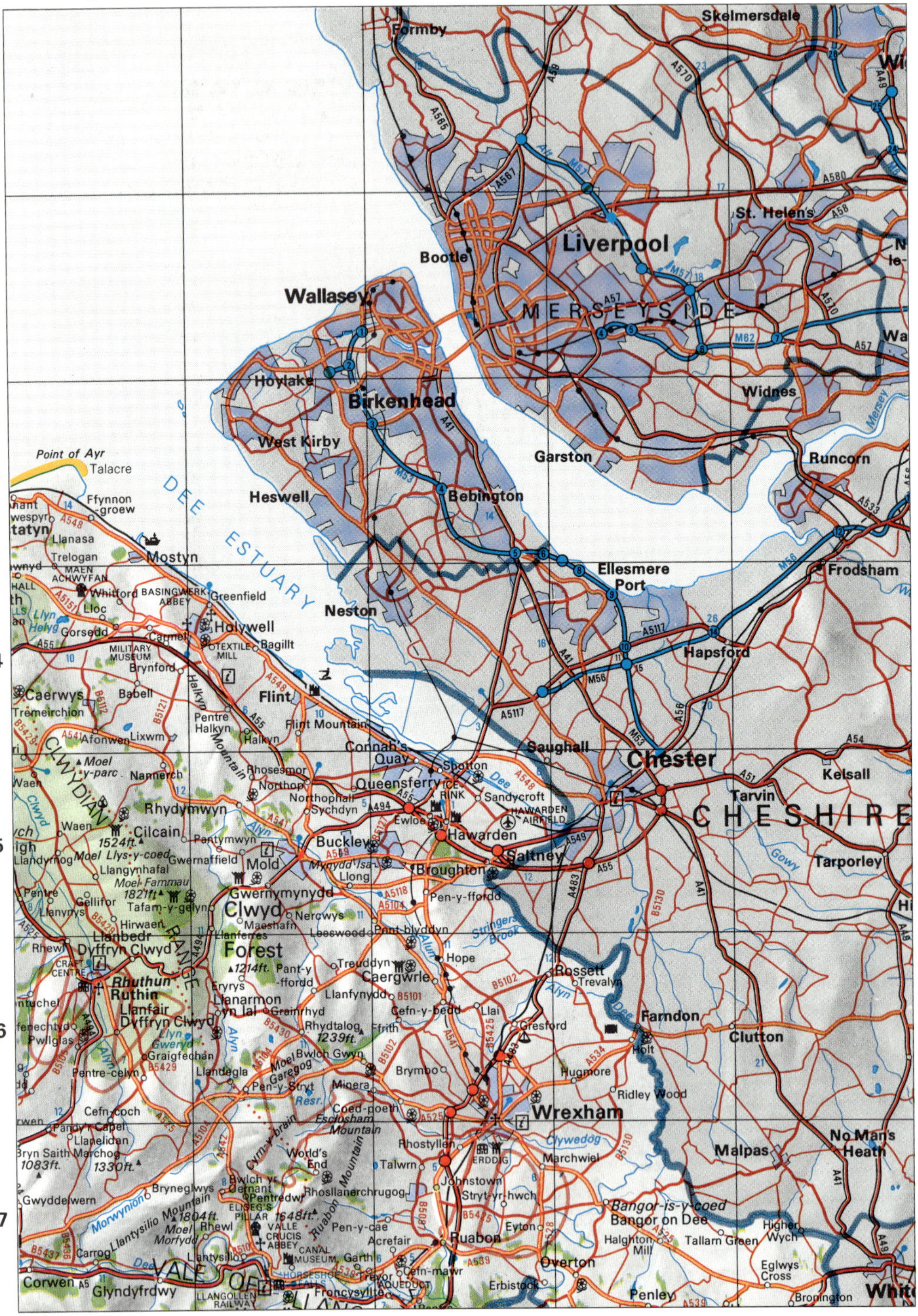

Map D

N
Miles 0 1 2 3 4 5
Kilometres 0 1 2 3 4 5 6 7 8
a
b
c
d
e
1
2
3
4
5
6
7
Beddgelert
Forest
FOREST PARK CENTRE
ABERGLASLYN PASS
Moel Hebog
Nantmor
GLODDFA GANOL
STWLAN DAM
Moelwyn Mawr 2527ft.
Cnicht 2265ft.
Moelwyn Bach 2334ft.
LLECHWEDD SLATE CAVERNS
Blaenau Ffestiniog
Bethania
Gylchedd 2059ft.
Cader Benllyn
2194ft.
Carnedd-y-Filiast
Llangwm
Foel Goch 2004ft.
Moel Emoel
Fron-goch
Dolbenmaen
Moel Ddu 1811ft.
Tan-lan
Garreg
Tanybwlch
FFESTINIOG RLY.
Dduallt
Ffestiniog
Migneint
Arennig Fach 2259ft.
SNOWDONIA
Graig Wen 1823ft.
Llyn Celyn
Penmorfa
Tremadog
WELSH HIGHLAND RLY.
Maentwrog
Penrhyndeudraeth
TOMEN-Y-MUR
Porthmadog
Borth-y-gest
Minffordd
TRAWSFYNYDD NUCLEAR POWER STATION
Llyn Arenig
2800ft. Arennig Fawr
Gwastadros 1182ft.
Y Bala
Llanycil
Llanfor
TOMEN Y BALA
VALE
Llandderfel
Portmeirion
Talsarnau
Traeth Bach
Llyn Trawsfynydd
Trawsfynydd
2461ft. Moel Llyfnant
2221ft.
Llyn Tegid
Rhos-y-gwaliau
Llanfihangel-y-traethau
Morfa Harlech
Eisingrug
Y Graig-ddrwg
2046ft.
NATIONAL
1766ft. Moel-y-Fiedlog
Mynydd Bryn-llech
Llanuwchllyn
Llangywair
BALA LAKE RAILWAY
Penllyn Forest
Harlech
Llyn Cwm Bychan
Crawcwellt
SLATE CAVERNS
Llanfair
Rhinog Fawr 2362ft.
MAESGWM FOREST VISITOR CENTRE
Coed y Brenin
Dduallt 2155ft.
Moel-y-Geifr 2054ft.
Talardd
Llandanwg
Gwynfryn
2333ft.
Rhinog Fach
Moel Hafod Owen 1428ft.
Rhobell Fawr 2408ft.
Llanbedr
Mochras (Shell Is.)
MAESARTRO CRAFT VILLAGE
Y Llethr 2475ft.
Ganllwyd
Foel Ddu 1527ft.
Aran Benllyn 2901ft.
Morfa Dyffryn
Moelfre 1932ft.
Llyn Bodlyn
PARK
Moel Cors-y-garnedd
Llanenddwyn
Dyffryn Ardudwy
Ty'n-y-groes
Llanfachreath
2970ft. Aran Fawddwy
Dyrysgol 2397ft.
Cefn Tre-Ysbyty 1681ft.
Llanddwywe
Diffwys 2462ft.
Y Garn 2063ft.
Moel Offrwm
Rhyd-y-main
Talybont
Moel 1328ft.
Llanymawddwy
RURAL LIFE CENTRE
Bontddu
Llanelltyd
ABBEY
Brithdir
Bwlchyfign 2149ft.
Dyfnant
Llanaber
Penmaenpool
Dolgellau
Cross Foxes
Bwlch yr Oerddrws
Aber Cowarch
Tir Rhiwiog 1787ft.
Abermaw
Barmouth
Ferry
TAL-Y-WAEN FARM TRAIL
Dinas Mawddwy
BARMOUTH
FAIRBOURNE RAILWAY
Arthog
Waen Oer 2197ft.
MEIRION WOOLLEN MILL
Tal-y-Meryn
Carreg-y-fran
Tyrau Mawr 2167ft.
CADER IDRIS
Mynydd Moel
BAY
Fairbourne
Friog
2040ft.
Penygadair 2927ft.
Mynydd Dolgoed
1708ft.
1244ft.
Mallwyd
Penygarn
Craig-y-llyn
Mynydd Pencoed
1504ft.
Minffordd
Corris Uchaf
Aberllefenni
Aberangell
Llwyngwril
Llanfihangel-y-pennant
CASTELL-Y-BERE
Tal-y-llyn
Craig Goch 2186ft.
Dyfi Forest
Corris
CRAFT CENTRE
Cemmaes
Cwm Llinau
Llyn Gwyddior
Llangelynnin
Abergynolwyn
TALYLLYN RAILWAY
NANT GWERNOL
Esgairgeiliog
ALT. TECH.NAT. CENTRE
VALLEY
Cemmaes Road
Pandy
FFORDD GLYNDWR
Rhoslefain
Llanegryn
ROOD SCREEN
Foel Cocyn 1013ft.
Dol-goch
Moelygeifr
Llanwrin
Commins Coch
Aber Gwydol
Llanbrynmair
Twmpath Melyn 1444ft.
Tonfanau
Aber Dysynni
Bryn-crug
Pandy
Taren Hendre 2076ft.
Darowen
Tafolwern
Trum Gelli 1755ft.
Machynlleth
Penegoes
Llan
Pont dolgadfan
Talerddig
Tywyn
Corlan Fraith
Happy Valley
Cwrt
Pennal
Forge
Talywern
837ft.
Aberdyfi
914ft.
DOVEY
Derwenlas
Pennant
Bryn Amlwg 1603ft.
Aberdovey
Glaspwll
Aberhosan
Carno
Glandyfi
Bryn y Fedwen 1784ft.
Pont Crygnant
Traeth Maelgwyn
Furnace
Eglwys-fach 1467ft.
Pen Carreg-gopa
Cwm Einion
Bryn yr Oerfa 1507ft.
Waen Garno 1293ft.
Ynyslas
Foel Goch 1557ft.
Rheidol
Llyn Pen-rhaiadr
Dylife
Staylittle
Bryn Crugog 1463ft.
Llancynfelyn
Tre'r-ddol
OLD CHAPEL MUSEUM
1703ft. Moelylyn
1607ft. Bryn Moel
Fedw Ddu 1597ft.
Llawr-y-glyn
Trannon
Talybont
Tre Taliesin
Hafren Forest
Borth
Dol-y-bont
Forest
Drosgol 1806ft.
Source of R. Severn
Source of R. Wye
Mynydd y Groes 1578ft.
Nant-y-moch Reservoir
Pen Plynlimon-fawr 2468ft.
Bryn Tail 1321ft.
Fan
Llandre
Elerch
Tor Du 1659ft.
Wallog
Bow Street
Disgwylfa Fawr 1661ft.
Drum Peithnant
PLYNLIMON
Y Foel 1791ft.
Llanidloes
Clarach
Penrhyn-coch
Eisteddfa-gurig
Pen-Bwlch-y-groes 1487ft.
Cwm-belan
CLIFF RLY.
Aberystwyth
Capel Dewi
Waun-fawr
Capel Bangor
Goginan
LLYWERNOG SILVER LEAD MINE
Dyffryn Castell
Ponterwyd

Map E

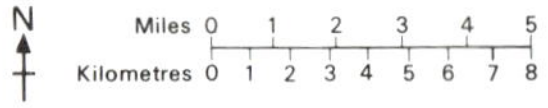

N
Miles 0 1 2 3 4 5
Kilometres 0 1 2 3 4 5 6 7 8

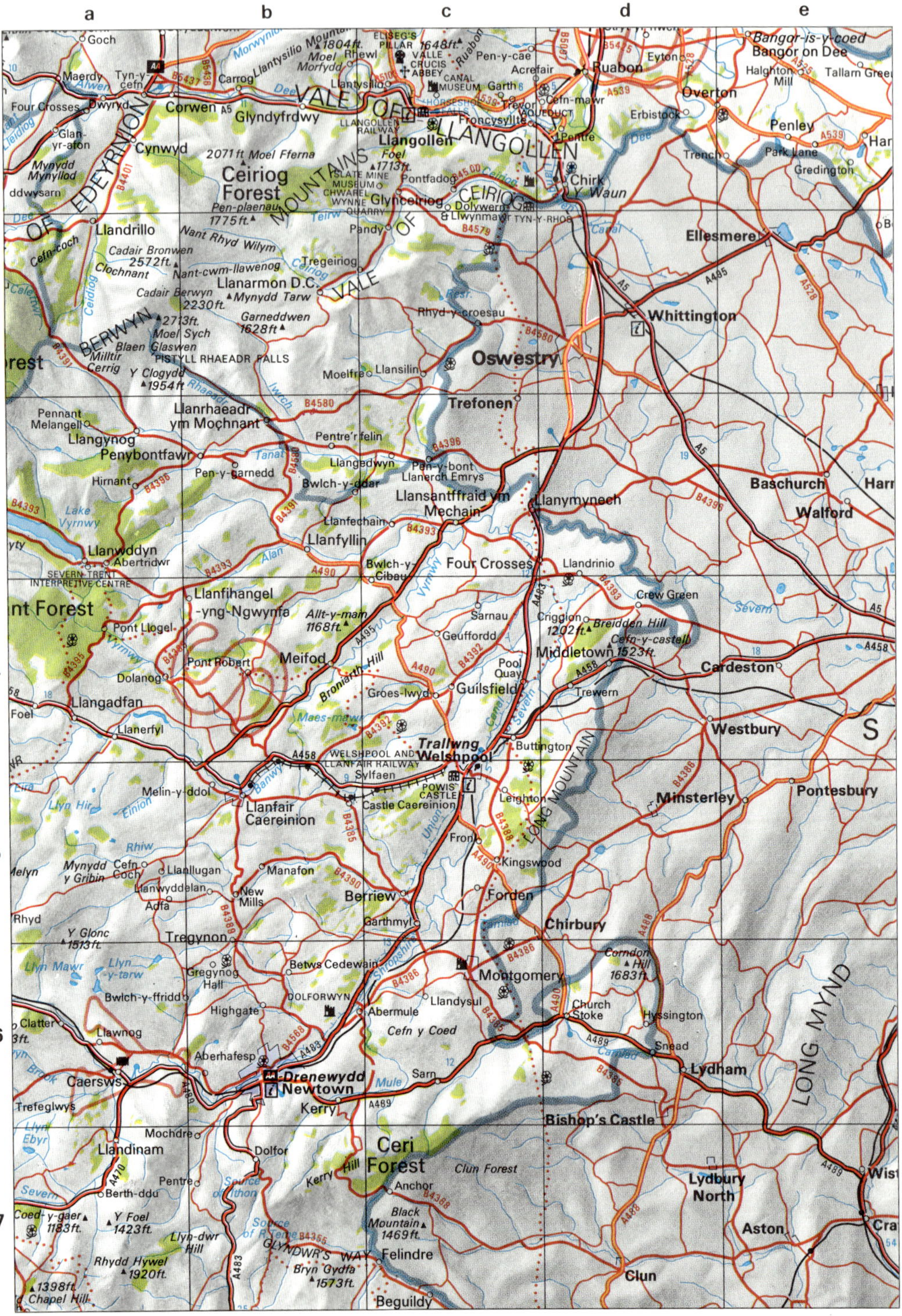

a
b
c
d
e
1
2
3
4
5
6
7
Goch
Maerdy
Tyn-y-cefn
Alwen
Four Crosses
Dwyryd
Glan-yr-afon
Cynwyd
Corwen
Carrog
Llantysilio Mountain
1804ft.
Moel Rhewl
Moel Morfydd
Morwynion
ELISEG'S PILLAR
VALLE CRUCIS ABBEY
1648ft.
Ruabon Mountain
Pen-y-cae
Acrefair
Ruabon
Eyton
Bangor-is-y-coed
Bangor on Dee
Halghton Mill
Tallarn Green
Overton
Erbistock
Penley
Park Lane
Gredington
Trench
Glyndyfrdwy
Dee
VALE OF LLANGOLLEN
Llantysilio
CANAL MUSEUM
Garth
Cefn-mawr
Trevor
AQUEDUCT
Froncysyllte
LLANGOLLEN RAILWAY
Llangollen
Pentre
Chirk
Y Waun
Mynydd Mynyllod
ddwysarn
EDEYRNION
Ceiriog Forest
2071ft Moel Fferna
MOUNTAINS
Foel 1713ft.
SLATE MINE MUSEUM
CHWAREL WYNNE QUARRY
Pontfadog
Glyn Ceiriog
Dolywern
Llwynmawr
TYN-Y-RHOS
CEIRIOG
Pen-plaenau 1775ft.
Pandy
Llandrillo
Cefn-coch
Nant Rhyd Wilym
Cadair Bronwen 2572ft.
Clochnant
Nant-cwm-llawenog
Tregeiriog
Cadair Berwyn 2713ft.
Llanarmon D.C.
Mynydd Tarw 2230ft.
VALE OF
Ellesmere
Whittington
Garneddwen 1628ft
Rhyd-y-croesau
BERWYN
Moel Sych
Blaen Glaswen
Milltir Cerrig
PISTYLL RHAEADR FALLS
Y Clogydd 1954ft
Moelfre
Llansilin
Oswestry
Trefonen
Pennant Melangell
Llangynog
Llanrhaeadr ym Mochnant
Penybontfawr
Tanat
Pentre'r felin
Llangedwyn
Pen-y-garnedd
Pen-y-bont Llanerch Emrys
Hirnant
Bwlch-y-ddar
Llansantffraid ym Mechain
Llanymynech
Baschurch
Walford
Lake Vyrnwy
Llanfechain
Llanfyllin
Llanwddyn
Abertridwr
SEVERN-TRENT INTERPRETIVE CENTRE
Bwlch-y-Cibau
Vyrnwy
Four Crosses
Llandrinio
Crew Green
Severn
Llanfihangel-yng-Ngwynfa
Allt-y-main 1168ft.
Sarnau
Criggion
Breidden Hill
1202ft.
Cefn-y-castell
Middletown
1523ft.
Pont Llogel
Geuffordd
Pool Quay
Cardeston
Pont Robert
Meifod
Broniarth Hill
Dolanog
Guilsfield
Trewern
Llangadfan
Groes-lwyd
Foel
Maes-mawr
Westbury
Llanerfyl
Trallwng
Welshpool
Buttington
WELSHPOOL AND LLANFAIR RAILWAY
Sylfaen
POWIS CASTLE
LONG MOUNTAIN
Melin-y-ddol
Llanfair Caereinion
Castle Caereinion
Leighton
Minsterley
Pontesbury
Banwy
Einion
Llyn Hir
Union
Fron
Rhiw
Mynydd y Gribin
Cefn Coch
Llanllugan
Manafon
Kingswood
Llanwyddelan
Adfa
New Mills
Berriew
Forden
Garthmyl
Chirbury
Y Glonc 1513ft.
Tregynon
Llyn Mawr
Llyn-y-tarw
Gregynog Hall
Betws Cedewain
Montgomery
Corndon Hill 1683ft.
Bwlch-y-ffridd
DOLFORWYN
Llandyssul
Highgate
Abermule
Church Stoke
Hyssington
Cefn y Coed
Clatter
Llawnog
Aberhafesp
Snead
Lydham
LONG MYND
Caersws
Drenewydd
Newtown
Mule
Sarn
Trefeglwys
Kerry
Bishop's Castle
Mochdre
Llandinam
Dolfor
Ceri Forest
Clun Forest
Kerry Hill
Lydbury North
Pentre
Berth-ddu
Source of R. Ithon
Anchor
Coed-y-gaer 1183ft.
Y Foel 1423ft.
Llyn-dwr Hill
Black Mountain 1469ft.
Aston
Source of R. Teme
Rhydd Hywel 1920ft.
GLYNDWR'S WAY
Bryn Gydfa 1573ft.
Felindre
Clun
1398ft. Chapel Hill
Beguildy
A5
A458
A483
A489
A490
A495
A470
A488
A528
A539
B4401
B4500
B4579
B4580
B4396
B4391
B4393
B4395
B4392
B4390
B4385
B4389
B4386
B4388
B4568
B4355
B4368
B4385

Map F

N
Miles 0 1 2 3 4 5
Kilometres 0 1 2 3 4 5 6 7 8
a
b
c
d
e
1
2
3
4
5
6
7
Talybont
Borth
Dol-y-bont
Llandre
Wallog
Bow Street
Clarach
Penrh
CLIFF RLY
Aberystwyth
Capel Dew
Waun-fawr
Llanbadarn-fawr
Pen-parcau
VALE OF RHEIDOL RAILWAY
Rhyd-y-felin
NANTEOS
Llanfarian
Blaenplwyf
Llanilar
Llanddeiniol
Llanrhystyd
Llangwyryfon
Trefenter
MYNYDD BACH
Llanon
Aeron
Llyn Eiddwen
Nebo
Forest
Aberarth
Pennant
Cross Inn
Bethania
Blaenpenal
Aberaeron
SEA AQUARIUM
Penuwch
Ffos-y-ffin
Llanaeron
Cilcennin
Llangeitho
Cei Bach
Llwyn-celyn
Cei Newydd
New Quay
Llanina
Ciliau Aeron
Bwlchllan
Betws Leucu
Cwm Tudu
Cross Inn
Llanarth
Llanfihangel Ystrad
Tal-sarn
Gartheli
Ynys Lochtyn
Llwyn Dafydd
Dihewid
Felinfach
Mydroylin
Temple Bar
Synod Inn
Llangybi
Llangrannog
Mwnt
Traeth Penbryn
Penbryn
Plwmp
Cribyn
Bettws-Bledrws
Aberporth
Sarnau
Brynhoffnant
Gors-goch
Tre-saith
Capel Cynon
Talgarreg
Llanbedr Pont Steffan
Lampeter
Blaenannerch
Glyn Arthen
FARM PARK
1062 ft.
Cwrt-newydd
Verwig
Tre-main
Blaenporth
Rhyd Lewis
Llanwnnen
Penparc
Aberteifi
Cardigan
Ffostrasol
Cwm-sychpant
Dre-fach
Allt-y-blacca
Ram
Beulah
Penrhiw-pâl
Pont-siân
Llanwenog
Pencarreg
Llangoedmor
Brongest
MAESLLYN WOOLLEN MILL
Tre-groes
Rhyd Owen
Pen Tas-eithin 1361ft.
Llechryd
Troed-yr-aur
Maes-llyn
Pren-gwyn
Llanybydder
Mynydd Pencarreg
Llandygwydd
FELIN GERI MILL
Aber-banc
Horeb
Capel Dewi
Cilgerran
Cwm-cou
Cenarth
Llandyfriog
Penrhiw-llan
Llanllwni
Pumsa
Aber Cych
Castell Newydd Emlyn
Newcastle Emlyn
Aberarad
Landysul
Maesycrugiau
Henllan
Bangor
Pont-tyweli
Llanfihangel-ar-arth
1256ft.
Mynydd Llanybydder
Rhyd-cymerau
Rhos-hill
Newchapel
Felindre
Tre-fach
MUSEUM OF WOOLLEN INDUSTRY
Pentre-cwrt
Boncath
Pentre-drefelin
Banc-y-ffordd
Mynydd Llanllwni 1209ft.
Blaenffos
Capel-Ifan
Penboyr
New Inn
Moelfre 1100ft.
Rhos
Pencader
Gwyddgrug
Edwinsford
Bwlch-y-groes
Star
Frenifawr 1297ft.
Cwm Morgan
Brechfa Forest
Abergorlech
ABBEY
1070ft.
1080ft.
Mynydd Cynros
Tegryn
Y Glog
Hermon
Allt Walis
Halfwa
869ft
Hermon
Cwm-duad
827 ft.
Waun-deg
Mynydd Figyn
Llanfyrnach
Dinas
Trelech
Llanllawddog
Brechfa
Llanpumpsaint
Glandwr
Cynwyl Elfed
Pont ar Sais
Llanfynydd
Hebron
Coed
Trelech a'r Betws
Blaen-y-coed
GWILI RAILWAY
Rhyd-ar-gaeau
Salem
Eglwys Fair a Churig
Cwm-bach
Llanglydwen
Talog
Cwmdwyfran
Peniel
Felin-gwm-uchaf
Pen-y-banc
Deufor

Map G

N — Miles 0 1 2 3 4 5 — Kilometres 0 1 2 3 4 5 6 7 8

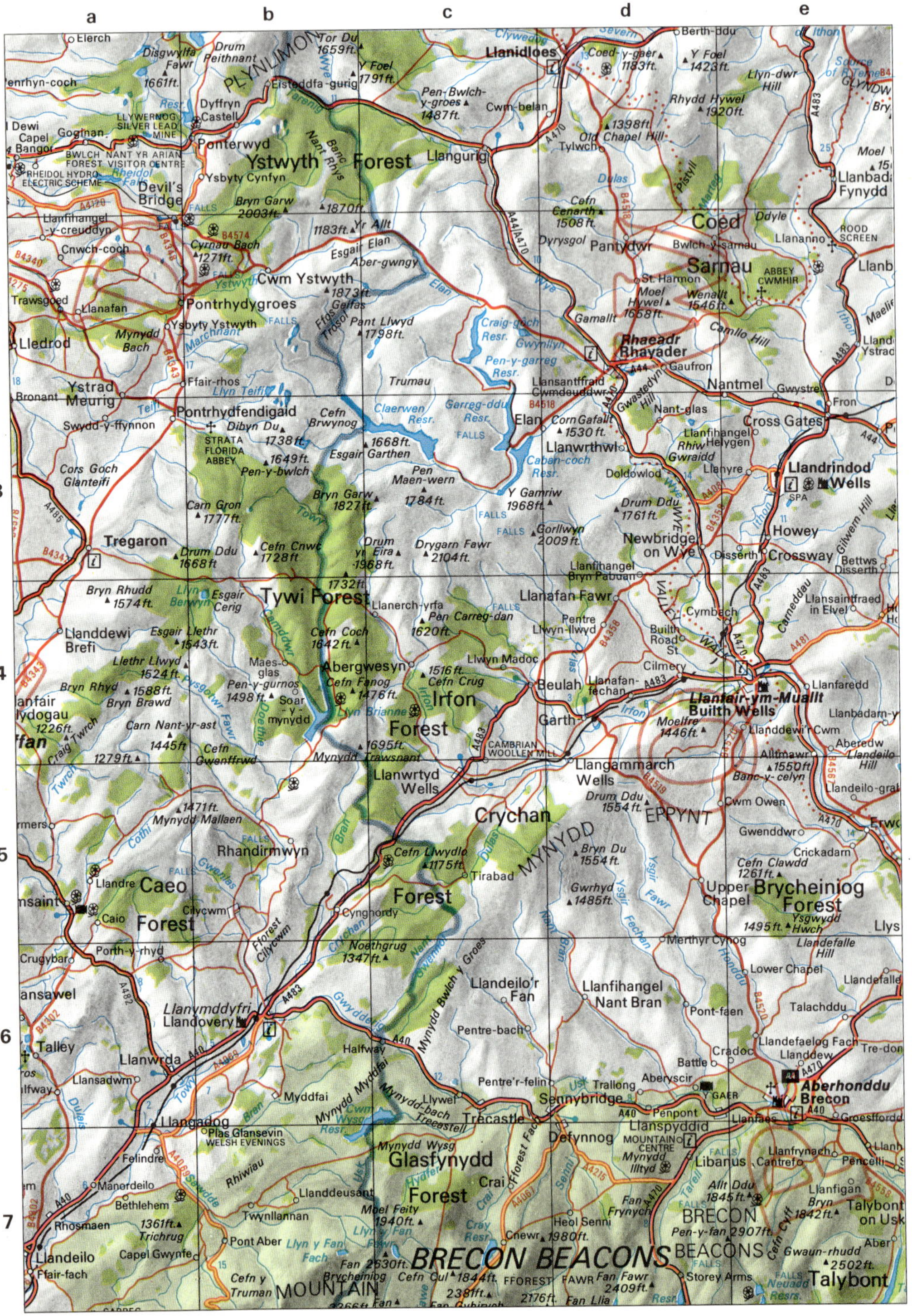

Map H

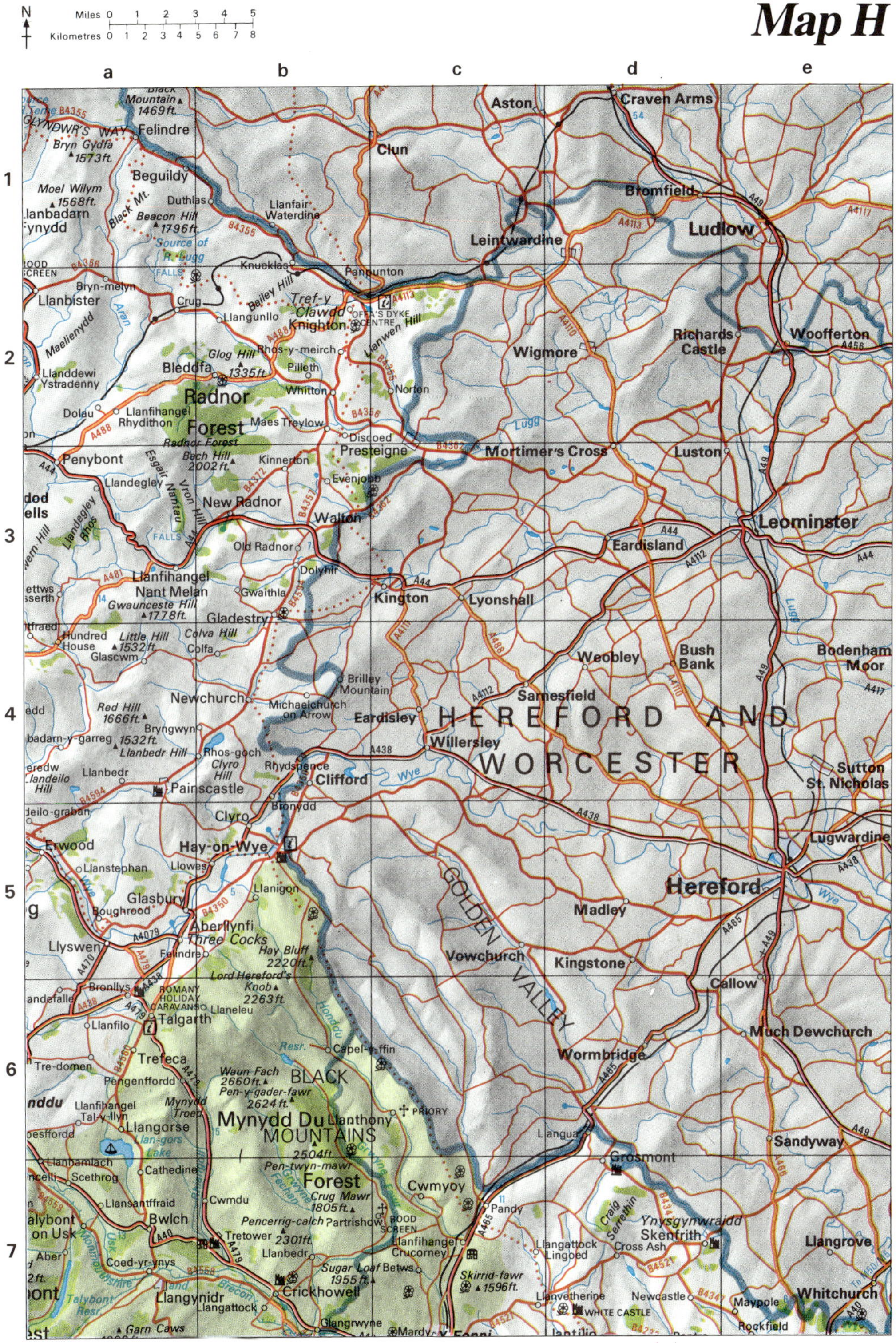

Miles 0 1 2 3 4 5
Kilometres 0 1 2 3 4 5 6 7 8
N
a
b
c
d
e
1
2
3
4
5
6
7
Black Mountain 1469ft.
Felindre
GLYNDWR'S WAY
Bryn Gydfa 1573ft.
Beguildy
Moel Wilym 1568ft.
Llanbadarn Fynydd
Black Mt.
Beacon Hill 1796ft.
Source of R. Lugg
Duthlas
Llanfair Waterdine
Clun
Aston
Craven Arms
Bromfield
Ludlow
Leintwardine
Knucklas
Panpunton
Llanbister
Bryn-melyn
Crug
Bailey Hill
Tref-y-Clawdd
Knighton
OFFA'S DYKE CENTRE
Llangunllo
Maelienydd
Llanwen Hill
Glog Hill 1335ft.
Rhos-y-meirch
Bleddfa
Pilleth
Llanddewi Ystradenny
Radnor
Forest
Whitton
Norton
Wigmore
Richards Castle
Woofferton
Dolau
Llanfihangel Rhydithon
Maes Treylow
Discoed
Presteigne
Mortimer's Cross
Luston
Lugg
Radnor Forest
Bach Hill 2002ft.
Penybont
Kinnerton
Evenjobb
Llandegley
Esgair Nantau
Vron Hill
New Radnor
Walton
Leominster
Eardisland
Old Radnor
Dolyhir
Llanfihangel Nant Melan
Gwaithla
Kington
Lyonshall
Gwaunceste Hill 1778ft.
Gladestry
Hundred House
Little Hill 1532ft.
Colva Hill
Colfa
Glascwm
Weobley
Bush Bank
Bodenham Moor
Brilley Mountain
Newchurch
Red Hill 1666ft.
Michaelchurch on Arrow
Sarnesfield
Eardisley
HEREFORD AND WORCESTER
Bryngwyn
1532ft.
Willersley
Llanbedr Hill
Rhos-goch
Cyrro Hill
Rhydspence
Clifford
Wye
Sutton St. Nicholas
Llanbedr
Painscastle
Clyro
Bronydd
Erwood
Hay-on-Wye
Llowes
Lugwardine
Llanstephan
Llanigon
GOLDEN VALLEY
Hereford
Glasbury
Boughrood
Aberllynfi
Three Cocks
Madley
Llyswen
Felindre
Hay Bluff 2220ft.
Vowchurch
Kingstone
Lord Hereford's Knob 2263ft.
Bronllys
ROMANY HOLIDAY CARAVANS
Talgarth
Llaneleu
Callow
Llanfilo
Much Dewchurch
Capel-y-ffin
Trefeca
Tre-domen
Wormbridge
Waun Fach 2660ft.
Pen-y-gader-fawr 2624ft.
BLACK
Pengenffordd
Llanfihangel Tal-y-llyn
Mynydd Troed
PRIORY
Mynydd Du
Llanthony
MOUNTAINS
Llangorse
Llan-gors Lake
Llangua
Sandyway
Grosmont
Llanhamlach
Cathedine
2504ft.
Scethrog
Pen-twyn-mawr
Forest
Cwmyoy
Llansantffraid
Crug Mawr 1805ft.
Craig Serrethin
Ynysgynwraidd
Skenfrith
Cwmdu
Pandy
Talybont on Usk
Bwlch
Pencerrig-calch 2301ft.
Partrishow
ROOD SCREEN
Llangattock Lingoed
Cross Ash
Llangrove
Tretower
Llanfihangel Crucorney
Llanbedr
Coed-yr-ynys
Sugar Loaf 1955ft.
Betws
Skirrid-fawr 1596ft.
Llangynidr
Crickhowell
Llangattock
Llanvetherine
WHITE CASTLE
Newcastle
Maypole
Whitchurch
Rockfield
Talybont Resr.
Garn Caws
Glangrwyne
Mardy
Y Fenni

Map J

N
Miles 0 1 2 3 4 5
Kilometres 0 1 2 3 4 5 6 7 8
a
b
c
d
e
1
2
3
4
5
6
7
PEMBROKESHIRE COAST NATIONAL PARK
Car Ferry Rosslare-Fishguard
Cardigan Island
Cemaes Hd.
Gwbert
Pen-yr-afr
Poppit Sands
Ceibwr
Llandudoch
St. Dogmael's
Trewyddel
Moylgrove
Glan-rhyd
Bridell
Trwyn y Bwa
Dinas Head
Pwll Gwaelod
Cwm-yr-eglwys
Newport Bay
Parrog
Nanhyfer
Nevern
Felindre-Farchog
Eglwyswrw
Trefdraeth
Newport
Carningli Common
Pentre Ifan
Ffynnongroes
Brynberian
Crymych
Strumble Head
Carreg Wastad Pt.
Pen Brush
Pen
Caer
Llanwnda
Goodwick
Abergwaun
Fishguard
Fishguard Bay
Aber-Bach
Dinas
Tref asser
Tremarchog
St. Nicholas
Llanllawer
1008ft.
1021 ft.
Mynydd Melyn
Mynydd Caregog
Aber-bach
Aber-mawr
Pen Morfa
Manorowen
Llanychaer
Gwaun Valley
Pontfaen
Mynydd Preseli
Granston
Abercastello
Scleddau
Jordanston
Trecwn
1096ft.
1535ft.
Foel Eryr
1760ft.
Mynydd Cilciffeth
Pen Clegyr
Porth-gain
Tre-fin
Mathry
Castle Morris
Cas-mael
Puncheston
Morfil
1137ft.
Coed Preseli
Mynydd Castlebythe
Foel Cwm-cerwyn
Rosebush
Clyn
1209ft.
Foel Drych
Pentre-galar
Aber Eiddi
Llanrhian
Treletert
Letterston
Castlebythe
Mynachlog-ddu
Croes-goch
Llanreithian
Cas-newydd-Bach
Little Newcastle
Tufton
Henry's Moat
Maenclochog
St. David's Head
Tretio
Llanhowel
Caerfarchell
Casblaidd
Wolf's castle
Newton
Llangly
Whitesand Bay
Rhodiad
Llandeloy
Woodstock
Mot
New Moat
Ramsey Island
Whitchurch
Middle Mill
Hayscastle
Hayscastle Cross
Ambleston
Llys-y-fran
Llan-y-cefn
Login
Tyddewi
St. David's
Solfach
R.A.F.
Treffgarne
Trefgarn
Cilymaenllwyd
Chapel
Caerbwdi
Solva
Brawdy
583ft.
Dudwell Mt.
Walton East
Caerfai
Porthclais
Dinas Fawr
Green Scar
Nectarium
Spittal
Pen-ffordd
Ramsey Sd.
Niwgwl
Newgale
Roch
Wolfsdale
Scolton
Rudbaxton
Clarbeston
Bletherston
Llandysilio
Camrose
Withybush Airfield
Clarbeston Road
Egremont
St. Bride's Bay
Rickets Head
Simpson Cross
Keeston
Keeston Hill
Wiston
Clunderwen
Llanfallteg
Nolton
Pelcomb Br.
Llawhaden
Castelldwyran
Druidston
Lambston
Robeston Wathen
Llanddewi Velfrey
Haroldston West
Hwlffordd
Haverfordwest
Canaston Br.
Redstone Bank
Portfield Gate
Dreenhill
Coed Preseli
Crinow
Broad Haven
Broadway
The Rhos
Minwear
Slebech
Arberth
Narberth
Lampeter Velfrey
Tavernspite
Little Haven
Walton West
Ratford Br.
Graham Sutherland Art Gallery
Landshipping
Cold Blow
Princes Gate
Talbenny
Rosepool
Freystrop
Hook
Martletwy
Templeton
Ludchurch
Martin's Haven
The Nab Head
St. Brides
Hasguard
Walwyn's Castle
Tiers Cross
Llangwm
Yerbeston
Garland Stone
Skomer Island
Musselwick Sands
Marloes
Johnston
Sardis
Reynalton
Stepaside
Rosemarket
Begelly
Mew Stone
Gateholm
Marloes Sands
St. Ishmael's
Herbrandston
Milffwrd
Milford Haven
Houghton
Lawrenny
Jeffreston
Kilgetty
Broad Sound
Westdale Bay
Dale
Sandy Haven
Gellis-wick
Waterston
Neyland
Burton
Cresswell
Cresselly
Hill
Wiseman's Bridge
Skokholm Island
Castlebeach
Milford Haven
Llanstadwell
W. Williamston
Redberth
Broadmoor
Doc Penfro
Pembroke Dock
Cosheston
Carew
Sageston
E. Williamston
Saundersfoot
Thorn Island
Watwick Bay
Mill Bay
St. Ann's Head
Angle
Pwllcrochan
Rhoscrowther
Penfro
Pembroke
Tidal Mill
Milton
Carew Cheriton
New Hedges
Monkstone
Dinbych-y-pysgod
Tenby
Bishops Palace
Lamphey
St. Florence
Gumfreston
Sheep Island
Freshwater West
Hundleton
Museum of Gypsy Lore
Kingsfold
Manor House Leisure Park
St. Catherine's
Newton
Maiden Wells
Jameston
Penally
Castlemartin
Castlemartin Br.
Hodgeston
Lydstep
Giltar Pt.
Orielton
Freshwater East
Swanlake Bay
Caldy Sd.
Warren
St. Petrox
Cheriton
Trewent Pt.
Manorbier
Monastery
Caldy
Linney Head
Merrion
Stackpole
Old Castle Hd.
Barafundle Bay
Bosherston
Stack Rocks
Chapel
Stackpole Head
Broad Haven
Saddle Hd.
St. Govan's Head

Map K

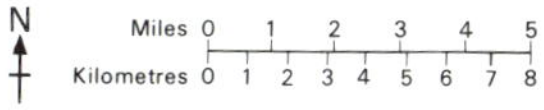

N
Miles 0 1 2 3 4 5
Kilometres 0 1 2 3 4 5 6 7 8

a
b
c
d
e
1
2
3
4
5
6
7
Hermon
869ft
Llanfyrnach
Glandwr
Hebron
Eglwys Fair a Churig
Llanglydwen
Login
Llanboidy
Rhyd-y-wrach
Llanfallteg
Dinas
Trelech
Coed Deufor
Cwm-bach
Cwmfelinmynach
Gelliwen
Trelech a'r Betws
Talog
Blaen-y-coed
Waun-deg
Cwm-duad
827 ft.
Allt Walis
Llanpumpsaint
Cynwyl Elfed
GWILI RAILWAY
Cwmdwyfran
Bwlch-newydd
Newchurch
Abernant
Bronwydd Arms
Peniel
Rhyd-ar-gaeau
Pont ar Sais
Llanllawddog
Brechfa
Mynydd Figyn
Halfway
Llanfynydd
Salem
Pen-y-banc
Felin-gwm-uchaf
Whitemill
Felinwen
Nantgaredig
Broadoak
DINEFWR
Felindre
Llangathen
DRYSLWYN
Dryslwyn
Golden Grove
Llanarthney
Caerfyrddin
Carmarthen
AMPHITHEATRE
Abergwili
Ffynnon-ddrain
Merthyr
Meidrim
Llangynin
Bron-y-Gaer
Sarnau
Llanllwch
Banc-y-felin
Llangynnwr
Llangunnor
Capel Dewi
Nant-y-caws
Cwm-Ffrwd
Llanddarog
Pen-rhiw-goch
Carmel
Maesybont
Foelgastell
Porth-y-rhyd
Pentre Gwenlais
Hendy-gwyn ar Daf
Whitland
Lampeter Velfrey
Pwll-trap
San Clêr
St. Clear's
Llangynog
Croes-y-ceiliog
Brandy Hill
Llanddowror
Llandeilo Abercywyn
Llanybri
Laugharne
Llansteffan
DYLAN THOMAS' BOATHOUSE
Llandawke
Eglwysgymmin
Eglwycummin
Llansadyrnin
Red Roses
Crunwear
Llanteg
Pentywyn
Pendine
Amroth
Marros
Wiseman's Bridge
Pendine Sands
Ginst Pt.
Ferryside
Broadway
Llansaint
St. Ishmael
Kidwelly
Gwendraeth
Llangyndeyrn
Gwendraeth Fach
Crwbin
Dre-fach
Cross Hands
Ammanford
Pen-y-groes
Tir-y-dail
Capel Hendre
Ty-croes
Pontantwn
Llandyfaelog
Meinciau
Tumble
Pontyberem
Pont Henry
Four Roads
Pontiets
Cynheidre
Mynydd Sylen
Brondini
Five Roads
Horeb
Trimsaran
Mynydd Pembrey
Llan-non
Craig Fawr
Hendy
Pontarddulais
Pembrey Forest
Towyn Burrows
Pembrey
Cefn Sidan
Burry Port
Pwll
Felinfoel
Llangennech
Dafen
Bryn
Llwynhendy
Bynea
Groves End
Gorseinon
Penllergaer
Loughor
Llanelli
BURRY INLET
Whiteford Pt.
Llanrhidian Sands
Penclawdd
Salthouse Pt.
Gowerton
Fforest-fach
Three Crosses
Waunarlwydd
Cockett
Llanmorlais
Dunvant
Killay
Upper Killay
CLYNE VALLEY
Clyne Common
Saundersfoot
Monkstone Pt.
Dinbych y Pysgod
Tenby
St. Catherine's Island
MONASTERY
Caldy Island
CARMARTHEN BAY
Broughton Bay
Whiteford Burrows
Llanmadoc
Landimore
Cheriton
Burry Holms
Llanrhidian
Oldwalls
Llangennith
GOWER
Reynoldston
Cefn Bryn 609ft.
PARC LE BREOS
Parkmill
SWANSEA AIRPORT
Rhosilli Bay
Llanddewi
Rhosili
Knelston
Penrice
Nicholaston
Bishopston
Southgate
Newton
Worms Hd.
Mewslade Bay
Port-Eynon
Horton
Oxwich
Oxwich Pt.
Slade
Three Cliffs Bay
Pobbles Bay
Pwll-du Hd.
Pwll-du
Caswell Bay
Langland
A40
A48
A477
A4066
A484
A485
A476
A483
A4138
A4118
A4070
A478
B4299
B4298
B4300
B4310
B4306
B4309
B4317
B4308
B4312
B4314
B4328
B4295
B4271
B4247
B4436
B4297

Map L

N

Miles 0 1 2 3 4 5
Kilometres 0 1 2 3 4 5 6 7 8

Map M

N

Miles 0 1 2 3 4 5

Kilometres 0 1 2 3 4 5 6 7 8

WE'RE HERE TO HELP

NORTH WALES

OPEN–ALL YEAR

COLWYN BAY, Clwyd, LL29 7LN.
Wales Tourist Board,
North Wales Regional Office,
77 Conway Road.
Tel: (0492) 531731. **BB**

COLWYN BAY, Clwyd, LL29 8BU.
Wales Tourist Information Centre,
Station Road.
Tel: (0492) 530478 **BB BABA**

LLANDUDNO, Gwynedd, LL30 2SY.
Wales Tourist Information Centre,
Chapel Street.
Tel: (0492) 76413. **BB BABA**

LLANDUDNO, Gwynedd.
Information Office, Arcadia Theatre.
Tel: (0492) 76413 Ext. 264.

LLANFAIR P. G. Isle of Anglesey
Gwynedd, LL61 5UJ.
Wales Tourist Information Centre,
Station Site, Isle of Anglesey.
Tel: (0248) 713177.

LLANGEFNI, Isle of Anglesey,
Gwynedd, LL77 7JA.
Isle of Anglesey Borough Council,
Pen Yr Orsedd.
Tel: (0248) 724666.

LLANGOLLEN, Clwyd, LL20 8PD.
Tourist Information Centre,
Town Hall.
Tel: (0978) 860828. **BB BABA**

RHYL, Clwyd, LL18 5NL.
Wales Tourist Information Bureau,
Promenade.
Tel: (0745) 55068. **BB BABA**

RUTHIN, Clwyd, LL15 1BP.
Craft Centre.
Tel: (08242) 3992. **BB BABA**

Tourist Information on North Wales also available at:-

CHESTER, Cheshire CH1 2HS.
Town Hall & Visitor Centre.
Tel· (0244) 40144 or 313126.
BB BABA

SANDBACH, Cheshire, CW11 0FB.
Road Chef Service Area,
M6 Motorway Northbound.
Tel: (09367) 60460. **BB BABA**

OPEN–SUMMER ONLY

BANGOR, Gwynedd, LL57 2RE.
Wales Tourist Information Centre,
Theatr Gwynedd.
Tel: (0248) 352786. **BB BABA**

BETWS-Y-COED, Gwynedd,
LL24 0AH.
Wales Tourist Information and
Snowdonia National Park Centre,
Royal Oak Stables.
Tel: (06902) 426 or 665. **BB BABA**

BLAENAU FFESTINIOG,
Gwynedd, LL41 3HD.
Wales Tourist Information and
Snowdonia National Park Centre,
Isallt, High Street.
Tel: (0766) 830360. **BB BABA**

CAERNARFON, Gwynedd,
LL55 2PB.
Wales Tourist Information Centre,
Oriel Pendeitsh.
Tel: (0286) 2232. **BB BABA**

CONWY, Gwynedd, LL32 8AY.
Wales Tourist Information Centre,
Castle Street.
Tel: (0492) 592248. **BB BABA**

CRICCIETH, Gwynedd, LL52 0DF.
Information Office, The Square.
Tel: (076671) 2489.

HOLYHEAD, Gwynedd, LL65 1DG.
Wales Tourist Information Centre,
Marine Square. Salt Island Approach.
Tel: (0407) 2622 **BB BABA**

HALKYN, Clwyd, CH8 8DF.
Wales Tourist Information Centre,
Little Chef Services, A55 Road.
Tel: (0352) 780144. **BB BABA**

LLANBERIS, Gwynedd, LL55 4UR.
Wales Tourist Information Centre,
Oriel Eryri.
Tel: (0286) 870765 **BB BABA**

MENAI BRIDGE,
Isle of Anglesey, LL59 5EA.
Wales Tourist Information Centre,
Coed Cyrnol.
Tel: (0248) 712626. **BB BABA**

MOLD, Gwynedd, CH7 1AB.
Tourist Information Centre,
Town Hall, Earl Street.
Tel: (0352) 59331. **BB BABA**

PORTHMADOG, Gwynedd
LL49 9LP.
Wales Tourist Information Centre,
High Street.
Tel: (0766) 512981. **BB BABA**

PRESTATYN, Clwyd, LL19 9LH.
Wales Tourist Information Centre,
Scala Cinema.
Tel: (07456) 4365.

PWLLHELI, Gwynedd, LL53 6HE.
Wales Tourist Information Centre,
Y Maes.
Tel: (0758) 613000. **BB BABA**

WREXHAM, Clwyd, LL12 7AG.
Information Centre, Memorial Hall,
Town Centre.
Tel: (0978) 357845. **BB BABA**

Tourist Information on North Wales also available at:-

OSWESTRY, Shropshire.
Information Centre,
Mile End Services.
Tel: (0691) 662488.

MID WALES

OPEN–ALL YEAR

ABERYSTWYTH, Dyfed, SY23 2AR.
Ceredigion District Council
Information Centre, Eastgate.
Tel: (0970) 612125/611955.
BB BABA

KNIGHTON, Powys, LD7 1EW.
Offa's Dyke Association,
The Old School.
Tel: (0547) 528753/528529.

LLANDRINDOD WELLS, Powys, LD1 6AA.
Wales Tourist and Radnor District Council Information Centre, Rock Park Spa.
Tel: (0597) 2600. **BB BABA**

LLANWRTYD WELLS, Powys, LD5 4SS.
The Bookshop.
Tel: (0591) 3391.

MACHYNLLETH, Powys, SY20 8EE.
Wales Tourist Board, Mid Wales Regional Office, Canolfan Owain Glyndwr.
Tel: (0654) 2401. **BB BABA**

WELSHPOOL, Powys, SY21 7DD.
Wales Tourist Information Centre, Vicarage Garden Car Park.
Tel: (0938) 2043/4038. **BB BABA**

OPEN – SUMMER ONLY

ABERAERON, Dyfed, SA46 0BT.
Ceredigion District Council Information Centre, The Harbour.
Tel: (0545) 570602. **BB BABA**

ABERDOVEY, Gwynedd, LL35 0ES.
Snowdonia National Park Centre, The Wharf.
Tel: (065472) 321. **BB BABA**

BALA, Gwynedd, LL23 7AB.
Snowdonia National Park Centre, High Street.
Tel: (0678) 520367. **BB BABA**

BARMOUTH, Gwynedd, LL42 1NL.
Wales Tourist and Barmouth Publicity Information Centre, Station Road.
Tel: (0341) 280787. **BB BABA**

BUILTH WELLS, Powys, LD2 3BL.
Wales Tourist Information Centre, Groe Car Park.
Tel: (0982) 553307. **BB BABA**

CARDIGAN, Dyfed, SA43 1HY.
Ceredigion District Council Information Centre, Prince Charles Quay, The Harbour.
Tel: (0239) 613230. **BB BABA**

CORRIS, Gwynedd, SY20 9RF.
Craft Centre.
Tel: (065473) 343. **BB BABA**

DOLGELLAU, Gwynedd, LL40 1LF.
Snowdonia National Park Centre, The Bridge.
Tel: (0341) 422888. **BB BABA**

ELAN VALLEY, Powys, LD6 5HP.
Elan Valley Visitor Centre.
Tel: (0597) 810898. **BB BABA**

HARLECH, Gwynedd, LL46 2YB.
Snowdonia National Park Centre, High Street.
Tel: (0766) 780658. **BB BABA**

LLANFYLLIN, Powys, SY22 5DB.
Wales Tourist Information Centre, High Street.
Tel: (069184) 8868. **BB BABA**

LLANIDLOES, Powys, SY18 6EF.
Wales Tourist Information Centre, Longbridge Street.
Tel: (05512) 2605. **BB BABA**

NEW QUAY, Dyfed, SA45 9NZ.
Ceredigion District Council Information Centre, Church Street.
Tel: (0545) 560865. **BB BABA**

NEWTOWN, Powys, SY16 2PW.
Wales Tourist Information Centre, Central Car Park.
Tel: (0686) 25580. **BB BABA**

PRESTEIGNE, Powys.
Wales Tourist Information Centre, Memorial Hall.
Tel: (0544) 260193.

RHAYADER, Powys, LD6 5AB.
Wales Tourist Information Centre, The Old Swan, West Street.
Tel: (0597) 815091. **BB BABA**

TYWYN, Gwynedd, LL36 9AD.
High Street.
Tel: (0654) 710070. **BB BABA**

SOUTH WALES

OPEN – ALL YEAR

CARDIFF, South Glamorgan, CF5 2EJ.
Wales Tourist Information Centre, Cardiff Visitor Centre, 8-14 Bridge Street.
Tel: (0222) 27281. **BB BABA**

MONMOUTH, Gwent, NP5 3BX.
Wales Tourist Information & National Trust Centre, Church Street.
Tel: (0600) 3899. **BB BABA**

NEWPORT, Gwent, NP9 1HZ.
Wales Tourist Information & Newport Museum Centre, Newport Museum & Art Gallery, John Frost Square.
Tel: (0633) 842962. **BB BABA**

PONT ABRAHAM, Dyfed, SA4 1FP.
Wales Tourist Information Centre, Pont Abraham Service Area, (Junction 49, M4), Nr. Pontarddulais.
Tel: (0792) 883838. **BB BABA**

PONTYPRIDD, Mid Glamorgan CF37 4PE.
Pontypridd Historical, Cultural & Tourist Information Centre, Bridge Street.
Tel: (0443) 402077. **BB BABA**

SARN, Mid Glamorgan, CF32 9SY.
Wales Tourist Information Centre, Sarn Service Area (Junction 36, M4), Nr. Bridgend.
Tel: (0656) 4906. **BB BABA**

BAGLE BROOK, West Glamorgan.
Wales Tourist Information Centre, Beefeater Restaurant, Sunnycroft Road, Baglan.
Tel: (0639) 823049.

SWANSEA, West Glamorgan, SA1 3QN.
Tourist Information Centre, Singleton Street.
Tel: (0792) 468321. **BB BABA**

SWANSEA, West Glamorgan, SA1 1TY.
Wales Tourist Board, South Wales Regional Office, Tŷ Croeso, Gloucester Place.
Tel: (0792) 465204.
Written and telephone enquiries only.

TREDEGAR, Gwent.
Wales Tourist Information Centre, Bryn Bach Country Park.
Tel: (0495) 711816. **BB BABA**

OPEN – SUMMER ONLY

ABERDULAIS, West Glamorgan, SA10 8EO.
Wales Tourist Information Centre, Aberdulais Basin, Nr. Neath.
Tel: (0639) 53531. **BB BABA**

ABERGAVENNY, Gwent, NP7 5NA.
Wales Tourist Information & Brecon Beacons National Park Centre, 2 Lower Monk Street.
Tel: (0873) 3254 or 77588.
BB BABA

BARRY, South Glamorgan, CF6 8TJ.
Wales Tourist Information Centre, The Promenade, Barry Island.
Tel: (0446) 747171. **BB BABA**

BLAENAVON, Gwent, NP4 9XP.
Wales Tourist Information Centre, Big Pit Mining Museum.
Tel: (0495) 790122. **BB BABA**

BRECON, Powys.
Wales Tourist Information Centre, Market Car Park.
Tel: (0874) 2485 or 5692. **BB BABA**

CAERPHILLY, Mid Glamorgan, CF8 1AA.
Tourist Information Centre, Old Police Station, Park Lane.
Tel: (0222) 863378. **BB BABA**

CARMARTHEN, Dyfed, SA31 3AQ.
Wales Tourist Information Centre, Lammas Street.
Tel. (0267) 231557 **BB BABA**

CHEPSTOW, Gwent, NP6 5LH.
Wales Tourist Information Centre, The Gatehouse, High Street.
Te: (02912) 3772. **BB BABA**

CROSS KEYS, Gwent.
Wales Tourist Information Centre, Cwmcarn Forest Drive Entrance, Cwmcarn.
Tel: (0495) 272001. **BB BABA**

FISHGUARD, Dyfed, SA65 9HE.
Town Hall, Fishguard.
Tel: (0348) 873484. **BB BABA**

HAVERFORDWEST, Dyfed, SA62 6SD.
Wales Tourist Information & Pembrokeshire Coast National Park Centre, 40 High Street.
Tel: (0437) 3110. **BB BABA**

KILGETTY, Dyfed, SA68 0YA.
Wales Tourist Information & Pembrokeshire Coast National Park, Kingsmoor Common.
Tel: (0834) 813672. **BB BABA**

LLANDOVERY, Dyfed, SA20 0AR.
Wales Tourist Information & Brecon Beacons National Park Centre, Central Car Park, Broad Street.
Tel: (0550) 20693. **BB BABA**

MERTHYR TYDFIL, Mid Glamorgan.
Wales Tourist Information Centre, 14a Glebeland Street.
Tel: (0655) 79884.

PONT NEDD FECHAN, West Glamorgan, SA11 5NR.
Wales Tourist Information Centre, Pont Nedd Fechan, Nr. Glynneath.
Tel: (0639) 721795. **BB BABA**

PORTHCAWL, Mid Glamorgan, CF36 3DT.
Wales Tourist Information Centre, Old Police Station, John Street.
Tel: (065671) 6639. **BB BABA**

SWANSEA, West Glamorgan, SA3 4DQ.
Tourist Information Centre, Oystermouth Square, Mumbles.
Tel: (0792) 61302. **BB BABA**

TINTERN, Gwent, NP6 6TE.
Wales Tourist Information Centre, Tintern Abbey.
Tel: (02918) 431. **BB BABA**

WHITLAND, Dyfed, SA34 0PY.
Wales Tourist Information Centre, Canolfan Hywel Dda.
Tel: (0994) 240867. **BB BABA**

BRITISH TOURIST AUTHORITY OVERSEAS OFFICES

BTA Your enquiries will be welcome at the offices of the British Tourist Authority in the following countries:

AUSTRALIA – British Tourist Authority, Midland House, 171 Clarence Street, Sydney, N.S.W. 2000.
Tel: (02) 29-8627

BELGIUM – British Tourist Authority, Rue de la Montagne, 52 Bergstraat, B2, 1000 Brussels.
Tel: (02) 511 43 90

BRAZIL – British Tourist Authority, Avenida Ipiranga 318-A, 12° Andar, Conjunto 1201, Edificio Vila Normanda, 01046 Sao Paulo, SP.
Tel: 257 1834

CANADA – British Tourist Authority, 94 Cumberland Street, Suite 600, Toronto, Ontario, M5R 3N3.
Tel: 416 925 6326

DENMARK – British Tourist Authority, Montergade 3, DK-1116, Kobenhavn.
Tel: (01) 12 07 93

FRANCE – British Tourist Authority, 63 Rue Pierre-Charron, 75008 Paris.
Tel: (01) 42 89 11 11 Minitel: 36 14 Type OTGB

GERMANY – British Tourist Authority, Neue Mainzer Str 22, 6000 Frankfurt am Main 1.
Tel: (069) 2380707

HONG KONG – British Tourist Authority, Suite 903, 1 Hysan Avenue, Causeway Bay, Hong Kong.
Tel: 5-764 366 Telex: 80201 BTAHK HX

IRELAND – British Tourist Authority, 123 Lr Baggot Street, Dublin 2.
Tel: (01) 614188

ITALY – British Tourist Authority, Corso Vittorio Emanuele II n° 337, 00186 Rome.
Tel: 654 0821 or 654 0464
Telex: (43) 622690 BTA ROM I

JAPAN – British Tourist Authority, 246 Tokyo Club Building, 3-2-6 Kasumigaseki, Chiyoda-ku, Tokyo 100.
Tel: (03) 581-3603

MEXICO – British Tourist Authority, Edificio Alber, Paseo de la Reforma 332-5 Piso, 06600 Mexico DF.
Tel: 533 6375/76

NETHERLANDS – British Tourist Authority, Aurora Gebouw 5e, Stadhouderskade 2, 1054 ES Amsterdam.
Tel: (020) 85 50 51 Telex: 13395 bta br

NEW ZEALAND – British Tourist Authority, 8th Floor, Norwich Insurance House, Cnr Queen & Durham Streets, Auckland 1.
Tel: (09) 31446

NORWAY – British Tourist Authority, Fridtjof Nansens plass 9, 0160 Oslo 1.
Postal address:
Postboks 1554 Vika, 0117 Oslo 1.
Tel: (02) 41 18 49

SINGAPORE – British Tourist Authority, 05-03 Singapore Rubber House, 14 Collyer Quay, Singapore 0104.
Tel: 535 2966 5352967 (Ansaphone)
Telex: 28493 BTA SIN Fax: 534 4703

SOUTH AFRICA – British Tourist Authority, 7th Floor, JBS Building, 107 Commissioner Street, Johannesburg 2001, PO Box 6256, Johannesburg 2000.
Tel: (011) 296770

SPAIN – British Tourist Authority, Torre de Madrid 6/4, Plaza de Espana, 28008 Madrid.
Tel: (91) 241 13 96

SWEDEN – British Tourist Authority.
For visitors: Malmskillnadsg 42 1st Floor.
For mail: Box 7293, S-103 90 Stockholm.
Tel: (08) 21 24 44

SWITZERLAND – British Tourist Authority, Limmatquai 78, 8001 Zurich.
Tel: (01) 47 42 77 or 47 42 97
Telex: 58632 BTACH

UNITED STATES OF AMERICA

CHICAGO – British Tourist Authority, John Hancock Center, Suite 3320, 875 N. Michigan Avenue, Chicago, Illinois 60611.
Tel: (312) 7870490

DALLAS – British Tourist Authority, Cedar Maple Plaza, Suite 210, 2305 Cedar Springs Road, Dallas, Texas 75201.
Tel: (214) 720 4040

LOS ANGELES – British Tourist Authority, World Trade Centre, 350 Sth. Figueroa Street, Suite 450, Los Angeles, CA 90071.
Tel: (213) 628 3525

NEW YORK – British Tourist Authority, 40 West 57th Street, New York, N.Y. 10019.
Tel: (212) 581-4700

HOTLINE CENTRAL RESERVATIONS SERVICE BOOKING CONDITIONS

1. Payment – A deposit of £20 per person is required on booking. If required, your premium for holiday cancellation insurance will be added to the sum required as a deposit. The balance is payable 42 days (6 weeks) prior to departure. If the booking is made within 42 days (6 weeks) of departure full payment is required at the time of booking.
2. Cancellation Charges – If you have to cancel your holiday for whatever reason, we reserve the right to make a cancellation charge as follows:

More than 42 days (6 weeks)	Deposit
29-42 days	30%
15-28 days	45%
1-14 days	60%
Departure date or after	100%

3. Prices include VAT at the current rate of 15%, where applicable. In the event of any changes in the VAT regulations, these will be passed on to the client (only applicable if VAT has been included in the price).
4. The Wales Tourist Board reserves the right to alter any arrangement or to cancel the holiday owing to unforseen circumstances. In the latter case, any sum paid by clients will be refunded but the Wales Tourist Board accepts no further liability whatsoever.
5. The Wales Tourist Board gives notice that all bookings for accommodation, etc., are made by them as agents for the establishment concerned upon the understanding that they shall not accept any liability whatsoever for any injury, loss, damage, accident or delay caused by or in any way connected with the acts or defaults of any proprietor or servant, or any liability whatsoever arising in any way directly or indirectly in connection with the making of the said booking.
6. The Wales Tourist Board accepts no liability for losses, additional expenses or any claim whatsoever due to changes in accommodation establishment, sickness, weather, strikes or any other cause. All such losses, additional expenses or claims will be borne by the client.
7. Your reservation constitutes a legal contact which requires you to pay for the reserved accommodation in the event of cancellation or curtailment of your holiday. Many of the risks which may give rise to the need to cancel can be easily and cheaply covered by an insurance policy. Our broker has arranged such a policy. Please enquire at the time of booking.

NOTE: Bookings other than through this service are subject to the operator's own booking conditions.

GERALD OF WALES–800th ANNIVERSARY

1988 marks the 800th anniversary of a journey through Wales made by Gerald, a medieval traveller and writer. Gerald of Wales, who was born in Pembrokeshire's Manorbier Castle (he called it 'the pleasantest spot in Wales'), penned a unique account of medieval life here following an historic tour in 1188. To commemorate this journey, Cadw: Welsh Historic Monuments (Brunel House, Cardiff) are organising a series of events and exhibitions throughout Wales.

WANT TO LEARN WELSH?

All kinds of special interest holidays are available in Wales – including, appropriately enough, Welsh language learning courses. For further details, please contact the Welsh Joint Education Committee, 245 Western Avenue, Cardiff CF5 2AY.

FURTHER INFORMATION

If you want further details on holidays in Wales, please contact Wales Tourist Board, Davis Street, Cardiff CF1 2FU. Tel: (0222) 27281.

BED AND BREAKFAST GUIDE 1988
BOOKING FORM

Send this form to the accommodation of your choice, or to the appropriate Holiday Hotline Office as applicable.

Note to applicants and establishments using this form.

It must be clearly understood that other than for bookings through the Wales Central Reservation Service, the Wales Tourist Board is in no way connected with the booking and accepts no liability whatsoever in any way connected with, arising out of the booking, or the use of this form. In the case of direct bookings applicants (or their agents as the case may be) should check direct with operators as to any Terms of Booking.

Clients Name and Address (or Agent's Stamp).

Booking Ref.

Details of Party

Mr/Mrs Miss	Initials	Surname	Age if Under 16

Total Number in party ☐ Number of children ☐
Number of adults ☐ Number of children (under 2) ☐
Pets ☐

INSURANCE REQUIRED	YES	NO

(please delete as appropriate)

(For Hotline Central Reservations only)

Accommodation

Accommodation name ____________

Accommodation address ____________

Date of arrival   /   /   Length of stay ☐ Nights

Type of accommodation required

HOTELS, MOTELS, GUEST HOUSES AND FARMHOUSES
Enter number in box.

Single room(s)		Double-bedded room(s)		Twin-bedded room(s)		Family room(s)	
With bath/shower	☐	With bath/shower	☐	With bath/shower	☐	With bath/shower	☐
Without bath	☐	Without bath	☐	Without bath	☐	Without bath	☐

Special Requirements ____________

Payment

Payment Method Cheque ☐ Postal Order ☐

Cheque/Postal Order Number ____________

If you wish to pay by credit card, please tick the appropriate box and enter your account number below.

Please check that the establishment of your choice accepts your particular credit card.

☐ American Express ☐ Diners Card
☐ Access ☐ VISA

TOTAL COST OF HOLIDAY (including supplements, where applicable) £

DEPOSIT (where applicable) £

BALANCE PAYABLE (where applicable) £

By (date) ____________

I agree to the terms of the Wales Central Reservation Service booking conditions, or the booking conditions of the operators concerned as advised to me at the time of booking.

I enclose a deposit of £

Signed ____________ Date ____________